BEFORE
MARCH
MADNESS

BEFORE
MARCH
MADNESS

THE WARS FOR THE SOUL
OF COLLEGE BASKETBALL

KURT EDWARD KEMPER

**UNIVERSITY OF
ILLINOIS PRESS**
Urbana, Chicago, and Springfield

Library of Congress Cataloging-in-Publication Data
Names: Kemper, Kurt Edward, author.
Title: Before March Madness : the wars for the soul
    of college basketball / Kurt Edward Kemper.
Description: Urbana : University of Illinois Press, 2020.
    | Series: Sport and society | Includes bibliographical
    references and index.
Identifiers: LCCN 2019054578 (print) | LCCN
    2019054579 (ebook) | ISBN 9780252043260
    (hardcover) | ISBN 9780252085185 (paperback) |
    ISBN 9780252052149 (ebook)
Subjects: LCSH: Basketball—United States—History—
    20th century. | Basketball—Economic aspects—
    United States. | College sports—United States—
    History—20th century. | College sports—Economic
    aspects—United States. | National Association of
    Intercollegiate Athletics—History—20th century. |
    National Collegiate Athletic Association—History—
    20th century.
Classification: LCC GV885.7 .K46 2020 (print) | LCC
    GV885.7 (ebook) | DDC 796.323/630973—dc23
LC record available at https://lccn.loc.gov/
    2019054578
LC ebook record available at https://lccn.loc
    .gov/2019054579

For
Rosamond Wilson, Clarence Walker,
Lowell Stewart, John Wilson, LeRoy Watts,
and the others, whose names we will never know

An important trait among men is their ability to assert themselves in relation to other men. It is not necessary to win all the little battles, but if and when human issues arise—we must take a stand— and this we must do by assertion.

—Clarence Walker, 1948

CONTENTS

ACKNOWLEDGMENTS

This book began as a result of a keyword search into the *American History and Life* database on college sports and desegregation, which turned up Milton Katz's excellent work on John B. McLendon, the NAIA, and college basketball. Having had no previous interest in basketball (much to my wife's chagrin), I had never heard of McLendon and was intrigued by the institutional difficulties of black players and black schools participating in national tournaments. I had intended to write a very different book from what appears presently, but each new area of inquiry pushed the project in a new direction. I vowed many years ago that I would never write a book on intercollegiate reform, mostly because Ron Smith has so thoroughly and excellently examined that subject that it seemed impossible to say something new. But the more I looked at the difficulties of race in college basketball, the more I realized the impossibility of explaining its resolutions, particularly the expansion of the NAIA tournament and the creation of the NCAA College Division tournament, without examining the question of reform and smaller institutions of higher education. I am deeply grateful for an almost countless number of archivists, scholars, and others who helped me unearth and connect those two seemingly disparate threads of the book.

I simply could not have written this book without the limitless support of Ellen Summers at the NCAA and Chad Waller and Staci Schottman at the NAIA (neither of whom are still with the NAIA). As my project kept morphing into something slightly different from my last inquiry, Ellen patiently identified an ever-widening circle of documents relating to NCAA governance, the organization's basketball tournaments, and the activities of the Small College Committee. I am forever in Ellen's debt, because without even realizing it, she had provided me with the first hint that the expansion of the basketball tournament was intimately related to the deep fissures among the association's liberal arts and smaller colleges. At the NAIA, Chad and Staci had to take a substantial leap of faith by letting me look at their materials. The NAIA does not maintain an archive in any sense of the word, has no staff to oversee its historical materials, and has materials in various places within its Kansas City headquarters. In essence, they gave me the run of the building and unlimited access to their copy machine on little more than the optimistic expectation that I would be a responsible steward and a benign interloper. I can only hope that I justified their confidence and generosity.

This project relied on more than two dozen university archival facilities, but three were of the utmost importance, and their staffs are owed substantial gratitude. Tamar Chute at Ohio State University remains an archivist of the first order; with a pleasant and generous personality, she is the rare archivist who can hear a researcher's incoherent ramblings and come back twenty minutes later with "Is this what you're looking for?" It never occurred to me that Ohio State's University Archives might contain material not specific to Ohio State, but after hearing of my project, Tamar turned me on to OSU's sizable holdings of the NABC. After my first book, for which Tamar provided invaluable assistance, I promised her a round of drinks. I now owe her at least a second round. I also benefited tremendously from Letha Johnson's able assistance at the University of Kansas in helping navigate the immense collection of Phog Allen's Papers. The Phog Allen collection contains not just Allen's correspondence but also that which he organized as an administrator, and it is not to be approached unsupervised. Letha did much to help me interpret the collection's vagaries and avoid missing valuable material. The collection is now available almost entirely online, but that would have deprived me of the experience of working in the Spencer Research Library, a classic old-school repository with a massive reading room, floor-to-ceiling windows, and heavy wooden tables. For that too I am grateful. Finally, I am professionally and financially indebted to Oberlin College and college archivist Kenneth Grossi. Oberlin maintains the John H. Nichols Papers, which not only convinced me that serious divisions existed within the NCAA in the 1940s and 1950s but in which I finally found the entire contents, including correspondence, appendixes, and hearing notes, of the otherwise elusive Crowley Committee report. Oberlin also graciously awarded me a Frederick B. Artz Summer Research Grant, which allowed me to spend a week in residence in the archives and the historic town of Oberlin, Ohio. Ken's hospitality and familiarity with Nichols's paper collection made the week an exceptionally enjoyable and intellectually profitable experience.

My book relied on the unending willingness of dozens of archivists and their willingness to find sometimes little more than a single piece of correspondence or perhaps a folder or two worth of relevant information. I am deeply grateful to Kayim Shabazz of the Atlanta University Center Archives, Jen McCullough at Baker University, Bill Shaman at Bemidji State University, Richard Lindemann and Kathy Petersen at Bowdoin College, Sheila Darrow at Central State University, Jessy Randall of Colorado College, Laurie Langland at Dakota Wesleyan University, Emily Jones of Delta State University, Meghann Toohey at the University of Dubuque, Thomas White at Duquesne University, Kathleen Shoemaker at Emory University, Christopher Rabb at Franklin and Marshall College, Karen Drickamer at Gettysburg College, Jim Stempert at Johns Hopkins University, Amy Surak at Manhattan College, Christina Vos at Morningside College, Kevin B. Leonard at Northwestern University, Emily Haddaway at Ohio Wesleyan University, Elise Blas at Southwestern College, Susanne Belovari and Molly Bruce at Tufts University, Nancy Miller at the University of Pennsylvania, Doris Peterson at the University of South Dakota, Joan Gosnell at Southern Methodist University, Teresa Gray at Vanderbilt University, and Martha Imperato at Washburn University.

My project is also deeply indebted to several people outside of academia. John McCarthy, a lifetime champion of small college basketball and now the driving force behind the Small College Hall of Fame, first put me in contact with Bill Wall and James Krause of the NABC. James graciously provided me a copy of his history of the association. Danny Stooksbury, whose excellent history of the early NAIB tournament was invaluable to me, not only provided me with some of his own research materials but also introduced me to the NAIA staff who facilitated my work there. Ted Graham of *Indystar.com*, who may be the most knowledgeable man alive regarding basketball and the state of Indiana, helped me get in contact with Clarence Walker's son and generally was a font of information regarding Hoosier basketball. And while the Clarence Walker story is becoming fairly well known, that of Rosamond Wilson remains far less so. I am deeply grateful to Jody Ewing for her article on Al Buckingham, Wilson's coach at Morningside, and for giving me contact information for Rosemary Tweet, Buckingham's daughter. Rosemary in turn generously provided me with information about her father and his commitment to racial justice. And Tim Gallagher of the *Sioux City (IA) Journal* offered me some background on Wilson and offered to help track down what became of Wilson after his shameful treatment in 1948. Sadly, he has apparently been lost to history.

The book has benefited immensely from the generosity of other scholars who have gone out of their way to offer inestimable assistance. Milton Katz, whose excellent biography of John McClendon has been a constant reference guide for me, has been a champion of the project from its inception. He has answered countless emails and, perhaps most important, provided me with copies of the records of the National Athletic Steering Committee that used to reside at the Big Ten offices in Chicago but have now apparently been lost. Charles Martin, who first befriended me while I was still a grad student and who is the definitive authority on the integration of American intercollegiate athletics, shared materials he came across for his own book and always graciously answered my never-ending questions on race and college sports. Ron Smith not only read and commented on the entire manuscript, offering much needed input on clarity and saving me from more than one questionable assertion, but also provided me with his unpublished paper on the NCAA and the freshmen rule and welcomed my foray into the domain of reform. And Chuck Shindo at Louisiana State University remains my friend, mentor, and confidante. Chuck was the first to read the entire manuscript and did much to help refine the introduction and conclusion, reading multiple drafts of each. I will always be indebted to Chuck in ways I can never repay.

Many thanks to Danny Nasset and the staff at the University of Illinois Press as well as the two anonymous reviewers. It takes a lot of work to transform a manuscript into a book, and UIP has done a wonderful job with both of my books. In addition to the Frederick B. Artz Summer Research Grant from Oberlin, I also received financial assistance from Dakota State University's modest Faculty Research Initiative and from its College of Arts and Sciences. Additionally, Greg and Shari Hospodor, old friends from our LSU days, graciously housed and fed me during my research trips to Kansas City.

Finally, I am forever grateful that the most important people in my life—my wife, Robin, and my two children, Nicholas and Madeleine—have been supportive of the process of academic scholarship. My wife cheerfully tolerated my numerous absences for research and accepted (perhaps less cheerfully) the distant and detached moods that mark my personality when I am writing. It's not easy living with me on a good day, more difficult still when I generally ignore the world and the people around me for something that happened more than half a century ago. Nicholas and Madeleine have given me much-needed perspective in life as both a father and a scholar. When I first read Clarence Walker's searing diary, I could not help but think of them, whose own athletic journeys have sometimes left them dependent on others. There is much of both of them in these pages, though each is more an aficionado of the diamond than the hardwood. They fill me with pride and wonder, never more than when they each chose a life behind the dish. Sorry it took so long, kids, but I am now free to go out and play catch whenever you want.

BEFORE MARCH MADNESS

INTRODUCTION

The NCAA hosted its second College Division Basketball Championship Tournament in Evansville, Indiana, in March 1958, won by the University of South Dakota (USD). The thirty-two-team tournament featured a mixture of small state schools like USD and private liberal arts colleges whose academic pedigrees often outstretched their athletics ones. It also featured the equivalent of a Jim Crow regional with all four entrants from historically black colleges placed in the South Central regional. Bracketing those colleges together meant that only one could emerge to face a team from a historically white school, and the tournament committee conveniently located the two segregationist Southern schools in the field in the opposite bracket to ensure that the two halves of America's racial conscience could meet only in the championship, if at all. This did not cordon off the contagion of equality, however, as USD featured an integrated lineup led by Jim and Cliff Daniels, two brothers from Brooklyn who had begun their careers at Lincoln University, a historically black college in Missouri. To get to the final, South Dakota had to get through Wheaton College, a private liberal arts school in Illinois with selective admissions and a multimillion-dollar endowment, and whose existence predated the onset of industrialization with its social justice bona fides intact when it secretly established an on-campus stop in the last days of the Underground Railroad. The other half of the Final Four that year featured national runner-up St. Michaels, a small private liberal arts college in upstate Vermont that was enjoying a substantial enrollment increase in the 1950s thanks to increased federal funding and the postwar expansion of higher education. While St. Michaels embraced an expansive intercollegiate and intramural athletics program that reached more than 60 percent of its entire all-male student body, it had recently and painfully decided it could no longer afford to compete in college football, dropping the sport in 1954, just three years removed from an undefeated championship season. On its way to the final, St. Michaels narrowly defeated the hometown Evansville College Aces, another small liberal arts school but also a basketball powerhouse, which already had four appearances in the National Association of Intercollegiate Athletics (NAIA) Tournament to its credit, and 1958 witnessed the first of six College Division Final Four appearances on its way to five national championships. In 1977 the Aces decided to move up to what had been the University Division, now called Division I.

The 1958 College Division Final Four, and the tournament itself, was a microcosm of the varying identities of most of the participants of intercollegiate athletics in the United States at the time. Although the media fixated on the handful of commercialized programs that dominated college football sponsored by the NCAA, the vast majority of college athletics programs did not and could not compete at that level, while almost as many schools were not even sure they should belong at all to the NCAA. Schools like Wheaton and St. Michaels were happy to limit their athletic aspirations to regional peers in accordance with their academic priorities while still maintaining a vigorous competitive athletic presence as part of a well-rounded liberal arts education. Evansville and USD, however, were willing to devote themselves to championship-caliber play, pursuing a smaller-scale model of commercialized athletics that sought to put an exciting, winning basketball team on the floor to draw paying spectators whose revenue helped pay for the venture. And though USD knew it was not going to match in athletics its big-time neighbors in Nebraska, Minnesota, and Iowa, it also knew that athletics was becoming a key component in postwar public higher education to new student recruiting, alumni engagement, and public attention, none of which spoke directly to the process of undergraduate instruction. Finally, the separate-but-equal condition of the historically black colleges marked their continued half-in, half-out status within the world of college sports in general and the NCAA specifically. In short, the 1958 College Division Tournament participants found themselves on the same floor in Evansville but with very different expectations of what role athletics should play in their institutional lives.

The existence of the College Division Tournament was the result of one of the most divisive and controversial periods in the history of college sports and was essentially a culmination of what this book describes as "the wars of college basketball." To examine the wars' combatants and partisans is to find oneself swimming in an alphabet soup of organizations, factions, and institutional identities whose interests sometimes interlocked, other times merely aligned, and at all times were evolving. The first outbreak of the conflict was a civil war in the 1920s and 1930s over the control and meaning of basketball's rules involving the Amateur Athletic Union (AAU) and the National Collegiate Athletic Association (NCAA). The intensity of the civil war forced virtually all of the game's constituent interests to choose a side with one of the two superpowers in whose orbits their respective satellites existed. Thus, the Young Men's Christian Association (YMCA), which included most of the game's supplicants in Canada, and a national association of game officials, aligned with the AAU, while the NCAA brought into its orbit the newly formed National Association of Basketball Coaches (NABC) and the national organization governing high school athletics. Having determined that collegians needed to control the game of basketball, varying groups within that faction attempted to create tournaments intended to mark the collegians' independence and triumph. Rivalries and recriminations among the National Association of Intercollegiate Basketball (NAIB, later NAIA) Tournament, the National Invitation Tournament (NIT), and the NCAA Tournament and their respective factions created a new round of internecine conflict that lingered into the 1950s.

Both conflicts, however, were mere preludes to a far larger, more complex, and more extended contestation within college athletics over the meaning and organization of college sports. College basketball, though not yet on the level of college football in terms of media attention, public perception, and profitability, was nonetheless a highly contested battleground in this larger struggle. One part of the struggle occurred within the NCAA and revealed deep divisions within the organization. The public presence of the NCAA largely emerged from the schools that pursued highly competitive, highly commercialized athletics, collectively referred to as "big-time athletics." And while these big-time schools dominated the NCAA and made up college athletics in the minds of the media and an undiscerning public, they were in fact only a minority. Often operating outside the public eye were the private liberal arts colleges that had set the tone for American higher education since its founding in the seventeenth century, which embraced college athletics as part of a classical curriculum but decried the commercial model of the big-time schools. These schools often criticized, sometimes with a jealous eye, the profits and motivations of the big-time schools.

The examination of this struggle between those who wanted to expand commercialized athletics in higher education and those who wanted to restrain those interests is traditionally seen as the struggle over reform, often simplified as one between high-minded intellectualism (read: good) and self-serving amoral financial opportunism (read: evil). The reform process, however, was not simply a question of those who were willing to prostitute higher education for profits on one side and principled idealists on the other. Rather, it was a struggle between two camps of ideologues. On the one side lay the forces of commercialized athletics, represented in the public eye most forcefully by big-time college football and housed increasingly in expanding state institutions. These schools saw college athletics as a multifaceted tool that not only supposedly funded additional components of those schools' missions but also served as a bridge to the substantial percentage of the populous with little connection to or understanding of higher education.[1] On the other side were the smaller, private liberal arts colleges that made up a majority of America's institutions of higher education and saw athletics as a wholly integrated component of an individual's intellectual development. These schools viewed the commercialization of those athletics as a threat to their academic missions, not an accessory to them.[2] Both sides were increasingly convinced that the practices of the other threatened their very existence.

At another level, however, examining intercollegiate athletic history as simply a binary struggle between big-time commercialism and liberal arts idealism ignores far too many constituencies, far too many institutional motivations, and far too much historical context. In reality, the landscape of college athletics contained a multitude of identities, aspirations, and agendas that only occasionally intersected with the traditional binary poles of reform. Located somewhere between the big-time schools and the private liberal arts colleges were the growing number of regional and smaller state schools that lacked the tradition and status to compete academically with the liberal arts colleges as well as the size and resources to compete with the big-time schools either academically or athletically. These so-called medium-time schools wanted to pursue moderately commercialized athletics to the extent that their institutional profiles allowed as part of a socially expected undergraduate experience. By the 1950s the big-time universities, the private liberal arts colleges, and the medium-time state schools all belonged to the NCAA, but each sought to bend the organization to their interests while trying to align with one of the others against the third.

In addition to the varying ideologies housed within the NCAA regarding commercialism, other intercollegiate athletics constituencies existed entirely outside the NCAA. Many schools saw the NCAA so in thrall to the commercialized big-time programs that they chose to remain outside of the organization entirely. Seeing the NCAA as attempting to carry forward a national agenda largely irrelevant to their own athletic interests and aspirations, these schools, if they joined any organization at all, gravitated toward the NAIB. This organization prided itself on serving smaller colleges and shunned the big-time commercial aspirations of many NCAA members. By refusing to accept the NCAA as "the voice of college sports," they presented an alternative narrative to critics both within and without the NCAA. Yet another group remained outside of both the NAIB and NCAA, but not by choice. Historically black colleges (HBCs) maintained proud athletic traditions, some dating back to the nineteenth century, but were entirely excluded from the mainstream national collegiate athletics establishment as an expression of segregation and the second-class status imposed upon black Americans. In the late 1940s and early 1950s, these schools began hammering at those exclusions, thereby forcing both the NCAA and NAIB to confront their exclusionary policies. As a result, the events that led up to the College Division Basketball Championship Tournament ultimately spoke to the shifting meanings of higher education itself in mid-century America.

At the center of *Before March Madness* lie these distinct, yet sometimes overlapping, constituencies within mid-century American college athletics: big-time state schools spread throughout the United States; private, academically elite liberal arts colleges, based mostly in the Northeast and the Midwest; HBCs, based mostly in the old Confederate South and the border states; and the growing regional public institutions with a more populist academic profile, spaced throughout the country but predominating in the Plains states and the far West. Each pursued college athletics for their own purposes and attached to them distinct functions. The big-time schools saw commercialized athletics, particularly football at first, as a way to make higher education appear less elitist and more accessible to a majority of Americans who still lacked high school diplomas, let alone any experience with college. The liberal arts colleges embraced competitive athletics as an integrated part of the academic curriculum, a venue in which students learned struggle, teamwork, and problem-solving skills just as valued in society as critical thinking skills. The HBCs certainly presumed that athletics delivered these skills, but the ability to compete fairly and honorably on level playing fields, particularly against white opponents, forcefully demonstrated the black yearning for equality in the face of segregation and the second-class citizenship of Jim Crow America. At the same time, the regional campuses of the growing state public education systems, many of them only a few years old, churning out graduates to shepherd the American economy from its industrial to postindustrial footing, had no pretensions of competing with their flagship brethren or established behemoths from more populous states. Instead, their pursuit of "medium-time athletics" elevated a commercialized model but one that was tailored to their budgets, markets, and enrollments, establishing their campuses in the popular mind as legitimate simply because they played well the same games as the more established schools. Thus, the big-time schools saw competitive athletics as a welcome mat, the liberal arts schools saw them as a component of an ideal, the HBCs saw them as a cudgel to win larger equality, and the smaller state schools viewed them as a route to legitimacy and popular acceptance.

Such diverse expectations of the function of college athletics illustrated the impossibility of a single organization like the NCAA or the NAIB crafting a coherent and unified expression of college athletics' role within American higher education or American culture. As such, the struggles of these constituencies created conflict within these organizations and within the larger American culture about the meaning of athletics, with no obvious outcome apparent by the mid-1950s. Yet, by the early 1960s the NCAA and its commitment to commercialized athletics triumphed, establishing it as the socially expected role of college sports and elevating it as something most of American higher education aspired to in some fashion. Although many participants in these struggles raised the prospects of secession, revolt, or reform, what resulted instead was a cooptation where the liberal arts schools, the HBCs, and the smaller regional schools each received just enough (and partially at the expense of the others) to maintain their commitment (sometimes begrudgingly) to the NCAA, which only wholly provided for the interests of big-time commercialized athletics. Though the earlier struggles over reform largely focused on matters of college football, the mid-century reform crisis—and indeed the struggle for the modern NCAA—was largely resolved over battles relating to college basketball.

Basketball was often only tangential to these larger struggles, but it was basketball that often served as the nexus through which these larger conflicts, interests, and rivalries intersected. The culmination of basketball's civil wars created big-time college basketball, which gave the big-time schools one more reason to look to the NCAA to protect their franchise. But it also gave the liberal arts schools one more reason to view with suspicion and frustration the willingness of the NCAA to privilege the big-time model. The successful creation of the NCAA Basketball Tournament as an expression of sporting and institutional legitimacy, however, made it highly desirable for the smaller state schools and the HBCs, particularly those that had no chance of competing in the ultra-expensive world of college football. In the contestations over the institutional identity of the NCAA—and indeed the very meaning of college sports in America—the big-time interests in the NCAA created the College Division Tournament to placate both critics and allies alike. Creating a separate tournament for smaller schools reserved the original tournament for the big-time programs; provided access for smaller state schools and the HBCs; secured Southern white schools from having to play the HBCs; and in so doing, directly confronted the rival NAIB Tournament, thereby stemming membership loss in that direction and thus satisfying the liberal arts desire to restore an NCAA in which they might continue to fight for academic reform. As college athletics faced its greatest crises in the 1950s, mostly stemming from college football, concessions in college basketball bought off the critics and placated opponents such that the NCAA emerged as a powerful regulatory agency. In short, it was the peace created over basketball that created the modern NCAA.[3]

Scholars of intercollegiate sports have generally focused on the world created by big-time commercialized schools with a justifiably heavy focus on college football. Much of this scholarship examines the abuses created by big-time football and the (mostly failed) efforts to restrain them. The story of early college football and how the game's brutality crisis in the early twentieth century led to the creation of the NCAA is well-trodden ground. But often missing are the divisions among the varying interested parties and how those divisions created a legacy that marked the history of the NCAA. Though this scholarship has provided thoughtful analysis of both college football's place in higher education and American culture, as well as the limits of reform, it has ignored both the agendas and varied identities of many who did not pursue commercialized athletics. Such scholarship generally tends to assume a certain air of inevitability, presuming to examine only how college sports emerged as it did and ask only why reform failed without examining the contingency played by other models and participants. *Before March Madness* attempts to show that the story of college sports in the middle of the twentieth century is far more complex than the creation of the NCAA simply to defend the interests of big-time college football.[4]

Part of that story entails placing new focus on the role of early college basketball, until recently a fairly ignored subject by sports scholars. If the scholarship of early college athletics is dominated by the inevitability of big-time football's triumph and the failure of reform, that of college basketball is similarly driven by an inevitability of college basketball's march toward the national three-week spectacle that has become March Madness. These authors tend to describe the early NCAA Tournament as the little engine that could within a consensus interpretation that minimizes or ignores conflict entirely. Put most simply, these histories tend to look back into the game's past only for a single trail of bread crumbs that leads directly to a multibillion-dollar television contract and a three-week, work-skipping bacchanalia of Cinderellas and chicken wings.[5] Within the last few years, however, a flurry of excellent scholarship has emerged offering a far more nuanced examination of the game's origins, conflicts, and place within the larger cultural landscape.[6] What remains missing, however, is the centrality of college basketball to the evolution of the NCAA and its importance to a large number of its members who did not or could not pursue big-time college football but who nonetheless remained vocal stakeholders in the landscape of college athletics. *Before March Madness* examines the power dynamics of mid-century college sports when their meaning in higher education was still uncertain, when their future in American culture was still undetermined, and when the ascendance—indeed the very survival—of the NCAA was not yet assured.

Before March Madness seeks to place a gallery of the dismissed, the ignored, and the marginalized in the world of American college athletics at the center of an examination of the forces that created the modern NCAA and contemporary assumptions about the role of college athletics in higher education and American culture. But the events of upheaval, scandal, and strife that marked the critical 1950s were themselves culminations of much earlier and, in some instances, more ruth-less contestations. The early years of college basketball were marked by intense conflict, some of them personal and petty, others institutional and savage, but all of them decisive and all of them ultimately won by the competitive and commercialized interests within the NCAA. To understand that story, we must go back to when the wars began—at the birth of the NCAA and basketball's infancy.

NOTE: As befitting the explosive growth of American higher educa-tion in the mid-twentieth century, a good many of the institutions that appear in the following pages have since changed their formal names. To avoid the countless cumbersome parenthetical references to alert readers to such names, all institutions are identified by the names used at the time.

CHAPTER 1

BASKETBALL'S CIVIL WAR

THE STRUGGLE FOR AMERICAN BASKETBALL
(1927-1936)

In April 1927 amateur basketball's Joint Rules Committee (JRC) met in New York for its annual discussion of the state of the game and the rules of play that governed basketball in both the United States and Canada. The JRC included delegates from both sides of the international border and from the varied organizations that played what then passed for amateur basketball: the Amateur Athletic Union (AAU), the Young Men's Christian Association (YMCA), and the National Collegiate Athletic Association (NCAA), as well as ex officio members from the association of officials and various high school federations. In an effort to improve the game, the JRC voted unanimously on April 9 to approve a proposal by the University of Wisconsin's Walter Meanwell to limit players from dribbling more than once per individual possession before requiring them to pass or shoot. More than 70 percent of all game fouls were called on the dribble, and many feared that the constant stoppage of play was grinding down the game. Additionally, dribbling required a more deliberate motion to corral the inconsistent bounces the laces on the ball created, allowing defenders to constantly swipe at the ball. The Indiana High School Federation had threatened to take matters into its own hands if the JRC refused to act, and all comment at the meeting suggested that the committee felt it had to do something. Advocates of the new rule hoped that limiting dribbling would increase passing and movement and drastically reduce the number of fouls. Unbeknownst to the delegates in New York City that day, they had just created the circumstance upon which rival factions would now make civil war upon each other in the world of amateur basketball.[1]

Opponents of the new dribble rule, most notably the University of Kansas's Phog Allen, howled in protest, describing the JRC as an "autocratic basketball rules committee," and alleged that it deviated from its usual process of discussion prior to rule changes. Both the Eastern Intercollegiate Basketball League, which made up what would eventually become the Ivy League, and the Missouri Valley Conference emphatically opposed the new rule, while the Pacific Coast Conference announced that they had no intention of following it at all. Allen and the other critics called their supporters to the barricades, grossly distorted the facts of what had gone on in New York City, and eventually helped create a rival organization that called for its own rules committee, decrying both the motivations and character of some involved in the New York meeting. Eventually, the city of New York itself came to be seen by the defenders of the dribble as a multiethnic den of inequity where all manner of the game's, and America's, corrupting influences might be found. Though the JRC rescinded the rule change a month later in response to the outcry, many within the college ranks happily accepted Allen's frenzied cries of undemocratic betrayal and readily accepted his logic that the college coaches housed in the NCAA needed their own organization to control a game that, in their opinion, was really theirs.[2]

To understand the outsized response to the JRC's decision is to understand the partisanship between the stewards of amateur sports in the United States in the first third of the twentieth century and, oddly enough, the incredibly long shadow cast over American intercollegiate athletics by college football. By the 1920s the NCAA and the AAU already maintained a thinly veiled hostility toward each other over which organization controlled and best exemplified supposedly amateur sports in America. And while some collegians supported the proposed dribble rule, most saw it as orchestrated to satisfy the demands of the AAU and, thus, fodder for their intensifying rivalry. Others, however, were far more influenced by patterns, both beneficial and destructive, established by college football.

College football originated in the late nineteenth century without central organization or coherent oversight, but its intense popularity rapidly elevated the game to big business in the form of gate revenues, substantial coaches' salaries, player subsidies, and intense media coverage. Because of the game's commercialization and its intense popular importance, football also witnessed preferential admissions for talented players, under-the-table inducements from alumni, and questionable academic practices. The intense and unregulated individualism of the late industrial period flourished in the world of big-time college football, and any attempts to restrain the game's abuses or regulate the game's organization were successfully met with substantial resistance.[3] By the early twentieth century, tactical and strategic innovations also brought to the game an unparalleled brutality that reached a crisis point in 1905 when eighteen players at several levels of football died over the course of the season from game-related injuries. The resulting public furor over the on-field violence merged with, and ultimately subsumed, the on-campus concerns about the game's academic and financial improprieties. Spurred by such pressures, a group of predominantly reform-minded but athletically uninfluential academics, mostly from traditional liberal arts colleges, met in December 1905 to consider football's fate on their campuses. The coaches and alumni supporters at big-time commercialized football schools, meanwhile, largely resented the proposed intrusion of those they perceived as meddling academics.[4] The reformers ultimately coalesced into the Intercollegiate Athletic Association of the United States, which became the National Collegiate Athletic Association in 1910, and while public pressure for rules reform forced the big-time programs to merge their rules committee with that of the reformers, almost all of them steadfastly remained aloof from the NCAA and generally refused to join. As a result, the early NCAA remained a collection of predominantly liberal arts schools based almost entirely in the Northeast and upper Midwest whose teams played football mostly out of the public eye.[5]

Although many in the NCAA sincerely wished to draft a program that addressed not merely on-field violence but the academic and financial issues as well, they recognized that they lacked the stature to make such reforms standard practice without the assent of the more influential schools. And to attempt such reforms without the involvement of the big-time schools was to all but assure those schools' continued alienation from the NCAA and that organization's potential irrelevance. Quite simply, in the words of scholar Burlette Carter, "The NCAA leadership realized that it could not claim national relevance without national membership." Consequently, the reformers hoped to attract the big-time schools while doing nothing in the meantime that might repel them. In 1907 the NCAA created a special membership committee aimed at increasing the number of members, particularly from the larger and more influential schools. Correspondence to potential members assured recipients that "your institution will lose none of its independence if it should join us in the work."[6]

Nonetheless, the big-time schools disdained the NCAA in its early years, largely out of fear that such an organization would deprive members of their athletic independence, imposing rigid codes of conduct that might limit decision making or, perhaps worse, impose rules that would reduce the quality of their football teams. Thus, while the NCAA's founding document called for "the regulation and supervision of college athletics throughout the United States," the absence of big-time schools deprived the NCAA of any prestige or authority, operating instead, in the oft-repeated words of historian Ronald Smith, as little more than "a faculty debating society for amateurism." Member schools attempted to persuade nonmembers that joining the NCAA would not come at the expense of their institutional autonomy, touting what became known as the "home rule principle." To institutionalize this principle, according to Smith, the NCAA amended its constitution in 1907 to include the following statement: "Legislation enacted at a conference of delegates shall not be binding upon any institution." According to Smith, "The colleges agreed collectively to act individually."[7] This allowed the barons of college athletics to operate largely without oversight, to disdain those who would presume to restrain them, and to view college athletics as their fiefdom. In this context, the collegians were aghast at the JRC's temerity to exercise any authorities beyond the control of the collegians and its rejection of the collegians' sense of prerogative.

In many regards the early NCAA was similar to the JRC in that it brought together several different and sometimes competing interests. But the outraged reaction of the college basketball programs to the JRC's abortive legislation on the dribble emerged in part because the JRC deigned to do what the NCAA could or would not—namely, hold the emerging basketball powers accountable to a national organization. Facing another brutality crisis in 1910, many big-time football schools recognized that in the public's perception the NCAA had successfully, if not completely accurately, cloaked itself in the mantle of athletic reform. The NCAA also successfully linked itself with educational reform when it joined groups like the YMCA and the Public Schools Athletic League to champion general fitness in the nation's primary school system. It also prominently lobbied the federal government in 1921 to pass the Fess-Capper Bill calling for federal aid to the states for universal K–12 physical education. Thus, to remain outside the NCAA fold appeared to the public as an overly narrow self-interested embrace of athletic spectacle bereft of any socially contributory function.[8]

Such schools began to see that the NCAA provided the veneer of legitimacy, particularly its high-minded, if utterly hypocritical, sanctification of amateurism, suggesting that all member schools sincerely sought to limit the game's commercializing and corrupting influences. With the home rule principle enshrined in NCAA bylaws and the growing necessity of public cover, big-time schools slowly joined the organization. According to the NCAA's own membership records, however, only 65 schools joined in the first five years and only 38 more joined in the following decade, reaching 182 members by the end of the 1920s. The significance of home rule was that the NCAA maintained no regulatory power to govern college athletics for roughly half a century. Nonetheless, many schools that belonged to the NCAA took advantage of the organization's annual meeting to espouse the principles of amateurism, faculty control, and athletics beholden to the mission of higher education. For these schools, few of which pursued big-time commercialized athletics, they saw in the NCAA a forum by which they might persuade the college athletics establishment to embrace such principles. The schools that did pursue big-time commercialized athletics, meanwhile, knew that the home rule provision kept such conversations from ever becoming enforceable national policy. Thus, the big-time schools successfully used the NCAA for their own purposes and held at bay any substantive restraints upon their athletic fiefdoms. The reaction to the JRC's decision on the dribble showed that while the barons controlled football and the NCAA, they did not yet control basketball and its organizations.

Within the NCAA the best that reformers could hope for was to cajole and guilt the membership into accepting such tepid advances as the 1922 acceptance of nine "fundamental principles" of the association, which enshrined amateurism, focused mostly on matters of player eligibility, and insisted on faculty control of athletics.[9] The 1922 document, however, must not be construed as any kind of sweeping or definitive national standards on institutional conduct or player eligibility rules. Defined as "fundamental principles," they were just that, principles upon which all schools should seek to operate and best practices to implement but that included no compulsion, requirement, or enforcement. Unable to govern the behavior of intercollegiate athletics, NCAA members devoted most of their energies to the rules committees governing various sports and championship committees that put on the NCAA-sponsored championship events, which by the mid-1930s included only swimming, track and field, cross-country, and gymnastics (not coincidentally, sports for which the AAU also sponsored championship events). The larger schools that pursued commercialized athletics generally gravitated toward and dominated these committees. The easy acquiescence of the smaller schools to the dominance of the rules committees by the larger commercialized schools only heightened the latter's sense of entitlement within the NCAA and helps explain their exaggerated response to the JRC's 1927 dribble rule. In the long run, it left most smaller schools as members of the NCAA but with little definitive role within the organization.[10] Thus, though many schools agreed to create and join a national organization nominally devoted to the oversight of college athletics, it did little to create consensus and moderation. Rather, it magnified the differing views of American collegiate athletics and soon allowed for the creation of outright factions.

The smaller reform-minded schools in the NCAA, housed overwhelmingly in the liberal arts colleges of the Northeast and upper Midwest, lacked the authority and institutional will to rein in their big-time colleagues, a fact that became glaringly apparent during the decade when college football emerged as a fully commercialized spectacle. Amid the consumerist, middle class–oriented financial growth of the 1920s, schools initiated a construction boom, building massive on-campus stadiums capable of seating seventy thousand fans in some instances, often through bonded indebtedness. With the ability to finance the debt pegged to filling the stadium, schools faced increasing pressure to field winning teams, themselves a product of superior talent and a single-minded devotion to football. Recruiting excesses flourished, as did a growing subjugation of the academic mission to the interests of winning football, and professional coaches, whose salaries skyrocketed during the decade, became de rigueur at many schools. In response to college football's increasing commercialization, in 1929 the Carnegie Foundation for the Advancement of Teaching released a scathing indictment of big-time college football, titled *American College Athletics*. The Carnegie Report, as it became known, revealed a wildly unregulated world of high-salaried coaches, lucrative gate receipts, lavish travel arrangements and special treatment afforded the players, and a veritable menu of programs and efforts designed to land new players—everything from minor cash payments to complete costs of tuition, room, and board. Though the Carnegie Report said little that the big-time schools did not already know, it was a major public embarrassment. And while the financial disaster of the Depression did help rein in some of the financial excesses mentioned in the report, other aspects relating to the game's commercialization—most notably bowl games, hosted off-campus by urban commercial entities—actually grew during the 1930s.[11]

The Carnegie Report soon receded in the public memory, but the criticisms it spawned remained and eventually focused more and more on bowl games as representative of college football's commercialized free-for-all. Hosted off-campus by municipal or financial boosters with no ties to any university, these games blatantly used college players to advertise and sell their own economic self-interest. With no bearing on conference championships, they were completely exhibitionary in nature, and because they were not sanctioned or governed by the NCAA, they did not determine any national champion. For those animated by the Carnegie Report, particularly the small-school reformers within the NCAA, bowl games were parasites that attached themselves to college football, flourishing in the environment of the game's unregulated in-dividualism. And to the big-time schools that played in them, the bowl organizers enjoyed a lucrative franchise at the expense of the schools that provided the spectacle.[12]

The stewards of college basketball cast a critical eye on football bowl games and eventually created their own postseason tournament to avoid any semblance of them, but that was only after big-time college bas-ketball emerged. What set basketball apart from college football, how-ever—indeed what affected in some way or another every significant aspect of early college basketball—is that unlike football, basketball did not originate as a collegiate enterprise. Like all team sports, basketball originated as an urban game, and it was created in a reformist environ-ment that spoke to the urban experience. Although some, particularly from Indiana and Kentucky, continue to speak of the game as a decisive expression of rural values and rural life, basketball was invented in 1891 at the YMCA Training School in Springfield, Massachusetts, by James Naismith for use in the physical education curricula of future YMCA athletic directors in their mostly urban postings. Under the guidance of Luther Gulick, the YMCA at the turn of the century sought to use athletics and physical culture as a way to attract to YMCA programming large numbers of young, single men, both immigrant and native-born, then teeming into the burgeoning cities of industrial America. Gulick transitioned the YMCA athletic program away from singular exercise and calisthenics and toward competitive athletics, creating in 1887 the physical education department at the YMCA Training School. By 1895 Gulick created an independent three-year curriculum for the physical education students. Under Gulick the physical culture mandate of the YMCA was clear: use sports to teach a distinctly Protestant set of values, stressing manliness, personal discipline, self-restraint, sobriety, and respect for the Sabbath, in what became known as muscular Christianity. Thus, muscular Christianity as practiced by the YMCA was intended as an antidote to the urban industrial experience, increasingly marked in the early twentieth century by eastern and southern European immigrant traditions that included alcohol and non-Protestant religious customs.[13]

Though the YMCA failed to convert many of its target demographic to Protestantism specifically or muscular Christianity in general, basketball began attracting supplicants to the game in record numbers to urban YMCAs in the industrial Northeast and upper Midwest by the end of the 1890s. Not only did YMCAs themselves field highly competitive teams—including the famed Buffalo Germans, winners of several national championships and holder of a 111-game win streak—but they also stewarded a game involving teams from ethnic settlement houses, urban youth organizations, and other religious-outreach programs. Quite literally, basketball threatened to become the raison d'être of the YMCA, potentially overwhelming urban YMCAs' outreach and ministry efforts. The Philadelphia YMCA disbanded its entire league because the game "retarded regular gymnasium work, fostered ill feelings among members, and attracted a rowdy element."[14] YMCA teams continued to participate at the game's elite levels, but the organization passed stewardship of the game and control of the rules to the Amateur Athletic Union (AAU) in 1896. The AAU, which claimed to oversee all "amateur" sports in the United States, was itself born from a significant turf war among Eastern elite clubs and their practice of providing under-the-table benefits to "auxiliary" members who were little more than athletic ringers. In 1888 several clubs sanctimoniously departed the existing governing body of club sports to form the AAU and assert "strong principles of amateurism." With the birth of the modern Olympic movement in the late 1890s, the AAU emerged as the clearinghouse for American amateur athletes and the sole sanctioning body of American Olympic teams. As such, it required clubs to affiliate with the AAU in order to compete against AAU teams and prohibited competition against unaffiliated clubs. When the AAU attempted to impose this restriction on

college basketball teams, the collegiate squads formed their own basketball leagues beginning in 1905 and shortly thereafter formed their
own rules committee. It was not coincidental that as the stewards of
college football attempted to create their own governing body in 1905,
the AAU attempted to expand its control over college basketball. When
the YMCA further distanced itself from elite competition, it too created
its own rules committee, such that by 1915 competitive basketball in
the United States included three different rules committees and very
little willingness on the part of the game's participants and leaders to
acknowledge the authority of any competing group.[15]

More than simply a juvenile quarrel over control, the split among
different groups also represented the intensely contested meaning of
"amateur" sports in the United States at the time. Proponents of amateurism in the United States sought to replicate the model followed
by the British whereby gentlemen of reputable social and economic
standing pursued sport solely among themselves for the purposes of
competition and manly class fellowship, with the pursuit of victory as a
secondary concern. Such athletic pursuits contained both cultural and
codified antipathies toward compensation. To be paid to play meant that
victory and profit motivated athletic pursuit rather than sportsmanship
and manly self-development. As a result, British amateurism reserved
respectable sport only for those with the financial means and available
time, thereby excluding commoners and the working class. Though
some Americans had been pursuing organized sports since before the
Civil War, amateurism only emerged as a direct response to the social
and cultural heterogeneity created by the industrial period. Immigra-
tion and socioeconomic mobility left a native-born elite uncomfortable
with the absence of formal social barriers defining industrial America.
American athletic elitists, however, were never able to fully replicate the
British amateur model because of the social egalitarianism of a democratic society as well as the intensely competitive nature of American
society created by a capitalist economic system. Put most simply, while
American elites aspired to amateurism, winning mattered too much to
them to fully embrace the term's British conception.[16]

Although the AAU emerged in response to blatant compensation of
allegedly amateur athletes, its members continued to provide to their
athletes varying inducements in the form of tournament entrance fees,
training and traveling expenses, and employment. By the 1920s the
AAU Basketball Tournament was dominated by corporate-sponsored
teams whose players were nominally employees but were hired for their

basketball skills and practiced on paid company time. When the legendary women's player Babe Didrikson was hired in 1930 to play for the Employer's Casualty team, she made seventy-five dollars a month as a stenographer when entry-level stenographers for the company were making only thirty-five dollars a month. And while the NCAA members also publicly stressed amateurism, their practices too revealed a broad and flexible definition of the term, as revealed in the Carnegie Report. With both the AAU and the NCAA claiming to espouse amateurism but neither able to demonstrate a rigid adherence to it, the two organizations generally decried the activities of its rival, chiefly as a way to deflect criticisms of their own practices.[17]

While the two organizations generally sniped at each other over which controlled amateur sports, the inability to agree on the rules of basketball finally led to a summit between the YMCA, the AAU, and college coaches that created the Joint Rules Committee in 1915. The JRC created peace in the basketball realm for twelve years before the 1927 dispute about dribbling shattered the tenuous consensus over the governance of basketball. Unbeknownst at the time, the dribbling controversy led directly to a series of events that transformed the game of basketball forever. It demonstrated that the game of basketball witnessed fully entrenched stakeholders who did not intend to meekly defer to the aspiring commercialized college programs, forcing the collegians to realize their subordinate position within the game of basketball to the hated AAU and leading them to create their own organization to counter the institutional influence of the AAU and YMCA. The dustup over dribbling also exposed the deep cultural divisions that existed in 1920s America between rural and urban and the mostly Protestant native-born and those of other faiths. Without question, it was a watershed moment.

The controversial 1927 vote on the dribbling rule took place while some of its most outspoken opponents were absent and, to critics of the new rule, was intentionally orchestrated with their absence in mind. One of the critics, University of Kansas head coach Forrest "Phog" Allen, indignant over the restriction on dribbling and mobility as well as what he perceived as the underhanded manner in which it was enacted, lobbied other college coaches attending that summer's Drake Relays to discuss the basketball rules and consider forming their own rules committee. On June 10, 1927, college coaches agreed to form the National Association of Basketball Coaches in order "to further dignify the basketball coaching profession" but also to assert for themselves the governance of the college game, with or without AAU-YMCA concurrence. As a condition of membership, the organization included only coaches affiliated with NCAA-member schools or conferences. Thus, while big-time football viewed the NCAA warily at first, the aspirations of big-time basketball embraced the NCAA from the beginning. The condition of NCAA membership for NABC membership obviously excluded AAU and YMCA coaches but also showed that college basketball understood it was not college football. College football existed without any competition from other organizations; however, college basketball not only faced competitors from the AAU and YMCA but also initially did so at a competitive disadvantage. Indeed, the dispute with the AAU-YMCA faction showed that the collegians needed the NCAA and its institutional authority, such as it was, as a counterweight, because big-time commercialized college basketball did not yet exist.[18]

The NABC sought to legitimate the institution of the professional coach in the college ranks, but the group's exclusion of those outside college athletics revealed the insistence of those within that they were best suited to protect the institution of amateur athletics and that those outside were not merely imposters but commercial shills who sullied the purity of amateur sport. The official rhetoric of the NABC not only charged the college coaches with the "protection" of the rules but also designated the coaches as "the guardians of the game."[19]

Thus aroused, the college coaches pressured the JRC to reconsider the ban on dribbling by threatening to form their own rules committee, which they backed away from when the JRC repealed the dribble rule. But the incident left them wary of the JRC, because they saw the linked interests of the YMCA and the AAU creating an undemocratic voting bloc that left college coaches, represented by the NCAA, in the minority. In response, committee chair Lynn St. John of Ohio State persuaded the committee to operate more consensually in an effort to avoid the partisan divisions created by the aborted dribble rule. Though the NABC did not directly serve on the JRC, the NCAA delegates were all members of the NABC, thus making the coaches organization a de facto subsidiary of the NCAA with regard to its interactions with the rules committee.

The NABC's first decade witnessed the group concentrate mostly on lobbying for a refinement of the rules, reaching for consensus on their application and teaching technique. The group's annual meetings in the late 1920s and early 1930s frequently centered on discussions such as "Should the Center Jump be eliminated?" and "Should the 3-second rule be expanded?" or admonitions to referees about inappropriate coaching conduct. Such priorities reveal a group aspiring for consistency and respectability for both the game and the institution of coach. By the mid-1930s the NABC's insistence on serving as the guardians of the game led the organization to see certain developments of the game's culture, rules, and style of play as a threat to basketball. In an editorial in the organization's 1936 annual bulletin, NABC president Henry Carlson wrote that the college coaches needed to concern themselves with more than the game's technical components. After surveying some of the problems confronting the game during the period in an editorial titled "A Change of Emphasis Is Needed," Carlson declared, "Our discussions have dealt with rules changes and player performances," but now needed to focus more upon the organization of the game. "Members of this Association might well concentrate on improving the administration of basketball."[20]

William H. Browne, head coach of the University of Nebraska, had exactly that in mind when he identified several issues that suggested the kinds of administrative reforms Carlson seemed to be referencing. In order to legitimate and distinguish the college game, as well as expand the game's commercial possibilities and "create more box office appeal," Browne offered his fellow coaches several suggestions: "Start the game on time. . . . Use experienced and, if possible, disinterested scorers and timers. . . . Provide sufficient police to take care of the rowdy element." The explicit reference to the box office not only revealed college athletics' ongoing contradiction of pursuing commercialized sport while claiming to pursue amateurism, but it also illustrated the still evolutionary nature of college basketball and the coaches' desire to rationalize the game.[21] But firmly ensconced in Lincoln, Nebraska, Browne took a thinly veiled swipe at how the game was organized and administered in Eastern urban areas with his comments about partisan environments and "the rowdy element" that gravitated to independent and AAU games. Tales of raucous spectators intimidating referees characterized early basketball, particularly in New York, Philadelphia, and Washington, DC, and the reference to "rowdy" spectators criticized an alleged lack of self-restraint and public respectability that rural Americans tended to see as endemic to big cities during the period and to which those associated with colleges and universities tended to link with the immigrant working class.[22]

While college coaches sought to legitimate the public presentation of the game, they also found a potential ally to equalize the AAU-YMCA voting bloc. In 1933 the NCAA Executive Committee deemed the game of basketball so thoroughly dominated by collegians that it proposed reorganizing the JRC to double the NCAA delegation, allowing for one representative from each of the organization's eight districts while also bringing in delegates from the high schools, who were already aligned with the collegians. Even more provocative, however, was that to keep the committee at what they deemed to be the same manageable size, the proposal also called for reducing the AAU-YMCA representation accordingly. The AAU-YMCA faction countered with a proposed expansion of delegates from each organization, as well as the inclusion of an officials' organization under the leadership of the YMCA's John Brown, to offset the addition of the high school group aligned with the NCAA. The proposal called for the ballooning of the committee to forty-four delegates, something Princeton University's Hamilton Salmon derided as the "44 dummies proposal."[23] When neither faction demonstrated any conciliation toward the other, the situation devolved into a seething environment of mistrust and vitriol, and the tenuous alliance jeopardized since the 1927 dribble rule now teetered on the brink of collapse. Connecticut high school administrator Harold Swaffield described the AAU-YMCA delegates as "picayunish and evasive" and saw Brown's opposition to St. John's continued committee chairmanship as both childishly partisan and indicative of an "ulterior motive on the part of the YMCA and the AAU . . . [to] secure absolute control" of the rules committee.[24] Swaffield wasn't the only individual to see John Brown as the chief malefactor of AAU-YMCA intransigence. C. W. Whitten, who headed the National Federation of State High School Athletic Associations, described Brown's organization as "a pure excrescence . . . upon the great body of basketball competition." Worse, according to Whitten, was that "the AAU people seem to be determined to exploit their dominance of the Olympic situation to bring the colleges and the high schools 'to heel.'"[25] Though basketball was not yet an Olympic sport, the possibility that it might become one meant that the college and high school faction antagonized the AAU at the peril of being excluded from future Olympic competition. Instead, the two sides hurled insults at each other and engaged in a flurry of confidential correspondence among allies mostly to allege some new transgression on the part of the other. Early amateur basketball became a viper pit of shifting alliances, naked prejudices, and ruthless recriminations. "Unless there is some change soon," declared American Olympic Committee president Avery Brundage, "I fear the lid will blow off."[26]

When the International Olympic Committee placed basketball on the 1936 Berlin Olympics program, the AAU-YMCA faction refused to accept any makeup of the JRC that put them at a disadvantage in terms of representation. The college and high school faction refused to go along, prompting representatives from the AAU and the YMCA to bolt from the spring 1935 rules convention to form their own National Rules Committee. In the eyes of the college coaches, the actions of the AAU-YMCA group now ensured that "the possibilities of future trouble for basketball are so great that it cannot be ignored."[27] Indeed, the Big Ten's John Griffith now saw the confrontation as unavoidable and, from his perspective, not unwelcomed. "I believe in peace," he informed St. John, "but I do not believe in peace at any price." Griffith, long a critic of the AAU, asserted that the confrontation was long overdue in the struggle to define amateurism in the United States and to win for the NCAA a seat at the American Olympic table. He acknowledged that conceding to the AAU's demands might be worth it if the NCAA stood to gain anything substantive with regard to the Olympics, but the AAU refused to grant the NCAA any legitimacy. In Griffith's mind the time to negotiate about the basketball rules was past: "As you know, several years ago when the fight was on, I was in favor of finishing it. . . . If we had continued on, we could have gotten a better line-up in the [American] Olympic [Committee]. As it is now, we take what they give us and then when we suggest that basketball is primarily a college and high school game, they will not yield the point."[28] What had begun with the proposed dribble rule in 1927 had now reached an endgame with the collegians seeking to "finish the fight," in Griffith's words.

Now engaged in an open struggle for the control of basketball, the two sides refused any charity or concession toward the other, and their correspondence took on an exaggerative tone that saw duplicity at every turn. Throughout the winter of 1935–1936, both sides made proposals designed to advantage one faction at the expense of the other. In a secret effort to undermine a proposal from the AAU-YMCA, St. John sent copies of the pertinent correspondence to Princeton's Hamilton Salmon so that Salmon could construct arguments against them. St. John sent the documents to Salmon "in strictest confidence. I do not want anybody to know that you have seen" the proposals. He also demanded that Salmon return the originals to him to ensure they did not fall into the hands of others.[29] Maybe the most ridiculous exchange occurred in the spring of 1936 when both sides held separate meetings in New York and unintentionally planned to use the same stenographer to take notes. It appears that when the JRC previously met as a whole in New York, they had retained the stenographic services of a Miss Smith. When each faction planned their own separate meetings, they again contracted with Miss Smith. It is unclear when each realized the potential liability her presence entailed, but John Brown hastened to ensure St. John, whose group met first, that he did not "intend to take advantage of the fact that Miss Smith" took notes for the NCAA meeting in New York: "I requested her to keep all her material confidential in every respect and when she turns it over to you, you will know that this is as far as it will go." It was an issue St. John was already anxious about, because he and University of Michigan's Floyd Rowe pulled Smith aside before they left New York to remind her of their expectation of confidentiality: "She assured us that everything she did for us would be strictly confidential, and that neither Dr. Brown or anybody else would have any access to" her notes. Nonetheless, St. John proposed "making other arrangements" in future years.[30]

More than just a petty squabble over which organization enjoyed more prominence, the basketball civil wars marked recognizable differences in the interpretation of rules. Neil Isaacs and Chad Carlson illustrate that the early years of basketball witnessed distinctly regional styles of play, with the Eastern urban game marked, at least in the eyes of its critics, by a far more physical, if not illegal, style.[31] The multiple rules bodies further exaggerated these differences both in their codifications as well as the interpretations of them by officials. The primary difference between the NCAA–high school rules and the AAU-YMCA rules regarded contact in the form of picks and screens, in which one offensive player provided a form of interference to free up another offensive player's path to the basket. The other area of disagreement focused on congestion under the basket with the so-called post-pivot play; the AAU-YMCA faction allowed for greater contact and the continuance of the post-pivot play. The play flourished in the days when the game was still below the rim and almost a decade before players began using the jump shot. It allowed an offensive player, usually the tallest player operating as the post man, to rotate on his pivot foot 180 degrees without engaging in traveling. Many teams stationed increasingly bigger and bigger players with their backs to the baskets to receive a pass and then turn on their pivot foot without needing to dribble to shoot a layup. The only way to defend the post-pivot play against such large players was to clog the lane with opponents to defend against the inlet pass or try to match the post player with an equally large player in what often devolved into a shoving match beneath the basket. One Ohio coach decried the ferocity of "the foul line pivot play."[32]

AAU and YMCA teams, mostly from large urban areas, generally welcomed this physical style of play and allowed for wide latitude on picks and screens to free up the post player. The problem, according to critics, was less a reasonable difference in rules interpretations between sanctioning bodies and more a dangerous cancer that was being nurtured from a singular host. "In this section," according to an Ohio coach, "we call holding or pushing by either player, but when we go to New York City, the defensive man can do anything but cut your throat."[33] At roughly the same time, University of Kentucky's Adolph Rupp decried the overly physical New York style as "one of the roughest and most rugged exhibitions of pivot play that has ever been shown."[34] Not for the last time did partisans of the game's ills link them with New York City. Similarly, an editorial in the NABC bulletin titled "Is Basketball Going Backwards?" surveyed the state of the college game, describing in apocalyptic and hostile rhetoric a future where basketball resembled a thuggish brawl contested by oversized immigrant behemoths, all overseen by multicultural minders ensconced in New York City. The unsigned NABC editorial alleged that the AAU-YMCA had initiated "a basketball civil war" with the collegians and highlighted the differences in style of play between Eastern urban areas, mostly New York, with the Midwestern style that was played farther away from the rim. To weaken the unity of Eastern college coaches, the AAU-YMCA rules committee named as its official rules interpreter City College of New York's (CCNY's) Nat Holman, who, the editorial noted, "will adopt the New York policy of screens and blocks."[35] St. John saw it as an act of desperation and illegitimacy "that this group found it necessary to draft somebody like Nat Holman in the attempt to give some stability and standing to their efforts." In St. John's opinion, college coaches in general, particularly those associated with the NCAA, enjoyed far greater reputability on the question of athletic integrity and amateurism: "It is certainly a confession of weakness on the part of the AAU-Y that they have to go into the college field to find somebody to give their basketball group a front."[36]

The desperation of the AAU-YMCA group to seek out somebody with Holman's college credentials was matched only by Holman's alleged perfidy in allowing himself to be so utilized against his compatriots. As far as St. John was concerned, Holman's decision was little short of sedition: "He is a sort of renegade misfit and should be run out of . . . National Collegiate circles."[37] Holman's willingness to throw in with the AAU and its style of play, however, was merely a proxy issue for what many

Midwestern college coaches saw as a trifecta of other unpardonable sins. Though Holman began coaching at CCNY in 1919 while still a student himself, he also played club basketball with the AAU and, beginning in 1921, professional basketball with the New York Original Celtics. In the eyes of amateur purists, Holman's time as a professional was made worse by the fact that he retained his college coaching responsibilities, utterly rejecting, in the eyes of his critics, the gentlemanly amateurism so many attributed to college athletics. As a result, he carried with him not only the taint of professionalism but a past history with the AAU as well. Additionally, Holman's New York origins and his embrace of the post-pivot play earned him the disdain of those outside the Eastern corridor who were suspicious of big cities and opposed to the changes affected by physical play and bigger players. Holman learned the game not in sterile YMCAs committed to the spirit of Naismith's original game but on the streets and tenement playgrounds of New York's Lower East Side, "where you had to move fast" or face rough consequences from aggressive and physical defenders. It was there that Holman first developed the post-pivot play, which maximized size and physicality. But in 1920s America, perhaps nothing so stigmatized Holman in the eyes of the elites ensconced in American academia and the increasingly Midwestern-dominated NABC as his Judaism. Holman openly cultivated his Jewish fan base during his playing days, admitting that the attendance of Jews made him play "even harder." Beginning in 1930, Holman also served as physical director of the Lower East Side's Young Men's Hebrew Association, a Jewish version of the YMCA, and in 1932 he helped organize the American delegation to the first Maccabiah Games in Palestine. Everything about Holman's background, it seemed, made him anathema to the nativist-leaning barons of college athletics.[38]

The veiled antipathy toward Holman and his faith was not unique during the period, particularly, if not especially, in sports. Jews in the early twentieth century faced the same paranoid suspicions long directed at Catholics and often for the same motivations. Since the onset of nationalism in the late nineteenth century, anti-Semites particularly criticized Jews for their lack of a nation-state, seeing them as parasites on the nations of others, more loyal to their Jewishness than their country and allegedly willing to sell it out at their financial convenience. Likewise, Protestant nativists saw Catholics as inherently and primarily loyal to the Vatican and the pope, thus questioning their loyalties. Within sports this warped logic took on its own meanings in that critics saw Catholic and Jewish fans and players as potentially subversive and cause "for the breakdown of unity and solidarity in a university community." When Ohio State University (OSU) chose not to renew its lucrative and highly competitive football series with Notre Dame in 1936, Lynn St. John alleged that all of OSU's Catholic faculty members and students rooted for Notre Dame and thus "placed their loyalty to the church over their loyalty to the Ohio State University."[39] Likewise, many saw Jews as so bereft of ideals and loyalties that critics challenged their impartiality in the setting and interpreting of rules. Writer Tom Graham asserts that Indiana University coach Branch McCracken admitted that the Big Ten prohibited Jews from refereeing conference games. McCracken had sponsored the certification of Nate Kaufman, whose reputation for fairness and knowledge of the rules won him the honor of refereeing five consecutive Indiana State High School Championships in the late 1930s. But when McCracken raised Kaufman's name, one unnamed Big Ten coach allegedly retorted, "There'll never be a kike in the bunch as long as I'm here."[40]

In identifying Holman as some kind of traitorous individual to college basketball, his critics lumped together their animosity toward Catholics, Jews, and the teeming city that housed them. In noting Holman's defection from the coaches' organization and his alliance with "the revolters," one NABC publication referenced the AAU-YMCA committee's alliances with Holman and the various urban ethnic immigrant aid groups that sponsored basketball. In a remarkable piece of thinly veiled Protestant paranoia relying on all of the usual nativist tropes of urbanization, political subversion, and religious pluralism, the editorial referred to these clubs and teams, who were ineligible for NABC membership because they were not affiliated with NCAA members, as having nonetheless "joined in the rebellion" against the college coaches. The editorial specifically mentioned the involvement of the Jewish Welfare Board, the American Sokol Union, and the Catholic Youth Organization. Having asserted that Catholic and Jewish organizations lay at the center of this "rebellion," the piece then described Holman in veiled terms as "a New York coach," noting that the "headquarters of each of these organizations is located in New York City" and that "the leaders of the YMCA and AAU who engineered the move are New York men." The piece thus suggested a Jewish–Catholic–New York cabal was afoot to undermine the game's democratic foundations and "challenge the right of the rest of the country to have a majority vote in the game's legislation." Furthermore, it suggested that unless such a challenge could be addressed, "the dark ages of basketball will return."[41] Phog Allen saw

Gotham as such a corrupting influence on the game that he thought "it very fortunate that the [1937 rules committee] meeting is to be held in Chicago this year instead of New York."[42]

The first fruit of this renewed "dark age" in basketball was a move away from the mobile offensive game that was first threatened with the now overturned 1927 limitation on dribbling. The question about the allowance of screens and blocks and the controversial post-pivot play was largely divided along regional lines: mostly Midwestern coaches favored a strict prohibition of such activities, while coaches in the urban Northeast, mostly affiliated with New York schools and the Eastern Intercollegiate Basketball League,[43] embraced them as evocative of a more aggressive style of play.[44] In the January 1936 issue of *Sport Pictorial* magazine, University of Kansas coach Phog Allen took after Holman by name for "acting as Official Interpreter for a group that espouses a rule which both the coaches' body and the rules body of the colleges declared as detrimental to the best interest of college and high school basketball." Allen implied that the New York style was really just dressed-up AAU basketball and thus illegitimate. He closed the article by alluding to the deceitfulness the collegians saw in the AAU-YMCA faction, claiming, "This dissenting group changed the rules to suit themselves, yet they want everybody to get together for the good of the game."[45] Stanford University coach John Bunn also picked up the criticism of the New York style of play when writing about intersectional basketball in the NABC bulletin. Bunn noted that "one may play anywhere in the United States except in New York City and the Eastern Intercollegiate Basketball League" and find a strict interpretation of the rules against screens and picks.[46]

An outgrowth of the rougher style and post-pivot play was the grow-ing reliance on taller and larger players to play the post, as well as simi-larly sized men to defend the post. In the eyes of many purists, big post players were ruining the game by congesting the area under the basket, making it nearly impossible for smaller, quicker players to release the two-handed set shot that was standard at the time. Phog Allen's solu-tion was to raise the rim from ten feet to twelve feet, thereby limiting the effectiveness of big men, creating both a higher arc on shots and longer rebounds, all designed to open the lane. Allen noted the arbitrary reasoning for the ten-foot rim: that was the height of the railing in the Springfield gymnasium to which Naismith nailed the original peach basket goal. Allen also argued that the presence of big men in a game played on ten-foot goals limited the game's growth internationally be-cause "the shorter races" in Japan and China could not compete against the Americans and the northern Europeans. The fact that Holman basically invented the post-pivot play and despised the twelve-foot proposal and that many affiliated with the New York style of play rejected Allen's suggestion out of hand only validated the idea in Allen's mind. Although the proposal never found a majority of supporters, its existence marked yet another point of contention between the two factions clamoring for sole stewardship of the game.[47]

Holman's defection now emerged as a signal lesson to the college coaches, heightening their sense of vigilance for any others who might abandon what so many saw as the true faith while also revealing the nefariousness they felt they confronted in the AAU. In the eyes of coaches like St. John and Allen, Holman represented an epic morality play along the lines of Judas or Benedict Arnold. St. John interpreted the AAU's offer to Holman as a willful expression of "their crooked way to take advantage" of some college coaches' willingness to adopt the post-pivot play. Worse, the offer to Holman revealed an attempt to lure other college coaches who find it "difficult . . . to resist the flattery and a measure of publicity which they may secure by accepting some appointment by the AAU."[48] Allen questioned St. John about the possibility of having the NCAA "contact our college people, advising them against working so close with the AAU." St. John responded enthusiastically to the suggestion while noting that any who followed Holman's lead were nothing more than traitors: "Anyone who does not stick with the NCAA in its activities and its organization work is disloyal to the best interests of the colleges. It is time we called things by their right name in some of these respects and time that we do some work to see that college men everywhere" support the NCAA agenda.[49] Even as Allen and St. John were corresponding, the AAU reached out to Creighton University's head coach, E. S. Hickey, to offer him a seat on their new advisory committee and asked University of Wisconsin head coach Walter Meanwell to aid them in visual instruction. Allen quickly advised Hickey to reject such an offer, declaring that the AAU was "warring on the National Collegiate basketball set-up," and noted "the danger the AAU group have presented" to the NCAA's vision for college basketball. Invoking the specter of Holman, Allen asserted that respectable college men now "characterize Holman as a renegade and personally, I would not want to be placed in the class that Holman has been placed in." Not surprisingly, Meanwell was so chastened he wrote to St. John essentially seeking permission, because he "did not wish to appear in any way out of step with the" NCAA committee.[50]

In the midst of the civil war between the game's factions, the college coaches now reinterpreted the 1927 effort to limit the dribble and saw it in the same nativist tropes as their criticisms of Holman. In this 1936 interpretation, the 1927 meeting had been designed to disregard the college coaches such that one NABC publication described how "the representatives of the AAU and the YMCA," located almost entirely in Eastern cities, "united to outvote the NCAA men on the question of the dribble." The decision brought vociferous protests from "coaches who not only opposed the change but resented such a dictatorial attitude." The Drake Relays meeting that led to the formation of the NABC was thus "a coaches' indignation meeting," designed "to check the arbitrary changes" of the New York–AAU–YMCA cabal, representing a false amateurism and a polyglot urban confederation, each motivated solely by the crass pursuit of victory and money.[51] While the coming of the 1936 Olympics heightened the confrontation over basketball's governance, the confrontation itself emerged as a decisive expression of the larger economic and cultural dislocation of the 1930s. It is no accident that such revisionist rhetoric emerged at the height of the Great Depression, when many Americans looked to salve their wounded psyches and find scapegoats for the destruction of America's economic and cultural fabric. The linking of Catholic and Jewish influences with the heterogeneous urban experience as a destructive force within the game was but one example of this. At a time when political demagoguery and extremism, both respectable and fringe, flourished across the American landscape, many sought refuge in the values of an earlier, simpler, allegedly more democratic America. As historian Elliot Gorn has shown, many Depression-era Americans saw in cities much that had gone wrong in America in the form of relative morals, religious and ethnic diversity, and the weakening of traditional gender roles while conversely exalting to the point of mythmaking an egalitarian social and economic system that emerged from a bygone rural society.[52]

The only trump card the AAU enjoyed—indeed the only thing that kept the NCAA from ignoring the AAU altogether—was its control over American Olympic team membership, particularly the decision to add basketball in 1936. Rather than compile an Olympic team of players from numerous existing teams, the US Olympic Committee (USOC) created a national playoff whereby the winning team would make up a preponderant majority of the American Olympic roster. In an acknowledgment of basketball's fractious kingdom, the US Olympic Basketball Committee created an eight-team playoff, with five teams coming from the NCAA, two coming from the AAU, and one coming from the YMCA ranks. Since both the AAU and the YMCA already maintained national tournaments, the Olympic Committee selected the YMCA champion and the two finalists in the AAU Tournament. For the NCAA, however, which maintained no national tournament, the Olympic Committee, made up overwhelmingly of personnel affiliated with the AAU, imposed a rigorous regional qualifying tournament that did not cover travel costs. From the start, advocates of the college game resented the entire process. According to basketball historian Carson Cunningham, convincing college teams to participate at their own expense "was so complicated that the [Olympic] Committee hired Creighton University's athletic director A. A. Schabinger" to help recruit teams. The NCAA charged that the process put the colleges at a competitive and financial disadvantage. While the AAU and YMCA tournaments were part of those teams' existing schedules, college teams completed their regular season and conference tournaments, then had to travel to their regional qualifying tournament, and then travel again to New York for the Olympic playoff, all at their own expense during the Great Depression. As a result, the NCAA had a hard time finding teams willing to participate.[53]

The tournament's hybrid, half USOC, half NCAA organization also brought criticism. The NCAA named Hamilton Salmon Jr. of New York to chair District 1, which represented the New England colleges. In a humorous reference that marked Americans' curiously shifting preoccupation with religion at the time, the appointment of the decidedly blue-blooded Protestant New Yorker Hamilton to run the New England committee elicited the curiously Jewish reference from the Catholic student newspaper at Providence College that "something doesn't look or smell kosher." The paper then asked rhetorically if there were no New England men esteemed enough in the game to chair their district. Besides concerns over regional chauvinism and perhaps some mild religious antipathy, it appears that the Providence students resented the oversized New England district, while the size of District 2 seemed to privilege the New York teams, an issue to which they felt Salmon was unresponsive.[54] A month later, and with far less attempt at humor, the paper criticized Salmon's imperious nature, caustically referring to him as "his excellency" and spoofing announcement of the qualifying process to the students "whether you like it or not."[55] Additionally, while college personnel organized the logistics of the qualifying tournament, it was nominally a USOC event; thus, the USOC laid claim to all proceeds to offset travel costs to Berlin for the Olympic team. By including all three sanctioning bodies in one event, the USOC put their claims to amateur status on equal footing, which the collegians resented by disdainfully referring to the AAU brand of the game as "independent basketball."[56]

The quarrel over the Olympic qualifying tournament merely brought to a head a decade's worth of resentment within the NCAA and of college officials toward the AAU and now their allies in the USOC. Critics decried the AAU's national tournament as little more than a showcase of semiprofessional teams, funded as they were by their corporate sponsors and ensconced in jobs designed to facilitate the playing of basketball, while the AAU had raked in significant gate receipts since the tournament's inception in 1921. Critics also noted the habit of AAU teams picking up players from college teams just before the tournament, while college rosters were limited to enrolled students. Although criticisms of the AAU Tournament were largely accurate, they were also criticisms (with the exception of adding players) that would just as accurately soon be lobbed at the NCAA. They were really an expression of college jealousy over the spectacle and financial profit the AAU Tournament and frustration over the colleges' inability to compete effectively in the AAU event. Prior to the 1936 Olympic qualifying process, college teams had managed to reach the finals of the national AAU Tournament only five times, and most defenders of college basketball felt the tournament put the collegians at a disadvantage. For years, supporters of the colleges lobbied the AAU to place all the college teams in one bracket and the "independent teams" in another bracket, whereby the two teams that emerged from each would then play each other for the national championship, but the AAU demurred. College supporters also saw in the sanctioning bodies distinctly different and unequal styles of play. One Kansas City sportswriter described the clogged-lane, post-pivot play style of an AAU semifinal as akin to watching "a champion boxer clinch and stall his way through 10 rounds of an exhibition," declaring "there was more excitement in ten minutes [of a college game] than forty minutes of the AAU games."[57]

For Phog Allen, the Olympic qualifying process and his preexisting disdain for "independent basketball" elicited a rhetorical temper tantrum that nonetheless was representative of how the collegians felt toward the AAU. Allen's diatribe simultaneously demonstrated the growing concern of not just control of the game and its finances but also the continued inability of those within the NCAA to coexist in a world where that organization was not the sole stakeholder and decision maker. Allen was originally to have served as the Olympic team's director of basketball operations but was eventually replaced by Joseph Reilly, the president of the Kansas City Athletic Club and an AAU official. Considering he had been one of the loudest and most vitriolic critics of the AAU faction in basketball's civil war, it is not at all unlikely that AAU supporters lobbied to have Allen replaced. Angry about what he perceived as both a denigration of the college game as well as his removal from the Olympic delegation, Allen tendered his resignation to the US Olympic Basketball Committee by famously describing the AAU as an "ambitious group of . . . quadrennial oceanic hitchhikers [who] chisel their way across the oceans every four years on the other fellow's money." Allen, who organized the regional tournament held in Kansas City, also took a swipe at his replacement by claiming his event had raised eight thousand dollars, none of which the colleges got to keep, while a local AAU event organized by Reilly held in the same facility for the same number of nights had raised only seven hundred dollars. This gross financial disparity showed "the difference in the public favor between college and independent basketball," according to Allen.[58]

In other correspondence on the matter, Allen claimed that AAU players were "technically amateurs but actually semi-professionals." Allen's animosity toward the AAU never abated, as he frequently claimed the organization's initials stood for "Asinine And Unfair." He also linked the group with the sin and disorder associated with big cities during the time by declaring in yet another swipe that AAU officials "resemble . . . Chicago racketeers who do not create a business or industry but who step in and tell those who did that they are going to run it." Allen signed off on the affair, asserting the moral supremacy of the collegians by noting that "NCAA members, coaches, and directors of athletics" had more integrity than Reilly and the rest of those affiliated with the AAU, because the former were paid "their annual salaries by their respective schools and they draw no monies from outside sources." Though Allen's response demonstrated his lifelong habit of hypersensitivity to perceived personal slights, it was indicative that for college coaches like Allen, college basketball *was* the game of basketball, and they mightily resented being told by others how to run it and what to do with its finances.[59]

The civil war over the rules and the Olympic qualifying tournament played a significant role in convincing the stewards of the college game that they could not coexist with the AAU in a basketball world where the NCAA was not the sole kingmaker. The creation of the NABC and a separate rules committee and the efforts to delegitimize the AAU were but two expressions of that. Like most civil wars, however, the struggle over college basketball soon divided allies and comrades, quickly devolving into recriminations, betrayals both real and imagined, and paranoid fears of agents provocateurs. And though the partisans of college basketball continued to view the AAU with hostility criticizing the commercialization of college sports while they pursued the same, they soon turned on each other to initiate a far longer and more consequential conflict that eventually affected all of college athletics.

The approach of the colleges in the 1930s to the oversight of college basketball was shaped by their experiences with college football and the circumstances that created the NCAA. The barons of college athletics responded to the public outcry over the brutality crisis and the internal academic concerns of faculty by slowly joining the NCAA and then dominating it through the home rule principle and the committee structure. The schools that made up a majority of the NCAA, desperate for the legitimacy that such schools gave the fledgling organization, had little choice but to acquiesce to their needs and demands. The barons, however, having accustomed themselves to such deference, resented mightily having to share governance of college basketball with the AAU-YMCA. But just as surely as their independent traditions learned from college football shaped their response to the JRC, their experiences with bowl games also shaped how they responded to outside ventures like the Olympic qualifying tournament. Consequently, the reform-minded aspirations of the smaller schools continued to run into the pragmatic realities imposed by the commercialized model of the big-time schools.

Basketball, however, originated outside of the colleges and was dominated by entrenched and unbeholden stakeholders. The NCAA faced the possibility of accepting the role of the AAU-YMCA as, at minimum, an equal partner in the enterprise or abandoning to them entirely the stewardship of the game. Unwilling to accept either option, the college coaches organized the NABC and linked it with the NCAA to produce a counterbalance in the world of college basketball. The civil war was only the NCAA's first step in the direction of seizing basketball once and for all as a game dominated by the collegians. The final provocation was the shift toward national tournaments hard on the heels of the Olympic qualifying fiasco and the divide over the rules, calling to mind the specter of college football bowl games. Finally, the barons and the reformers had something they could agree upon, or so they thought.

CHAPTER 2

SEARCHING FOR CHAMPIONS AND FINDING ENEMIES

THE RISE OF TOURNAMENT BASKETBALL (1937-1939)

Late in 1938 the NCAA announced plans for an inaugural basketball championship for their membership, to be held the following spring. Throughout the late fall and early winter of that year, University of Kansas's "Phog" Allen engaged in fervent correspondence with the NCAA Basketball Committee chair, Ohio State's Harold G. Olsen, regarding ways to neutralize interests they believed undermined or threatened the NCAA's new event. Desperate for favorable media coverage as well as seeking to undermine a potential rival, Olsen proposed that Allen offer a bribe to a writer from the *Kansas City Star*. Eagerly responding, Allen, convinced there were traitors in their midst, proposed a full-blown conspiracy and asked Olsen to fabricate a letter for him to use. Wary of the same forces animating Allen, Carleton College's Marshall Diebold called for a secret investigation of those who had been disloyal to the interests of the NCAA, while Ohio State's Lynn St. John was sure he saw the heavy hand of Nat Holman.[1] In short, the rise of college basketball and the creation of its major postseason tournaments in the 1930s was a story of paranoid jealousies, intense turf wars, and overactions that were both created by and representative of the civil war with the AAU-YMCA.

Far from a continuation of the first civil war with the AAU-YMCA faction, however, this next phase of conflict that surrounded the creation of postseason tournaments was among former allies and comrades within the college game, veterans of the civil war who took tactics and strategies from that conflict and now used them against fellow partisans in a second civil war. The internecine battles of the late 1930s revealed not only the winner-take-all mentality of college basketball's stewards but also the maturation of the NCAA from the uninfluential role of its first three decades to a presumption that it represented the only legitimate voice in college athletics by the end of the 1930s. If football birthed the NCAA, it was basketball that revealed its transition from adolescence. And like an intemperate teenager, many within the NCAA engaged in the petty recriminations and exaggerated challenges pursued by Allen, Olsen, and their confidantes in 1938–1939. But beneath that adolescent braggadocio lay an insecurity in the knowledge that the NCAA was not yet nearly as authoritative as it presumed to be. And worse, in wresting basketball from the AAU-YMCA, the stewards of big-time college basketball had not definitively cordoned off the external commercial interests that might profit from college basketball as they had college football. In the long shadow of college football, few by-products exerted more influence upon the wars of college basketball than bowl games.

Although the Great Depression restrained some of the financial abuses of college football during the 1930s, the unregulated bowl games serving the financial interests of those unaffiliated with higher education actually grew during the decade. This growth emerged from local municipal efforts to use tourism revenues to address the financial shortfalls of the Depression and the inability of the NCAA to regulate the creation of the games or prohibit teams from participating in them. In short order, similar forces turned their attention to college basketball. New York City, like most municipalities during the Depression, struggled to address the overwhelming poverty and human suffering witnessed before New Deal relief programs. Hoping to direct more effectively such efforts in New York City, Mayor Jimmy Walker created the Emergency Unemployment Relief Committee, which proposed staging college football and basketball exhibition games with the proceeds going toward New York's relief efforts. In December 1930 the city staged a series of three football games: New York University (NYU) versus Colgate, Army versus Navy, and a team of Notre Dame all-stars versus the New York Giants. Though the NYU–Colgate game lacked the gate success of the other two contests, the football games did well enough that the committee staged a triple-header basketball benefit in January 1931, which promptly sold out Madison Square Garden. Apparently the football benefits proved overly ambitious, as the following year only a single game was scheduled, but another basketball tripleheader was scheduled there for New Year's Eve 1931. The slate of games featuring six New York–area teams again sold out the seventeen-thousand-seat venue, pressuring the facility to add an additional two thousand temporary seats to accommodate demand. Inability to match the colleges' schedule with the availability of Madison Square Garden led to the 1932 benefit being staged at the city's Seventy-First Regiment Armory, which seated only fifteen hundred, but the benefit returned to the Garden in 1933 with a vengeance, offering a seven-game, day-night program with the afternoon sessions alone bringing in more than twenty thousand fans.[2]

Hoping to maximize exposure for the benefit games, the relief committee also included sportswriters who were expected to promote the games in the pages of the city's daily newspapers. One of these individuals was a young writer named Edward "Ned" Irish, who seized upon the success of the benefit games to propose to the management of Madison Square Garden, desperate to book events during the Depression, that he act as concessionaire to bring college games to the venue. Beginning in 1935, Irish scheduled eight weekend doubleheaders in the Garden featuring New York–area teams and attracting 99,995 spectators. Irish's doubleheaders at the facility launched a successful career in sports promotion that ultimately resulted in his owning the New York Knicks and serving as president of Madison Square Garden. A tireless self-promoter for whatever venture he was hawking, in the eyes of his critics he was arrogant, distant, and crassly driven by the profit motive. Utterly unconcerned with the college coaches' agenda to wrest the game from the AAU or to promote "amateurism," as they chose to define it, Irish was simply interested in promoting events for which fans were willing to pay. Striking upon the success of the 1936 Olympic basketball team and hoping to get the jump on other promoters wanting to schedule exhibitions with them, Irish famously hired the tug *Manhattan* to take him out into New York Harbor to meet up with the Olympic champions upon their return from Berlin before their vessel could even berth. Climbing aboard the liner, Irish greeted the heretofore-amateur players with the proposition "How would you guys like to make some money?"[3]

The Madison Square Garden doubleheaders were simply the most glaring example of college basketball's tremendous growth during the 1930s. The NYU squads, a fan favorite at the Garden, drew capacity crowds during the 1930s and in 1936 actually outdrew their well-regarded football team by nineteen thousand spectators over the course of the season.[4] Attendance increased not only in large urban areas like New York but in the game's hinterlands as well. At Bradley University in Peoria, Illinois, the school's basketball team quickly outgrew its small on-campus gym and began selling out the five-thousand-seat state armory and claimed a radio audience of five hundred thousand listeners. According to a piece on basketball's growth during the period, *Newsweek* asserted that basketball at all levels topped all sports with eighty million spectators in 1935. The same piece noted that at the high school level, 95 percent of schools with enrollments of four hundred or greater fielded basketball teams, while only 55 percent of those same schools fielded football teams.[5] The value of basketball also increased at Pittsburgh's Duquesne University during the period. Duquesne hired twenty-three-year-old head coach Charles "Chick" Davies in 1924, and by 1928 he was earning an annual salary of fifteen hundred dollars. As the Depression deepened, however, Davies's salary began a meteoric rise. In 1932 he earned twenty-five hundred dollars, a 66 percent raise from his 1928 contract. Two years later he received only a 20 percent raise to three thousand dollars, but his contract also stipulated free tuition so that he could earn his master's degree. Two years later he earned another 20 percent raise and continued tuition for his degree, such that he was making thirty-six hundred dollars annually with the cost of a master's degree thrown in gratis. Thus, within eight years Duquesne granted Davies a 171 percent raise at the height of the Depression when the average annual family income was only fifteen hundred dollars.[6] Rule changes during the period also assisted in the growth of the game. The imposition of the backcourt violation requiring teams to move the ball into the offensive end within ten seconds, and the elimination of the center jump after each made basket accelerated the pace of the game, making it more exciting and fan-friendly. Thus, increased fan interest, the profitability of large venues, and up-tempo rules all helped create the college basketball spectacle. According to writer Peter Bjarkman, "The true birth of college basketball . . . came in the 1930s." A significant piece of that process included the arrival of national postseason tournaments.[7]

The creation of the NCAA Basketball Tournament in 1939 was in fact a reaction to the creation of two earlier tournaments, themselves a product of outside forces. The 1936 Olympic qualifying process engendered tremendous resentment from college coaches who interpreted the NCAA Olympic qualifying process as engineered by the AAU with the intention of disadvantaging the college teams. However, the NCAA playoff, which the USOC described as the university section, included only NCAA member schools and thus did not include the vast majority of college basketball teams. Nonmembers, mostly smaller colleges, were not given their own tournament but were forced to participate in the AAU Tournament. The decision outraged many small college coaches who had gathered to discuss their frustration in January 1936 in Winfield, Kansas, at the annual Southwestern Invitational Basketball Tournament. The group coalesced under the leadership of Emil Liston, head coach at Kansas's Baker University, who wrote to the USOC, voicing his frustration with a process that placed smaller colleges at such a tremendous disadvantage. Claiming that at the moment, small college frustration had not yet reached a point of outright rebellion against the Olympic program, Liston tellingly noted that "the disgust of the present set-up" privileging both AAU and NCAA teams but disadvantaging the small colleges "might easily grow into such."[8]

Following the 1936 AAU Tournament, which had been hosted in Kansas City since its inception in 1921, the event relocated to Denver in search of better financial guarantees provided by municipal organizers. Kansas City boosters, led by Phog Allen's Olympic nemesis Joseph Reilly, proposed filling the void left by the AAU Tournament with a college-only event. Reilly and Liston eventually joined forces, deciding to stage a national collegiate invitational tournament in 1937. The two initially proposed a sixteen-team bracket to include only conference champions, though logistics eventually reduced the initial event to eight teams. Indicative of the tournament's initial rationale, the group rebuked the Olympic qualifying process and embraced what would become a consistently populist message by proudly noting, "No college team will be barred." Supportive coaches of the event optimistically believed "such a tournament would receive recognition from 1940 Olympic officials," thus avoiding the situation that had developed in 1936.[9]

No theme proved stronger in the creation of the small college tournament—which originally operated under the name "Intercollegiate Tournament" to demonstrate its independence from the AAU—than as a form of deliverance from AAU professionalism. With the AAU Tournament having decamped to Denver, Kansas City sportswriters now turned on the event they had once hyped by pillorying it as the bête noir of the newly proposed college tournament. Describing the growing support for the Intercollegiate Tournament, the *Kansas City Star* noted, "Coaches everywhere have endorsed the idea, believing that college teams should have a national tournament of their own rather than elbow their way through national AAU fields in which are 'tramp' players who make basketball a business." The *Star* played not only on themes of professionalism but also on the desire for collegiate control of the game: "For too long, the colleges have resented being tossed into the maelstrom of the AAU basketball tournament competition against pro-tainted teams. The lure of competition is strong, but nevertheless, the college coaches have complained at the injustice of the thing even while taking part. The college tournament plan offers them a way out. . . . Under college management and control with the colleges collecting and distributing the gate receipts among themselves, the idea may appeal." On the eve of the first Intercollegiate Tournament in Kansas City, the *Star*'s main section editorialized, saying, "Always, the colleges have resented the manner of conducting the National AAU tournament in which college teams are thrust into competition with the high powered independent teams, many of which carry the taint of professionalism."[10]

Though the first tournament took in less than seven hundred dollars and Reilly dropped out of further involvement after the initial event, Liston was encouraged enough by other small college coaches to continue the event. His vision won the support of Dr. James Naismith, who invented the game, and Naismith consented to Liston's suggestion that the championship trophy bear Naismith's name, with Naismith on hand to award the inaugural trophy in 1937. Convinced the small colleges had no place in the AAU, Liston journeyed to the AAU Tournament in Denver to proselytize small college coaches there. Envisioning a tournament of thirty-two teams "to include every section of the country . . . and thus lend excuse to the title of National Collegiate Championship," Liston created a Board of Management that included many of the luminaries of big-time college basketball, including John Bunn at Stanford University, Henry Iba at Oklahoma A&M University, Arthur Lonborg at Northwestern University, and Adolph Rupp at University of Kentucky, though the extent of their involvement has never been made entirely clear. What is clear is that NABC president and Missouri head coach George Edwards chaired the Intercollegiate Tournament's seeding committee in 1938, helping Liston select teams and place them in the brackets. Liston was emphatic, however, that the tournament was not a commercial affair. Tournament proceeds underwrote the lodging and meals of the participating teams: "No one will make any money out of this tournament. In the event that receipts amount to more than the local expenses, said amount will be placed in the reserve fund under the control of the Board of Management."[11] As the *Star* put it in defending Liston's trolling for teams while in Denver, "He has no ax to grind. . . . He is a widely respected college man with an idea he thinks may appeal to college men."[12] Thus, under the direction of Emil Liston of tiny Baker University, a college-only tournament emerged under the leadership and direction of college coaches on a not-for-profit basis that stood a good chance of being recognized by the US Olympic Committee as a legitimate venue in which to determine the collegiate participants in the Olympic qualifying process. Seemingly, it was everything the coaches had wanted since the fracture of the old Joint Rules Committee in 1927 over the dribble rule.

Just as the AAU Tournament's ambivalence toward college teams created the Kansas City event, the profitability of the Madison Square Garden doubleheaders, which continued unabated into the late 1930s, helped create the National Invitation Tournament (NIT). In 1938 the Garden doubleheaders attracted a record 162,309 paying spectators, which provided the seed for a postseason, college-only tournament. Almost assuredly prompted by Ned Irish, New York's Metropolitan Basketball Writers Association (MBWA) announced in February 1938 their intention to host "a nation-wide intercollegiate invitation tournament." As both an expression of generating local fan interest and local assumptions about New York's place at the center of the basketball universe, the tournament's initial plan called for the two leading city teams to play two top-ranked teams from the East. The winners of those two games advanced to play two top teams from elsewhere in the country, with the winners of those games playing for the championship.[13]

So while the New York area teams had to play an extra game to reach the championship, two of them were guaranteed entry. When the first tournament tipped off in March 1938, organizers tweaked it slightly so that the two metro teams played each other, ensuring that only one metro team could make the semifinals. But just as the game's Protestant Midwest interests disdained the polyglot urbanity of the East and the rough-and-tumble game as marked by the post-pivot play, the NIT's New York–centric organizers had little patience for a game played by those they dismissed as undersized farm boys and even less regard for the teetotaling temperance views their fans brought with them. The writers' primary concern was to stage an event with teams that enjoyed national attention that filled not only the Garden but local bars, restaurants, and hotels as well. As a result, they rarely invited to the Big Apple one of the small, mostly Midwestern schools who found Emil Liston's Kansas City tournament so attractive.[14]

While those within New York found no trouble with the privileging of metro teams, many outside the city were less enamored with the caveat, simply because it ensured a spot for one less potentially deserving team merely as an accident of geography. Even more troubling to fans was that without any defined selection criteria, they consistently believed that competitively deserving teams were excluded in favor of teams who better served the financial interests of the event's sponsors. In a letter that modern fans of college basketball will find all too familiar, Maurice Murphy of Rhode Island wrote to the *New York Times* in 1938 to lambaste the NIT committee for excluding his home-state school. After incredulously asking, "How can the Metropolitan Basketball Writers' Association justify the omission of Rhode Island . . . from its tournament?," Murphy went on to cite not only the Rams' scoring average but their margin of victory and the quality of their opponents to establish the University of Rhode Island's (URI's) tournament credentials and to highlight (in his mind) the selection committee's obvious disregard for Rams basketball.[15] Not for the last time, college basketball fans in one region decried the perceived ignorance of their team's abilities from the decision makers in another region, all the while seeing that decision through the lens of disrespect.

A more substantive issue that troubled some critics of the NIT was its promotional nature. Held at the discretion of the writers, organized to privilege the inclusion of metro teams, and beholden to Irish and the Garden, all aimed at driving gate revenue and the hospitality industry, the NIT was a commercialized venture from the start. To create the appearance of shared oversight, the writers invited two prominent collegiate sports figures with New York ties—Asa Bushnell and Hamilton Salmon Jr.—to serve on the NIT's advisory board, but most within college basketball saw that as little more than window dressing. In reality it appeared that college basketball was following a similar path as college football by allowing local commercial and booster organizations to host unregulated, for-profit events entirely detached from the universities participating in them. The ease with which so many accepted this assumption was illustrated by the immediate and ever-present comparison to the football bowl system in the NIT's early years. Irish initially referred to the NIT as "the Rose Bowl of [b]asketball," illustrating his vision for college basketball's postseason future. Irish was not alone in seeing college basketball's future through the lens of college football's past. In 1934 a group of Atlantic City boosters attempted to create a year-end exhibition of the best of college basketball by hosting what they too described as "the Rose Bowl of basketball." It was a comparison both writers and readers in New York constantly made. After the MBWA initially proposed the NIT, several fans wrote letters to the editors of New York papers to propose teams, with one reader referring to it as the "Rose Bowl basketball tournament being sponsored by the MWBA." Arthur Daley, the dean of the *New York Times* sports page, referred to "the 'Rose Bowl' court tournament the writers are planning at the Garden," describing the NIT's intent as basketball's culminating event as "a Rose Bowl climax." Beat writers too described the NIT as "the basketball Rose Bowl classic" and "the closest thing that basketball has to a post-season Rose Bowl."[16] The comparison to the Rose Bowl also illustrated what the writers and promoters of the NIT intended for the public to perceive of their event: the most prominent finale of the basketball season, preferably for the public to think of the tournament's champion as the best in college basketball. It was a claim the writers did not back away from. On the eve of the 1939 tournament, the *Brooklyn Daily Eagle* asserted that the NIT "is already considered the top championship in the country. The winner . . . will be recognized as" the best in college basketball, while the winners of other events were merely also-rans. The following year, Everett Morris of the *New York Herald Tribune* similarly asserted that although the writers made "no national championship claims for its tourney, you will have to stretch your imagination more than somewhat to find a more likely pretender to the throne of collegiate court king" than the NIT champ.[17]

For proponents of the idea of college athletics run by the college establishment, particularly those still stung by the findings of the 1929 Carnegie Report on college football, such a naked comparison with college football's most commercialized aspect was troubling. Indicative of the MBWA's own self-consciousness on the matter, writer Louis Effrat defended the group, saying, "The metropolitan association does not wish to be classified as a promotion office. Nor is it seeking personal profit of any kind."[18] Nonetheless, Henry Van Arsdale Porter, NABC secretary in 1939, feared a college tournament that might "get into the hands of any unofficial group which may have the nerve and commercial backing to undertake control. . . . I do not think for one minute that the various athletic boards of control in the colleges will sanction an organization which is entirely independent of any regularly approved collegiate organization."[19] Though Porter exaggerated the concern that many schools' administrative oversight boards would show the NIT, he revealed the holier-than-thou attitude of many within the college coaching ranks at the time about the appearance of commercialized college athletics outside the college's control. And to surrender the future of postseason big-time college basketball to the likes of Ned Irish and his multiethnic New York cronies was simply untenable to the game's Midwestern ideologues like Phog Allen and Lynn St. John.[20]

The idea of a national championship tournament was not new. Chad Carlson has unearthed several events that were hoped would become a single championship tournament event. In 1935, after appearing in one of Irish's Garden doubleheaders, Kentucky coach Adolph Rupp openly pined for such an event, suggesting, "If the leading teams of each section would agree to play a round robin tournament in some centrally located city . . . a sort of Rose Bowl champion in basketball would be crowned each year."[21] Faced now with outside commercial interests controlling basketball's postseason as they did football's, the NABC began discussions in 1938 to host a national college tournament run entirely by the coaches' organization in alliance with the NCAA. Harold Olsen, head coach at Ohio State, wrote a letter to the coaches' convention that year not only explaining the potential benefit of such an event but also asserting that the NIT did not serve the interests of college basketball, implying that the tournament instead benefited promotional and financial interests of the writers' association, Madison Square Garden, and the New York hospitality industry. Olsen's rationale for such a tournament revealed much about the mind-set of the college coaches, speaking to both their anxieties about outside commercialization and their aspirations for the future role of the coaches' association. Since its inception the NABC increasingly resented the actions of others as they affected the college game, assigning to themselves the imposing moniker "Guardians of the Game." The existence of both the Intercollegiate Tournament and the NIT demonstrated "a demand for deciding by some means a national collegiate championship" but also raised the specter of football bowl games. According to Olsen, "The proper group to sponsor such championship play is the Coaches Association" in conjunction with the NCAA. As far as those two organizations were concerned, any tournament organized by any other group was inherently improper and illegitimate and promised the same headache that bowl games delivered to college football. A genuine college event should be sanctioned by "the NCAA . . . rather than some less desirable sponsor." By creating an NCAA national championship in basketball, the group knew such an event would be regulated by the NCAA's committee structure and avoid criticisms that the games did not lead to any recognized championship.[22]

Olsen's proposal addressed several other concerns of the coaches, such as their commercial aspirations, while simultaneously discrediting the game's commercialization by others, describing the tournament as "bringing in some very welcome revenue to the National Association of Basketball Coaches" that would go directly to the coaches, with "no outside promoters to get their first 'cut.'" Olsen also asserted that hosting their own tournament served as "a means for insuring proper collegiate representation in the next Olympic game try-outs." Finally, Olsen played to the coaches' loyalty to the NABC and their desire to see the association's influence grow, suggesting that a tournament "held in conjunction with our annual convention would be the finest tie-up that we could possibly have."[23] Olsen envisioned a two-pronged climactic event in the college basketball world, featuring both the tournament and the coaches' annual meeting.[24]

After the reading of Olsen's letter to the convention floor, Phog Allen seconded Olsen's sentiments by reviewing the 1936 Olympic qualifying process from his perspective, claiming that "the college people got basketball into the Olympics" and then were sacrificed to the financial interests of the AAU. Allen maintained that subsequently the NCAA decided not to host a basketball championship "and left basketball in the hands of the AAU." Though Allen's version of events reveals more about his perspective than reality, Georgia Tech University's Roy Mundorff called for a motion to create an NABC committee to examine the possibility of hosting a national basketball tournament in conjunction with the NCAA. Not surprisingly, that committee consisted of Phog Allen and Harold Olsen, as well as Stanford's John Bunn.[25] Clearly, Allen, Olsen, and Bunn pushed the tournament proposal hard, but according to at least one NABC member, the rest of the membership was largely ambivalent. Howard Hobson, head coach of the University of Oregon, which eventually won the first tournament, declared that "interest was not great" among the membership for creating the tournament, and Terry Frei asserts that it was largely the prestige of the tourney supporters that carried the day.[26] The committee nonetheless proposed to NCAA president William Brownlee Owens a tournament involving eight teams, one from each existing NCAA district, with the four regions in the East playing off to create a champion to meet the winner of the four-team playoff from the districts in the West. The proposal raised the issue of bowl games, stressing "that the conduct of collegiate basketball events should be in the hands of the colleges or some association of colleges and not in the hands of any outside promoters" as was the case in college football. It was an issue that resonated sufficiently enough with Owens that, using Olsen's words almost exactly, he felt it necessary to stress it in a year-end piece in the annual *Basketball Guide* put out by the NCAA. From there, the NCAA's executive committee discussed the tournament proposal at its October 1938 meeting, approving the tournament and naming its own organizing committee with Olsen as chair and including Allen and Bunn as well as William Chandler, Marquette's head coach, and Hamilton Salmon Jr., the former bane of the Providence College student newspaper.[27]

The tournament selection committee now faced a unique situation that no NCAA postseason event had yet confronted and illustrated some of the conflicts and factors that shaped the early NCAA. By the late 1930s the NCAA offered championships in track, swimming, cross-country, and wrestling, in large measure because those were sports in which the AAU also offered championships and were Olympic sports. (In contrast, football, which the AAU did not sanction and did not enjoy a place on the Olympic program, happily continued without a national championship.) All of those sports qualified participants through objective standards of time or head-to-head victory, and, while awarding team championships based on point aggregations, were essentially individual events. In sanctioning the first team sport championship, the NCAA now handed a hornet's nest to the tournament selection committee. Olsen's committee named district selection committees in December 1938, charged with identifying teams from their respective districts to fill the eight-team bracket. In instances where a single team in a region was clearly dominant, the committee was empowered to offer an invitation outright. In instances where a region witnessed several strong teams, the selection committee attempted to arrange some kind of playoff, although as was soon demonstrated, that caveat allowed for significant variations and inequalities.[28]

Of greater significance in the short run was the tournament's oversight and intent. Sanctioned by the NCAA, it was organized and run by the NABC that first year as a hybrid sponsorship meant to serve the mutual interests of each group. In addition to Olsen's desire to use the tournament as bait for the NABC's annual meeting, it could also be used to solidify control over the game's rules and governance. Olsen ensured that a member of the NCAA Rules Committee chaired each district selection committee and that "the great majority of the committee members are members of the [NABC]," thereby excluding any potential dissidents from either the AAU-YMCA faction or even those overtly linked with the New York style of play (notably absent was CCNY coach and NABC member Nat Holman). In an effort to secure favorable media coverage and thus extend the prominence of both the NABC and the NCAA, Olsen also provided for half of the selection committees to include members of the media: Everett Morris of the *New York Herald Tribune*; Kenneth Gregory, an Atlanta-based stringer for the *Lexington (KY) Herald*; C.E. McBride of the *Kansas City Star*; and George White of the *Dallas News*.[29]

Finally, the NABC and the NCAA apparently conceived of the tournament not as a national clearinghouse for all of college basketball but as an event designed essentially as a perk for NCAA members and perhaps as an incentive to increase membership. Prior to the beginning of the first tournament, Harold Olsen wrote to Phog Allen to insist that "it is incumbent upon each member of the committee to spread the word . . . that this is not a 'National Intercollegiate Championship' sponsored by the NCAA, but rather a tournament run by the NCAA for its membership only."[30] Olsen was not the only one wary that the NCAA event might become an oversized collegiate version of the AAU Tournament, whereby basketball mercenaries with little ideological affinity with the NCAA marauded annually. Henry Van Arsdale Porter, a member of the NABC's executive committee and secretary of the rules committee, "envision[ed] all kinds of attempts on the part of commercial clubs and promotional groups" to involve themselves "lead[ing] up to the national championship."[31] Consequently, Olsen was at pains to ensure that such teams stayed out of the NCAA event: "Obviously, there are a number of schools with good basketball teams who are not members of the NCAA, but we are not interested in them in connection with our tournament."[32] Thus, the NCAA Tournament sought to avoid comparison in its participants with the AAU and in its organization with college football.

The inaugural 1939 tournament was only a moderate success. After struggling to settle on dates and secure appropriate locations, the committee hosted the final in Northwestern University's on-campus Patten Gymnasium in one of the last events held there before the university demolished it the following year. The tournament also struggled to attract quality teams. The Eastern Intercollegiate Basketball League remained largely indifferent to the tournament just as most of their members remained largely indifferent to the NCAA. For example, the conference champion, Dartmouth University, refused the NCAA invitation and would continue to do so for another two years, although another conference member, Brown University, played as an independent team in the 1939 tournament. The University of Rhode Island—the highest-scoring team in the nation, averaging a then unheard of seventy points a game and featuring one of the leading players in the nation in Chet Jaworski—also refused to play in the NCAA Tournament. Arguably the two best teams in the country, Loyola University of Chicago and Long Island University, both undefeated, chose to play in the NIT. Though both schools were ineligible because they did not yet belong to the NCAA, neither even considered joining the NCAA to be eligible for the event as was common in the tournament's early years. Loyola's decision was particularly galling to the NCAA, which hoped to drive gate revenue for a championship game in Evanston, Illinois, that might feature a Chicago team. Finally, and the one shortcoming that most concerned the sponsoring coaches, the inaugural tournament lost money. In a quick handwritten memo to Lynn St. John after the tournament, director Harold Olsen was forced to qualify his optimism by noting, "The tournament was a success in every way except financially and in our failure to enlist the support of the Eastern Intercollegiate League." Later, he also described as a "bad spot" the existence of the NIT and the teams that played in that event rather than the NCAA and again remarked on "the apathy of the Eastern Intercollegiate League." The following year, things did not get much better when Rice Institute, the University of Colorado, and Oklahoma A&M, all conference champions, spurned the NCAA by choosing instead to play in the NIT.[33]

Because of this situation, the selection process of the early NCAA Tournament was a haphazard affair. Olsen's committee proposed, and the NCAA accepted, a tournament field selected entirely by the selection committees, with no explicit provisions for including conference champions or criteria for how a team might qualify. In correspondence with other members of the committees, Olsen acknowledged the unease of many within higher education, sparked by their experiences with college football bowl games, about the naked pursuit of postseason activity, which not only prolonged students' distraction from the classroom but also was often linked with commercialized entities. In announcing the tournament format to the media, he mentioned the possibility of district playoffs to select each district's representative but said that such playoffs were not "necessary or desirable."[34] He urged committee members to "bear in mind the very general objection to any amount of post-season play," and thus "we want to select *the* best team in each district without any playoffs" if possible. In the event that such a determination between two teams was impossible and "these two teams are willing to play off to see who will represent the district," Olsen encouraged the committee to arrange such a game.[35] So while some teams might gain entrance into the tournament through some kind of elimination process, others appeared based simply on the district committee's assumptions of their excellence. With no explicit criteria to evaluate teams and no mandate for an elimination process, the committee unsurprisingly deferred to conference champions who, by dint of conference play, had hopefully demonstrated some level of superiority. While this carried a certain degree of logic, it inherently put at a disadvantage the tremendously large number of schools that did not belong to conferences at all. Doing so privileged the most prominent schools and conferences and was an issue that the tournament consistently faced in its early years.[36]

In 1939 Wake Forest University was upset by Clemson University in the first round of the Southern Conference Tournament on a basket at the buzzer. Even though Clemson went on to win the tournament, the selection committee felt that Wake Forest was still the best team in the district and invited them instead. Similarly, North Carolina State University (NC State) won the Southern Conference Tournament in 1947 but was passed over by the selection committee in favor of the US Naval Academy. The year before, when the tournament committee remained divided over the University of North Carolina and Duke, it proposed a playoff game for the NCAA berth. North Carolina refused, believing it was the deserving team, and the cowed selection committee extended the invitation to the Tar Heels, a bluff that did not work in 1950 when the committee proposed a playoff between the University of Kentucky and NC State. Kentucky's Adolph Rupp refused, and the committee invited NC State instead. The same year witnessed the committee's inability to decide between CCNY, Duquesne, and St. Johns University, so it simply decided to invite whichever team went furthest in the NIT, which had changed the dates of its event, now conceivably allowing teams to participate in both events.[37] Thus, the nebulous process by which teams gained entrance into the NCAA Tournament allowed for all sorts of allegations of bias and favoritism, where reputation, prominence, conference affiliation, as well as the tournament's own agenda, benefited the larger schools in the established conferences and excluded the kinds of smaller schools that played outside of the major conferences and media markets that the Intercollegiate Tournament attracted.

No example better illustrates this than the case of New York University (NYU) in 1940. The Violets were one of college basketball's best teams that season, undefeated and playing what many perceived as one of the toughest schedules. Both the NIT and the NCAA Tournament eagerly desired NYU to participate in their event, with both organizations thinking they had a claim to the Violets. As a metro New York school, NYU felt "terrific pressure" from both fans and the media to support the hometown NIT, as well as from fans who simply wanted to see them play locally. But NYU's Board of Athletic Control was chaired by faculty member Phillip O. Badger, NYU's representative to the NCAA, who was an ardent supporter and future president of that organization, and a personal confidante of Harold Olsen and Lynn St. John, who both hoped they might sway Badger to deliver the Violets to the NCAA Tournament. The 1940 NCAA Tournament took place more than a week after the NIT and almost three weeks after NYU's last regular season game. Badger acknowledged that the board of control would not look favorably upon keeping the players "in training" and away from their studies for such an extended period. Conversely, the board also looked warily upon the NIT's connection to Ned Irish and the commercial nature of that event.[38]

In response to Badger's protestations, and hoping to secure the Violets for the NCAA Tournament, Olsen wrote a rather fantastic letter to Badger in late February 1940. After acknowledging that NYU was a lock to receive the bid from District 2 in the NCAA Tournament—no stretch considering they were undefeated—Olsen then played upon Badger's loyalty to the NCAA by saying he hoped "that you would feel as I do about [NYU's] participation" in the tournament and the benefits to be accrued. Olsen then noted how the initial tournament in 1939 had incurred a debt, but with the possibility of the Eastern regional played in New York City featuring the undefeated Violets: "I am certain we can wipe out completely the deficit which the tournament incurred last season." Having thus placed the financial future of the NCAA Tournament at Badger's feet, Olsen offered a questionable quid pro quo, implying that if NYU agreed to play in the NCAA Tournament, he would make sure that the Eastern regional was played in Madison Square Garden. Olsen offered one final inducement to Badger that if such a result could be delivered, "Garden arrangements, looking after NCAA interests,

etc. could very well be handled by you." In case Badger was not yet sufficiently obligated or enticed, Olsen closed thusly: "Thanks in advance
for what I am sure will be a favorable reply. I don't see how it could be
otherwise and I feel definitely that if we can't secure a team like New
York University under conditions such as we have this year that the
whole idea of the National Tournament ought to be thrown right out
the window."[39] Nonetheless, NYU's Board of Athletic Control decided
in 1940 not to extend the season or trade with commercial interests by
rejecting invitations from both tournaments, and contrary to Olsen's
suggestion, the NCAA Tournament managed to survive.

In addition to privileging some teams while holding others at arm's
length, Olsen attempted to distance the NCAA event from the other two
collegiate tournaments: "We are not competing with other tournaments
as may be run throughout the country; we are simply trying to put over
in the best possible manner this NCAA tournament, but I think it should
be rather clear to everybody that if we do a good job, this tournament
will be the outstanding basketball tournament in the country." Thus,
having declared that the NCAA event was not a national championship
but simply an in-house tournament for NCAA members, the basketball
committee promptly began positioning the tournament as the premier
college basketball championship. In announcing the date of the final,
the tournament was forced to move the championship game to a different date to accommodate another event, but Olsen saw the benefit
of the basketball game not having to compete for media attention and
"publicity." To maximize media coverage and public attention, he urged
members to "start a campaign to make the public a little bit 'national
intercollegiate tournament conscious.'"[40] These contradictions—along
with Olsen's assertion that the NCAA Tournament was not in competition with other events while simultaneously claiming that he envisioned
making those other events eventually obsolete—reveal the contradiction
of the NCAA claiming the tournament was a simple in-house affair for
its members.

Phog Allen certainly saw the other events as competition with the
NCAA Tournament, and when NCAA teams chose to play elsewhere,
it invoked in him the same kind of response that Nat Holman's actions had. When Rice, Colorado, and Oklahoma A&M accepted bids
to play in the 1940 NIT, Allen disgustedly wrote Olsen, "The ridiculous
has happened," with the three conference champions "all entering the
promotional tournament in New York." Having himself made several
decisions regarding the profitability of the tournament, Allen rather

disingenuously railed, "There is no justifiable reason for this except that these NCAA teams are entering for the money." More than lack of loyalty, however, for Allen, such actions endangered the entire NCAA Tournament along with both the public perception of college athletics and attitudes of faculty athletic oversight: "This will cause confusion in the minds of the academicians who will resent [the NCAA] tournament. Ours is an educational project and the other is nothing but a promotional venture which strikes at the heart of our tournament." Allen wanted to see the NCAA create punitive measures requiring eligible teams to participate in the NCAA Tournament or face consequences: "This is what some of our so-called loyal NCAA people need. They are taking all the benefit from the NCAA and then playing both sides."[41]

Some members of the media saw the tournaments in competition with each other as well but in terms Allen would have found distasteful, and the comparison of the Intercollegiate Tournament with the NIT and NCAA events was not flattering to the latter two. Writing on the eve of the first NCAA Tournament, Associated Press columnist Whitney Martin compared the three events, writing, "It may be a question of which is the keener—the competition among the teams or the competitions among tournaments." In assessing the three events, Martin suggested, "The Kansas City tournament would seem the most representative and consequently carry more prestige," because unlike the other two events, the Intercollegiate was "open to all accredited four-year colleges." In evaluating the 1938 champions of the NIT (Temple University) and Intercollegiate Tournament (Warrensburg College), Whitney noted that Temple played its way through a bracket of teams from a limited pool, chosen not by competition but by the whims of a selection committee beholden to commercial interests. And while Temple had to play only three games in the NIT's eight-team field, Warrensburg had to navigate a thirty-two-team bracket to win five games in as many days. Temple might well have beaten Warrensburg, according to Whitney, "but the fact remains that it didn't and as Warrensburg was competing in a meet in which no teams were barred it would seem to be entitled to No. 1 national rating." Whitney embraced Liston's populist rhetoric by further suggesting that the NCAA Tournament's exclusion of all nonmembers denied that event of any legitimacy to claim a collegiate champion.[42]

The coaches' decision to include the media in the selection process indicated their interest in promoting the event as a commercial venture but nonetheless continued to criticize commercialized collegiate athletic events. In discussing the new tournament, NCAA president Owens declared it "fitting" that such an enterprise should not "be left to private promotion and enterprise."[43] The difference, as Olsen made clear in his committee's report to the NABC, was that "the conduct of collegiate basketball events should be in the hands of the colleges . . . and not in the hands of any outside promoters."[44] Like Allen, he drew the distinction between outsiders making money on amateurs as opposed to the NCAA making money on them. Having now created their own tournament and convinced themselves that only the NCAA, in conjunction with the coaches, could properly chaperone the meaning of such an event, organizers of the NCAA Tournament set about attempting to undermine, delegitimize, and vilify both the NIT and, to a much greater extent, the Intercollegiate Tournament in Kansas City.

For reasons that remain unclear, the NCAA's hostility toward the NIT always remained just below the surface, never achieving the venomous ferocity directed toward Emil Liston and his group. Nonetheless, the comments of people like Henry Van Arsdale Porter, William Owens, and Phog Allen about commercialized ventures and outside promoters were clearly aimed at the NIT. Ohio State's Lynn St. John feared the undue influence of the media upon the conduct of the games themselves, invoking the specter of college football by noting in 1938 the clamoring from the media, which lacked "any reason, or sense or judgement," that resulted in the football rules committee moving the hash marks in from the sidelines and liberalizing rules governing the forward pass. Allowing the media into the organization of collegiate basketball, according to St. John, would likely result in the basketball rules committee's being similarly "inveigled into doing something as a result of this thinking and writing on the part of various and sundry sports editors."[45] Thus revealed a fundamental paradox of the early NCAA Basketball Tournament: a desire to cultivate and exploit the commercial media to the advantage of the tournament's growth while keeping the media and its populist (read: uninformed) constituency at arm's length when it came to influences and profit.

At some point in 1938, representatives of the NCAA Tournament approached the writers association to encourage them to abandon the NIT. A flurry of correspondence between those associated with the NCAA Tournament and New York writers and Irish prior to December 1938 led the writers' association to agree tentatively to end the NIT in deference to the NCAA event. In Olsen's year-end report to the NCAA, he declared that the proposed NCAA Tournament was "meeting with a fine response" from nationwide media, "particularly the Metropolitan Sports Writers Association in New York," who "have agreed that they will get behind the NCAA Tournament rather than to continue with the one they inaugurated last year."[46] NYU's Phillip Badger, writing to Olsen in late December, also believed "that the local tournament with which these writers are concerned will be discontinued" and that Everett Morris, of the *New York Tribune* and president of the NIT's executive committee, "is very kindly disposed to us and would be in favor of abandoning the writers' tournament."[47] As late as January 21, 1939, the writers decided that in light of the NCAA Tournament, "plans for the [NIT] are being held in abeyance." Within four days, however, the writers changed their tune decidedly, claiming they had approached the NCAA and offered up the NIT as the NCAA's Eastern regional.[48] Either the writers' sentiments on the matter changed dramatically, or Olsen and Badger badly misread the signals coming from the writers' association. On the same day as Badger's letter to Olsen, the writers expressed their desire to continue the NIT.

It is unclear how strongly the writers seriously considered abandoning the NIT. Louis Effrat explained, "It isn't that the association has tired of the idea, . . . but the proposed tournament by the NCAA creates a situation which places the metropolitan scribes in an uncomfortable situation."[49] The writers were wary of being held up as pariahs by the college establishment for potentially encroaching on the NCAA's domain: "Above all, the scribes definitely are against being called obstructionists by those whose opinions hold that the NCAA tournament shall be the only one." But the writers knew they also had advantages, most notably that as long as Ned Irish remained involved, the NIT enjoyed the advantage in competing for dates at Madison Square Garden. The group also felt that the NIT's primacy gave it priority, conveniently ignoring the Intercollegiate Tournament in Kansas City that began play a year earlier, by declaring, "the idea was born here." They were inclined to continue the NIT, because "public opinion is with the [writers] and the tournament should go on."[50]

Eventually, the two tournaments declared an uneasy truce, the motivations for which remain unclear. Hoping to avoid "incur[ring] the enmity of the NCAA," the NIT's executive committee agreed to study the problem and seek some compromise. The writers passed a resolution hoping to sway public opinion, asserting "that their tournament was not under any circumstances to be regarded as a rival to the proposed NCAA championships."[51] One obvious solution would have been for the NIT to move their tournament to earlier in the season so as not to conflict with the NCAA's end-of-season event. To do so, however, would have required the NIT to abandon the implication that its tournament produced an annual champion of college basketball, something it was unwilling to do. Another solution would have been for the NCAA to accept the writers' proposal to allow the NIT to serve as the Eastern regional for the NCAA Tournament. But this would have required the colleges to get into bed with Irish and the appearance of outside promoters. It also surely would have involved sharing tournament revenues, a proposal that would have brought the tightfisted Allen howling at the barricades, but either proposal would have faced heavy opposition within the college ranks.

In announcing the continuation of the NIT, the writers also extended an olive branch to the NABC and the NCAA by "vot[ing] to give the NCAA all the help possible in the conduct of its national championship tournament."[52] Phillip Badger, in writing to assure NCAA president Owens "that all of us here in [New York] did everything that we could" to bring about the end of the NIT, contended that "certain coaches gave these writers to understand that the coaches as a whole were not very enthusiastic about [the NCAA] tournament." Badger alleged that the flattery of New York writers, who often took coaches to lunch on their expense accounts, wooed coaches who, "in their efforts to get favorable publicity for their teams, are very likely to play up a bit to the writers." He reported specifically that Marquette University's William Chandler had encouraged the writers in this fashion. More than simply feeding their own vanity, some coaches also conveyed to the writers some confusion as to the impetus for the NCAA Tournament, echoing Howard Hobson's sentiments that they never really wanted it in the first place, a sentiment Badger was at pains to dispel with the media.[53] Ohio State's Lynn St. John, however, saw more nefarious forces at work; according to him, it was none other than Nat Holman who had spread the notions that the coaches were ambivalent about the NCAA Tournament and that Harold Olsen had plunged ahead on his own "without benefit of clergy."[54]

More than simply seeking to convince the writers that the coaches did in fact support the NCAA Tournament, allies of the tournament sought to put the writers on the defensive and continued to pressure them to abandon the NIT. On the eve of the inaugural NCAA event, Phillip Badger wrote a lengthy and remarkably bold letter to Ned Irish, laying out the NCAA's claim to govern all of collegiate athletics, the necessity of amateur control, and the subordinate position of the media within the enterprise. Badger wrote that "it is distinctly to be regretted" that an agreement could not be reached to end the NIT. But lest Irish see the NCAA Tournament as merely a trial venture or simply tangential to NCAA affairs, Badger hastened to assure him that there was "no question . . . that the NCAA will continue" its tournament in the same vein as its other championships in track, wrestling, swimming, boxing, and tennis. Asserting the NCAA's amateur legitimacy in overseeing these events, Badger mentioned how the United States Golf Association deferred to the NCAA in allowing that body to assume control of its amateur championship, thereby also adding golf to the growing list of NCAA championships. And while acknowledging that the writers in general, and Irish personally, "have done much to publicize intercollegiate basketball" and grant access to Madison Square Garden, Badger bluntly informed Irish "that the function of the writers is that of reporting the games and should not be that of promoting them. The conducting of tournaments in which college teams play should be in the hands of the colleges."[55]

More than simply asserting the primacy of the NCAA in sponsoring such events, however, Badger went on to assert that continued promotional involvement of the writers or other commercial entities ultimately threatened college athletics. According to Badger, the creation of the NCAA Tournament was essentially forced upon the association by the NIT and the Intercollegiate Tournament: "Something had to be done in an effort to head off the development of post-season tournaments all over the country which were being promoted and, in some instances, styled as intercollegiate championships." Badger again raised the specter of bowl games in asserting, "If this promotional and professional movement were to be allowed to run rampant, it would do much to hurt intercollegiate basketball," creating an unregulated commercialized environment similar to college football. And exhibit A in that movement in the opinion of many was Ned Irish. Indeed, the colleges were already facing "considerable criticism," according to Badger, "for staging games on our regular schedules under your auspices in Madison Square Garden." Although Badger acknowledged that the lack of collegiate gym space in New York made the playing of games at the Garden a necessity, he pronounced, "We must do everything in our power to see that no further fuel is added to the fire. In short, any post-season invitation tournament held here in New York City, such as the Basketball Writers are now sponsoring, does incite further criticism" such that "if the writers persist in continuing their tournament, a very unwholesome situation will develop with respect to the intercollegiate program of basketball games held in the Garden during the regular season." The continuation of the NIT thus opened up college athletics not only to damaging criticisms of commercialization but also to the repercussions from which would ultimately directly harm Ned Irish and his lucrative scheduling concession at one of the most famed addresses in American sports. If Irish somehow missed that shot across his financial bow, Badger urged him to consider the outcome of a long-term struggle between the writers and the NCAA, a struggle Badger assured Irish that the NCAA would win. Though the NCAA Tournament in its infancy was a moderate affair, "in the long run, such a plan will be perfected and will be made to stick. I think it behooves all of us to think of this situation in terms of the future rather than the present and to think, particularly, of the general welfare of the intercollegiate game in which we are all interested." The willingness of Irish and the writers to directly challenge what the NCAA perceived as its prerogative to stage postseason tournaments potentially contained significant consequences for the writers: "If it is true that the Basketball Writers have been helpful in arousing interest in college basketball in this area, it is equally true that college basketball has been extremely helpful in furnishing them with something extremely interesting about which to write." Having thus implicitly yet ridiculously threatened Irish and the New York media with no access to college sports, Badger closed by saying, "I think it behooves the writers to realize thoroughly that, in the long run, their own welfare is bound up with the success of the college game."[56]

Certainly, several factors shaped the writers' thinking with regard to their continued involvement with the NIT, and it is unclear how influential was Badger's rather heavy-handed letter to Irish, but the following year, the Metropolitan Basketball Writers Association voted to turn the NIT over to the eight metro-area colleges. Though the *New York Times*' Arthur Daley claimed that the decision came because "the scribes did not want to stay in the promoting business," such a claim seems moderately disingenuous considering that Ned Irish continued to make the financial arrangements with the Garden and that Everett Morris of the *New York Herald Tribune* remained on the NIT's executive committee as a representative of the writers' association. The NIT, however, moved its event up a week so that it did not conflict with the NCAA Tournament, conceivably allowing teams to enter both events amid the prospect of the NCAA prohibiting its member schools who rejected the NCAA Tournament from entering the NIT.[57] Whatever occurred, Badger found Irish compliant enough that he happily informed Harold Olsen in February 1940 that Irish was "anxious to cooperate with . . . the NCAA in every way possible." Moreover, according to Badger, Irish "realizes that in certain respects the future of the intercollegiate basketball program at the Garden is related to the matter of maintaining friendly relations with us."[58]

In the immediate years after the truce of 1940, the relationship between the two tournaments maintained the veneer of forced cordiality. Proposals to match the champions of the two tournaments were initially brushed off by both sides, with the NIT likely unwilling to grant the NCAA event any legitimacy of equality while the NCAA organizers likely found distasteful an alliance with such a commercialized venture. However, the necessities of World War II soon intervened and briefly brought the two events together under the aegis of charity. Promoters and sportswriters across the country quickly proposed hosting various football and basketball games for charitable aid organizations like the American Red Cross and the Army Emergency Fund. With such a precedent already established in New York from Jimmy Walker's Depression-era games, New Yorkers quickly fell in love with the idea of matching the NIT and NCAA Tournament champions in a charity event to benefit the Red Cross. While the metro sportswriters drummed up support, the NCAA decided to host the 1943 NCAA championship at Madison Square Garden, thus conveniently placing the two tournaments in the same location for the first time. Because there was no logistical reason to oppose the matchup, the NCAA acquiesced to the public clamoring, and from 1943 to 1945 the two champions met to raise funds for the Red Cross. The NCAA champion won all three games, doing much to establish its tournament as on par with the NIT. With the NIT uneasy about giving the NCAA any further opportunities to establish itself at its expense and the NCAA feeling it no longer needed to prove anything, the series was abruptly canceled with war's end under the disingenuous claim that Americans were no longer as willing to donate to the Red Cross without the pressing emergency of global war.[59]

Illustrating that it was not lack of public interest or media coverage that killed the NIT–NCAA matchup, the possibility of matching the two tournament champions arose again in 1947, a scenario that gained even greater credence when coaches from each of the teams favored to win their respective tournaments—Kentucky's Adolph Rupp in the NCAA and Holy Cross's Alvin "Doggie" Julian in the NIT—both expressed their interest in playing for a "mythical national championship." The prospect so titillated the *New York Times* that it discussed the possibility for a solid week in its sports section, and when organizers failed to bring the game about, *Newsweek* magazine decried the failure, dismissing the stated reason that "the season has run too long as it is, and the boys had better be getting back to their books." The benefit games of the war years demonstrated that NCAA Tournament champions could hold their own against the NIT teams, but popular clamoring for the two champions to meet in what was commonly known during the period as a "mythical national championship" illustrated that the public did not yet reflexively grant supremacy to either tournament.[60] By the late 1940s the two events unpleasantly acknowledged each other's existence while quietly carping about its illegitimacy.

NCAA efforts to undermine Emil Liston's Intercollegiate Tournament, however, were more ruthless, more prolonged, and, ultimately, more successful. Unlike the jousting with the NIT, the confrontation with the Intercollegiate Tournament involved an organized NCAA belligerency in the form of the tournament committee. Even before the first NCAA Tournament was held, Olsen defined the two tournaments in literal "us-vs.-them" rhetoric. In a letter to Phog Allen, Olsen "noted that a number of the members on their 'Board of Management' are people whose allegiance belongs to us." Additionally, Olsen took it upon himself to contact NCAA president William Owens, urging him to "circularize each member of the NCAA immediately asking for their active support. . . . I have no doubt that when it comes to a showdown[,] these coaches who are at present tied up in a general sort of way with this Kansas City tournament will see that they belong with us rather than with them."[61] Without waiting for Owens, Olsen's committee asked NCAA members directly to "refrain from promoting or supporting any other so-called 'intercollegiate basketball championship.'"[62] It is apparent that Olsen's strategy of including members of the media in the NCAA Selection Committee was aimed at least in part at isolating the NIT and the Intercollegiate Tournament. Of the four media personalities included on the NCAA committee, two were openly aligned with the other tournaments: Everett Morris of the *New York Herald Tribune* was a member of the Metropolitan Writers Association and intimately linked with the NIT's organization; similarly, C. E. McBride of the *Kanas City Star* had been involved with the promotional efforts of the Intercollegiate Tournament from the beginning. It's unclear what kind of machinations Olsen might have proposed concerning Morris at the *Herald Tribune*, but correspondence between him and Phog Allen regarding McBride reveal nothing less than a conspiracy to turn the Kansas City newsman against the Intercollegiate Tournament. Olsen admitted his purpose of appointing McBride to the committee: "I believe that if we can get men like McBride on the committee . . . that this tourney will receive a lot of fine support in the newspapers and that we will be able to put across this tournament over and above such attempts as are being made by fellows like Emil Liston."[63] After acknowledging to Allen in another letter that McBride and Liston "have some pretty definite tie-up," Olsen nonetheless hoped that McBride "can see that the interests of Kansas City might be equally well-served, or better served, by getting behind the NCAA project." In a scenario eerily similar to his questionable efforts to entice Philip Badger to shepherd NYU to the NCAA Tournament, Olsen instructed Allen to engage in subtle bribery by insinuating to McBride that in exchange for his loyalty, "the final game of the NCAA championship, plus the NABC convention[,] might be brought to Kansas City if there were proper support given to our plans." Olsen urged Allen to see McBride on the matter "at the earliest possible opportunity" but said, "If McBride isn't interested and can't be sold on our tournament," he would be replaced on the selection committee.[64]

Allen hastened to reply, matching Olsen's connivance and duplicity step for step while also engaging in rumor and inuendo. Allen instructed Olsen to "write me a letter importuning me to see C. E. McBride at the earliest possible opportunity, and then give me a sales talk about the importance of McBride being on that Committee. I want to take this letter of yours to McBride and let him read it." To complete the ruse and avoid offending McBride's relationship with Liston, Allen noted, "Now of course, I want nothing detrimental to Liston or anything about that tournament in Kansas City." Such a ploy was necessary because "in each of your other letters, there has been some reference to Liston or something about the withdrawing of these coaches from the Kansas City setup that I could not show him." Thus, Allen also revealed how much correspondence had already changed hands regarding plans to strike at the Intercollegiate Tournament. Allen then rather cryptically closed by referencing McBride's connection with Joseph Reilly of the Kansas City Athletic Club (KCAC), salaciously passing on the rumor that Reilly took in "as much as $10,000" organizing an AAU event with McBride's promotional assistance. Allen wrote that "it is alleged" that McBride took no money for himself but arranged "for other people who did," perhaps suggesting that if it came down to it, McBride's scruples could be at least compromised if not bought outright.[65] Allen was not the only one to engage in uninformed gossip about the finances of the old AAU Tournament in Kansas City. Big Ten commissioner John Griffith informed Stanford's Bill Owens that "some of the Kansas City Athletic Club men used to promote the annual National A.A.U. Basketball Tournament. I am told, however, that the local group turned over very little money to the A.A.U.," implying that financial impropriety was the reason the AAU event decamped for Denver, and the members of the KCAC, who were then no longer actually involved with the Intercollegiate Tournament, "would like to build up Liston's tournament" for their own financial benefit.[66]

Although Olsen and Allen failed in their efforts to turn McBride, Allen's own duplicity toward Liston eventually bordered on outright personal betrayal. Allen had begun his coaching career at Baker University in 1905 and won his first championship there a year later by winning the Kansas Collegiate Athletics Conference basketball title. When Baker dedicated its new gym on the thirtieth anniversary of that title, Liston thought to honor Allen's undefeated 1906 title team by inviting Allen and his University of Kansas Jayhawks to play Baker in the new gym's inaugural contest. Liston not only honored Allen at halftime but also personally arranged for many of Allen's players from the 1906 team to attend.[67] Though Liston considered Allen "a good friend" and often referred to him warmly in his correspondence to others, Allen apparently saw the continuation of Liston's tournament as a betrayal that took on unexplainable venom. Allen seldom missed an opportunity to level caustic references at Liston or his tournament in his correspondence with others, once describing Liston's activities regarding "the National Intercollegiate Tournament [as] under the straw-bossing of Emil Liston."[68] And when the secretary of the NABC sent a public letter to its members lambasting Liston and the Intercollegiate Tournament, Allen enthusiastically replied in a manner as if he had never met Liston: "Bully for you, mister! You not only took one pot shot at this young man from Baldwin City, Kansas . . . but you fired sixteen 'Big Berthas' at him all at the same time. You are aggressive and you say what you mean, but a lot of these fellows are afraid to speak out. I would rather worship at the shrine of a man who is not afraid to speak his convictions. Thank you very much."[69] Even supporters of the NIT piled on the Kansas City tournament when the opportunity presented itself. Everett Morris described Liston and his event as "a bush league meet."[70] NCAA Tournament organizers also seldom passed up an opportunity to demean or diminish the Intercollegiate Tournament or

Liston. After the initial NCAA Tournament, the NABC donated the championship trophy and deemed it the Naismith Memorial Trophy. Even though James Naismith himself presented the inaugural NAIB Tournament trophy and his widow presented the trophy the following year after Naismith's death, the NCAA bulletin in 1940 incorrectly and cattily announced, "This memorial trophy, by the way, is the only trophy officially approved and authorized by the Naismith family."[71]

Beyond the petty personal rivalries and the catty sniping, NCAA and NABC officials continued to view the Kansas City event in dire, threatening terms. Following the successful 1939 tournament, Liston and other supporters formally created the National Association of Intercollegiate Basketball (NAIB), whose initial aim was to sanctify the tournament as an open national collegiate championship but whose culture also sought to ensure equal access for small colleges. Marshall Diebold, athletic director at Minnesota's Carleton College, wrote to Allen in "alarm" upon hearing of the NAIB's formal organization. In a separate letter dripping with paranoia to Butch Grover, the new president of the NABC, Diebold declared that the organization of the NAIB "represents a problem for our association." He pondered how the NAIB, which claimed in its constitution no authority or prerogative over the rules, might affect the NABC or "basketball in general, . . . to say nothing of what the motive involved might be." Insisting that the NABC "must be prepared to protect our own interest" against the incursions of the NAIB, Diebold suggested to Grover that the NABC "investigate this new association," declaring, "I shall appreciate whatever information you have on this group."[72] Unwilling to wait for Grover to take action, Diebold sent the letter to other NABC members he knew to be hostile to Liston and the NAIB, most notably Phog Allen.[73] John Bunn at Stanford similarly saw the creation of the NAIB as cause for the NABC to man the barricades. Declaring the group "in direct competition with the NCAA," Bunn then dismissed its members as "largely those which are ineligible to join the NCAA because they are not willing to abide by our rules." Since the NCAA had no rules on national eligibility and NAIB schools were accredited, it is unclear what "NCAA rules" NAIB schools were then in violation of. Having derided the NAIB's member institutions, Bunn then attacked Liston, describing him as "most antagonistic and critical of the whole set-up of the NCAA."[74]

Although excitable, and largely inaccurate, claims that the NAIB was a threat either to the NCAA or to the NABC dominated such rhetoric, what bothered leaders of both organizations was the involvement in

NAIB activities by NCAA and NABC members. The correspondence of Allen, Olsen, Diebold, Bunn, and others noted the names of coaches serving on the NAIB Board of Management. In response to this, NCAA and NABC leaders initiated a campaign to drive such coaches away from the NAIB and dissuade others from looking favorably on the organization. Much as some college coaches turned on Nat Holman and others who had joined with the AAU in the first of basketball's civil wars, they again turned on some of their own in the second civil war with the NAIB. Harold Olsen, NCAA committee chair, acknowledged that he had pressured Northwestern's Arthur "Dutch" Lonborg about the latter's service on the NAIB Board of Management, stressing "that he should cut loose from this Kansas City tournament."[75] Olsen was also aware of more organized pressure, writing in December 1939, "With respect to the . . . association that Liston is sponsoring, Butch Grover is getting busy with the membership of the NABC to try to set them straight with respect to this move."[76] By far the most audacious maneuver was an open letter from Edward Hickox, the NABC's secretary-treasurer, to its membership. Dismissing the NAIB as little more than a poor imitator of the NABC, Hickox declared that the objectives and membership requirements "differ very little from those of our Association." He also derided the group's central event by referring to the "so-called NAIB Tournament conducted by E. S. Liston," ignoring the organizational structure created by the group in 1939.[77] Phog Allen also often portrayed the NAIB Tournament as if it were run by a group in thrall to Liston, describing the NCAA Tournament as "a real national tournament sponsored by the NCAA and not by some small group of individuals."[78] Ignoring the NAIB, Hickox amazingly claimed that the 1939 NCAA Tournament was "the first actual U.S. Basketball Championship among colleges where provision was made for representation from all sections of the United States." With such accomplishments in mind, he wrote, "I am disturbed that members of our organization should wish to ally themselves with what might well become a devisive [sic] movement." Hickox closed by putting the matter in the context of the coaches' struggles with the AAU-YMCA faction: "If we . . . withhold support from this competing organization which is still in the embryonic stage, we strengthen the real power of the coaches to bring about what we wish for the best interests of the game. . . . I appeal to you . . . to consider carefully before giving encouragement or aid to a movement that might well weaken the power and influence of the Basketball Coaches in the United States." Having suggested that the NABC essentially strangle the NAIB by withholding membership, Hickox's letter was nothing less than a declaration of war against the NAIB.[79]

Hickox sent the letter to every member of the NABC except Emil Liston, who nonetheless received a copy through a supporter and hastened to reply, rebutting Hickox point by point. Liston rebuked Hickox as "too seriously concerned" about viewing any developments as threatening the institutional presence of the NABC. He also noted that since NAIB membership was institutional, not individual, and since many coaches of NAIB member schools belonged to the NABC and wholeheartedly supported their program, the NAIB could hardly be seen as a threat to the NABC. After dismissing all of Hickox's logic, Liston cut to the unspoken issue that animated Hickox's letter in the first place: the competing existence of the groups' tournaments. "The main controversy," according to Liston, "is that of determining the national champion." Liston then threw down the gauntlet by suggesting that the NCAA Tournament teams enter the NAIB Tournament, or for the NCAA to admit teams that qualified for the NAIB Tournament: "Until that is done, there will be a National Intercollegiate Champion (Open Championship), and an NCAA Champion (Closed Championship)." As far as Liston was concerned, the NCAA's favoritism toward the large schools was a denial of democracy, and their refusal to invite smaller colleges only demonstrated the need for the NAIB event. Having challenged the NCAA where it was most vulnerable, Liston closed by taking one final dig at Hickox and the NABC's patronage of the NCAA Tournament: "Then in the spirit of cooperation, Mr. Hickox, . . . wouldn't it be better to go along . . . without fear that one association will do what the other has not yet been able to do?" While Hickox's letter amounted to the establishment's declaration of war on the NAIB, Liston's response demonstrated that neither he nor the NAIB was going to be bullied on the matter.[80]

The animosity between the two tournaments remained throughout the 1940s and accelerated in the 1950s before the NCAA gained the upper hand near the end of the decade. But before then, the shared arrangement between the NABC and the NCAA over their tournament reached a climax. The initial tournament in 1939, run by the NABC and sanctioned by the NCAA, lost more than twenty-five hundred dollars, and both sides considered dropping the idea. Phog Allen, however, promised that if Kansas City were granted the right to host the NCAA Tournament in 1940 under his management, "I will not only pay back the deficit, but we will make you some money." The NABC asked the NCAA to take over the management of the tournament and, not inconsequentially, bail the NABC out of the red; Allen delivered on his pledge, netting more than ninety-five hundred dollars. While Allen, Olsen, and John Bunn decided that the NABC would grant to the NCAA 20 percent of the revenues, in addition to the amount necessary to cover the 1939 shortfall, Olsen never conveyed to NCAA leadership that the NABC expected to continue controlling the tournament's finances and profits. Having rescued the event from its 1939 financial shortcomings and undertaken the risk to underwrite the 1940 event, the NCAA reserved for itself 60 percent of the 1940 revenues, leaving the remaining 40 percent to the NABC to cover the travel expenses of participating teams.[81] Not surprisingly, such terms prompted Allen to turn his caustic pen on the NCAA just as he had the AAU five years earlier. Allen described the NCAA's demands as "an outrageous discrimination against the sport of basketball," declaring rather disingenuously that the NCAA's executive committee "has killed the NCAA Tournament by grabbing everything within sight."[82] While Allen demonstrated throughout his life a penchant for exaggerated responses to perceived personal slights, his animosity also stemmed from his concerns that the financial arrangement demanded by the NCAA undercut the tournament's ability to compete with the NIT for quality teams. According to Allen's biographer Blair Kerchoff, "The NIT not only paid expenses for its eight teams but handed each a nice lump sum as a parting gift." Allen urged the NCAA to cover all traveling expenses and "then divide a very handsome profit" for the teams as well.[83] The fact that the NIT operated this way allowed many to criticize it as a commercial venture but also allowed it to continue drawing teams even after the NCAA event began play. That Allen and many other coaches wanted to criticize the NIT but then pursue the same model demonstrated one of the fundamental contradictions of American intercollegiate athletics.

Allen's call to divide some of the profits among the participating teams was rejected for the moment, but the preoccupation with the tournament as a revenue stream remained strong. Chad Carlson asserts that the making of the NCAA Tournament came in its decision to finally play its Eastern regional and the national championship game in New York's Madison Square Garden beginning in 1943. In 1942, the tournament's last year in Kansas City, it drew a few thousand fans and made $1,362 after expenses. In 1943, however, the first night in the Garden outdrew the entire tournament from the previous year and the event cleared $10,200. By 1946 the Garden's clamoring fans and the media rights delivered a profit of $50,664 to the NCAA.[84] In 1950 the tournament committee considered moving the event to a more convenient date, the result of which would have jeopardized their availability to stage the Eastern regional in Madison Square Garden and enjoy the lucrative gate that Garden dates always delivered. In commenting to the NCAA's Walter Byers, committee chair Arthur Lonborg wrote, "Possibly, we can in the near future, get out of the Garden completely but I don't believe that time is now." Lonborg pointed out that other locales simply could not deliver the gate as could Madison Square Garden, but, wary of appearing to lobby for any particular venue, he closed by stating, "The only thing I am trying to do, Walt, is to make a little money for the [NCAA]. I certainly do not care particularly where the tournament is held as long as it makes us money."[85] For Phog Allen, who resented the new financial arrangement that privileged the NCAA over the NABC, the bitterness of having the tournament taken out from under him in Kansas City could only have been exceeded by its financial success in Nat Holman's backyard.

Throughout the 1920s and 1930s, the NCCA's big-time schools spent much of their energies undermining efforts to allocate more power to the NCAA that might in any way limit their football activities. Yet at the same time, they also encouraged and facilitated that organization to become much more activist and empowered within the realm of college basketball. The utilization of NCAA resources to win over allies and persecute perceived enemies was but one example of such endeavors, as well as Phog Allen's desire to see the NCAA compel its members to participate in its events while punishing those that participated in rival events. It was the big-time college basketball schools that called the NCAA to war against all comers, and for their efforts they won themselves a national tournament that privileged their own kind to the exclusion of most members of the NCAA. But in so doing, they inadvertently created the origins of division and possible dissolution of the NCAA.

By the close of the 1930s and the onset of World War II, the issues confronting basketball soon intersected with broader struggles over college athletics and larger social changes in American society. No sooner had the civil wars with the AAU-YMCA faction been resolved than a second civil war erupted between college basketball's tournaments. The bitter animosity between the NCAA and the NAIB that originated in the 1930s took on immense significance in the 1950s when those two organizations battled for the soul of American collegiate athletics. The NAIB Tournament attracted an increasing number of smaller NCAA schools when they realized the big-time commercialized programs had little intention of letting a sizable number of the organization's members have access. But the disenchantment of those schools with the NCAA did not begin with basketball; basketball only became the prism through which that angst emerged. Rather, that angst arose from the unresolved tension between the liberal arts schools that founded the NCAA with one vision of college athletics and the big-time purveyors with a different vision whom they had to lure into the organization. Basketball would eventually fracture the NCAA that football had created. But first the NCAA's smaller schools sought to organize and assert a single identity in opposition to the big-time schools. Their ultimate failure portended immense consequence for all of college athletics.

CHAPTER 3

THE CITADEL OF HOME RULE

THE LIBERAL ARTS' FAILED WAR AGAINST COMMERCIALISM (1936–1951)

In January 1950 delegates for the NCAA's Annual Convention arrived in New York to conduct the business of a decidedly beleaguered organization. Most observers expected the convention to feature various proposals addressing the perceived threat of television to college football's live gate receipts, as well as various proposals to amend, abolish, or neuter a series of constitutional amendments regarding recruiting and subsidization known as the Sanity Code. Although few observers then or since saw the actions and agenda of the Small College Committee meeting as providing much of a bellwether for the NCAA, the sense of disenchantment and desperation exhibited at that year's committee meeting revealed an organization in crisis mode. Oberlin College's John H. Nichols gaveled the session to order and offered his prefatory remarks. Nichols, an Oberlin alum and physician by training but an academic by trade for more than two decades, had been coming to NCAA conventions since the 1930s. He had watched the organization grow while weathering the financial crisis of the Depression, the manpower shortages of World War II, and a series of crises and scandals in the years following the war. Through it all he remained a staunch advocate of the small liberal arts colleges that had founded the NCAA and made up a majority of its members, and an eternal optimist about the ability of the liberal arts colleges to convince their larger colleagues, mostly state-run universities, to abandon the path of commercialized, big-time intercollegiate athletics devoted to profit and victory.

In 1936 Nichols had addressed the entire NCAA Convention, ringing the alarm about dangerous and unethical athletics practices that barnacled the educational process, reducing college sports to an entertainment spectacle limited to only a few students. He and his colleagues had operated under the old antebellum reformist assumptions of moral suasion in that such evils might be avoided if everyone saw them in the light of day. But as he prepared to speak at the 1950 convention, his optimism had darkened considerably. In his opening remarks, Nichols described college athletics as being at "a crossroads. We can go one way or the other." The inability to effectively enforce the Sanity Code reforms enacted two years earlier had brought the NCAA to this crossroads, according to Nichols, and it was an intersection of fateful choice. Down one path lay the unregulated excesses of commercialized big-time athletics; down the other path lay a responsible "attempt to direct and control athletics along educational lines." Nichols left no doubt about his preference for the latter by saying that "to many of us it would seem that the other direction lies in the direction of chaos." At such a crossroads, the time had arrived "to stand up and be counted as to which direction we prefer." According to Nichols, college athletics was standing at Armageddon.[1]

Nichols's 1950 address illustrates that he and many of his colleagues housed in America's small liberal arts colleges had spent the previous fourteen years as Cassandras, able to foresee where the current path of intercollegiate athletics would lead but unable to convince the controlling interests in the NCAA of its destructiveness. As a result, Nichols and his band of reformers spent more than a decade railing into the wind of commercialized college sports, optimistically looking for new allies and to each other, convinced that each turn of events would finally bring the opposition around to their position, loyally clinging to the idea that a single national organization committed to gentlemanly, amateur, and collegial athletic competition could prevail. But by 1950 the optimism was mostly gone, replaced by a frustration borne of failed reforms, spurned concessions, and indifferent allies. Many delegates from small liberal arts colleges were bereft of patience and ready to abandon the NCAA, convinced that it ignored their interests, manipulated them for its own benefit, and accelerated the destruction of a participatory athletics model that not only served as the bulwark of their academic curricula but also, they felt, was vital to the fabric of America. The NCAA was at a crossroads indeed.

America's small liberal arts colleges too believed they faced a crossroads, although many exaggerated their vulnerability. The democratizing influences of the twentieth century struck at higher education just as they had other aspects of American society, and the private liberal arts college witnessed the loss of its monopoly on higher education. By 1940 the number of young adults enrolled in higher education jumped to 1.2 million, a growth rate of more than 400 percent over the previous twenty years. And while many of those students still found their way to private liberal arts colleges, most of them, from decidedly farther down the economic spectrum, matriculated to more affordable state schools with their subsidized tuition and fees. There, students found an educational curriculum less insistent on broad intellectual skills steeped in the arts and sciences and embedded in universal notions of critical thinking. Instead, they increasingly embraced the emerging social sciences and new fields of quantification, helping to create the direct linkage between a college education and post-college economic fulfillment. By mid-century more and more American college students lustily embraced a traditional undergraduate life as a rite of passage but did so outside of the caste-oriented social and kin networks of the private liberal arts colleges that had previously assured economic security for those young adults. This impetus toward using education to remake oneself separate from their birth family's social and economic status only accelerated in the wake of the Depression and World War II. For many, the Great Depression marked a failure of the old order and of established sources of authority. For this new generation of college students, higher education was much less about where one came from and more about where one aspired to go. A significant cultural aspect of this new democratic educational style was the growth of commercialized athletics that John Nichols and others in the private liberal arts school so decried.[2]

The inability of the small-time, reformist-minded schools within the NCAA to make any substantive headway in curtailing the big-time schools motivated many by the late 1930s to reconsider the notion of the NCAA as a single entity capable of governing all of college athletics. To be sure, the small school reformers, housed overwhelmingly in private liberal arts colleges in the East and upper Midwest, did not bring any new criticisms to the discussion. At the 1936 NCAA Convention, Nichols criticized the "trend toward professionalism" in college football, proposing the end of commercialized college athletics as it had been practiced since the 1890s. Echoing much of what the Carnegie Report had either criticized or proposed a decade earlier, Nichols outlined what would be the general platform of the small college agenda for the next two decades: the abolition of gate receipts, funding the athletic department through the regular university budget process, giving faculty rank and tenure to coaches, the abolition of preferential admissions, and the restriction of financial aid to academic qualifications based on need only. The logic of Nichols and the other reformers was the same in 1936 as it had been in 1929 with the Carnegie Report: freeing schools from having to make money on their athletic departments by abolishing gate receipts and funding them as a standing line item minimized the pressure to win, thus allowing them to hire coaches primarily for their instructional qualities and to create teams consisting of regularly enrolled students who represented a cross-section of the male student body.[3]

While the reformist proposals that Nichols laid out in December 1936 offered nothing particularly new to the ongoing criticisms of commercialized collegiate sports, they were borne from a growing tension pressing in on American higher education and college athletics in the years before and after World War II. In the eyes of small college educators like Nichols, big-time commercialized athletics not only created corruption and abuse in the thirst for victory but also bastardized the discipline of physical education and cheated the majority of the student body. Small liberal arts educators accepted that physical athletic training was part of the classical curriculum, alongside such mainstays as literature, the natural sciences, and calculus. After the Civil War most institutions of higher learning understood physical education within very limited and historically specific contexts. Embracing the classical notion that a sound mind flourished only in a sound body, liberal arts schools sought to develop their all-male students' bodily health through calisthenics, gymnastics, and other aerobic-oriented individualist pursuits. Additionally, educators and social theorists saw such activities as part of the larger Victorian campaign to teach self-abnegation and discipline in the face of the stresses and anxieties that accompanied industrialization. The purpose, according to Harvard's professor of physical training and director of the gymnasium, Dudley Sargent, was "to improve the physical condition of the mass of our students, and to give them as much health, strength and stamina as possible, to enable them to perform the duties that await them after leaving college."[4] These schools tended to require three to four years of physical education classes for all students, regardless of major; some of them also required demonstration of certain "life-skills," such as passing a swimming test. In the minds of liberal arts educators, physical education courses and skills were thus expected requirements, not merely random supplemental components, of an educational model that sought to develop critically minded, manfully engaged citizens of the republic. By the early twentieth century, liberal arts schools began shifting away from general fitness to more competitive sports programs that encouraged mass participation, fitness, and socialization; according to one physical educator, "the vital objective and outcome should be the production of participants."[5]

The upheavals of the Great Depression and the rise of fascism and totalitarianism also affected the role of sports in American higher education. The economic crisis of the 1930s, coupled with the apparently stunning dynamism of totalitarian political economies in Germany, Italy, and the Soviet Union, temporarily put defenders of capitalism and representative government on the defensive. One outgrowth of this was to charge higher education with the added responsibility of inculcating an appreciation for representative government and free market economic activity. In the words of historian David Levine, "Education was increasingly viewed as the salvation of progress and democracy."[6] And competitive sports emerged as a crucial cog in the process. Quite simply, few activities crystallized the benefits of egalitarian access and the meritocracy of excellence as did athletics. By the 1930s liberal arts colleges embraced the physical theories of Jesse Feiring Williams, who espoused "education *through* the physical rather than *of* the physical," with the objective "to develop character and learn activities that could be utilized later" in the life and career of students.[7]

Thus emerged what this book calls the "liberal arts agenda," an almost unchallenged pursuit by liberal arts faculty and administrators of broadly accessible competitive athletics that coexisted with and reinforced a civic-minded, academic curriculum. According to Nichols, "An education which trained young people for work but not for play, for labor but not for leisure, for toil but not recreation, was a half-done job."[8] The centrality of competitive athletics to this curriculum meant that it needed secure funding within the academy and could not be left to the vagaries of a commercial market where spectators paid only to see winners. Because some felt it was as important as calculus, foreign language, and literature, it also had to be available to as much of the student body as possible, not just the most athletically talented students. According to the liberal arts agenda, intercollegiate athletics at its most valuable level was what best served the academic and intellectual needs of the students, not what most intrigued the media and the paying public.

From the late 1930s to the mid-1950s, few voices articulated the liberal arts agenda and its grievances with the commercialized model of the NCAA as forcefully and consistently as Nichols. And so many liberal arts educators at the time were willing to follow his lead because he not only espoused their views, but his background so closely mirrored their own. Like many of his peers, Nichols was a product of a liberal arts education, earning his bachelor's degree from Oberlin in 1911 while playing basketball, baseball, and football, earning nine letters for the Yeomen. After medical school and service in World War I, Nichols began his tenure in academia at Ohio State, where he shifted OSU's physical education program from one of mass calisthenics to competitive sports and saw up close the effects of commercialized varsity teams on the broad curriculum. Nichols's time in Columbus convinced him that varsity intercollegiate athletics was a cancer on the student body. When Oberlin's athletic director came calling in 1928, it did not take much to convince Nichols to return to his alma mater; seven years later he became its athletic director, a position he occupied until his retirement in 1955.[9] In taking up the liberal arts argument against the commercialized model enshrined in the NCAA, Nichols was not articulating the party line of his employer; he was defending the crucible that made him.

The rise of big-time athletics, particularly the growing stress on winning and the devotion of resources to that end, jeopardized that crucible. The stress on winning led schools to field varsity teams of the best players, provide them access to professional coaches and training regimens, and create infrastructure such as stadiums to support those endeavors. All of those resources, however, came at the expense of a broad, competitive athletics program available to the student body as a whole. What liberal arts physical educators like Nichols envisioned were numerous teams in dozens of sports competing against similar-size schools in competitive athletics, whereby almost all members of the student body found a home on some competitive team. As Oberlin president Ernest Wilkins said of Oberlin at the time, "Our program fully recognizes the value of athletic activity not for Varsity men alone, but for all the men in the College."[10] The best example of such thinking came from Atlanta's Emory University. Besides requiring multiple years of physical education and a swimming test for all graduates, Emory also developed a fully funded competitive athletics program for the majority of the student body that was the envy of the liberal arts establishment.

The 1929 Carnegie Report, after lambasting the commercialized athletic programs, set aside Emory's policy of "athletics for all" for special commendation. By the late 1940s Emory fielded four tackle football teams and dozens of basketball teams. According to one observer, "While nearly everybody at Emory plays one game or another, hardly anybody watches." Such a broad-based participatory model could not exist, according to Emory chancellor Warren Akin Candler, alongside a commercialized athletics program. As far back as 1919 Candler declared that hyper-commercialized "intercollegiate athletics is evil, only evil and that continually." Thomas McDonough, Emory's athletic director and confidant of Nichols and others who advocated for a broader application of the liberal arts model, noted caustically, "I seriously doubt whether colleges are obligated to provide entertainment for the public."[11]

After his address at the 1936 convention, Nichols received both criticism and compliments from around the nation, and his response to both critics and supporters alike remained consistent in all of his correspondence. He patiently explained that the staff of Oberlin's physical education department "is not selected alone on their ability to coach one or two varsity sports" but rather on their contribution to the broad mandates of the program, not the least of which was a required two years of physical education for all students regardless of academic major. Nichols also noted that intercollegiate athletics was part of, not separate from, that academic department in terms of funding, staffing, and mission.[12] And the growing costs of commercialized athletics jeopardized this model. Beginning in 1935, the Southeastern Conference (SEC) openly provided for the granting of full athletic scholarships in the search for better talent. Many schools, mostly in the Big Ten and the Pacific Coast Conference (PCC), avoided offering outright scholarships, because they provided jobs to athletes, often little more than make-work tasks or jobs that existed only on paper. The SEC's decision, however, now attracted potential students who were uninterested in the sham of the jobs programs, forcing other schools to lose players to the SEC or increase their own costs by funding scholarships as well. Funding these scholarships put ever more pressure on athletic departments to produce the revenue to pay for them; this was the "trend toward professionalism" that Nichols criticized at the following year's NCAA Convention.[13]

As the 1930s ended, the PCC and Big Ten Conference looked with angst at the ability of Southern schools to offer scholarships to lure recruits away from those conferences. One possible counterweight would be the transformation of the NCAA into a regulatory agency, effectively ending the home rule principle upon which so many of the big-time schools had been lured into the organization in the first place. Big Ten members discussed the adoption of uniform national standards for all NCAA members that would implicitly ban the kinds of scholarships then offered by the SEC. Even at the football hotbed of the University of Texas, one official claimed that circumstances now required "a more aggressive attitude toward the administration of intercollegiate athletics." The Big Ten and the PCC, however, mistakenly interpreted comments from small college reformers like Nichols as evidence of those delegates' willingness to see the NCAA more actively regulate commercialized athletics, ignoring entirely that small college criticisms of the period were not of unregulated commercialized athletics but of commercialized athletics overall. Thurston Davies, president of Colorado College and a strong advocate for the liberal arts version of competitive athletics, condemned the Big Ten proposal, warning of, in the words of historian Ronald Smith, "the danger of the NCAA becoming a regulatory agency with enforcement powers." Small college advocates like Davies feared that empowering the NCAA would only tend to serve the reformist needs of the big-time commercialized schools and thus deliver neither true reform nor an environment that protected the liberal arts physical education curriculum.[14]

Liberal arts colleges across the United States before World War II attempted to hold the practices of big-time programs at bay without resorting to an empowered NCAA. The liberal arts–oriented Association of New England Colleges passed a series of new protocols for its members aimed at restricting the growth of commercialized athletics but also explicitly opposing practices that ran counter to the liberal arts physical education ideology of broad participation. In December 1940 the group declared that requiring students to take part in athletic tryouts before admission was an "unethical practice and should not be tolerated."[15] As G. Wilson Shaffer at Johns Hopkins University espoused the ideal, "every able-bodied student" should participate in "competitive sports," because they were "both psychologically important and an integral part of the education curriculum."[16] The opposite model, according to Nichols, created an ever widening and unbridgeable divide between those who desired the place of competitive athletics in the academic curriculum and those who simply pursued it for filthy lucre: "I think we are seeing developed one group that will carry on their athletics as a part of the educational programs on an amateur basis and another group that will become more and more professional and will make football a more and more commercial and public enterprise." For Nichols, Shaffer, and their colleagues, the moral authority of the former position was never in doubt. But what bothered them was that the public remained ignorant of commercialized college football's nefarious and destructive consequences to the physical education curriculum. Instead, they read exposés like the Carnegie Report and assumed that football itself was what ignited the abuse and that all purveyors were equally guilty. "The tendency" of the public, according to Nichols, "is to throw all institutions in together because you know that the practice is so general and the system is shot through and through with hypocrisy and deceit as it relates to college football."[17]

In response to these phenomena, Clarence Bilheimer of Gettysburg College, who had been attending NCAA conventions longer than most of his colleagues could remember, informally surveyed many of those liberal arts colleagues at the 1937 NCAA New Orleans convention about their growing frustration with the NCAA and its seeming disinterest in the concerns of the small colleges. If Nichols was the articulate voice of the liberal arts reformers, Bilheimer was their organizer. Sharing a background similar to that of Nichols, he matriculated to Lehigh University in Pennsylvania's Bethlehem Valley, playing football for the Engineers before becoming a professor of mathematics at York College, a position he relinquished when Gettysburg College asked him to serve as athletic director beginning in 1927. Like Nichols, Bilheimer would remain in that position until retirement in 1953. And like so many of his liberal arts brethren, he abhorred funding college athletics through gate receipts and other fluctuating revenues, proudly declaring that at Gettysburg "the Athletic Council . . . is not a separate and distinct organization, but a cog in the educational wheel."[18] Many of the small college representatives whom Bilheimer surveyed expressed their frustration that the NCAA's historic efforts to entice the big-time schools to join the association had led the organization down a path that seemingly placated the interests of big-time athletics at every turn.

It was this very concern that made small college advocates like Thurston Davies look so warily on the Big Ten's 1939 proposal to create a regulatory function within the NCAA. Bilheimer eventually gathered eighty-three signatures from delegates representing schools with enrollments of one thousand students or less, requesting the creation of a permanent NCAA committee "to integrate and make more definite points of view on athletic and institutional policies" for small colleges "to the end that their distinctive institutional problems may receive more constant and effective discussion and attention." Although Bilheimer, who lost his sight to cataracts in the 1940s, would wonder in future years "if the small colleges really appreciated the things I had to do and what I did to finally obtain this recognition," the NCAA's executive council approved the request, appropriating a modest budget of three hundred dollars, and the following year, the NCAA Small College Committee held its first meeting based on the topic of "What methods can the smaller colleges pursue in order to promote confidence and a better understanding among competing institutions in intercollegiate sports?"[19] The group frequently stressed the integral nature of physical education not merely to a liberal arts education but also to a healthy and happy life. For example, in the late 1930s Shaffer at Johns Hopkins offered a paper titled "Recreation as a Preventative and Therapy for Social Maladjustment."[20] Absent from these early meetings were organized sessions about remaking the NCAA or efforts to put greater regulatory teeth in the organization to serve the reformist desires. The agendas of the early Small College Committee meetings illustrate that most members simply wanted to get the most out of the NCAA relative to the level of athletics they chose to pursue, not necessarily wage a crusade against commercialized athletics. And while reformers like Nichols and Bilheimer were vocal, they did not presume to speak for a single small college identity.

Nonetheless, one of the subjects that the Small College Committee never strayed too far from was the growing difference between how the smaller schools pursued intercollegiate athletics and the practices of big-time schools. Shaffer, like Nichols, described at the 1939 committee meeting of that year's NCAA Convention this widening disparity, decrying the mind-set within the organization that "we shall continue to spend our time during the year getting away with as much as possible, and our times at these conventions trying to keep others from getting away with as much."[21] For the first several years, the Small College Committee meeting unfolded within its own bubble, operating like an academic conference with formal papers on themes central to the liberal arts physical education curricula, such as the benefits and consequences of compulsory physical education, or competitive versus intramural athletics, all the while casting a critical eye toward the excesses of the big-time football purveyors meeting just down the hall. Most opposed the practices of the commercialized schools, but few were as animated as the reformers.

The austerity measures resulting from the Great Depression did much to animate the concerns of these liberal arts physical educators.

Fears that the dependence of athletic departments on the budgetary successes of commercialized athletics could have disastrous financial consequences became reality during the 1930s. The Big Ten Conference in 1931 cut wrestling except for the single all-conference meet and limited gymnastics and fencing rosters to six and three participants, respectively, while Ohio State abolished varsity programs in polo, rifle and pistol, and fencing. Only basketball and football remained untouched, a phenomenon that Nichols saw as the inevitable consequence of commercialized athletics. Even worse, while schools reduced faculty salaries and froze library expenditures and the Big Ten dropped or restricted sports, Ohio State administrator Justin Morrill proposed seeking a direct legislative appropriation to support Ohio State's competitive athletic program because of the financial crisis of the Depression. As Brad Austin has written of Ohio State's response to the Depression's effects on big-time athletics, "Even if the state could not provide enough money for library subscriptions, some administrators believed that it could, and should, find enough tax money for its athletic teams."[22] In a letter to the *Chicago Tribune*'s Arch Ward, Nichols denounced this unbalanced privileging of one part of the curriculum over another as well as the perceived sanctity of the commercialized revenue sports over other teams. Without mentioning Ohio State by name, Nichols took a veiled swipe at his former employer and larger in-state neighbor by proudly noting in 1940 that "for the past 15 years," Oberlin offered the same number of athletic teams while participation doubled, "and during the Depression we did not drop a single sport."[23] To another correspondent, Nichols critically noted of Ohio State, "Some colleges in this state . . . are putting practically all of their time, effort, and money into a few income producing, intercollegiate sports. They find it necessary to do this due to the fact that the physical education and athletic program is not being financed from college funds."[24]

Nichols was not the only one to raise some concern with the effects of privileging big-time commercialized athletics. In early 1940 *New York Times* columnist John Kieran ran a series of columns that examined the effects of profit-driven athletics on the larger competitive physical education program. Kieran echoed the traditional liberal arts ideology by claiming, "Athletics are as integral a part of the program as chemistry or Romance languages." When some readers responded that it was no longer possible to run intercollegiate athletics on such a model, Kieran noted that the model was functioning just fine at Johns Hopkins University, which stopped charging gate admission to all of its athletic events in 1934.[25] The assistant sports editor from Hopkins' student paper wrote in to confirm that since the financing of the athletic department had reverted to receiving budgetary allocations like all other departments on campus, participation actually increased at Hopkins, and the school offered fourteen different varsity sports.[26]

As World War II drew closer, the defenders of the traditional liberal arts physical education curriculum saw an opportunity not only to assert the long-term benefits of such a curriculum but also to demonstrate that commercialized athletics ultimately harmed national security. In 1940 John Nichols remarked, "The present world conditions demand a searching study of educational procedures and especially a reappraisal of our health and physical education programs. The physical education and athletic programs in our colleges have a special contribution to make to our national preparedness." The problem, as Nichols and others saw it, was that the colleges that pursued commercialized athletics put too many resources into creating an athletic spectacle designed to make money rather than into an athletic program designed to make manly citizens: "Our special and primary function, then, is the physical preparedness of college and university men, some 650,000 of them, and this means all of them, *not just a selected few.*"[27] T. Nelson Metcalf, the athletic director at the University of Chicago, offered much the same sentiments, declaring that the highly commercialized model put a lot of resources into just a few students: "While we may have been doing a pretty good job in preparing for service in the military forces a few specialized athletes in our institutions, we have sort of missed the boat in the kind of training we have been emphasizing in our college for the general run of students."[28] What advocates like Metcalf envisioned was a liberal arts physical education curriculum similar to what existed at Johns Hopkins and Emory, where hundreds of students played competitive sports, or Franklin and Marshall College, which required every student to take four years of physical education. The problem was not just that highly commercialized competitive athletics did not reach enough students but that its reliance on gate receipts and the whims of public interest left it vulnerable to changing tastes or economic downturn, as they saw during the Depression. Nichols asserted the vital importance of "intercollegiate athletics in national preparedness" and that "the best thing that most of our colleges can do would be to place their entire athletic program in the college budget." To do otherwise was to leave a vital aspect of national defense to the vagaries of the market.[29]

Not surprisingly, many liberal arts administrators and faculty saw the question of preparedness for World War II within the context of their experiences from World War I. Oberlin's Charles Savage reminded the 1941 Small College Committee meeting that during World War I, then Secretary of War Newton D. Baker addressed the NCAA and acknowledged that while star varsity athletes "were of tremendous value," the limitations of commercialized athletics meant the military wasn't "getting enough of them." Competitive athletics at any level, according to Baker on the eve of American involvement in World War I, served as "preliminary training for potential officers . . . [and] promoted physical development, team unity, and served as a recreational outlet during military camp life."[30] Facing another period of national emergency, Savage suggested that the embrace of commercialized athletics placed the nation in no better stead in 1941 than it had in 1917. He also made a sly reference to Ohio State when he called upon colleges and universities to "stiffen up on the kinds of programs we are developing in the field of athletic competition and not to spend (as I know they are doing in one particular institution) $20,000 for their staff of intercollegiate coaches and $1,800 for part-time intramural directors." Savage declared that such emphasis was economically unsound but also "not the sort of thing that Mr. Baker wanted."[31] Such a program would not only address the wartime emergency but also position the United States for a postwar world. According to Colorado College's Thurston Davies, "We should be thinking in terms of programs which not only meet the present emergency, but which are sound, continuing programs of physical education throughout the United States so that we can look ahead."[32] Nichols more bluntly announced, "My belief is that in our college athletic programs, we are training for peace as well as for war."[33] Davies echoed this sentiment after the war as he ruminated on the possibility that the physical education gains of the war would be lost as they had been in 1919. In "considering what form intercollegiate athletics should take after the war," Davies hoped that the wartime devotion to broad competitive athletics would be retained so that "this physical fitness will not have to be built up from the start," and that "if it should be necessary again," the education establishment might avoid the debate.[34]

The embrace of the liberal arts preparedness model in the face of the wartime emergency required not merely an ideological shift but a dramatic reallocation of resources. Early in the war, the Small College Committee recommended that NCAA meetings be held in conjunction with that of "the College Physical Education Association, and other interested organizations, for the purpose of a discussion of common problems, arising from our new responsibilities in the war-training program."[35] Likewise, Rear Admiral Randall Jacobs, head of the navy's V-12 officer training program, addressed the NCAA in September 1942, calling on the colleges and universities to set aside the profits of commercialized athletics to adapt their athletic departments to wartime service: "It is hoped that the men of the universities will institute among themselves a regime of self-discipline and condition in order to better complete the immediate job at hand." Jacobs proposed a compulsory physical training program for all male undergraduates five days a week.[36] The NCAA Executive Committee endorsed Jacobs's request on principle, though acknowledging the home rule principle, they admitted that "the Executive Committee did not have the power to invoke a program of physical hardening among the members of the group."

As soon became apparent, however, the liberal arts colleges embraced the recommendation more readily than others. Oberlin College, for example, immediately proposed a required eight semesters of physical education for the duration of the war (an increase from their existing four-semester requirement) as a necessity for "pre-induction training." A doubling of physical education enrollment required redirecting the energies of varsity coaches toward more general physical education training, a commitment Oberlin willingly made but one that Nichols suspected others would not.[37] Such efforts not only affected staffing but had consequences on resources and facilities as well. At the University of Kansas, the physical education department never witnessed more than 450 students enrolled in any one semester before the war. But by the fall of 1942, 1,800 students were taking such classes each semester. This increased demand occupied existing staff and facilities such that Kansas's vaunted basketball team was not able to get gym space until 8:00 P.M. and the length of practice was cut in half.[38] In the state of Ohio, naval officers assigned to campus training programs met with a committee of athletic directors to convince them of the need for restricting their intercollegiate programs. The officers elicited an agreement to limit practice times to free up personnel for non-varsity activities and limit travel for away games to limit the amount of time athletes were away from on-campus military training. The agreement, however, had to be consistently enforced, such as when Case Institute of Technology scheduled their home game against Oberlin for a 6:00 P.M. kickoff in Cleveland's Luna Park in an effort to increase the gate receipts. Oberlin's resident naval training officer vetoed the game time, citing the difficulty in getting students back to campus for Sunday morning military exercises after a potential night of revelry in the city. Similarly, when Oberlin's own football coach requested that several petty officers with coaching experience be given extra leave time to help coach the football team, the training officer unsurprisingly vetoed that request as well.[39]

The redirection of intercollegiate athletics in favor of preparedness was something the NCAA too tried to avoid as much as possible during the war. In an effort to help save college athletics during World War II, the NCAA drafted a resolution calling for the explicit participation of military service training programs. Admiral Thomas J. Hamilton, the head football coach at the US Naval Academy before the war, organized and administered the navy's V-5 training program. Both the university-based V-5 and the V-12 officer programs allowed for trainees to participate in intercollegiate athletics. The Army's Specialized Training Program (ASTP), however, took a dimmer view of the distraction of intercollegiate athletics and refused to allow ASTP trainees to participate in intercollegiate competition. In January 1943 Asa Bushnell, Thurston Davies, and Karl Leib journeyed to Washington, DC, to lobby the US War Department on behalf of the NCAA on the matter. Although they managed to secure the navy's strong commitment to retaining the provision for the V-5 and V-12 programs, the army remained steadfast in its refusal to incorporate intercollegiate athletics for its university-based ASTP.[40] With such inevitable consequences for their athletic programs, many schools loudly proclaimed their support for the war effort but quietly pursued business as usual. Indeed, even as Admiral Jacobs addressed the NCAA Executive Committee urging a conversion of broad-based fitness, the *Chicago Tribune* remarked that "the NCAA is apparently determined to continue its national athletic events" during the war by holding its national championship events. An NCAA survey during the height of the war discovered that 83 percent of all members required two years or less of physical education, with 60 percent requiring one, two, or no semesters of physical training.[41] Thus, while the war placed demands on many schools, it never forced them to fundamentally reconsider or curtail the practices of big-time commercialized athletics.

Champions of liberal arts physical education complained about the continued adherence to a commercialized model throughout the war. In January 1945 the Small College Committee devoted its entire meeting to discussing the possibility of changing intercollegiate athletics after the war. Lyle Butler of Oberlin noted that the liberal arts concept of "athletics for all" was neither innovative nor foreign. Butler declared that support for such a model had existed within the NCAA almost from its inception. Purdue University's Clarence Waldo had asked at the 1909 convention, "Instead of a few gladiators of transcendent prowess and national notoriety, shall we not try to secure an athletic spirit throughout the whole student body, a spirit that drives the many out onto the field . . . for the joys . . . of athletic competition?" Butler observed that every decade since its birth, NCAA delegates had held up the broad-based program that existed at the liberal arts colleges, only to be shoved aside by the big-time purveyors of commercialized athletics.[42] And the crises of preparedness and war did little to quell their insistence on a commercialized model. Lloyd Messersmith of DePauw University noted near the war's end that intercollegiate athletics had "been confronting the same problems for the past three years." The biggest "weakness," as Messersmith defined it, was an unwillingness to fully support the war effort by insisting on "limit[ing] the scope of the intercollegiate athletic program solely to" one provided by "gate receipts." And the insistence of schools funding their intercollegiate athletic program based on what could be collected at the paying gate led directly to "the failure to provide a sufficiently wide variety of sports so that large numbers of students may have an opportunity to compete" and develop the fitness necessary for the war effort.[43] Clearly, many were unwilling or unable to redirect their big-time commercialized athletic aspirations to the practices called for by the reformers. As a result, many big-time programs subjugated their commitment to the war effort when it came in conflict with their commitment to commercialized athletics.

Not surprisingly, such sentiments did not recede after the war. A. W. Marsh from Amherst College asserted in 1947, "It has been obvious that during the war years and subsequently, one of the important things that we should do in our program is to provide for the inclusion of more men." Marsh's sentiments were echoed almost identically by Nichols at Oberlin, who said, "I think we have all realized, after the war, that we are not reaching anywhere near the men that we should reach."[44] As the Cold War increasingly revealed itself to be an indefinite feature of postwar American life, the College Committee on Physical Education and Athletics, which featured Marsh and Emory's Thomas McDonough, issued a statement in 1949 titled "College Physical Education and National Defense." In its preamble the report asserted "the world leadership" of the United States and the centrality of higher education in helping to curtail "those forces that would propel us into a third great war." The report explicitly criticized commercialized athletics "merely as an attractive but basically 'non-academic' impediment to the main business for which the college exists." In contrast the report called for activities in the "gymnasium, athletic field, or swimming pool . . . which aid in the development of the citizen ready to assume his obligations for peace and defense." In the view of liberal arts physical education advocates, big-time commercialized athletics not only distracted from the academic mission of higher education but now also hindered the development of citizens fit for service in a Cold War military and political economy.[45]

Nonetheless, the small college hopes that the fitness needs of World War II and the Cold War would rein in commercialized, competitive athletics proved illusory. Faced with few other alternatives, liberal arts colleges reconsidered making common cause with those who wished to elevate the NCAA to a regulatory function. The prewar escalation of the recruiting arms race on the part of the SEC, and the postwar participation in it by seemingly everyone else, convinced many liberal arts schools that sweeping national reform was now necessary. As was soon apparent, however, the two camps had entirely different visions of what a "reformed" college athletics program should look like. Many small colleges came to realize their numerical superiority within the NCAA, but their failure to exercise the balance of power worked to the detriment of both them and the NCAA. Clarence Houston of Tufts University declared in 1946 that the small colleges "as a matter of fact make up considerably more than a majority of the membership of the NCAA," but that institution too often busied itself only with the "problems pertaining to the larger institutions and had to do with major sports such as football." The small college advocates felt that such single-mindedness imperiled the NCAA and college athletics as an academic institution.[46] Carl Dellmuth of Swarthmore College thought that the ability of small colleges to "see the whole picture" of the academic process afforded them a view "which cannot be obtained in the large universities" that practice athletic "specialization."[47] Houston and Dellmuth held that the distinctive liberal arts mission better positioned those schools to see a more academic application of competitive athletics. And many came to believe that the holistic, liberal arts view was gaining traction. As one small college group member optimistically declared, "I think we all feel that the NCAA has been more conscious of the Small College Group and their best interests as the result of some of the frank and honest criticisms of the way in which some things have been handled in the past."[48]

One of those frank and honest criticisms came from the small college delegates' general exclusion from NCAA governance. Like any bureaucracy, the NCAA has multiple layers of organization. At the top is the NCAA Council, functioning as the de facto "board of directors" for the association. Serving as the policy board, its function is to establish and direct the general policy of the association between annual conventions, themselves serving to crystallize and express the will of the membership. The executive committee reports to the council but serves as the final authority in three areas: association finances, championships, and the direction of national office staff. Both the council and the executive committee are made up of delegates from the membership. The annual convention is where amendments or new legislation are submitted, discussed, and voted on. The agenda for the annual conventions largely emerges from the work of the varying committees, also made up of the delegates from the membership. In many regards the bulk of power within the NCAA emanates from its committee assignments, and the small colleges' exclusion from them inevitably left them without a seat at the table. Coe College's C. Ward Macy commented after the war "that it is unfortunate that small college conferences have not been given more consideration in the governing of the NCAA." Macy noted that while representatives from schools like Coe were some "of the strongest supporters for reform in principle and practice," not one school from their conference was represented on NCAA committees, "and as far as I can see, there is no one who is even remotely connected with middle western small institutions" involved in NCAA governance.[49] Similarly, John Truesdale from Grinnell College frustratingly criticized the Small College Committee's limitation within the NCAA as an advisory body only, declaring that both the Grinnell faculty and their president "deplore[d] the lack of 'teeth' in the recommendation of the small colleges committee [sic]." The upshot of such frustrations was that the Small College Committee at the end of 1945 recommended reorganizing the NCAA so as to base committee representation on the organization's existing eight regional districts, thereby allowing the small liberal arts colleges to benefit from their concentration in the upper Midwest, Northeast, and New England regions. It was a proposal that the NCAA eventually adopted in 1954, when they had good reason to fear the small colleges. But in the immediate postwar years, the proposal was dismissed and largely forgotten such that a year later, Kenneth "Tug" Wilson's assistant had to be prodded to "remind the Committee on Committees of the Small College recommendation" before it was ultimately defeated at the 1946 convention. The defeat of a proposal that would have given greater representation to the smaller colleges was one of several occurrences during the period that did much to chasten small college optimism that their collective voice might be more welcomed and influential in NCAA affairs.[50]

While the interests of big-time athletics most certainly hoped for the support of the small college majority, they had no intention of dismantling commercialized intercollegiate athletics as they knew it. Rather than see a swing of the big-time interests toward the vision of the Small College Committee, Tug Wilson, the NCAA's secretary-treasurer and longtime defender of whatever was good for the Big Ten, believed that the committee had already aligned its interests with the prewar proposal to grant regulatory powers to the NCAA so as to rein in the renegade SEC. Nichols's naiveté that the NCAA had now come round to the small college position was matched only by Wilson's equal naiveté that a consensus had formed among NCAA members, regardless of size, "to curb the practices that are not in accordance with our constitution." In a letter to Thurston Davies, a prewar opponent of a regulatory NCAA, Wilson incredibly suggested that such reforms would have already been affected had not "the war interfered" and short-circuited such efforts. Nothing illustrated the distance between those who wanted to see the NCAA regulate commercialized athletics and those who wanted to end commercialized athletics like the postwar designs for an expanded organizational structure.[51]

If small college advocates maintained any illusions that the big-time schools were content to maintain the status quo following the war, they were quickly disabused of that notion when the NCAA's executive committee proposed establishing a permanent office, with a paid executive director and necessary full-time staff. Many understood that such an expansion was but the first step in transforming the NCAA into a regulatory body while also illustrating the fears of the small college advocates that a new, larger NCAA intended to serve only the commercialized interests of the organization's big-time purveyors. "Apparently," announced Clarence Houston to his small college brethren in January 1946, "the Association has come to a parting of the ways, and they must set up a larger office in order to . . . conduct [championship] meets and tournaments." Houston had foreseen such efforts a year earlier and had been optimistic that under his leadership the Small College Committee might be able to forestall them. Like so many of the reformers, Houston, from the same generation as his peers but whom everyone called "Pop," enjoyed the privilege of teaching at his alma mater, where he played ironman football for Tufts University from 1911 to 1914. After completing a law degree from Northeastern University, he found his way back to Tufts in 1921 to serve as athletic director, where he promptly enacted what would be a mainstay of liberal arts reformers by banning freshmen eligibility in varsity football. Having been handed the leadership during World War II of the Small College Committee from the cantankerous Bilheimer when the latter's vision deteriorated to the point of incapacity, Houston saw the maneuverings of the commercialized interests even before the war ended. In January 1945 Houston, though a "firm believer in rotation in office," who was ready to hand over the chair of the Small College Committee to Nichols, nonetheless consented to stay on. In a letter to Nichols he explained that "it is conceivable that in the next period the Small College Committee may assume considerabl[y] more importance than in the past." Foreseeing the coming expansion of NCAA administrative and publicity bureaucracies, Houston felt that such growth would be rejected by "the rank and file of the member colleges, many of which fall into a class which is not primarily interested in that type of publicity." Not for the last time, a liberal arts reformer envisioned a day when the NCAA's small colleges could exert their electoral majority on the organization. Scrapping for a fight that had been at least a decade in the making, Houston wanted his ducks in a row. "For these reasons," he assured Nichols, "I am not inclined to relinquish the job until I am sure that you will take it and will be acceptable to the Committee, and it will take a little time to ascertain the latter."[52]

To finance a permanent office with full-time staff, the proposal called for a 400 percent increase in membership dues. Thus, at a time when small college reformers believed that less, not more, commercialized athletics was on the horizon, the NCAA Executive Committee proposed an entrenchment of that model, asking the membership, including the small college members who did not generally pursue national championships, to fund them. Unsurprisingly, this brought about no small amount of criticism from the small college camp on the grounds of both the institutionalization of the championship model and the increased financial cost.[53] In an effort to preempt the latter opposition, some advocates of the expanded NCAA proposed a sliding scale of dues based on student population, with the largest and most athletically inclined schools paying the largest share of NCAA operating costs. Houston, who sought unsuccessfully to forestall the entire expansion, denounced such proposals because of the inevitable marginalization of the smaller schools. Describing the NCAA as "a democratic institution," where every school paid equal dues and "had equal rights in the organization," such a proposal would instead create a scenario where schools that paid the most dues "will naturally and by implication expect greater representation . . . and the smaller college will feel gradually pushed out of the picture."[54]

Small college unhappiness over the dues increase and expansion of the association was nothing, however, compared to the displeasure of the group with another initiative that Houston had foreseen. The executive committee also endorsed a proposal from the American Football Coaches Association (AFCA) to establish within the confines of the NCAA a publicity bureau, essentially a national sports information department under NCAA auspices, charged with disseminating to media outlets information about intercollegiate athletics, mostly football. Nichols saw through the publicity bureau immediately as a vehicle "merely to serve the financial interests of big-time athletics." Edward Parsons of Northeastern University was even more explicit, charging that the AFCA's "principal object" was "to enable college football to more successfully compete with professional football for the public interest and [financial] support." At the 1946 Small College Committee meeting, Parsons proposed a resolution urging the NCAA's executive committee to reject such a publicity bureau. When Parsons asked the room for further discussion, Malcolm Morrell of Bowdoin College immediately moved instead for its outright adoption, which was quickly seconded by Nichols. The resolution passed unanimously. Although the Small College Committee managed to defeat the AFCA proposal, it, along with the increase in dues and the creation of permanent office staff, demonstrated that a primary motivation of the big-time schools' call for an expanded postwar NCAA was their expectation that it would further the interests of big-time athletics and their existing revenue streams through greater media exposure.[55]

Such proposals illustrated how the big-time commercial programs sought to dominate the NCAA as a servant of their interests, triggering many small colleges to question whether they belonged in the NCAA at all. By the 1940s Nichols was just beginning to wrestle with the idea that perhaps the NCAA could not serve the interests of all the various players within intercollegiate athletics. For years he assumed that the big-time schools could be convinced to abandon the commercialized athletics and embrace the liberal arts view of collegiate athletics. But the war years did much to shake Nichols's optimism. The unwillingness of big-time commercialized programs like Ohio State to subjugate their athletic departments to wartime necessities was more than an unseemly pursuit of athletic profit; it was a barrier to ending the war and to putting the country on a sound postwar fitness foundation. And the desires of those same programs to continue business as usual after the war prompted him to call for greater cooperation among the Small College Committee. He realized that without concerted participation in any postwar reform efforts, the small colleges were doomed to watch the big-time schools seize the NCAA for their own purposes. Such efforts required him to seek out "the colleges that have not gone frankly commercial. I do not see much chance of changing the situation in those institutions that are interested primarily in athletic prestige and making money."[56]

The SEC's decision before the war to grant athletic scholarships and wantonly recruit outside of the South, in conjunction with the recruiting free-for-all that accompanied postwar demobilization, allowed for questionable ethics, financial excess, and, in some instances, downright illegality. The events of the period only strengthened the prewar desires of the Big Ten and the PCC to create within the NCAA a national rule-making body with enforcement powers to govern college sports. Advocates of the liberal arts view of competitive athletics also saw the period as a turning point. In their estimation, if they were ever going to position intercollegiate athletics to serve a broad section of the male undergraduate enrollment while also de-commercializing the entire enterprise, the time was now. Their arguments for broad male fitness, competitiveness, and national preparedness would only weaken as the urgency of World War II receded, and they realized that if they deferred to Tug Wilson and the big-time reformers, the small college voice might be marginalized indefinitely. Finally, the public tended to ignore the attempts by liberal arts physical educators to distinguish between their broad participatory program and the highly commercialized big-time athletics that witnessed the postwar excesses. The entrenchment of such views in the mind of the public made it that much more difficult to convince people that competitive intercollegiate athletics contained educational benefits. As a result, 1947 saw the initiation of parallel reforms from entirely different constituencies aimed at drastically different ends. The big-time commercialized programs in the NCAA began debating the reforms eventually known as the Sanity Code, to be administered by a newly empowered NCAA as a regulatory agency overseeing intercollegiate athletics, while the small college reformers proposed reforms that spoke to their fundamental concerns about the role of the small colleges and the liberal arts physical education curriculum within the NCAA.

At the same convention that small college delegates unsuccessfully called for a regional reorganization of the NCAA to win greater committee access, delegates from the Big Ten and PCC formally introduced constitutional amendments that collectively made up the Sanity Code, rules that prohibited off-campus recruiting and special admission standards for athletes but that now fully legitimated need-based scholarships for athletes. The code sought to establish a series of amendments to the NCAA constitution, intended to establish amateurism as the NCAA chose to define it, but failed to address the only issue that actually defined amateurism: the commercialized basis of big-time college athletics. The commercialized programs found the code appealing because it promised to control labor costs in terms of both acquisition (off-campus recruiting) and compensation (scholarships). Small colleges, however, that did not engage in these practices in the first place, were disappointed that no mention was made of restraining or ending commercialized athletics outright. And numerous parties in both camps were anxious about the elevation of the NCAA to regulatory status. Tug Wilson and other supporters of the code continued to delude themselves that their version of reform was the same as that of the small colleges. Others, however, more shrewdly understood the deep divisions and varied identities within the NCAA. The University of Michigan's Fritz Crisler, after surveying the differences between the big-time purveyors, also noted the desire for truly "amateur" athletics in other quarters. Rather prophetically, Crisler noted, "I can foresee the possibility of a group of schools seceding from the NCAA."[57]

To drum up support for the code, Tug Wilson wrote letters to various college and university presidents, describing the NCAA's earnest concern for the elevation of postwar athletics to an ethical plane: "It is the belief of the Association that the suspension of many rules during the war emergency has resulted in a certain amount of relaxation and that it is time to renew our fundamental faith in the values of amateur college athletics." With no sense of irony, Wilson asked for the "sympathy and support in our effort to hold intercollegiate athletics to the same place as other collegiate activities" by supporting a code that made no effort to place commercialized athletics within the same budgetary limitations as other academic endeavors. When the Tufts president received Wilson's letter, he asked Clarence Houston how he should respond. Houston, long a supporter of holding intercollegiate athletics to the same budgetary limitations as the physics department and the glee club, dryly suggested that the president merely assert, "This College has already subscribed to these principles."[58]

Even the most optimistic small college reformers held out little hope that the Sanity Code alone could address some of the problems besetting postwar college athletics. Wary of a regulatory NCAA in thrall to the commercialized big-time interests, most small colleges assumed that enforcement of the code would simply legitimate many existing commercialized practices. Hoping to avoid the foxes guarding the proverbial henhouse, the Small College Committee unanimously proposed the creation of a presidential advisory committee to govern any expanded NCAA structure. The promise of presidential leadership, always more tantalizing than real, operated under the assumption that college and university presidents, with their institutional authority and prestige, would be able to ride herd over maverick athletic directors and starry-eyed faculty athletic representatives. Small college reformers now latched on to the idea that a commission of presidents would be able to keep the big-time interests at bay and make academic considerations their primary concern. So fully did the small colleges distrust the entrenched big-time interests in the NCAA that their proposal called for such a commission to be appointed not by NCAA leadership but by the American College Association, and requiring such a commission to provide to the NCAA membership an annual report on the state of intercollegiate athletics with recommendations to the membership for study and action.[59]

Many small college advocates agreed with the idea of the presidential advisory committee as a means to ensure the liberal arts agenda enjoyed a place in the discussion. G. Wilson Shaffer of Johns Hopkins declared that "the effort to secure more participation on the part of our college and university presidents should be pursued to the fullest extent, since the responsibility for our program must finally rest with them," while some small college presidents, such as Grinnell's Samuel Stevens, eagerly volunteered to serve on such a committee.[60] The Small College Committee offered their proposal for the presidential advisory committee to the NCAA's executive committee at the organization's 1948 convention. The executive committee unanimously accepted the proposal, declaring that it "merited worthy consideration and the officers of the [NCAA] were delegated to study ways and means most effective for putting such a plan into effect." The 1948 convention also saw the enactment of the

Sanity Code. Although it passed almost unanimously, few delegates had any real optimism for the code, though to oppose it openly suggested a rejection of the mythic principle of amateurism upon which the NCAA was based. As one cynic said at the time, "Many will vote for the code but are already figuring out ways to beat it." Many delegates were wary of the code because it explicitly meant the end of the home rule principle and the elevation of the NCAA to a regulatory body; the South resented it because it was created in direct response to their actions in the 1930s; and the small colleges felt it did nothing to actually de-commercialize college sports. Indeed, as Ronald Smith has noted, the code "contributed to the hypocrisy of the NCAA as an amateur institution," because while it claimed to elevate amateurism, it actually sanctioned professionalism by codifying compensation in the form of scholarships.[61]

The depth of ambivalence toward the Sanity Code within the small college group is hard to exaggerate. The code prohibited practices that small colleges did not engage in from the standpoint of either ideology or financial reality. It was largely proposed by one faction of those who played college football for the highest stakes against another faction of the same group to establish something resembling a level playing field. The fact that members of the Small College Committee were deeply ambivalent about it is not surprising, but the depth of that ambivalence also revealed how fragile was their commitment to the NCAA. Marshall Turner of Johns Hopkins asserted that "the practices mentioned in the Sanity Code in no way touch the activities of the small school. . . . That is why I don't see why we, as a small college, are particularly interested in the Sanity Code." Similarly, Drexel Institute's delegate bluntly asked, "What is the place of the small college in the Sanity Code discussion?" Indeed, he wanted to know "What is the place of the small college in this whole program [NCAA]?" Responding to the implication that the small colleges needed to get involved for the good of the body, one delegate tartly compared it to a "fellow trying to get out the vote of the irresponsible citizen," suggesting that if the big-time schools weren't interested in creating truly amateur athletics, why should the small college reformers bother to try?[62] The fact that big-time schools so actively lobbied the smaller colleges indicated that while the big-time schools still dominated the NCAA's organizational landscape, they could no longer take for granted smaller college acquiescence to their agenda. Clarence Houston offered perhaps the most telling benefit that many small college advocates hoped to reap from the code: "It is hoped that any justifiable criticism now aimed at our college athletics may be partly and perhaps wholly eliminated."[63] Unable to effectively impose the liberal arts athletics model, the small college advocates hoped to at least change how the public thought about affairs of the big-time commercialized programs.

Thus, the 1948 convention witnessed the apparent culmination of two parallel reform efforts, each wary of the other and designed to accomplish different ends. Each emerged without broad-based support within the NCAA and as a result of the rapidly changing landscape of collegiate athletics in the 1930s and 1940s. In both instances they were reactive. And perhaps not surprisingly, both failed to achieve implementation, let alone true reform. While grumbling about the Sanity Code began almost immediately, it was the presidential advisory committee that ran asunder first. Considering the executive committee's unequivocal endorsement of the proposal, the Small College Committee expected them to move quickly in identifying for the membership how to implement it. Throughout the spring and summer of 1948, however, the executive committee made no apparent progress on the matter, and by the fall Nichols's frustration emerged in a letter with Tug Wilson's assistant at the NCAA, Walter Byers. Feeling that the executive committee was stonewalling the proposal, Nichols reminded Byers of the unambiguous language of the executive committee resolution at the convention. Furthermore, wary that the committee might sit on the matter indefinitely, Nichols rather cheekily requested the executive committee produce a report for the membership on the status of the resolution.[64] In response, Byers promptly threw the matter back onto the Small College Committee. After acknowledging that the executive committee had discussed the matter extensively in its June meeting, Byers, a diligent and robust correspondent, rather lamely said, "I thought I had written you about that discussion, but apparently I failed to do so." Byers then noted that the executive committee "was not certain" as to the "procedure" for establishing the committee nor as to who should serve on such a committee and asked if the "the Small College Committee could make its recommendation more specific [and] present a more detailed plan."[65]

In frustration, Nichols wrote to Clarence Houston, the chairman of the compliance committee and one of the few small college representatives to achieve a leadership role in the NCAA, expressing his frustration with Byers's dissembling and pleading with Houston to urge some accountability upon both Byers and Wilson. Houston observed that the real issue within the NCAA leadership was the preoccupation with the Sanity Code. Any hope in getting the presidential advisory committee off the ground had to account for the opposition to the code, particularly in the regions where opposition was strongest. Houston suggested that Nichols find "a strong college president who is willing to face facts [and] discuss the position of the NCAA and the Code of Principles [Sanity Code], . . . and I think it politic to get someone from the South or Southeast." Here was the clearest statement yet that the NCAA leadership was primarily concerned with the Sanity Code reform and that any assistance with implementing the presidential advisory committee would require a quid pro quo from the small college reformers.[66]

For reasons that remain unclear, the presidential advisory committee as it was originally envisioned never came to fruition; most likely it fell victim to several forces. First, the efforts to impose the Sanity Code consumed virtually all the reformist energies in the late 1940s, and its ultimate failure left a deep and lasting mark upon college athletics. Second, as Ronald Smith has ably demonstrated elsewhere, the notion of presidential reform in intercollegiate athletics has always been a chimera, evaporating amid the varying self-interested agendas of academic executives and their own egos and presumptions.[67] Finally, the Small College Committee remained unable to exercise its electoral majority in the NCAA. Radicals and reformers alike fantasized about the possibility of imposing their will upon the organization with the collective votes of the small college majority. That they could not do so indicated that while schools below the supersize state schools did in fact make up a majority of the NCAA and even thought of themselves as "small colleges," they seldom maintained a singular agenda. Only some of them were actually liberal arts colleges, and they often struggled on a singular definition of "small college" or what a reformed intercollegiate athletics model looked like. In the 1940s many advocates defined a small college as one with a thousand students or less; by 1950 Nichols expanded the designation to schools with two thousand students or less, but even that was an unworkable definition according to some.[68] The real issue dividing schools in the NCAA was not their numerical size but their philosophical approach to athletics. And that marked a divide that was simply unbridgeable across the spectrum of institutions that criticized the big-time commercialized model. After Nichols had tried to show how much uniformity existed among the Small College Group at its 1950 meeting, Montana State University's Schubert Dyche mildly rebuked Nichols for imposing a single description of the small college mentality: "Now, what is a small school and what is a large one hasn't been determined, but the average small school that I know of has to rely on gate receipts in order to maintain an intercollegiate schedule. . . . We shouldn't draw any more conclusions about this until you know more about small schools, and there are a lot of them."[69]

The diversity of outlooks varied from one extreme to the other with an inability to agree even on minor details somewhere in the middle. Consider, for example, the statements of Lafayette College's president R. C. Hutchinson, who declared in 1950, "Intercollegiate athletics has very little to do with physical education, because the entire training of intercollegiate athletics along physical lines is given to those students who have no need of any training." In Hutchinson's mind the sole benefit of intercollegiate athletics was to create "emotional integration for the American college campus," designed to raise the loyalty and spirits of the university community and its constituencies. As such, intercollegiate athletics was "a spiritual matter" and "should be under the control . . . [of those] whose business it is to provide the spiritual leadership of the college." Even Nichols thought Hutchinson's proposal was a little much when he incredulously asked a colleague of his at Lafayette, "Is he seriously considering putting such a program into effect at Lafayette?"[70] Malcolm Morrell of Bowdoin College, usually an ally of Nichols, had no problem acknowledging the off-campus constituencies of college athletics but brought up some of the practical concerns that abolishing gate receipts entailed: "How would we decide who could come to the game? How would we know in advance when a big crowd was coming?"[71]

Jesse Feiring Williams of Columbia University correctly asserted that the entire question of reform in intercollegiate athletics—and indeed its very role in American culture—centered on "the principle of pecuniary gain." According to Williams, the fundamental problem was that those charged with reform and oversight were creations of the very financial system so many of them were decrying: "To ask individuals who are the product of forces that produced 16 Bowl Games last January to put an end to such business by acts of personal volition is merely to profess faith in moral magic. To ask individuals who are caught up in the meshes of an economic system to give up Madison Square Garden by simply foregoing thousands of dollars is a species of faith that may move mountains but not athletic boards and councils." The problem, according to Williams, was not so much that college athletics made money; it was that educators had allowed the making of money to be the sole condition on which decisions were made. The only way to resolve the role of money was to change the purpose for which intercollegiate athletics existed.[72]

Perhaps the clearest statement of such an effort, which marked both the position of the hardline liberal arts critics and the divide within the Small College Committee, came from Johns Hopkins' G. Wilson Shaffer at their 1947 meeting, and it deserves to be quoted at length here:

> We decided about ten years ago that we thought we had gone pretty far in trying to keep amateur standards. I was opposed to going the whole way without taking the dollar mark out of it, and so we decided to take that step. We have almost ten years' experience now without gate receipts for any athletic contest. I don't want to seem flippant, but we keep saying we are not playing football for money, and we are playing for money. So long as you take in ten cents at the gate, you are playing football for money. The difficulty is that you can never get people into groups. If you lined up all the colleges in the country and tried to put them into a group, you would find it as difficult a job as that of a psychiatrist when he tries to put people into groups of introverts and extroverts. You can't do that.
>
> Instead of saying we play for money or we don't play for big money— when we actually do—let's prove we are really not playing for money by actually not playing for money at all. I know there are other propositions involved, but I don't believe we can better the situation by pointing the finger at somebody else and saying, "We people don't play for money and these people do." It is just a matter of degree.
>
> You will find it difficult to classify yourselves in[to] any group. I thought ten years ago that it might be done. I was rather hopeful then, but I have about lost hope, because it doesn't seem possible to convince most of the people that a few cents isn't important. As most colleges say, "We really don't make any money on our athletic program. It is a pittance. It is only a dime here or there." We don't seem to be able to get them to throw that dime away. I don't believe you can make any distinction until a fairly large number of [us] decide to throw it away.[73]

Shaffer understood, perhaps better than others, that the small colleges' efforts to impose their electoral majority upon the NCAA and remake competitive athletics on the liberal arts model were hopelessly mired in their own divisions. Some small colleges that opposed the commercialized model were just as opposed to what the liberal arts reforms might mean for their budgets. In this context the cure might be more destructive than the disease. Worse, having pointed the finger at the big-time commercialized programs, too many were unwilling to take the steps that would definitively set them apart from those same schools. As a result, Shaffer implied, their self-righteousness emerged as little more than asserting gradations of sin.

The Sanity Code also soon ran aground on the shoals of a fractured constituency. The lack of genuine support for the code appeared almost immediately as many conferences and schools debated whether to abide by it and what kind of leeway, if any, existed within it. Of the schools willing to accept the elevation of the NCAA as a regulatory agency, few enjoyed much consensus with their peers on what that presence should look like. The punishment for violating the code was expulsion from the NCAA, which seemed too harsh to many in the tightly knit, overly familiar world of college athletics. And many who had questions about the code's application could hardly be accused of looking for loopholes to serve their self-interest. Indeed, of the seven institutions that openly defied the new code in its first year, soon dubbed the "Sinful Seven" by the media, only one pursued big-time commercialized football. The violations of the remaining six were often trivial in nature, such as providing meals to players, and many people were unwilling to see the single kingdom of college athletics Balkanized with a vote for expulsion. Although a majority did vote for expulsion, it was far short of the two-thirds majority needed to carry. The unwillingness to expel the Sinful Seven left the code in an ambiguous position. Though few knew it at the time, and critics and supporters continued to discuss the code, the unwillingness to expel effectively emasculated it. Clarence Houston, however, understood what had happened, and it was the drop of excess that overflowed his cup of patience. Having orchestrated his extended term as Small College Committee chair solely to see the liberal arts forces triumphant in just this kind of battle for the NCAA's soul, he now gave up in disgust. When Nichols and Northeastern's Ed Parsons tried to get Houston to carry on the fight, Houston bluntly replied "definitely that I would not be a candidate for re-election. . . . After three years of rather intense effort" to carry out the liberal arts agenda and leverage their electoral majority, "I see no real evidence that [the Sanity Code] will be supported by a sufficient force of the members to overcome the minority actually in opposition to it."[74]

In the wake of the Sanity Code's emasculation, Walter Byers maintained the same delusional optimism about reform and the commitment of the small colleges to go along with the big-time programs as Tug Wilson had in the early 1940s. Writing to Nichols, Byers said that although "we are picking up the pieces from the New York convention, . . . as we put them back together, it seems the NCAA might very well emerge from this whole matter as a stronger group than it was before."[75] Byers's letter was a perfect example of the sentiments that simply exasperated and infuriated the liberal arts reformers because of its irrational optimism, its continued ignorance of the liberal arts agenda, and its presumption that solving the concerns of the big-time commercialized programs benefited others. Consequently, the NCAA continued to expand its revenue streams and set policy based on what served its commercially oriented membership. Beginning with the 1950 convention, the NCAA for the first time charged a registration fee for its annual convention. And although this brought a storm of criticism from small college delegates, the NCAA actually doubled the fee just two years later.[76] Thus, while people like Wilson and Byers attempted to claim in their correspondence an affinity for the small college position, their actions continued to reveal that they did not have a clue about what animated that group's concerns for college athletics. Before Nichols had his secretary file Byers's letter, he scribbled under Byers's name his own off-the-cuff editorial on the NCAA's soon-to-be executive director: "Not greatly impressed with ideals or standards."[77]

Delegates to the Small College Committee consistently claimed that the NCAA largely ignored the problems and concerns of the small colleges, and nothing during this period better symbolized that than the question of freshmen eligibility. The question of ruling freshmen ineligible for varsity play dated back to the end of the nineteenth century, and by the end of the 1920s all major college athletics conferences ruled freshmen ineligible, under the assumption that giving these students a year to concentrate solely on their academics more effectively acculturated them to college-level academic rigor. While the NCAA's tradition of home rule kept it from attempting to impose national eligibility rules, it did succeed in 1939 in creating a "freshman rule" for championship events. The manpower shortages created by World War II led to a temporary suspension of the rule, but it was restored in 1947. The freshman rule was not seen by all small schools in the same light. Many small college reformers embraced the academic logic of allowing freshmen to concentrate solely on academics their first year on campus. Yet the rule obviously made ineligible roughly 25 percent of the male student body, a significant barrier to fielding competitive teams from schools more concerned with competitive equity and with only one or two thousand students.[78] In March 1950 Kenyon College requested from the Ohio Athletic Conference a two-year exemption from the freshman rule in order to more competitively fill their football roster. Kenyon's plight elicited "sincere sympathy" from the other conference delegates, who nonetheless overwhelmingly rejected the request knowing full well that it likely meant Kenyon's withdrawal from the conference. In turn, many small schools abandoned the freshman rule and either accepted their ineligibility for conference or NCAA events or refrained from joining the NCAA at all.[79] As one administrator noted in the postwar years regarding the NCAA's stand on the freshman rule, "Some small schools do not follow NCAA rules. They can't."[80]

What most troubled reformers was not the inability of the NCAA to resolve this conundrum among the small schools but its pursuit of the freshman rule as a means to serve big-time athletics. The freshman rule's intent of allowing freshmen to concentrate on their academics was obliterated when big-time schools created freshmen teams who often practiced as much as the varsity. With the number of coaches and the amount of equipment required to field two football squads, most small colleges could not afford freshmen teams. As Kansas State Teacher's College's F. G. Welch pointed out in 1950, "In many small colleges, student enrollment and staff is insufficient to provide distinct programs of freshman and varsity competition," while the big-time schools "provide a full schedule of freshman competition and thereafter permit three years of varsity competition."[81] Thus, freshmen teams became a loophole that only the big-time commercialized programs were able to exploit. Here was a classic example of how even when the NCAA embraced a reform called for by some smaller schools, it did so to the benefit of big-time athletics. As a result, many within the Small College Committee felt that NCAA membership contained no real consequence or meaning as far as the small schools were concerned. As Nichols wrote in May 1950, "From the point of view of the type of school I represent, it actually would make no difference at all as to whether the NCAA had any [Sanity Code] legislation or whether we even were members."[82]

Small college doubts predating World War II about their role in the NCAA now morphed into doubt about the efficacy of the entire organization and whether those schools should seek some athletic organization of their own in the postwar years. E. Wilson Lyon, president of Pomona College in Southern California, argued that schools such as his "should remain in the NCAA" only as long as their "influence and voting power" allowed them to "secure a more sensible program" along small college lines. Failing that, however, "I would certainly be in favor of forming a new association of smaller institutions."[83] It was a sentiment shared by Amherst College's A. W. Marsh, who acknowledged that his school had discussed withdrawing from the NCAA "but have stuck to it to help them with a program of reform." If that could not be effected, however "the small colleges are better off with their own organization." In responding to Marsh, Nichols admitted that the only advantage of NCAA membership for schools like Amherst and Oberlin was "to use our limited influence to keep the NCAA from becoming even weaker" than its current state.[84]

The problem with such sentiments was, as Nichols's comment referenced, the "limited influence" of the small colleges, particularly in the form of their committee service. The two most senior NCAA committees, the council and the executive committee, formulated policy and coordinated activities with the paid staff. In the decade of the 1930s, only nine small college representatives served on the executive committee, compared to fifty from the big-time commercialized programs. And by the 1950s, while small college representation remained frozen at nine participants throughout the decade, the number of big-time schools represented swelled to sixty-two. Those numbers were proportionally equivalent on the more powerful NCAA Council, which, throughout the 1930s and 1940s, witnessed representation of the big-time schools at a ratio of five to one over the small colleges.[85]

For all the public attention focused on things like the Sanity Code, the meat of NCAA authority appeared in the form of its smaller committees, particularly those that established rules, set up its championship events, and determined allocations of funds. From those expressions of NCAA prestige, the small colleges were almost completely excluded, and it was a subject that rankled whenever it emerged. In the 1940s and 1950s the football rules committee began moving away from the original rules that limited substitution, ensuring that most players played both offense and defense. The movement toward two-platoon football and, eventually, open substitution drove up costs as the size of teams skyrocketed. Small colleges and their limited budgets faced an increasing strain, and small college advocates railed against the increasing costs of the game. Bowdoin's Mal Morrell noted indignantly, "There is no small college with a voice on the Rules Committee." Acknowledging that no small college would have supported increasing their costs and decreasing their competitiveness, Morrell asked rhetorically, "What small college requested a change in the rules?"[86] The extent to which the big-time programs dominated NCAA committee service can be seen in the resignation of the University of Pennsylvania's LeRoy Mercer. In

1950 Penn, then still a big-time athletic program, separated its athletic department from its College of Physical Education, of which Mercer was dean. Because he was no longer affiliated with the athletic department, he felt compelled to resign his *seven* NCAA committee positions, including his chairmanship of the eligibility and finance committees and his position on the NCAA Council. In comparison, no small college delegate served on more than one committee.[87]

Many advocates saw the futility of trying to influence the NCAA from within. Cornell's Robert Kane was one such small college man unwilling to wait, declaring in April 1950 that small college efforts to influence NCAA legislation were hopeless: "I am more convinced than ever that the NCAA should pull out altogether of trying to legislate" both the big-time programs and the small liberal arts colleges.[88] In response, Nichols expressed his increasing pessimism about not only the future of college athletics but also the role of small colleges in the NCAA: "There has been a strong undercurrent of feeling for some time that probably the small institutions of our type would be better off not in the NCAA."[89] To another correspondent, Nichols was even more pessimistic, declaring that "small colleges" should simply "withdraw from the NCAA and form their own organization."[90] Indeed, it was not just that the NCAA could not serve both the commercialized big-time interests and those of the liberal arts colleges but that the interests of the former were a contagion that would eventually spread to the sporting body politic. It was a concern shared by Pepperdine College's Al Duer, who pointed out at the 1951 Small College Committee meeting that Sanity Code prohibitions, such as training table meals, were not problems for the small schools simply because they could not afford them. The problem, according to Duer, was that the small schools learned from the commercialized programs that the only way to maintain competitive equity was "the bypassing and the chicanery of the rules."[91] Declaring that "football is a lost cause as far as education is concerned in the larger institutions that have gone into the entertainment business on a huge scale," Nichols proposed to contain the game's "vested interests" from corrupting the small schools, saying they "might be better off if we entirely cut ourselves off from the NCAA and formed our own organization." To remain in the NCAA, according to Nichols, was to be "tarred with the same brush" in the minds of the public.[92] Not even the advocates of big-time athletics could deny the dysfunction of the NCAA in attempting to serve the small college interests. Justin Morrill, president of the University of Minnesota, acknowledged in 1952 that the NCAA's "tent has to cover too many" and that perhaps the small schools would be better off elsewhere.[93]

For all of the handwringing over the postwar recruiting excesses and the failed Sanity Code, nothing rocked the college athletics establishment like a series of scandals that emerged over six months in 1951 involving gambling, grade fixing, and outright academic cheating. In late February of that year, New York district attorney Frank Hogan revealed extensive evidence that professional gamblers had offered bribes to numerous college basketball players to "shave points" in games, thereby keeping the final scores within the pregame point spread established by the bookmakers. By spring Hogan handed down indictments to almost three dozen players at schools not just in New York but also at Toledo University; Bradley University in Peoria, Illinois; and Adolph Rupp's vaunted University of Kentucky. No sooner had the basketball scandal fallen out of the news than stories emerged from William and Mary College that in an effort to position itself as a big-time football program, university and athletic officials had altered transcripts of incoming players, given grades to players for classes they never attended, and fixed grades for players to maintain their academic standing. And hard upon the heels of the William and Mary scandal, West Point announced in the first week of August that it was expelling ninety cadets, including almost half the football team, for engaging in a campus cheating ring. Over the span of slightly more than six months, the worst of college athletics found itself on the front page of the *New York Times* in no less than eighteen separate instances, with each scandal appearing to bring new levels of public outrage and disenchantment with college sports. Culminating with the scandals of 1951, the postwar years, in the words of John Thelin, marked "the closest that organized college sports came to a complete collapse of safeguards and standards."[94]

Small college advocates saw the scandals as the inevitable outgrowth of an athletics model that privileged victory over academic priorities and sought to attract public and media interest so as to accrue financial gain. Others saw the scandals as examples of how the corruption of commercialized athletics could spread even into liberal arts colleges. Many reexamined their own standards and protocols to ensure that such excesses could not occur at their campuses while reaching out to colleagues on the same wave length on other campuses to share proposals and policies that might hold their own campuses and conferences at arm's length from the increasingly fetid stench emanating from college athletics.[95] With the failure of the Sanity Code and the inability of the

NCAA to achieve any national consensus about reform, such efforts also marked a temporary resurgence of what Ronald Smith has called "Inter-Institutional Control." Realizing that unilateral restrictions on athletic practices tended to accomplish little other than putting one's own school at a competitive disadvantage, schools dating back to the late nineteenth century circularized athletic and academic peers in hoping to forge a consensus among like-minded schools. Although such efforts had failed in the late nineteenth century to achieve any lasting, wide-scale success, their resurgence in the early 1950s marked the growing desperation of the period.[96] These efforts also emerged from the realization that the public and the media made no effort to distinguish between the excesses of the cheats and the virtue of the reformers. As a result, these communiqués often criticized the wanton practices of college athletics' big-time purveyors that tended also to besmirch the reputations of those who denounced such practices.

Even before the scandals of 1951 broke onto the pages of the nation's newspapers, liberal arts reformers bristled at how the public and media defined college athletics as a monolith rife with corruption and decay. Malcolm Morrell of Bowdoin College remarked, "When some large colleges go out and make themselves into football institutions and football is criticized, we are all tarred with that same brush no matter how decent our programs may be."[97] Tufts' Clarence Houston, who had been the Small College Committee's town crier for more than a decade, grasped that he and his colleagues were losing the battle for public opinion. They had consistently committed themselves to the broad participatory model of the liberal arts agenda, and yet, as far as the public was concerned, Tufts might as well have been the University of Oklahoma or the University of Southern California (USC): "Abuses and evils have grown up to a point where it has become a public scandal. Whether intercollegiate football is a racket is beside the point, but the public has become to think it is a racket."[98] As the events of 1951 settled into the public mind and colored all college athletics, not just football, Nichols argued that the public needed to be reminded that not every school lived outside the boundaries: "As a result of the tremendous amount of adverse publicity, I believe that some people think all college athletics are rife with fraud, hypocrisy, and over-emphasis. We need . . . to show that athletics can be conducted in harmony with education."[99]

Such sentiments marked the mood of the NCAA as a whole on the eve of its 1952 annual convention. In the preconvention materials sent out to members, the agenda mentioned the "severe censure and criticism" of college athletics in the wake of the scandals. Unable to restrain himself, Nichols angrily handwrote in the margins of his copy, "Intercollegiate athletics have been subject to severe criticism during the past year and justly so. However, it is unjust to condemn all intercollegiate sports for the malpractices of some."[100] It was a refrain that the liberal arts reformers returned to again and again—at conventions, in their correspondence, and in their internal administrative reports to faculty and administrators. The frustration of these reformers in their inability to convince the big-time athletics programs to embrace the liberal arts model was exceeded only by their frustration at the public's implication that all college athletics had become an immoral den of iniquity. Mal Morrell forlornly noted in his annual report to Bowdoin's president that "intercollegiate athletic programs have been the subject of widespread and in most cases justified criticism" that unfairly lumped together "the football institutions" with the liberal arts programs. "Actually," he wrote, "many of the small . . . liberal arts colleges have kept athletics on a high plane."[101] Likewise, in his report to the Ohio Wesleyan University (OWU) faculty in the wake of the scandals, George Gauthier noted that OWU's policies were "based on a firm resolve to avoid the excesses which characterize the popular trend in intercollegiate athletics and an equally strong conviction that physical education, intercollegiate athletics, and intramural athletics are an integral part of total educational program."[102] Perhaps none, however, were as indignant as Johns Hopkins' Marshall Turner. It was Turner who had overseen Hopkins' full embrace of the liberal arts model, abolishing gate receipts and establishing dozens of competitive teams in multiple sports for all students and to establish college athletics, creating an environment aimed at both the physical and moral development of students. And yet, "One thing I have been more disturbed about than anything else . . . is the fact that the attention of the public is now centered on the moral aspects of our intercollegiate athletics."[103]

In the midst of college athletics' greatest crisis since the NCAA's founding in 1905, the organization's council met in Chicago at the end of August 1951. Confronted with six months of scandal and embarrassment, the council issued a five-page statement addressing the "recent developments" of the previous half year in an effort to assert the NCAA's moral and institutional legitimacy and convey to the public the appearance of a watchdog organization sufficiently aroused to action. In reality the statement aroused only the liberal arts and small college reformers, giving them further proof that the NCAA was a house divided against itself that could not stand. The statement began by asserting the council's conclusion "that there is nothing wrong with intercollegiate athletics that a release of the pressures upon it will not cure." After linking themselves to a tradition of "wholesome intercollegiate athletics," the council noted that they "share[d] the widespread opinion that the moral tone of the nation has declined. . . . College athletics are but a cross-section of our national citizenry, and it is not surprising that a few of them are affected by the lowered morals." And rather amazingly, the council contended that such moral declension was the fault solely of the young men who played the games rather than the adults charged with their moral development: "The sins of a nation are reflected in magnified proportions in the misdeeds of a comparatively few athletes." Thus, the council claimed in the wake of college athletics' greatest crisis in half a century that there was nothing systemically wrong with the commercialized big-time model of college sports, that the scandals were the fault not of college athletics but a declining American morality, and that the adults could not possibly be held accountable for their eighteen-to-twenty-one-year-old charges. Having asserted that nothing ailed college athletics and that it was not their fault anyway, the council nonetheless proceeded to urge schools to consider several recommendations, such as "rigidly supervising" out-of-season practice, "re-examining [bowl] games," "reducing undesirable recruiting activity," and "eliminating excessive" recruitment practices. Two years after Nichols addressed the entire NCAA Convention with essentially the exact same message, the council closed by maintaining "that the public is now sufficiently aroused," implying that college athletics was at a crossroads. And without any sense of irony, the report concluded with the line, "The time for platitudes is past."[104]

Since at least the late 1920s, many small college advocates had hoped to elevate the liberal arts model allowing for broad participation of a regularly enrolled student body with a primary aim on fitness, individual development, and student spirit. The schools' athletics programs would be funded not through gate receipts and outside capital that incentivized winning but through annual line item appropriations that placed athletics on par with other curricular expenses, such as academic departments and the music and drama programs. They had hoped that the embarrassing revelations of the Carnegie Report, the financial crisis of the Depression, and the sense of national emergency and patriotic obligation of World War II and the Cold War would be the impetus to establish the liberal arts model as the dominant form of competitive intercollegiate athletics but had been rebuffed and disappointed at every turn. And with each missed opportunity, their sense of frustration and pessimism deepened about the NCAA's ability to craft a singular vision of what college athletics should look like. In their frustration, however, they missed the growing diversity within the NCAA of the small colleges. No longer were almost all small college members private liberal arts colleges; by the 1950s the postwar growth of higher education created medium-size private universities, more academically pedestrian parochial schools, and smaller state schools that considered athletics a vital part of their identity. Unable to compete against the big-time commercialized programs, they sought simply to create a college athletics world that allowed for their parallel participation.

It was not lost on the liberal arts colleges that they had founded the NCAA and spent three decades wooing the big-time purveyors to create a singular philosophy for American college athletics. But the cost of that effort had been the sacrifice of their vision and indeed their role in the NCAA itself. As the NCCA's small colleges grew increasingly embittered with how that organization's larger members held them at arm's length from its leadership and viewed with ambivalence or contempt their desires for college athletics on something less than a commercialized model, some began pondering the possibilities of life outside the NCAA. The Sanity Code witnessed the first suggestions that perhaps the small colleges would be better off leaving the NCAA to the clutches of the big-time commercialized athletic programs. Although liberal arts reformers shied away from such talk, their more vocal colleagues from smaller, but athletically aspirant, schools openly doubted the value of the NCAA. Such talk had been abstract, in large measure because they had nowhere to go and no real model to follow. But the early 1950s soon saw those abstractions blow up into outright rebellion leading to calls for both division of and secession from the NCAA. In either case, the discussion was informed when small colleges looked to an organization in Kansas City that seemed to place their interests at the forefront rather than the periphery. And unlike the NCAA, whose dominant members were preoccupied with football and its revenues, the Kansas City organization originated out of a basketball tournament. It not only threatened to blow apart the NCAA, but it also threatened to fracture the tenuous consensus between the liberal arts reformers and the smaller colleges that wanted athletics somewhere between the big-time model and simon-pure amateurism.

CHAPTER 4

BARBARIANS AT THE GATE

BASKETBALL, THE NAIA, AND THE PROMISE
OF A SMALL COLLEGE REVOLT (1941–1953)

The delegates to the NCAA's 46th Annual Convention uneasily convened at Cincinnati's Hotel Netherland Plaza in January 1952. Some, like those from the University of Kentucky, were unsure if the next few days held in store for them the public humiliation of being sanctioned by—or worse, expelled entirely from—the NCAA for their role in one of the most salacious sports gambling scandals of all time. Others, knowing that the public made little distinction between the guilty and the innocent, bitterly bore the media criticism and resented their big-time peers not only for creating the morally ambiguous world in which the gamblers found entrée into college sports but also for the embarrassing aspersions that were now cast upon their own programs in the wake of the William and Mary and West Point revelations. Although Kentucky staved off expulsion, they were forced to sit out the upcoming basketball season. This, however, did little to mitigate the rage that seethed through members of the association's College Committee, which had spent years claiming that engaging in commercialized athletics exposed higher education to the kinds of outside influences that led to exactly the kinds of outcomes witnessed in the gambling scandal.[1]

At the College Committee meeting that year in Cincinnati, Franklin and Marshall College's J. Schober Barr, "Schobie" to his friends and colleagues, sat listening to his fellow delegates condemn the NCAA's big-time members and the environment they created that all delegates now had to inhabit. As a student in his undergraduate days at Franklin and Marshall, Barr was both an athlete and aesthete, just as at home on the gridiron for the Diplomats as in the extensive extracurricular activities that flourished at liberal arts colleges. His easy persona and his ability to wax rhapsodic about great works of literature fit well with his trademark bow ties and his ever-present pipe. History does not record if Schobie wore leather elbow patches on his blazers, but he otherwise emulated the caricature of a liberal arts faculty member. However, when it was Barr's turn to speak, he gave voice to the collective rage that percolated throughout the room, surprising some with the heat and intensity that his remarks contained. After noting the disgust he felt about the scandals and the personal anger he felt over the fact that the actions of others cast aspersions upon his own character, Barr claimed that the time for debate was over: "I think it is time we do something about it. . . . The time is at hand where we ought to stand up and be counted!" Knowing that the small and liberal arts colleges made up a majority of the NCAA, Barr now proposed nothing less than the equivalent of a peasant uprising against the landlords, seizing control of the NCAA from the big-time commercialized programs that were, in his mind, currently driving college athletics into the ground.[2] The convention delegates from the big-time commercialized schools tended to dismiss the College Committee members, with their bow ties and ideals of athletics-for-all, as out of touch with the power and benefit of big-time commercialized athletics, but in January 1952 they had no idea how enraged and dangerous were the men of the College Committee.

The frustrations of the small school reformers and the excesses and scandals of the big-time purveyors finally caused many small schools to seriously consider creating some small college institutional identity within the NCAA or leaving it entirely. The first step in that direction actually began before the 1951 scandals broke and was part of the death throes of the Sanity Code. After the NCAA membership refused to expel the Sinful Seven in 1950, the big-time schools sponsored an amendment to the code that legitimated their recruiting and subsidization practices and essentially stripped the code of any real reformist strength. Realizing they had lost the opportunity to use the Sanity Code as a cudgel to force the big-time schools to embrace the liberal arts model, reformers proposed two different Sanity Codes, A and B, the former for "those that either do not have the funds to subsidize athletics or do not desire to do so," and the latter for "those that use financial means of assisting athletes in their athletic program." Almost no liberal arts or small college pursued most of what the Sanity Code prohibited anyway, but it did allow those schools to distinguish themselves more thoroughly in the public's mind from the big-time schools. Although the small college conference commissioners who originally proposed the dual code system claimed, "It is not our thought to break up the NCAA," what they proposed in the summer of 1950 was the direct origins of the division of the NCAA.[3]

The January 1951 Small College Committee meeting spent much time discussing the demise of the original Sanity Code and its meaning for the NCCA's future. The lack of institutional commitment evident in the Sanity Code's demise led many to doubt the efficacy of not only a regulatory NCAA but that of any single national organization. William McCarter of Dartmouth University acknowledged that "it is becoming more and more obvious that the entire country cannot follow the same regulations." Though many at that year's meeting tended to agree with him, they found less agreement on how to address that fact. S. W. Cram, representing the Central Intercollegiate Conference, proposed the dual code, suggesting the possibility of a two-tiered NCAA. Al Duer from Pepperdine College suggested that a formal "division be made . . . between the smaller and larger conferences and institutions" within the NCAA, mostly along the lines of the dual code. Others argued that if the small colleges could not affect the behavior of the commercialized programs, perhaps there was no point remaining in the NCAA at all. Foreshadowing the divisions within the small college camp, however, Johns Hopkins' Marshall Turner definitively told his colleagues in the meeting, "We have no intention of dropping out of the NCAA."[4]

When the dual code found no support at the 1951 meeting, George Springer, the executive secretary of the West Virginia Intercollegiate Athletic Association, sent out letters to the leaders of 27 athletic conferences whose member schools averaged male enrollments of less than 1,000 students. According to Springer, 239 schools belonged to these 27 conferences, but only 28 of them belonged to the NCAA. Springer saw in these figures that these nonmember schools "feel . . . that competition in all sports in the NCAA is just way over our heads." He went on to propose the creation of the National Small Collegiate Athletic

Association (NSCAA), with the usual language about fostering amateurism, maintaining institutional control, ensuring strong consensus on eligibility and recruiting, as well as a post-scandal nod to restraining gambling. But his first rationale was to allow "small college conferences to give to their teams and their individuals the same right to compete on a national basis that the larger conferences do."[5] For Springer, the competitive depth of the NCAA was far more exclusive of the small schools than any ideological rift over commercialized athletics versus a liberal arts physical education curriculum. It is unclear how far Springer's proposal for an independent NSCAA went or what kind of reception it enjoyed. The Mason-Dixon Conference, which included Johns Hopkins University, met to discuss the proposal, and while its representatives acknowledged the "dissatisfaction" of the small colleges in the NCAA, they believed "that every effort should be made to exhaust" options "within the foundation of the NCAA before setting up a separate organization."[6]

Quite unintentionally, however, Springer's proposal illustrated the divide within the small school contingent of the NCAA. The most vocal critics of the NCAA from within that organization throughout the 1930s and 1940s came from the liberal arts colleges based overwhelmingly in the Northeast and upper Midwest. With fairly imposing admission requirements and tightly knit bands of loyal alumni contributing to annual endowments, these schools aspired to produce an American elite—perhaps not on the scale of the Ivy League but a refined professional class nonetheless—whose paths after their undergraduate days often took them to medical school, law school, and the professions that tended to influence and direct American life. As a result, their desire for a broad-based physical education curriculum spoke to their assumptions about producing an intellectually, morally, and physically fit graduate capable of taking his place in the upper echelons of American society. According to historian Hugh Hawkins, "Political ambition might be better served by going to the state university, but for other forms of 'leadership,' the small colleges were increasingly the choice of upper-middle-class youth." And displays of sophistication and "advanced literacy . . . still mattered in cultivated company."[7] Springer's proposal, however, was motivated less by liberal arts ideological concerns and more by the general desires of small colleges for competitive equity. The response from the Mason-Dixon Conference demonstrated that at least some small schools were as yet unwilling to forsake the NCAA's legitimacy and the chimeric possibility of long-term reform for the simple gratification of championships.

Springer's efforts were soon aligned with the expansion efforts of a new organization borne from the NAIB Basketball Tournament that originated in 1937. Having been spurned by the game's elites, Emil Liston devoted himself to legitimizing the Intercollegiate Tournament and in 1941 founded the National Association of Intercollegiate Basketball, becoming its first executive director. The organization espoused principles similar to that of the National Association of Basketball Coaches, charging itself with the fostering and stewardship of the intercollegiate game and establishing uniformity in rules. The NAIB also explicitly asserted the benefits of tournament play by noting the "socializing values of intersectional and national competition" and declared that by reserving "the management and control . . . with the administrators of college basketball," their event avoided "the dangers of commercialization by private promotion." The NAIB required only that members be accredited and welcomed all comers but explicitly marketed itself to schools that had no hope of competing against the big-time purveyors of commercialized athletics. Regardless of its lofty rhetoric, though, for several years the NAIB's sole activity was hosting the Intercollegiate Tournament, which soon became known as the NAIB Tournament. The NAIB imposed modest annual membership dues of ten dollars, but nonmembers could still be invited to the tournament with a twenty-five-dollar fee, a figure that jumped to fifty dollars in 1946. After the cancellation of the 1944 tournament and a wartime reduction in the size of the 1945 field to sixteen teams, the tournament rebounded in 1946 to a thirty-two-team field.[8] Membership in the 1940s, however, remained a haphazard experience. Indiana Central College's athletic director wrote to Liston in 1947, sheepishly acknowledging that "we have been unable to find whether or not we are a member" of the NAIB. They were not, but Liston happily forwarded an application.[9] The allure of the open tournament saw many schools in the postwar years join the NAIB when they believed they had a basketball team worthy of consideration by the tournament, a prospect made even more appealing because the NAIB covered participants' travel fees. By the late 1940s interest in the tournament was such that the NAIB raised the nonmember fee to one hundred dollars and still had no problem filling its brackets.[10] The postwar success of the tournament illustrated its staying power but also consumed a growing amount of Liston's time, which had been divided between NAIB business in Kansas City and his coaching responsibilities at Baker University. As a result, Liston retired from coaching and devoted his full energies to the NAIB beginning with the 1945–1946 academic year.[11]

Another indicator of the tournament's success and its growing competitive legitimacy came in 1947 when the US Olympic Committee declared that the NAIB champion would be granted one of the eight slots to determine the US Olympic basketball team. Inclusion in the Olympic qualifying process had long been a goal of Liston's as an adjunct to his bitterness over how small schools were treated in the AAU Tournament. Because the NCAA qualifying process was open to NCAA members only (and, as soon became apparent, favored the big-time programs) and the AAU Tournament put the college teams at a disadvantage against their pseudo-professionals, small colleges had no real opportunity to win the Olympic berth. To have earned a seat at the table on somewhat equal footing with the NCAA and the AAU gave Liston not only a measure of personal satisfaction but also a validation of the NAIB's competitive quality. The NAIB witnessed slow, but steady, growth in the postwar years and reveled in its role of hosting the only truly "open" collegiate tournament. In October 1949, however, Liston suffered a massive fatal heart attack, depriving the NAIB of its driving force. Liston wasn't just the founder of the NAIB; he *was* the NAIB, handling virtually every detail, relying on a lifetime of connections in intercollegiate athletics, calling in favors when necessary, and maintaining every logistical aspect of the tournament in his head without benefit of a secretary. In Liston's obituary the student newspaper at his alma mater and previous employer, Baker University, noted his activities on campus as both a student and a coach but focused on his creation of the NAIB. The tournament was not simply another event, according to the author, but an annual statement about the possibility inherent in athletic competition, where all competitors might meet on a level playing field, regardless of size, associational influence, or national prominence. "It was [Liston]," said the writer, "who made it possible for standard teams of small colleges to compete on an equal basis with those of larger schools." The populist prophet of small college basketball had died, and many now wondered whether his beloved tournament would die with him.[12]

In late October and early November 1949, the NAIB's executive committee engaged in a flurry of correspondence to discuss its options in the wake of Liston's death. No one wanted to abandon the tournament that had provided a championship venue for the small colleges shut out of the NIT and the NCAA events. They also understood that partisans from those two events relished the possibility of witnessing the NAIB's demise. Two days after Liston's death, the executive committee met in Kansas City to discuss their options. Virtually everyone involved with the tournament understood that it had been an extension of Liston's personality and sheer force of will. Sponsors in Kansas City, the management of the Municipal Auditorium, and coaches from NAIB schools all wrote in to inquire if the event could survive without Liston. After examining the organization's books and polling their collective will, the executive committee had an answer by the first week of November. Announcing their preparation "financially and psychologically to go forward" as an affirmation of Liston's memory and his commitment to small college basketball, the committee knew there was really only one man for the job.[13]

In October 1949 Al Duer sat in his coaching office at Pepperdine University preparing for the upcoming basketball season, then only a few weeks away. Duer had been on the job at Pepperdine since before the war and made the small Los Angeles–area Christian liberal arts college a regional basketball powerhouse. In the five seasons from 1942 to 1946, Pepperdine averaged twenty-three wins a year, qualifying for postseason play all five years, reaching the NAIB Final Four in both 1945 and 1946. Duer appreciated the NAIB not only for the opportunities it afforded small colleges like his own to showcase their talents in a truly national tournament but also for the commitment to a model of intercollegiate athletics counter to the big-time commercialized one embraced by members of the NCAA. In 1947 he proudly touted the tournament's national selection process as being "completely democratic" due to its district play-in format that allowed any member school to have a chance to compete for a tournament bid. But Duer was also a reformer and saw the events of the postwar years in the same terms as Oberlin's John Nichols and the others. "College athletics is in danger of being used and its tremendous positive power sapped by selfish interests," he warned in 1947.[14] Duer became a close confidant and regular correspondent of Liston, encouraging Liston's vision, defending the NAIB at every turn, and helping the executive committee vet teams from the far West. After Duer wrote to Liston acknowledging Santa Clara College's disappointment in being left out of the 1947 NCAA Basketball Tournament, despite going 21-4, including beating USC, UCLA, and UC Berkeley twice, Liston left it up to Duer to "impress upon them that the NCAA is a closed program and Santa Clara should get into" the NAIB, where all schools were treated equally.[15] By the late 1940s Liston made virtually no significant decisions on the tournament without seeking Duer's counsel. Whether Duer knew it or not, Liston had groomed him to take over the NAIB, and the executive committee never truly considered anyone else, naming him the next executive director that fall.

Duer resigned his position at Pepperdine with a heavy heart and hurriedly made his way to Kansas City, understanding two things: (1) that the NAIB had tapped into a deep wellspring of small college desire for equal access to a national basketball championship, and (2) that the NAIB had an equally deep resentment for how small colleges were treated and ignored by the NCAA. In his first annual message as executive director, Duer took a swipe at the NCAA Basketball Tournament noting the "democracy" of the NAIB as compared to the format of the NCAA Tournament, which created "competition between winners of a few selected conferences."[16] Recognizing the growing disenchantment of small schools in the NCAA by the late 1940s, including his own, Duer felt the time was ripe for the NAIB to consider expanding its program. Describing the NCAA as "certainly in an unsteady position" and having "lost face with both the colleges and the public all over the United States," Duer saw this as "a good time to take up some slack."[17] Excited about the prospect of coordinated action outside the NCAA, conference commissioners, some of whom were aligned with George Springer's NCSAA proposal, urged their member schools to attend the NAIB meeting in March 1951. S. W. Cram, chair of the Central Intercollegiate Conference, noted that in the wake of the Sanity Code disaster, the reformers "realize we need to have some uniformity nationwide—at least the small colleges might well establish some type of pattern." Cram urged his member schools to determine "if the NAIB is an appropriate organization in which to do this."[18]

At that year's annual meeting, the NAIB, in a nod to the reformers, imposed what essentially amounted to its own Sanity Code addressing financial aid and scholarships. It also hosted a seminar for campus sports information directors (then referred to as "sports publicity officers") to regularize interactions with the press and maximize athletic media exposure for those schools looking to engage in commercialized athletics on a smaller scale. And it finally abolished the loophole that allowed nonmember schools to participate in the tournament simply by paying a nonmember rate. The centrality of the championship tournament, not to mention efforts to aid sports publicity efforts and rules against athlete subsidies, demonstrated that while the NAIB's growth came overwhelmingly from small colleges, it was not from the liberal arts schools that were so concerned with commercialization in the NCAA.

Nothing marked a more assertive vision for the NAIB like its decision to expand beyond basketball. The clamoring of small schools both within and without the NCAA to participate in tournaments and events with schools whose enrollments and annual budgets more closely resembled their own was what led to Springer's attempt to create the NSCAA, and it was a sentiment that the NAIB capitalized upon. Dozens of schools already in the NAIB orbit in 1950 began discussing the possibility of an annual track meet, an event that first came to fruition in 1951 at Emporia State College.[19] It is unclear exactly what transpired after Springer circulated his proposal for the NSCAA in September 1951, but he emerged as leader of the same group of conference commissioners who had proposed A and B versions of the Sanity Code. By December of that year, his efforts were wrapped up in the growing program of the NAIB. Springer was appointed to chair an NAIB committee of national conferences, ostensibly to help bring about under the NAIB banner the NSCAA proposal made earlier in the fall.[20] After circularizing its membership, the NAIB agreed to host an annual spring championships event featuring track and field, golf, and tennis in Abilene, Texas, in June 1952. At the 1952 annual meeting, the membership agreed to change their name to the National Association of Intercollegiate Athletics, sponsoring championships in several sports across the academic year, and pledged "to stand as a bulwark against the perils which have plagued college athletics." While the NAIA's stipulation that "the athletic department should have a place in the institutional structure comparable to all other departments" surely drew the approving notice of the liberal arts reformers, the NAIA endorsed championship play from the outset and made no moves to condemn commercialized athletics.[21]

Duer, however, addressed another subject near and dear to the heart of many liberal arts reformers by authoring a sixteen-hundred-word manifesto titled "How to Save College Football." Since at least the 1940s, many small college representatives realized they could no longer win much attention compared with the large, big-time football programs, and the emerging prominence of television only widened that disparity. As West Texas State College's Gus Miller said, "There is no use trying to do anything about football. The schools that can't afford it had better start a strong intramural football program."[22] For liberal arts schools and their presumptions to train an American professional class, few things matched football's ability to develop masculinity, leadership, and "moral character"; in short, it was "the focal point of athletics in America."[23] As a result, the marginalization of smaller schools in the sport was particularly painful, and they resented the effects of commercialized football on their own programs. Nichols lamented bitterly in 1950, "Football is a lost cause."[24] The inevitable outcome, according to Duer, was the complete abandonment of the smaller schools: "The great American sports public would travel long distances to see a big game between two national publicized teams . . . but only a faithful few would pay at the gate to watch Siwash and the old traditional rival of fifty years decide the championship of the 'little seven' conference."[25] Without state subsidies and large open enrollments, according to Duer, the ability of those schools to pay for their athletic programs through moderate public support was now at an end: "Commercial football for the small college is dead." To save college football for these schools, Duer proposed exactly what Nichols and liberal arts reformers had been calling for since the mid-1930s, by allocating to the football program "the same financial support from the college budget as does science, music, . . . and other laboratory departments." Duer also argued that an integral part of this campaign to save small college football required that "colleges must participate with institutions of like size, manpower, and standards of competition." He declared that such a two-tiered separation between "the highly commercialized programs" and those programs "who play for the love of the game and the benefits to be derived from participation" was inevitable. Duer never mentioned either the NCAA or the NAIA by name, but he took a thinly veiled swipe at the former by noting that such a path would "serve to bring us back to 'sanity' in college athletics, and without the necessity of formally adopting a 'sanity code.'"[26]

Though Duer honestly came by his outrage over the NCAA's disdain for and indifference toward smaller schools, he and the NAIA never completely aligned themselves with the liberal arts reformers. They both criticized the commercialized model as unduly emphasizing victory and coming at the expense of greater competitive equity, but the NAIA's growth occurred because it took some of the same incremental steps. No one could deny that the NAIA Basketball Championship offered a tantalizing incentive for many member schools. While Bilheimer and Nichols thought the NCAA needed to place less emphasis on championships, Duer and the NAIA never apologized for their efforts to build a national tournament that by the 1950s many saw as the legitimate small college national championship. While Duer and the NAIA's advocates stressed the egalitarian nature of their event compared to the NCAA's, the liberal arts reformers pointed to its existence at all, thus illustrating the "gradations of sin" argument that Johns Hopkins' G. Wilson Schaffer had elucidated at the 1947 Small College Committee meeting. Though Duer and the liberal arts reformers saw in each other much in common, this fundamental difference existed from the beginning.

The recent scandals in college athletics and the NAIA's formal expansion into a national small college organization most decisively put the NCAA on the defensive but also broke some of the institutional lethargy regarding the small schools. Seeking to avoid the semantic distraction of setting a minimum enrollment to determine whether a school was a "small college," as well as an acknowledgment that the issue was more about values and practices than enrollment, in 1951 the NCAA renamed the Small College Committee simply the NCAA College Committee. Indicating the depth of division within the NCAA between these schools and the large universities that played big-time sports, some advocates began immediately thinking in terms of a "college division" within the NCAA, even though the designation would not exist for another five years. And recognizing that the inability to participate in NCAA championships drove a lot of college interest in the NAIA, the committee began "considering the possibility of establishing tournaments and meets for the college division in the NCAA. We feel that this would undoubtedly strengthen the college interest in the NCAA."[27] After receiving some NAIA promotion materials, Oberlin's John Nichols forwarded them to Walter Byers, the NCAA's new executive director, with a note reading, "I don't know how much it [the NAIA] cuts in on our membership, but I can imagine it does affect it some."[28]

The scandals and ideological division of the period led many to discuss seriously the dismemberment or abandonment of the NCAA, but such conversations increasingly illustrated the differences between those who wanted to impose the liberal arts agenda and those who simply wanted to cordon themselves off from the commercialized abuses while enjoying some manner of competitive equity. At the 1951 Small College Committee meeting, Pomona College president E. Wilson Lyon said he doubted the ability of the NCAA to govern all of college athletics and called on other schools to join Pomona in pulling out of the NCAA entirely. Marshall Turner conceded that the small colleges that pursued "non-subsidized" athletics had no clear role or function in the NCAA but could not bring himself to lead a stampede out of the organization, opposing Lyon's proposal.[29] Having himself suggested that the NCAA might never provide an adequate home for the liberal arts colleges,

Nichols, like Turner, nonetheless had a hard time formally abandoning the organization and the prestige that it conveyed, if even in the limited outlets afforded to the small colleges. Grinnell's John Truesdale, though offering his support for a division along the A/B code within the NCAA, also could not bring himself to completely abandon the NCAA. Asserting that he would never propose disbanding the NCAA or removing the small schools entirely, he noted, "There is a proper function [for the NCAA] to perform in playing rules, championship meets, Olympic plans, publications and statistical services." Leaving the NCAA entirely stripped the small schools of the prestige of governing American amateur sport, particularly the Olympics.[30]

Even as Nichols and the NCAA College Committee ruminated on the idea of hosting college division championships within the NCAA fold, most of the old-guard liberal arts reformers were adamantly opposed. The grievances of these reformers had rarely, if ever, involved the lack of competitive opportunity for small schools. Rather, they criticized the abandonment of broad-scale competitive athletics for the whole male undergraduate population in favor of the commercialized model. They particularly took issue with the exclusion of small college representatives from the NCAA committees that exercised the preponderant amount of institutional power. Many recognized that creating championship opportunities for small schools only allowed for those schools to also orient themselves toward victory and potentially embark on the road to perdition. Nichols himself noted, "I personally do not favor the NCAA promoting national championship meets for smaller colleges. I think we already have enough emphasis on championships, . . . and [they] tend to lead to still further over-emphasis, especially in basketball."[31] The college group's old lion Clarence Bilheimer was even more emphatic: "I should never favor asking the NCAA to run tournaments for the small colleges." Opposing all postseason games, Bilheimer decried them as anathema "with sound principles or practices."[32] Others feared the financial repercussions of sanctioning meets and events they assumed would have less public appeal. Colorado College's Howard Olson also noted his lack of "favor of national championship meets especially set up for the smaller colleges," because such an endeavor "might be a financial flop."[33] Fearing that the NCAA leadership was overly fixating on hosting championships merely to save small college membership without addressing some of the root causes of small college disenchantment, all of these men suggested instead that committee membership be more equitably distributed. As Bilheimer put it, "There ought to be better representation for the small colleges on all our committees. We are just as much entitled to that as the larger institutions."[34]

Lying just beneath the surface of this tournament opposition within the NCAA was the realization that the former NAIB already operated a well-respected, financially successful event for those very same schools. For the NCAA to offer a similar event would require it to compete with the NAIA Tournament in a finite market and possibly come up the loser. Olson acknowledged that "the [NAIA] meet in Kansas City has done quite well financially and has furnished an outlet" for the small colleges while "a Small College NCAA meet might be a financial flop." For Olson, however, the bigger issue was that in plowing the ground early, the NAIA had already established a legitimacy and prestige that the NCAA could not match: "At this time, the [NAIA] is considered by many middle western schools as being as important as that of any NCAA basketball tournament. . . . For the NCAA to run competition with the [NAIA] at this time would be hazardous at best."[35] Nichols also noted the financial and competitive success of the Kansas City event and recognized that several small schools in the NCAA pursued the tournament. He also saw it as evidence that the NCAA did not need to offer its own tournament for smaller schools since the NAIA offered that outlet: "The . . . meet in Kansas City has done quite well financially and has furnished a championship opportunity for those schools that are interested in that kind of meet."[36] By Nichols's own estimation, "practically all of the [NCAA] colleges that are in the NAIA are interested in having championship competition."[37]

As far as Nichols was concerned, the NCAA could easily coexist with the NAIA, allowing the latter to provide what he deemed as moderately distasteful, while the former might still enshrine the liberal arts model, thus allowing them to occupy the moral high ground. In Nichols's mind the barons of college athletics in the NCAA could tolerate the NAIA in the same way that some nineteenth-century gentlemen advocated the legalization of prostitution as an outlet for the baser instincts of others. NCAA president Hugh Willett of USC, however, saw the issue in far more complex terms. Whether he agreed or not with Nichols's condescension about the tournament and the ability simply to use the NAIA for its own benefit was irrelevant; the fact was that some member schools desired this event and they found it under the auspices of another organization: "Some of us have bemoaned the fact that the NCAA did not assume the responsibility for the college basketball tournament held annually in Kansas City. It could have been, in my opinion, an 'NCAA Championship—College Division' ranking side by side with the 'NCAA Championship—University Division.'" Willett, far more than Nichols, understood the NAIA as a competitor, not a confederate. The NAIA Tournament also marked a lost opportunity to institutionalize the two-tiered NCAA identity that many had begun calling for in the early 1950s between the big-time universities and the reform-minded colleges. For many, the creation of a University Division and a College Division was a panacea that would grant to the smaller schools their own dominion without requiring the dissolution of the NCAA or asking the commercialized schools to forsake their profit-minded pursuits. Willett, however, seemed to think that in 1951 such an outcome was fantasy: "Of course, I'm only dreaming!"[38]

Willett's desire to create separate divisions as a way to placate the smaller schools and hold together the NCAA marked a growing divide within the NCAA that emerged into a full-blown crisis by 1953. College athletics did not fall into any greater disrepute during the period, but the NCAA's unwillingness or inability to acknowledge the depths of college athletics' depravity, as evidenced by the NCAA Council's unintentionally ironic 1951 statement in the wake of that year's scandals, only accelerated the frustration and alienation of the small colleges. For the liberal arts reformers like Nichols, the NCAA's response to the 1951 scandals was tone deaf and appalling. After the University of Kentucky's involvement in the basketball fixing scandals emerged, including head coach Adolph Rupp's own outrageous ties to gamblers, many assumed the NCAA would expel the University of Kentucky and others in the scandal. According to Nichols in May 1952, "There are certainly a number of institutions that should be dropped from the NCAA." After singling out Kentucky and Bradley University by name, Nichols described their actions as "pitiful," calling for a "very thorough housecleaning of the NCAA." Willett agreed with him, sharing his "great concern over the Kentucky matter," but he disappointingly reminded Nichols that "we cannot afford to enter into any investigation which we cannot carry through to the end." Willet understood both the then limited enforcement powers of the NCAA as well as the membership's unwillingness to expel its own, as evidenced in the earlier Sanity Code vote. Notably, some schools simply abandoned the NCAA and joined the NAIA.[39] By the mid-1950s NAIA membership exceeded NCAA membership, 465 to 395. Others, however, unwilling to abandon the stature and gentlemanly collegiality of the NCAA, decided to stay and fight for its soul, perhaps for one last time.

In an effort to determine exactly what the small schools in the NCAA wanted from the organization, Hugh Willett and Penn's E. LeRoy Mercer proposed in 1951 a survey of the small schools. Colorado College's Howard Olson offered conditional support as long as the results actually accomplished something. "There is little point in collecting data aimlessly," he said. "The collection of the data should be only the beginning of a rather extensive project" aimed at a thorough reevaluation of NCAA governance and membership. Olson also noted that such a survey had been conducted previously, "but nothing was ever done with it so far as I know."[40] Mal Morrell of Bowdoin College was even more cynical about the proposal. Having served his alma mater's athletic interests for more than two decades and being a typical liberal arts "college man," Morrell put in place Bowdoin's "athletics for all" policy and had little patience for those who still pretended that the problem was simply that the NCAA did not fully know what the small colleges wanted. "The questionnaire suggested by Dr. Mercer has been sent out about once every two years for as far back as I can remember," he said, and nothing ever came of it. Morrell indicated that schools that would be surveyed all operated their athletic departments on similar lines with similar values and approaches: "We know these things now, and I dislike spending another year on the same old study."[41] Nonetheless, the committee agreed to send out the survey, which was discussed at length at the College Committee meeting of the 1952 NCAA Convention. The committee noted the usual suspects of exclusion from NCAA committees and the NCAA leadership's general ignorance of the issues confronting the small colleges. One example of the latter appeared as the NCAA renegotiated its athletic insurance policy for member schools. Although the policy contained a death and dismemberment clause in deference to the concerns of the big-time football powers, it did not cover intramural athletics, which was a crucial allied component of the liberal arts schools' athletic programs.[42] Utterly unwilling to abandon the intramurals program so vital to their athletics-for-all model, liberal arts schools were faced with the choice of taking out their own costly insurance policies or risk going without one. In the wake of the insurance betrayal, Schober Barr of Franklin and Marshall College distilled the survey's results down to a single question: "What do we get out of the NCAA?" Gordon Clark of the University of the South answered "not much" by noting that the overwhelming sentiment from his district showed that "a great many [schools] don't think . . . the NCAA is out for anybody but the big-league boys."[43]

While the 1952 College Committee meeting featured an unrelenting level of frustration and anger over the direction of college sports and the NCAA in general, underneath that frustration lay a growing divide between the private liberal arts colleges that wanted to reform the NCAA and the small state colleges that simply wanted to find competitive outlets for schools of their size. After listening to many of his colleagues note the depth of the divide between the small colleges and the big-time schools, Schober Barr believed a model aimed at pursuing financial profit and victory would lead to further crisis and scandal. The scandals of 1951, however, were not merely an embarrassing revelation for the schools involved or even a broader indictment of commercialized college sports, according to Barr, but rather a condemnation of seemingly everyone who pursued college sports at any level, including the liberal arts programs that had spent so much effort seeking to avoid the very revelations that now besmirched men like Barr, and he took it personally. Like so many of his colleagues, Barr so fervently defended the liberal arts tradition because it was at the core of his identity. As a student at Franklin and Marshall (F&M), he "represented the quintessential 'college man,'" having starred on the football team, sung in the glee club, and acted in campus theatrical productions. Shortly after he completed his bachelor's degree, Barr began teaching secondary mathematics while F&M joined so many of its liberal arts brethren and abolished freshman eligibility for the varsity. In need of someone to run its now expanded intramural program, F&M's president turned to its recent prodigal son; having returned to Lancaster, Barr remained a fixture on campus for the next thirty-seven years.[44] In a venting of pent-up frustration, anger, and embarrassment that many of his colleagues shared, Barr angrily denounced the consequences of the 1951 scandals: "It seems every member is involved in the present criticisms that are being carried on in the sports pages. And I get kind of hot under the collar" about being linked with such unethical and disreputable revelations. The small colleges made up a majority of the NCAA and followed sound academic and athletic policies, "and yet we are criticized because we belong to the same organization [as the malefactors]." Thus inflamed, Barr now proposed the small college seizure of the NCAA. For Barr, the morally bankrupt practices of the big-time schools were a contagion that was infecting them all. Even worse, they demonstrated that if the commercialized programs were willing to accept the recent abuses as acceptable occasional outcomes of commercialized sports, then the small schools were much further than they thought in convincing them to embrace the broad physical education curriculum of the liberal arts reformers.[45]

Barr was not the only delegate troubled by the 1951 scandals, but their meaning to a different constituency contained a far less morally outraged conclusion. Small state schools also saw the 1951 scandals as indications of the ready acceptance of commercialized excesses by the big-time schools. But their displeasure was less over the moral outrage the scandals represented and more over the hopelessly uneven playing field the scandals revealed. The schools unwilling to pursue victory at all costs realized they could never hope to achieve any competitive success against such practices. For them, the problem with the NCAA was not its inability to engage in moral reform but its unwillingness to allow these smaller schools their own championship opportunities in which to pursue athletic excellence against like-minded peers. After Barr finished flaying the big-time programs, South Dakota State College's faculty representative H. C. Severin took up the theme of disenchantment, though Severin and Barr came from different perspectives. Severin never presumed to dictate terms to the commercialized programs, nor did he believe his school aspired to see Oberlin or Franklin and Marshall as peers. Thus, South Dakota State, like many small state schools at the time, fell somewhere in the middle of the liberal arts moral reformers and the commercialized big-time programs. They pursued what Mark Bernstein has called "medium-time" athletics, a competitive program that relied on gate receipts and wanted to compete for championships against peers but with little or no intention of ever competing against the nearby state schools like the Universities of Minnesota, Iowa, or Nebraska. Thus, in 1951 South Dakota State, with little ethical difficulty, made the decision to cancel its golf and tennis programs for lack of budget in the same year they installed lights at the football stadium and installed retractable glass backboards, a four-sided electronic scoreboard, and a new press box in their basketball venue. They also saw no issue of divided loyalties by belonging to both the NCAA and the NAIA, indeed playing in the NAIA Tournament the same year they joined the NCAA.[46]

Though Barr and Severin came from different worlds and thus maintained different aspirations, they both entertained the same solution: separation from the big-time purveyors. Barr, having spent the better part of a decade pillorying the NCAA's privileging of commercialized athletics and its unwillingness to grant equal status to the small schools, was still unwilling to completely abandon the NCAA. He proposed "enlisting the membership of the [College Committee]. Then if you want to classify it NCAA Class A and NCAA Class B . . . then let's go along on that basis." Barr and the liberal arts reformers now saw division within the NCAA as the only remaining alternative to secession.[47] The small state colleges like South Dakota State, however, accepted the existing presence of the NAIA as the emerging champion of the small school, foreseeing some kind of alliance where the small schools in the NCAA might retain their voting presence in that organization but turn to the NAIA as a source of championship meets and tournaments. Los Angeles State College's Ferron Losee declared, "Perhaps we have now arrived at that time when we could have two classifications in the NCAA," with the smaller schools finding their championship options via the NAIA. The frustration of many schools unable to participate in the NCAA Tournament caused the basketball committee chair to stress during the 1953 College Committee meeting that the NCAA sanctioned "championship possibilities for all members" but took special pains to note the recent expansion of the NCAA Tournament: "I might add at this point that the Council and the Executive Committee have recently approved a reorganization in the basketball tournament which will provide a truly representative tournament for the membership." Unsatisfied with such concessions, Dan Emery of the state-supported University of Omaha motioned to create a committee to examine the suitability of creating a distinct small college identity within the NCAA. It passed unanimously.[48]

In his annual report to the NCAA Council, College Committee chair Marshall Turner sounded the alarm over the increasing pessimism of the small schools. Turner identified three factors that tended to alienate the small schools from the organization as a whole: (1) difference in the conduct of athletic policy, particularly regarding player recruitment and subsidization; (2) difference in the problems faced, mostly in the form of commercialized versus budget-supported models; and (3) resentment over the "publicized malpractices" of the commercialized programs. These factors, according to Turner, left most small colleges feeling as if they "have no place in a large organization such as the NCAA." In an effort to address that sentiment, Turner rather disingenuously suggested only one remedy: greater committee representation.[49] Though committee service and a voice in the organization were vital issues in the small college discontent, they were mostly limited to the liberal arts reformers like Turner. A 1937 Phi Beta Kappa graduate of the liberal arts–oriented University of the South, Turner arrived at Johns

Hopkins in 1946 and rapidly embraced the university's "play-for-all" model championed by the liberal arts schools.[50] Nowhere in his report was there mention of the other faction in the college group and their primary concern for competitive events more suited for their level of play. In his post-convention correspondence on the matter, Nichols too discussed the issue of ensuring small college participation on the committees but noted "it was certainly not desirable to break the NCAA up into splinter groups," thus suggesting that, like Turner, he was also unwilling to join the growing coalition calling for division.[51] Just as the big-time schools ignored the liberal arts discontent at their peril, those same liberal arts schools now ran the risk of doing the same toward the medium-time schools.

Faced with the possibility of full-scale revolt, NCAA leadership quickly realized that they could no longer delude themselves into thinking that the small colleges were on their side or that small college discontent could be diffused simply through the outlet of the annual College Committee meeting. Confronted with Turner's report, partial as it was, the NCAA Council asked for a full examination of "the Small College question" within the NCAA, with a full report due directly to the council. Chaired by Santa Clara College's Father Wilfred Crowley, the committee also included Nichols and Vanderbilt University's Fred J. Lewis. As an indication of how serious the council viewed the unrest, they authorized the Crowley Committee to hold hearings and gave them a budget to reimburse the travel of those who appeared. The fact that the committee was staffed by representatives from three academically established private schools, two of which openly called for the liberal arts model of athletics, did not bode well for a balanced report representing the interests of the small state schools and their primary concern for a competitive quarantine of the big-time schools.[52]

Almost immediately the Crowley Committee ran into difficulty in determining exactly what constituted a small college. Crowley noted a Northern California school (likely University of San Francisco) with a male enrollment of only seven hundred students but a football stadium that seated thirty-four thousand and a schedule that included "three or four" big-time opponents from within the region and "two or three strong intersectional [games] in football. In what class does such an institution belong?" Crowley also understood that the situation was not limited to football, noting that "the majority of teams in the NIT are from institutions commonly considered 'small colleges.' And yet, would they want to be considered small in basketball?" The previous year, in the

College Committee survey that so exasperated many of the committee's members, schools were asked to classify themselves as a big-time school or a small college. In aggregating the survey results, several individuals noticed "the large number" of schools in the mid-Atlantic and upper South districts that most observers "considered 'big-time' colleges" but that nonetheless linked themselves with the small college identity. In his handwritten notes to Crowley's letter, Nichols remarked that in his mind "the real criteria for the division" was more about "athletic philosophy" and the nature of athletic financing. Schools that expected their athletics program to pay for itself through gate receipts and media contracts, regardless of enrollment size, were not "small colleges" according to Nichols.[53]

When the Crowley Committee held its first hearings in April 1953, Marshall Turner provided a summary of the College Committee's activities as well as the most recent survey submitted to the council. Turner noted that the "College Committee had found it virtually impossible to define the term 'small college.'" He also highlighted the concern over small college exclusion from committee representation within the NCAA, noting that only two small colleges were represented on the council and none on the executive committee. Indeed, the dominance of the larger schools and the exclusion of the small schools altogether prompted proposals for term limits on NCAA committee service as a way to keep the powerful interests from dominating.[54] In the afternoon session, Al Duer and Al Wheeler from the NAIA provided material on the NAIA and made an appeal to link its activities with the NCAA's smaller schools. Duer noted that 145 NCAA members already held dual membership in the NAIA and "all are accredited four-year institutions." He also pointed out that such schools found that NCAA rules and programs simply did not account for the existence and realities of small colleges, citing specifically the "freshman rule and the restriction of the NCAA [basketball] tournament to larger institutions." After hearing from representatives of both the College Committee and the NAIA, the Crowley Committee met privately to discuss the information they had received from both groups. What emerged from that discussion reveals that the committee doubted from the start any profitable alliance between the NCAA and the NAIA. Suspicious of the NAIA's membership "standards," the committee pondered what "guarantee" the organization "could provide that a similar athletic policy was in effect in all member institutions." More damaging to the NAIA's hopes, however, was the committee's conclusion "that the NAIA appealed to a different type of institution than that represented by the members of the College Committee, and that the principal, if not the sole, benefit to be derived from NAIA membership would be national tournament participation." Determining that schools interested in the NAIA were different from the elite liberal arts colleges, apparently in large measure because those schools sought championship opportunities, the committee then punted. Having "decided that the matter was too cloudy and obscure to justify any definite conclusions or recommendations," the committee decided to survey the members' understanding of what constituted a small college and "to express their opinion concerning the NCAA–Small College relationship."[55]

If the Crowley Committee was hoping to minimize the differences within the small college membership or stifle efforts to link with the NAIA, it made an egregious mistake by soliciting the membership. The five-question survey received 205 responses and provided clear statistical and anecdotal majorities desiring a change in how the NCAA dealt with its smaller members. The responses accounted for almost 52 percent of the entire NCAA membership, and of those responding, 78 percent represented schools with enrollments of less than three thousand students; thus, the vast majority of the NCAA's smaller schools participated in the survey. The first three questions of the survey sought to ferret out the definition of "small college" and how schools identified themselves, but by far the most revelatory was the first question, which gave five criteria and asked respondents to rate their significance "in classifying an institution's athletic program in the 'small institution' category." The options were caliber of competition, budget, revenue, enrollment, and integration of athletics with physical education. Assigning five points to the most significant, descending to a single point for the least significant, respondents overwhelmingly ranked caliber of competition first, with 596 points, followed closely by budget (550 points), then revenue (488 points), enrollment (415 points), and integration with physical education at 313 points. Thus, the majority of respondents tended to define themselves against their competition and viewed that factor as almost twice as significant as the liberal arts model, which they overwhelmingly rated as the least significant. Question 4 asked what services respondents wanted to see the NCAA provide; not surprisingly, this elicited a gamut of opinion, with no answer receiving more than 13 percent of concurrence from respondents. However, the answer that more respondents agreed to than anything else was the desire for NCAA championship events for small colleges. That number did not include a separate group that simply wanted to revise the existing basketball and baseball tournaments to allow small schools an opportunity to compete in those events. The final question simply asked if respondents wished to see the NCAA create a classification system, which witnessed an affirmative response by more than two to one. The numbers to the final question were even more stunning when broken down by region. The home of the liberal arts colleges, the Mid-Atlantic states and the Northeast/New England states, supported separate classifications by less than 60 percent, but the upper Midwest, the Plains, and the South, which witnessed growing state schools in the postwar years, supported reclassification well in excess of 70 percent, with the South supporting it by a whopping 80 percent.[56]

Equally unequivocal were the voluminous comments that respondents provided, which, when aggregated in the final report, ran to thirteen single-spaced pages. Interestingly, while a measurable minority of respondents opposed classification, the NAIA, or much change at all, they chose to offer almost no comments. As a result, the comment section spilled forth as a one-sided siren call to acknowledge the path carved out by the NAIA. Kentucky State College's William Exum baldly stated, "The reason the NAIA is expanding so rapidly is due to its slant towards the small colleges." By comparison, according to Exum, "very little policy procedures are made [in the NCAA] with a recognition . . . of the small colleges. I'm thinking particularly . . . of the methods of selecting district representatives for the basketball playoff. We in the small colleges have practically no chance, . . . because they are far from our immediate domain." Besides ability to offer a competitive balance on the field, South Dakota State's H. C. Severin ascribed the NAIA's growth to the exclusion of the small schools from the NCAA power structure. Severin mentioned what other respondents echoed again and again in their comments: "[The NAIA is] trying to do for the smaller colleges what the NCAA [does] for the larger colleges and universities." Both Exum's and Severin's comments illustrated not only a belief that the smaller schools were likely to find a more hospitable environment in the NAIA but also, more problematically for the NCAA, the a priori assumption that the NCAA represented not all of college athletics, just the big-time commercialized model. For those who had desired since the early 1890s to see a single kingdom of athletic governance, such matter-of-fact assertions to the contrary must have stung indeed. John Bunn of Springfield College noted the intensity of the pressure from and appeal of the NAIA, but "if the NCAA does not provide for these small colleges, [small colleges] may be forced to withdraw from the NCAA. . . . I don't believe the NCAA can afford to ignore the NAIA any longer." The obvious solution, according to Oscar Strahan at Southwest Texas State College, was to allow the NAIA to deliver to the small colleges the same kinds of targeted programming that the NCAA delivered to the big-time programs: "Perhaps close integration with the NAIA is the best answer," he said. "This association is well on its way toward doing for the small college that which the NCAA possibly can never do" so long as it remained beholden to its commercialized big-time members.[57]

In its final report, the Crowley Committee observed the number and clarity of responses, revealing their understanding of its statistical legitimacy, and acknowledged the tremendous "dissatisfaction" of respondents. It also revealed the extent to which the NAIA shaped their thinking by acknowledging the existence of "a competitive organization appealing to about one-third of the NCAA membership." In light of such circumstances, "the Council could not afford to dismiss the problem lightly or fail to take some tangible and concrete steps." Having recognized the severity of discontent and the danger of inaction, however, the committee nonetheless revealed its liberal arts bias while trying to deny the one thing that survey respondents overwhelmingly called for and that the NCAA was most vulnerable to from the NAIA. Its recommendations marked both the tilt of the committee toward the liberal arts agenda as well as the institutional inertia of the NCAA, accepting "that additional steps should be taken to insure" the satisfaction of the small colleges, but it should be done "without effecting a cleavage in an organization which is national in scope and should be concerned with all phases of intercollegiate athletics." As if the first resolution did not effectively display the committee's opposition to the NAIA, its second asserted its "belief that any helpful solution for the problems of small institutions should be achieved within the cooperative and comprehensive framework of the Association."[58]

The Crowley Committee found itself in a bind in 1953; faced with overwhelming data pointing toward a conclusion the committee members desperately wanted to avoid, the final report simply pretended to ignore the evidence. Unwilling to parley with the NAIA or create a classification system within the NCAA, the committee recommended only that the council sponsor an amendment to create a vice-president-at-large position to be filled by a representative from the small college delegates and that small college delegates have greater access to the various NCAA rules committees. Though short of the competitive classifications that smaller state schools wanted, the institutional reforms spoke to the liberal arts anxieties regarding the bureaucracy's indifference to smaller schools. Ralph Henry, secretary of the elite liberal arts–oriented Midwest Conference, declared that winter with some trepidation, "If our best efforts are not successful and if the NCAA does not succeed in passing legislation satisfactory to the small colleges, I am personally afraid you will not be able to hold the allegiance of the Midwest Conference much longer. I should hate to see a real break."[59] The Crowley report claimed that the recommendations advantageously did "not bring about a division in the organization, which . . . would not be beneficial to the Association or the small institutions." The report also claimed that "while the recommendations do not clearly bring about the classification so predominantly favored in the responses to the questionnaire," they did call for a small college vice presidency "that may be instrumental in establishing" future reforms for the small colleges.[60]

That the Crowley Committee report refused to accept the legitimacy of the NAIA or propose a separate classification for member schools within the NCAA should come as no surprise. It was what Walter Byers had basically told them to conclude beforehand. At the same February 1953 meeting that authorized the Crowley Committee to examine "the small college question," Walter Byers offered a detailed "analysis of the 'Small College' situation" to the NCAA Council. Allegedly aimed at examining the larger question of the role of small schools, it was instead little more than a declaration of war against the NAIA. Byers began his report by providing a brief history of the NCAA College Committee, describing its sole purpose as an outlet for the discussion of topics unique to smaller schools. He remarked that it was "charged primarily with the responsibility of formulating the portion of the Convention program devoted to small colleges" and generally served as a watchdog for small college issues. However, Byers swiftly asserted that "this move was never designed or contemplated to be a separation of the two classes of institutions and until now has not worked toward that end." Having declared that the College Committee was never intended to create a separate identity within the NCAA and decried that it had in fact become so, Byers then more scathingly turned his attention to the NAIA. After accurately describing the NAIA's early focus on basketball and its recent expansion into other sports, Byers then accused Al Duer of actively poaching NCAA members at the recent NCAA Convention. Byers acknowledged that 40 percent of NAIA members were NCAA members solely in order to participate in the NAIA Basketball Tournament. He then made the rather dubious assertion that "the remaining 60% of NAIA membership is composed of unaccredited institutions ineligible for NCAA membership." Having leveled some strong accusations with some fairly hard statistical information, Byers then had the temerity to acknowledge that "accurate figures are not available because . . . Mr. Duer has not made available a list of NAIA members," a claim that was patently false, as Crowley had already requested and received from Duer evidence to his own satisfaction documenting his testimony to the committee about the number and accreditation of NAIA member schools.[61]

Byers said that the "the only reason the NAIA was created was because . . . the smaller institutions had no opportunity to qualify for our basketball tournament," and that since then, the NAIA had done nothing but "duplicate existing NCAA services." In Byers's mind here was the NAIA's real transgression and why it should be pursued to its extinction. Byers called on the council "to deal with this matter promptly" and laid out the crimes that the NAIA had committed against the NCAA. First and foremost, Byers alleged that the NAIA willfully and duplicitously misrepresented itself by describing itself as a "national association": "It is an association of small colleges which is not national in scope, yet the title carries the word 'national' and carries no reference to 'small college.'" Furthermore, Byers claimed that the NAIA insisted on describing its championship meets as "national intercollegiate championships." By precedent and recognition, according to Byers, the NCAA events were the only "'national collegiate championships.'" Byers conveniently ignored that the NAIB event had originated two years before the NCAA Tournament but nonetheless described it as "a direct infringement." He also suggested that the NAIA's statistical service could potentially "disrupt" the NCAA's service to small schools and that by using the same rules for football and basketball, the NAIA violated the NCAA's copyright. Finally, Byers alleged that the NAIA's "failure to adopt standards of eligibility and like rules" threatened to "undermine . . . much of the progress the NCAA has effected through its enforcement of eligibility rules for NCAA events." Just as he conveniently ignored that the NAIA Tournament predated the NCAA's, he also refused to acknowledge that the NAIA had indeed put in place eligibility rules, just not those of the NCAA. Considering that NCAA members refused to carry out the organization's own Sanity Code and were then the malefactors of some of the most salacious scandals in the history of college sports, it was more than hypocritical for Byers to position the NCAA as a paragon of moral virtue only to be threatened by the lawless presence of the renegade NAIA.[62]

Having surveyed the historical issues and the sins of the NAIA, Byers unsurprisingly recommended to the council that it "record its support for a national organization for all classes of members" but then also proposed the consideration of whether the NCAA should create a member classification system and offer separate championships for those classes.[63] With Byers having already told the NCAA Council how to handle the NAIA, it is little wonder that the Crowley Committee came back with the same recommendations, even in the face of overwhelming evidence from its membership. With the Crowley report aligning itself with Byers's pre-stated position recommending no division within the NCAA and marginalizing the NAIA, the NCAA Council quickly endorsed the report and forwarded its findings and the proposed amendment to the membership to be enacted at the 1954 convention.[64] The council also addressed the state of relations between the NCAA and NAIA, observing that any "friction" between the NCAA and NAIA could easily be resolved if "the NAIA will cooperate with [Byers]" on a "satisfactory settlement" of the issues Byers raised in his analysis—namely, that the NAIA cease using the term "national," both in name and the billing of its championships; that it abolish its statistical service to avoid "confusion and misrepresentation"; and that the NAIA cease violating NCAA copyright by abandoning use of the accepted rules of college basketball and football.[65] Such demands were of course "satisfactory" only to the NCAA and akin to Rome's demands upon Carthage prior to the Third Punic War.

The Crowley Committee report revealed not only the depth of small college alienation but also the diversity of that disenchantment and the illustration that no single small college identity existed. There were chasmic divisions between the liberal arts reformers and the state college representatives who wanted competitive outlets of scale. The promise of Schobie Barr's peasant uprising against the landlords now looked like little more than fantasy in light of the fact that while most NCAA members were small schools, they represented distinctly different constituencies. If Byers and those who wished to see the NCAA pursue the status quo could exploit those divisions, the weakness revealed in the Crowley report could potentially become the NCAA's salvation.

A third constituency also existed, but outside the existing institutional framework of a collegiate athletics organization, who saw college athletics as a venue in which to engage in a much more significant reform of American society. Historically black colleges saw in athletics a way to demonstrate masculinity, achievement, and success in a venue most Americans already accepted as freighted with those values. However, to use athletics to challenge discrimination and demand equal access in society at large required them to challenge discrimination and win equal access within the world of college athletics first. Throughout the 1940s and 1950s, HBCs and individual black athletes found a sporting world riven with both formal and informal discriminatory practices. The challenges to these practices soon became wrapped up in the struggle of the varying small school constituencies and between the NCAA and the NAIA. It was a challenge that NAIA leadership handled with greater moral resolve and courage than that of the NCAA.

CHAPTER 5

REBELS WITH A CONSCIENCE

RACE, THE NAIA, AND COLLEGE BASKETBALL IN MID-CENTURY AMERICA (1939-1953)

On the eve of the 1948 NAIB Tournament, the *Kansas City Star* ran a standard hometown fluff piece masquerading as news with the hope of increasing the live gate. The *Star's* piece optimistically declared that the tournament's prominence made "Kansas City the nation's basketball capital this week" and pointed out the regional diversity of the participating teams. It also traded on the NAIB's egalitarian ethos by noting, "A feature of the tournament is that although it is not restricted in any way as to school size, it does afford a tournament chance to the small school." It was this feature that led the *Star* to claim that the tournament required teams to "meet in democratic fashion," a description that achieved unintended irony when it was soon revealed that the NAIB Tournament excluded black players.[1] Among the thirty-two schools invited to participate in the 1948 NAIB Tournament was Manhattan College, a progressive-minded Catholic school in the heart of New York. In looking over the materials forwarded to the school, Manhattan's director of athletics, Brother Eusebius,[2] noticed that buried at the end of the section on player eligibility was the parenthetical reference "Colored Players not eligible." Though Manhattan did not have any black players on that year's squad, Eusebius immediately sensed trouble.

Manhattan had a proud tradition of integrated academics and athletics going back to the 1920s, and the school embraced an avowed commitment to "promoting the idea of interracial justice." Before leaving his office for the weekend that Friday afternoon, Eusebius forwarded the information to the college president, Brother B. Thomas, and asked for guidance. Thomas called a special meeting of the college council for Monday morning to discuss "whether Manhattan College would be inconsistent regarding our policy of toleration and respect for the rights of minority groups, especially Colored people, by accepting an invitation to this tournament."[3]

Manhattan did indeed withdraw, a decision that pained Thomas for the consequence it would have on the team, saying he was "reluctant to take this action but cannot consistently do otherwise." By the end of the day, Eusebius had telegraphed Emil Liston to inform him of the college's decision and to let him know that Manhattan would still play if the NAIB was willing to rescind the rule. Indicative of Manhattan's savvy in negotiating the currents of mid-twentieth-century American racial politics, and wary that Liston might promise one thing to secure Manhattan's participating and then later renege, Eusebius made Manhattan's participation contingent upon the permanent elimination of the ban on black players and the NAIB's willingness to publicize the removal of the clause by Wednesday, March 4.[4] Liston immediately wired back, hoping to pressure Manhattan into playing in the tournament but also inadvertently revealing how little he understood about the team and the school. Liston "suggest[ed] Manhattan College reconsider" their refusal to play on account of "the colored player rule unless you have colored players on your team." Hoping to make Manhattan feel guilty by pointing out their earlier acceptance and acknowledging how much the issue exposed the NAIB, Liston implored Eusebius to "save an embarrassing situation by going through with your commitment." Eusebius tersely responded to Liston's impassioned plea with a twelve-word telegram that simply said Manhattan "still holds to original position."[5]

With Thomas's Wednesday deadline passing, Manhattan, though "not wish[ing] to interfere with . . . local customs" in pressuring the NAIB, was forced to announce its rejection of the tournament bid, setting in motion a blistering sequence of events. Seeking to fill Manhattan's vacated spot in the bracket, the NAIB invited upstate New York's similarly progressive Siena College, which initially accepted. But after conferring with Thomas at Manhattan College, Siena too backed out, claiming such a clause "was unchristian, undemocratic, and unsportsmanlike."

When approached with the now twice-rejected invitation, Long Island University (LIU) also demurred. Like Manhattan, LIU maintained a tradition of social justice. In 1936 the small university won thirty-three straight games and was considered one of the dominant teams in the nation at any level, but the predominantly Jewish team refused to try out for the 1936 Olympics to protest the games' location in Nazi Germany. Public opinion in the Northeast overwhelmingly supported Manhattan's stand. Both the *New York Times* and the *New York Herald Tribune* ran editorials lauding the college's "higher sportsmanship," and Manhattan received telegrams and letters of congratulations from alumni, social justice organizations, media outlets, and other institutions of higher education. The national publicity so overwhelmed the tiny Catholic school for a period that the president's office felt compelled to compile and provide a two-page press release, clarifying the timeline of events and deflating media exaggerations or inaccuracies.[6]

The mini firestorm over Manhattan College's stand exposed the extent to which black athletes were still so ambivalently excluded from the sporting mainstream, and perhaps nowhere more so than basketball. Although the National Football League (NFL), Major League Baseball (MLB), and the NBA (National Basketball Association) all made highly publicized advances to sign black players in the 1940s—with UCLA's Kenny Washington and Woody Strode integrating the NFL in 1946, their Bruin teammate Jackie Robinson doing the same for Major League Baseball the following year, and fellow Bruin Don Barksdale being invited to integrate the NBA in 1948[7]—many big-time college basketball programs remained not only closed to blacks but downright hostile toward them. While Southern schools rejected out of hand the possibility of integration, even Northern schools in the 1940s maintained the color line in basketball. As black athletes increasingly demonstrated their skills in college sports such as track, baseball, and football, the Big Ten Conference remained steadfastly closed to blacks in basketball, even as they integrated other sports. By the 1930s only a handful of black players appeared on the rosters of historically white schools around the country. In his definitive treatise on college sports and the color line, historian Charles Martin illustrated how few blacks there actually were in big-time college basketball before World War II by naming them all to a list that ended at seven. Martin's list may well have missed some, but clearly very few blacks played big-time college basketball.[8]

The most glaring and devout exclusion outside of the South appeared in the Big Ten Conference. Although at the time, and since, the Big Ten's exclusion has been referred to as "the unwritten rule," it was neither unwritten about nor unknown. In March 1937, student representatives from Northwestern University, Ohio State University, Purdue University, and the Universities of Iowa, Minnesota, Michigan, and Chicago petitioned the conference athletic directors to "rescind a so-called 'unwritten law' prohibiting . . . Negroes in Big Ten basketball," a request the meeting refused even to put on the agenda, let alone discuss. (They were also prohibited from swimming and wrestling.) Such institutional indifference to black students was deeply embedded at many Big Ten schools during the Depression and war years. At Ohio State the same year, the university privately worried about the negative publicity generated when students formed an Anti-Negro Guild on campus, distributing leaflets that read "THE KU KLUX KLAN HAD THE RIGHT IDEA!" However, the school suspended instead the leftist student organization that protested the guild rather than the guild members themselves.[9] Indiana University managed to keep the campus Reserve Officer Training Corps (ROTC) program all white by getting a local doctor to offer a standing diagnosis that all of the Bloomington campus's black students had flat feet, thereby disqualifying them from ROTC.[10] And throughout the 1930s and early 1940s, administrators at the University of Minnesota maintained a rigid, open, and unabashed exclusion of blacks from all manner of student life activities and venues. As black student enrollment increased, the university responded in 1941 by building International House residence hall, ostensibly for the university's foreign exchange students, but in reality it was where all native-born black students were assigned. Minnesota did not finally abandon its dorm segregation until after the war and did so begrudgingly.[11]

To be sure, the Big Ten's most glaring public hostility to blacks was its insistence on prohibiting them from playing basketball, an insistence that became increasingly difficult to uphold and justify in light of the United States' experience in World War II. Wartime rhetoric contrasting Nazi racial ideologies with American equality brought America's own racial policies uncomfortably into the spotlight, and racial activists on both sides of the color line took advantage. In 1943 white students at Ohio State challenged the dismissal of Ernest Savory from the basketball team, alleging discrimination after Ohio State freshman coach Jimmy Hull admitted that Savory was "a good player" and "an accomplished point-maker." Even though the student senate found no evidence that Savory was dismissed because he was black, female students within the university's YWCA launched a conference-wide investigation of the Big

Ten's color ban, with general secretary Elizabeth Leinbach asserting, "It is incredible that no Negro has ever attended a Big Ten college who could . . . make the basketball squad." Although the Ohio State YWCA investigation did little but demonstrate that the Big Ten was engaging in an unwritten exclusion of blacks, it did force both Ohio State athletic director Lynn St. John and Big Ten commissioner John Griffith to deny in writing that such an agreement existed.[12]

As the war drew to a close, activists and journalists continued to embarrass the Big Ten on the question. In 1946 John Wilson led unheralded Anderson High School to the all-class Indiana State Championship and was named the state's prestigious Mr. Basketball as the most outstanding player in the state. Yet when boosters asked Indiana University's (IU's) head coach Branch McCracken if Wilson could play for the Hoosiers, who had finished in the bottom half of the Big Ten, McCracken incredulously declared that he didn't think Wilson could even make the team.[13] After watching the number of outstanding black players in the 1947 Indiana High School State Tournament, John Whittaker, sports editor of Hammond, Indiana's *Hammond Times*, wrote an open letter to Kenneth "Tug" Wilson, the Big Ten commissioner following Griffith's death in 1944. After remarking that all observers agreed upon the superb play and commendable behavior of the black players in the tournament, Whittaker pointedly wrote, "We keep hearing that the Big Ten conference has an 'unwritten agreement' not to use Negroes in basketball. If so, WHY?" Whittaker also noted the inconsistency of the Big Ten's willingness to allow integrated football and asked, "If the . . . [Big Ten] . . . can use Negroes . . . to draw $200,000 crowds in football . . . and Negroes like Jesse Owens [Ohio State] and Eddie Tolan [Michigan] to win Olympic crowns, why can't it use them in basketball?"[14] The embarrassment and inconsistency only intensified when Indiana writers again named a black player who had led his team to the state title as Mr. Basketball in Shelbyville's Bill Garrett. When McCracken refused to recruit Garrett as he had similarly refused Wilson, supporters went directly to IU president Herman Wells before McCracken finally relented and agreed to give Garrett an opportunity to make the team.[15]

The Big Ten's willingness to participate in integrated activities in some sports while continuing to insist on segregated basketball, as well as wrestling and swimming, reveals much about America's discomfort with race at the time. In 1936 Tug Wilson, then athletic director at Northwestern University, justified the Big Ten's exclusionary practices by saying, "If an attempt were made to use a negro in these three events [basketball, swimming, and wrestling], it would cause the opposing team to withdraw from the contest, which would make it far more embarrassing for them than it is now."[16] Wilson's certainty that no respectable opponent would be willing to countenance such close contact with blacks was matched only by his concern for the possibility of embarrassing an opponent rather than the humiliation of the offending student athlete. Others too found discomfiting such close sporting contact with blacks. Though Notre Dame willingly played integrated teams in other sports, basketball coach George Keoghan prohibited the Fighting Irish from taking the floor against the University of Detroit's Laurence Bleach in 1934. When pressed on the matter, Notre Dame's acting president, John O'Hara, accepted his head coach's logic "that there is a difference in a game where there is such close physical contact between players scantily clad and perspiring at every pore." Likewise, Phog Allen at the University of Kansas persisted in his refusal to sign black players, suggesting in 1949 that they run track instead due to the fact that it "doesn't require as much body contact as basketball."[17] And coaches were not the only ones suffering discomfort with the increasing demand for an integrated America. Before the war, New York's Queensbridge College hired a black coach to run the school's otherwise white basketball team. While the school found nothing troubling with the arrangement, the local *Long Island Star Journal* refused to include a team photograph that also included its coach because of the paper's policy not to publish integrated photographs. Players and the campus paper described the decision as "un-American and undemocratic and a violation of the American policy of sportsmanship and fair play" and declared such practices as more appropriate to Nazi Germany.[18]

In this context, the NAIB was not any more discriminatory than other forces within college basketball; they were just one of the first to be held to account for their sentiments. In response to the Manhattan College decision, New York's Harry Henshel, a member of the US Olympic Basketball Committee, personally called Thomas to confirm the news reports and then formally requested that the USOC revoke the NAIB's inclusion in the eight-team Olympic tournament. Although Henshel's motives are not clear, he was an advocate of sport as a vehicle of fairness and an outspoken opponent of discrimination against Jews.[19] In an effort to defuse the rapidly embarrassing situation and save the NAIB's spot in the Olympic qualifying tournament, organization president Joseph Hutton of Hamline University derided Henshel's request as "poppycock." In an awkward and lame attempt to shift the discussion elsewhere, Hutton claimed that Henshel was misinformed that an integrated team had sought entrance to the tournament, implying that since no black players had actually been discriminated against, Henshel was merely grandstanding. Then Hutton suggested that since no integrated teams qualified for the tournament, the NAIB's discriminatory clause was irrelevant: "We do have a rule barring Negroes from competitions, but it has been in existence as long as the NAIB. So far as I can recall it has never been an issue in the selection of teams for Kansas City competition."[20] In fact, it was Hutton who was misinformed, both about the entrants in the 1948 tournament and in previous year's events.

Caught in the middle of the media firestorm as well as the threat of Henshel's request and the demands of a divided board of directors, the NAIB's executive director, Emil Liston, tried his best to placate as many groups as possible while still maintaining his own dignity and personal opposition to the discriminatory provision. The issue was not news to Liston, who had coached integrated squads in the 1920s. He had sought to have the clause removed the previous year and had already put the clause's removal on the agenda for the NAIB's executive committee meeting scheduled for the Friday before the tournament began in 1948.[21] Liston's private correspondence reveals a deep discomfort with the clause since at least 1947; one editorial during the time assured readers that "Liston . . . had nothing to do with the ban. Liz just isn't built that way."[22] In his communications with both Manhattan College and the news media, Liston made sure to note that the ban was not included in the NAIB's bylaws but merely a rule insisted upon by the tournament committee when that group was created in 1940 to take charge of what was by then a large national, annual event.[23] No minutes from the tournament committee's 1940 meeting apparently survive, and indeed no mention of a tournament committee appears in the records of the organizing committee, though that body did create three other committees whose activities do remain in the historical record.

Most historians who have studied the NAIB claim that the organizing committee of the NAIB, which met at Kansas City's Phillips Hotel on March 10 and 11, 1940, was the tournament committee, but the minutes from that event make no reference to race or player eligibility, nor do they concern themselves with the logistics of the tournament at all and instead are clearly concerned with bylaws and organizational matters. Considering that the 1940 tournament began the next day, it is difficult to gauge when a committee might have actually had time to meet and conduct business. The tournament owed much of its early financial solvency to support from interests deeply embedded in the local hospitality industry, including a very favorable rental agreement for the Municipal Auditorium. Thus, it is quite possible that such a prohibition was suggested by or enacted as a concession to Kansas City's highly segregated hotel and restaurant community.[24] In 1948 Liston described the refusal of local lodging and eating establishments to serve blacks as "a social condition in Kansas City in which the NAIB has no influence," and as late as 1959, a *Kansas City Star* survey found that only 22 percent of the city's eating establishments featured integrated access.[25] It is equally plausible that such a ban was enacted to encourage Southern schools to participate, as Liston privately claimed on one occasion.[26] Thus, both the origins and the enabling authority of the ban remain murky.

Even if an independent tournament committee did meet and formally enact a ban, it did not likely do so with much concurrence from those involved in the NAIB's creation. The NAIB's founding on March 10–11 involved no more than twenty individuals.[27] While the passage of time makes it impossible to identify the racial views of all those individuals, some reasoned assumptions about some of them, particularly those in leadership positions, are recoverable. Blacks maintained only the most marginal presence in big-time college basketball; they were far more common, however, at small, particularly church-affiliated, schools that tended to gravitate to the NAIB in its early years. Liston, who taught at the Methodist-affiliated Baker University and coached integrated teams, chaired the meeting and was elected as executive secretary and clearly opposed the clause. Charles Dee Erickson, who chaired the constitution committee and was the principal architect of that document, taught and coached at Kansas's Washburn University, which was affiliated with the Congregational Church, whose 1865 Articles of Association explicitly banned discriminatory practices. In the 1930s and 1940s Washburn refused to honor so-called gentlemen's agreements whereby teams agreed to bench their black players so as not to offend some opponents' racial sensibilities.[28] William Moneypenny, who chaired the nominating committee charged with naming the NAIB's first leadership slate, coached at Southwestern College in Kansas, which was affiliated with the Methodist Episcopal Church with its long-standing opposition to segregation, and which became integrated in the 1920s.[29] Other attendees included Duquesne's coach Charles "Chick" Davies, who just two months earlier made national news when he refused to accede to the University of Tennessee's demand that he bench Chuck Cooper, forcing the Volunteers to forfeit rather than compete against a black player. Davies endeared himself to racial liberals everywhere when he protectively said of Cooper, "They wouldn't play with him and we wouldn't play without him."[30] Also active in the 1940 meeting was Charles Belding of South Dakota's Dakota Wesleyan University (DWU), also affiliated with the Methodist Church and that had a long tradition of social justice consciousness and antidiscriminatory activities. By the 1920s DWU's athletic teams were integrated with both black and Native American students, and in the 1930s Belding's team played against the Harlem Globetrotters.[31] Finally, Reuben Frost of Minnesota's Bemidji College, who coached integrated teams at least as early as the 1940s, if not sooner, and Ray Hanson of Western Illinois College, who enthusiastically voted to reverse the ban in 1948, both seem like unlikely supporters of such a clause.[32] Surely, there were men in the room those two days in March 1940 who would not likely have been described as integrationists, but it is just as likely that a substantial number of attendees would have offered them vociferous opposition. Thus, the extant record leaves more questions than answers. No record of a tournament committee apparently exists, yet all involved insist the ban originated from such a committee. The ban dates from the NAIB's formal origins, yet it seems impossible to imagine individuals like Davies, Belding, and others sitting quietly by as the group built its organization upon a foundation of segregationist exclusion. Yet while no written evidence exists of a ban at all, nobody challenged its existence in the tournament's early years.

Thus, the origins of the ban on black players is entirely murky, and as the NAIB moved forward it is equally unclear how well known was the ban or how it was conveyed. Like most racial exclusions, the NAIB's ban was never mentioned in the mainstream media before 1948, and since whoever sponsored it left little or no paper trail, it is possible that they lacked the nerve to commit it to paper at all in 1940. Nonetheless, the very next year, the tournament invited San Jose State College and Santa Barbara State College, both of which featured integrated teams. San Jose turned down the invitation rather than leave their two black starters at home, while Santa Barbara chose to bench Lowell Stewart, its leading scorer, before being eliminated in the semifinals of the 1941 tournament. Local media coverage in both instances did not mention racial issues, and it was only because the *Pittsburgh Courier* noted the racial policy that the episodes appear in the historical record at all.[33] The experiences of San Jose and Santa Barbara were not well known at the time, and they were definitely unknown in Sioux City, Iowa, in March 1946.

Like most colleges after World War II, Sioux City's Morningside College looked to restock male student enrollment and male university personnel with the passing of the wartime manpower emergency. In looking for a basketball coach, Morningside hired Al Buckingham, a Morningside graduate, a standout for the Maroons in the late 1930s, and a World War II veteran. Like many vets exposed to the horrors of the Axis powers and imbued with the democratic and exceptionalist rhetoric of the American war effort, Buckingham returned to American society deeply suspicious of racial antipathy, choosing instead to take individuals on their own merits. He willingly and actively recruited black players throughout his career and never hesitated to take his integrated teams on trips into the South, fully aware of the segregationist sentiments they would run into, particularly in lodging and eating establishments. But those experiences lay in the future for Buckingham. In 1946 he was just a young, first-time head coach who wanted to win games, and he apparently never gave a second thought to recruiting a "quick breaking, fast moving forward" out of Sioux City's Central High School name Rosamond Wilson. Like many postwar teams in 1945–1946, the Morningside Maroons were a squad filled with older players who had their academic and playing careers interrupted by the war. Wilson was the only freshman and the only black player. Buckingham's inaugural season was a stunning success; the squad went 15-5 and was invited to participate in the NAIB Tournament, which thrilled Buckingham, who had played in the inaugural tournament as a student for the Maroons in 1937.[34]

When the Maroons arrived in Kansas City, they learned of the ban on black players and quickly realized the level of opposition to Wilson's participation. Hotel officials refused to allow Wilson to stay with the team, forcing him to stay at Kansas City's black YMCA. NAIB officials remained steadfast in keeping Wilson off the court, although he apparently sat on the bench. It was an evening that remained seared into the memory of Al Buckingham for the rest of his life. After Morningside's first-round ouster by the University of Nevada, Buckingham dropped Wilson off at the Paseo YMCA, humiliated, crushed, and isolated on the eve of his nineteenth birthday. Though Buckingham already opposed discrimination, he vowed to become much more aggressive in challenging segregation.[35] By circumstance the game immediately following the Morningside–Nevada contest involved Pepperdine University, coached by Al Duer, who also served as the Western District chairman for the NAIB Tournament. While waiting to take the floor, Duer couldn't help but notice the only black face in the building sitting forlornly at the end of Morningside's bench. After learning of Wilson's exclusion, Duer could not let go of the image of a bright, talented basketball player drifting on the edge of his team's huddle like some half-in, half-out interloper. After the tournament, Duer began asking pointed questions about the ban, never failing to bring it up in correspondence with Liston and remaining haunted by the image of Rosamond Wilson sitting at the end of Morningside's bench.[36]

The event also ostensibly forced the NAIB to more boldly attempt to uphold the color line. It is unclear if the NAIB's ban on black players was never conveyed to Buckingham or if it was conveyed and he ignored it, hoping to bully them into allowing Wilson's participation by showing up and forcing a confrontation. The NAIB was certainly unaware of Rosamond Wilson's racial background, because he was listed as part of Morningside's lineup printed in the tournament program.[37] And considering how devastated the event left both Buckingham and Wilson, it seems unlikely he would have knowingly put Wilson in the position to be formally and publicly excluded. It is possible that such a ban, perhaps never committed to paper in its creation, was also conveyed at the time only verbally and in ambiguities.

If the NAIB had previously left the ban unwritten before Rosamond Wilson, it began putting it in writing in the clause discovered by Brother Eusebius two years later. Either way, the ban gained greater attention, barred a growing number of talented black players, and generated an increasing internal opposition. Immediately after the 1946 tournament, Pepperdine's Duer began questioning Liston on the ban. In discussing with Liston possible California schools to invite during the 1946–1947 season, Duer suggested that "San Jose [State College] is not a possibility since they have a colored boy on their team." Liston replied with a tone of regret that a team as talented as San Jose State would be excluded but indicated that he was already aware of the situation by saying he "understood they had some colored boys."[38] Unwilling to let the matter drop, Duer again brought up San Jose State two weeks later, noting their interest in participating but then regretfully saying, "They have a colored boy on their team."[39] Such references struck directly at Liston's personal desire to see the tournament grow in national stature, asserting that the clause was now harming rather than helping the organization. The clause troubled Duer as horribly unfair and destructive to the NAIB: "On the matter of colored boys, I simply cannot justify that ruling in a national tournament such as ours. I think it is undemocratic and I definitely feel we should take it off the Constitution. . . . Personally I am ashamed that we hold an attitude of that kind in a national tournament. I know there are problems involved but I feel it is definitely discriminatory handling and as I said before, very undemocratic." Duer's misunderstanding about the location of the ban in the NAIB constitution only further clouds the exact prohibition, and his reference to "problems involved" with removing the ban suggests the opposition of entrenched interests such as the local hospitality industry or Southern schools.[40] The fact that Duer did not learn of the ban until the Wilson incident in the 1946 tournament also indicates how few people knew about it all.

Nevertheless, Duer found an ally in opposing the ban with Liston, who agreed with Duer "100% in your statement concerning the colored boys." However, Liston asserted that the problem was linked with the desire to grow the NAIB into a national organization and thus not easily resolved. "How soon the NAIB will be strong enough to rescind the rule, I do not know," he said. "It was put in there to bring in the 'solid south,'" he added, pointing out that the "membership south of the Mason-Dixon line . . . is quite heavy."[41] Even before Duer's prodding, Liston had already put together some scenarios in which the ban might be overturned and solicited the opinion of the *Kansas City Star*'s C. E. McBride. McBride too thought it best if the ban was removed. Liston remarked, "We would have no trouble getting the matter out of the regulations I am sure if the South would propose it," but he was not sure if that could be carried off anytime soon. Realizing the political opposition many Southern schools might face in repealing the prohibition, Liston called the matter "a hot potato" and said, "However it is handled it should [be] done quietly." Barring a Southern-initiated repeal effort, Liston also considered simply "removing the statement in the regulations and sit[ting] quietly by and see what happens." That is essentially what resulted with the inadvertent arrival of Rosamond Wilson the previous year, but the idea failed utterly. Nonetheless, it was a problem that Liston knew was not going to go away: "There is hardly a year goes by but that one or more cases are called to our attention."[42] Thus, Hutton's assertion in 1948 was either blatantly disingenuous or woefully uninformed for an NAIB officer.

Before Manhattan's public rejection in 1948, few of the cases Liston noted came to light, but as an indication of how much the clause was limiting the NAIB field, besides Manhattan, at least five instances emerged in 1947 and 1948 alone. The Presbyterian-affiliated University of Dubuque, like many of the NAIB's religiously affiliated schools, featured a proud tradition of social equality in their founding values.

Under Ken Mercer, the Dubuque Spartans were completing a five-year run of dominating the Iowa Athletic Conference with an overall record since 1944 of 61-13 and three outright conference championships. A key player in Dubuque's success was LeRoy Watts, a gifted all-around athlete who also was a star high jumper and would be named the following year as Dubuque's Outstanding Male Athlete of the Year. Mercer quietly exempted Dubuque from the regional playoffs in both 1947 and 1948 that would have won them a trip to Kansas City, because the Spartans refused to play without Watts. Dubuque, according to the student newspaper, "does not stamp a person for his color, creed, or nationality, but for his abilities as a human being. To do otherwise would be to violate their Christian principles." Mercer wrote that he had only one black player in 1948 but that Watts was "as fine a boy as one could ask for in every way, [and] without him our club would have been only a shell of its self." In the wake of the Manhattan incident, Mercer wanted to see the insertion of constitutional language disallowing such prohibitions in the future.[43]

In addition to Dubuque's quiet stand in 1947 and 1948, Anderson College of Indiana also featured a talented integrated team that was denied the possibility of playing in Kansas City. Anderson featured Johnny Wilson, the 1946 Indiana Mr. Basketball who had helped Anderson High School win the coveted all-class Indiana High School State Championship. Wilson, who very much wanted to go to Indiana University, was not recruited because of the Big Ten's ban on black players. It would take another year and another black Mr. Basketball helping his team to the state title before Bill Garrett finally and permanently challenged the Big Ten color line in basketball. In 1948 Anderson lost only one game and won the conference championship but was not even offered the chance to leave Wilson at home when the NAIB regional chairman, Canterbury College's Glenn Johnson, chose his own all-white team instead (not that head coach Edward Ronsheim would have considered playing without Wilson).[44]

By far the most celebrated and consequential cases involved Indiana State in 1947 and 1948, and those cases deserve to be examined at some length here. In 1946 Indiana State University, under head coach Glenn Curtis, completed a three-year run that saw the Sycamores win fifty-six games, capping off that season with an appearance in the NAIB championship, where they suffered a heartbreaking one-point defeat to Southern Illinois University. As was the custom in the NAIB's early years, both participants in the previous year's final received an automatic tournament invitation the following year, which Curtis accepted before moving on to a job in the fledgling professional leagues later that summer. Indiana State replaced Curtis with one of his former protégés at Martinsville High School, John Robert Wooden. Apparently, Curtis failed to inform Wooden of Indiana State's automatic entry into the 1947 tournament, and Wooden learned of it from the head coach at Southern Illinois. Although Indiana State eventually finished the season with a record of 17-8, when Wooden learned of the invitation in late December, the Sycamores were struggling to find a successful lineup with a record of 7-7. Perhaps fearing that Indiana State would finish with a mediocre or even losing record, Wooden, whose acute sense of fairness became part of his legend, was anxious about accepting the invitation, particularly if it meant taking the spot of a more deserving team from their region. Liston hastened to assure Wooden that Indiana State's inclusion "does not affect the allotment of teams assigned to a district" and that the district champion would also qualify. Thus mollified, Wooden agreed to play in the 1947 NAIB Tournament, at which point he received from Liston the tournament information. It was then that Wooden learned that participating in the NAIB Tournament would require him to leave at home his seldom-used freshman guard from East Chicago, Clarence Walker.[45]

Walker was Indiana State's first black player, but he was not the first for Wooden, who had readily coached integrated teams at Indiana's South Bend Central High School before the war. The number of black players on Wooden's teams throughout his career has allowed a fair number of commentators to compliment Wooden for his racially egalitarian views, but few have ever offered any comprehensive analysis of the origins of Wooden's views on race. Indeed, John Matthew Smith, author of the most recent scholarly examination of Wooden, expressed that one of his "frustrations in studying Wooden was really understanding where his views about racial equality came from."[46] What is clear in anecdotes that stretch his entire career is that Wooden remained steadfastly consistent in treating his black players equally and insisting that others do the same. Though Wooden grew up in the harsh racial environment of segregated and Klan-controlled Indiana in the 1920s, he seemingly put into practice his father's teachings that he was no better than any other man. Stationed in Georgia during World War II, Wooden was so appalled with Southern racial views that he reveled in deflating them, such as when he suggested his daughter ask her teacher on Abraham Lincoln's birthday about her opinion of the Great Emancipator. In an unpublished interview five months before his death, Wooden talked of getting to know the only two black families who lived in Martinsville and seeing the treatment they received, as well as his experiences with Negro League players when he played semiprofessional baseball. In 1962, two years before Wooden won his first national championship at UCLA, the NABC held its annual convention in conjunction with the Final Four in segregated Louisville, Kentucky. When the convention hotel refused to seat black coaches at the NABC banquet, Wooden refused to attend, joining the black coaches instead at a local "colored restaurant." Throughout his life, Wooden consistently responded to inquiries about his views on race by simply retelling the anecdote of his father's advice. While such deflections may appear overly simple, by the late 1960s and early 1970s Wooden often received criticism from his black players at UCLA for his unwillingness to embrace their racial militancy and for his overly simple view of race in America. Thus, while Wooden's views were considered fairly radical in the 1930s, by the tumultuous 1960s some viewed him as racially conservative.[47]

It's unclear how long Wooden mulled over the possibility of playing without Walker, but he conveyed enough uncertainty to Liston that the latter acknowledged to Duer on February 15 that "Indiana State has not yet made up their mind as to whether they will come."[48] Wooden always acknowledged that it was a simple decision and his alone, writing in one of his autobiographies, "The NAIB wanted me to tell Clarence to stay home while his fellow team members—who were a team in part because of him—enjoyed the benefits of what the team had achieved. . . . How do you do something like that to a young man? I quietly turned down the invitation."[49] Indeed, two days before Liston's letter to Duer, Indiana State declined the invitation, ignoring the race question entirely and citing instead the desires of the school's athletic committee that "no additional school work should be missed by participating in the tournament."[50] Whether Wooden ever conveyed the real reason to Liston is unclear, but it seems unlikely Wooden would have missed the opportunity to express his moral convictions. Indeed, Liston brought up the race ban at that year's executive committee meeting, and it "was discussed quite fully"; although the ban may have been debated previously, that year curiously marks the first time such debates appear in the historical record. Liston and Duer obviously failed to sway the majority, who "felt at that time that the regulation should not be rescinded but should be discussed at the executive meeting scheduled for 1948." As a result, the two ramped up their efforts to get the clause removed, with Duer, joined by Ray Hanson of Western Illinois College, quietly lobbying members of the NAIB's board in preparation for the 1948 meeting of the executive committee.[51] On the eve of the 1948 tournament, the two surely knew that the moral conflict of maintaining the ban while personally opposing it was going to become more perilous and complicating. Indiana State, along with Clarence Walker, stormed to a 27-7 record in 1948; the possibility of refusing another invitation would only bring more personal embarrassment to Liston and Duer and would eventually engulf the NAIB. Whether the two would have been successful in 1948 when they had failed in 1947 is unknown, but Manhattan's public refusal to play because of the ban and Henshel's call to revoke the NAIB's participation in the 1948 Olympic qualifying process forced the issue.

Now faced with the public embarrassment of the ban and the loss of the NAIB's legitimacy in the form of Olympic qualifying, Liston took the extraordinary step of conducting a telegraphic vote of the executive committee before the tournament field was set. The committee voted 9–2 with one abstention to remove the ban on black players; however, their individual responses reveal something less than a deep commitment to the matter. John Miller of Kentucky's Murray State College evidently abstained by not voting at all. Northwestern State College's H. Lee Prather of Louisiana voted unconditionally to "keep the regulation as it is." He was joined by Peru State College's Al Wheeler, in Nebraska, who feared that such an abrupt change literally on the eve of the tournament might cause "too many teams from the south [to] withdraw at the last minute," though Wheeler did favor discussing the matter at the upcoming executive committee meeting. William Herrington of Culver-Stockton College in Missouri personally favored allowing "Negroes to play" but acknowledged he would defer to "the executive committee either way" so as to make the vote unanimous. And while the chairman of the Illinois/Indiana District voted "in favor of colored boys playing," his telegram was more preoccupied with trying to get the committee to reconsider not choosing a second team from his district, thereby excluding Wheaton College. Nonetheless, Liston hastened to forward the results to Eusebius at Manhattan College, who immediately wired back that Manhattan had now reversed its earlier decision and would play in Kansas City.[52]

In response to the NAIB's decision, Liston received both praise and condemnation across the spectrum. Peggy Brown, New York chair of the National Commission on Interracial Justice, wired to offer her "congratulations on a move which marks another step forward in the fight against racial prejudice." Less encouraging was Carlos Harrison of Cincinnati, who expressed his "utter contempt" for those responsible for the "equal rights concession . . . at the insistence of New York teams," whom he derided as the "sticky melting pot gang." Seeing the growing, if still limited, national drift toward civil rights, particularly President Harry Truman's recent executive order desegregating the armed forces, as pandering to a Northern, racially liberal, supposedly pro-communist demographic, Harrison asked if Liston was "playing Peewee Truman's politics" in now allowing black players. After suggesting that Liston should take his cues on race from the South, Harrison closed by giving "the heave-ho to New York and its lousy Communist trend."[53]

Perhaps the most astute assessment of the NAIB's action appeared much closer to home in the pages of Kansas City's black newspaper, *The Call*. A news article on the episode described the executive committee's action as "the hasty erasure of the color line" and outlined the sequence of events beginning with Manhattan's refusal and Henshel's protest. *The Call*'s leading sports columnist, John Johnson, was even more direct. Johnson observed that most challenges to the color line were met with "multiple conferences by executive committees or long waits until 'the time gets ripe,'" solely for the purpose of delaying equality as long as possible or at least as long as necessary for the white folks to feel comfortable about the matter: "We would like to report that the [NAIB] committee saw the injustice of its racial prejudice bars and voluntarily voted to remove them, thus showing to the world that the motivation came from a spirit of fair play and sportsmanship. But that is not true." Although Johnson noted that black players were now allowed to participate, "we can't shout glory, glory hallelujah for the . . . committee as we would like to do, for their act was somewhat forced, and the hallelujahs belong to others."[54]

The decision to allow black players, however, did not remove all barriers and in fact represented only the first step in a process that would take more than a decade to reach its denouement. Liston now happily invited John Wooden and his powerhouse Indiana State team, complete with little-used guard Clarence Walker. After his return from Kansas City, Walker wrote about his basketball experiences with Jim Crow segregation, a brief memoir that spoke well of the character and introspection of Walker, was complimentary of Wooden, and revealed a dark hole in the soul of America. Walker wrote in the frontispiece of his memoir, "This was written, I think, as a way of getting something off my mind." What followed was a searing examination of the daily personal degradations and humiliations that segregation imposed, as well as an examination of self and black identity in pre–civil rights America. Walker explained his decision to write about that season simply by stating, "I am the only Negro on the team," suggesting that without anyone with whom to share the experiences of loneliness and discrimination, he would need to record them merely to be able to understand them. Even though Walker was treated generally well by his teammates, he vividly remembered the first discriminatory Jim Crow experience that season, what he termed his "encounter with Mr. J. C." With the dining hall closed for the Thanksgiving holiday in 1947, Wooden had arranged for the players to eat at Sankey's Café. On Thanksgiving, Walker arrived and was greeted cordially by the owner, Bob Sankey—"a nice fellow," according to Walker—but Sankey asked if he would not mind taking his meal in the kitchen. Given the circumstances, Walker said he would prefer to eat his meals at home instead, offering, "I know my presence is not preferred in the proper part of a café." "Mr. J. C." also appeared with opposing teams, such as when the team played Southeastern Oklahoma the first week of January and the opposing coach yelled at one of his own players after a jump-ball situation with Walker, "Jerk that nigger's head off!" To his credit, the comment prompted Wooden not only to confront the coach during the game but also to go into the opposing team's locker room after the game and start "a big argument."[55]

Road trips included similarly uncomfortable and demeaning encounters. On a trip to South Bend to play Notre Dame in early December, the counter worker at a diner took the food order of every member of the team except Walker, and on a trip to play Eastern Kentucky University, Walker had to stay in the local "Negro hotel." Of course, that was when Walker was able to travel at all; before a trip to play Marshall University in West Virginia, Wooden was unable to secure any lodgings for Walker, and Marshall personnel bluntly advised Wooden not to bring him.[56] Walker also had to stay home when the team played road games against Arkansas State University and St. Louis's Concordia Seminary. Even among his own teammates, Walker occasionally had to confront Mr. J. C. In the locker room after beating Valparaiso University in mid-January, Don McDonald, whom Walker described as "a very congenial and easy to get along with fellow," but who grew up in one of Indiana's notorious "sundown towns," absent-mindedly began singing a juvenile ditty that included the word "nigger." After uttering the word, McDonald realized what he had said and paused, creating what Walker described as "a tense atmosphere" for "2 or 3 seconds." Walker let it go without comment, later recollecting, "I find myself not being affected by such as much as I used to." He wondered to himself if his indifference to such unthinking racism was an expression of his "ignorance or unawareness . . . tak[ing] for granted that such sentiments were meant for" him.[57]

Walker returned again and again to this kind of introspection in his memoir, examining the cost of discrimination and segregation on his psyche. He described race as "a permanent stigma to be born, knowing that one cannot attain his ultimate desires." This realization led him to declare, "I . . . cannot say I am proud I am a Negro." At times, his cataloging of Mr. J. C.'s appearances that season became commonplace. Before the trip to Eastern Kentucky, Walker recorded, "It was plainly understood, without a word being spoken that I could not stay with the boys." Describing the year-end road trip to Concordia and Arkansas State, Walker wrote, "Next weekend is another one of those understandable deals. . . . This is a two-day trip, the last of the regular season. But officially, my season is over Tuesday the 24th when we play Illinois Normal at home." Such acceptance and indifference to discrimination only made the times when it caught him off guard that much more painful and disconcerting. Although Walker did not go into detail, he noted that he was unable to travel with the team to New York in his freshman year "because I, among many, was born a Negro." He described the experience as a "severe setback."[58] Strangely, he does not mention the possibility of playing in the 1947 NAIB Tournament, although the invitation was noted in the Terre Haute papers. It is possible that Wooden, aware of how being left at home for the New York tournament affected Walker, told the team the same story that the media printed about not wanting any more class time missed. Indeed, Duane Klueh, one of Walker's teammates, later described the season's end without tournament play in simple terms: "We just knew the season was over."[59]

But when Indiana State won the 1948 conference title and the accompanying invitation to the NAIB Tournament, the team was visibly excited. Before the game that clinched the conference championship for Indiana State, Walker described how happy he was and that before "the game, my mental attitude was tops." But when he realized that the team had earned a trip to Kansas City and that the tournament barred him, Walker's mood changed immediately. He remarked on how the news of being left behind for the New York trip the year before "rendered me most unstable for almost a week. This one didn't hurt as much because I made up my mind that one was enough. Yet when they come, believe me, it is hard to take." After expressing this disappointment, Walker departed from his usual writing style to add a single-spaced interjection: "NOTE: Let's be frank, can a boy of age or at my level in life be proud he is a Negro? The thing he aspires to can be done, I mean the opportunity comes, but cannot be taken, not because I am not capable, or my ability is not up to par, but only because I am [a] NEGRO. 'God bless this inane world.'"[60]

How, exactly, Clarence Walker got to Kansas City to become the first black player in any national basketball tournament remains shrouded in the Wooden myth with very little documentary evidence to recover events. Wooden later consistently claimed that he never hesitated to reject again the NAIB invitation when he learned that Clarence Walker would not be able to stay at the team hotel or take his meals with the team. However, in his 2004 autobiography, Wooden claimed that after turning down the invitation, he received a phone call from the NAACP urging him to reconsider, acknowledging that even under segregated circumstances, Walker's appearance would mark "the first black player ever permitted to play in a national college basketball tournament."[61] In an interview he gave a year later, he added that Indiana State president Ralph Tirey also urged him to reconsider playing in Kansas City and to have Walker speak with his parents to determine their comfort level with the matter.[62] Wooden never specified who in the NAACP contacted him or even whether it was the national office or a local chapter. It is highly unlikely that the NAACP's national office took note of the possibility of Walker desegregating the NAIB event. Even ten years after its inception, the event was not nationally known beyond basketball circles and had no cultural resonance beyond hard-core basketball fans. Additionally, at that time the NAACP generally ignored the discriminatory practices in sports or campaigns to challenge them, almost never mentioning sporting themes in the pages of its monthly newsletter, *The Crisis,* and was generally slow to pick up on the political and cultural value of sport as a venue for racial change. At the local level, Terre Haute did not found an NAACP chapter until 1960, and if the Kansas City NAACP contacted Wooden, it managed to stay under the radar of *The Call,* which never referred to any NAACP involvement in its reporting at the time, nor did Walker's own writings then. Nonetheless, Wooden did discuss the matter with Clarence Walker and his parents, and they agreed that Clarence and the team should go to Kansas City under the segregated conditions.

In any event, Walker's memoir and some media references at the time make clear that Indiana State accepted the invitation before being assured that Walker would be going. Manhattan's opposition did not become public until March 2, yet Walker reports that his Indiana State teammates were asked to sign some kind of tournament release form after their defeat of Valparaiso to clinch the conference championship on February 14, and the Terre Haute paper announced Indiana State's participation on Sunday, February 22.[63] In an interview with *The Call* during the tournament, Wooden excused some of Walker's rustiness in the first game, claiming, "He didn't know that he was coming along with the team until days before we left home. He has not had any practice for two weeks because we didn't know that he would be permitted to play in the tournament."[64] Similarly, it seems that Walker's name was added to the program after the initial typesetting, as it appears at the very bottom of the list of players and he is the only Indiana State player listed without a position.[65]

As a result, it was more than disingenuous for Wooden to later claim that he rejected the invitation until after being assured that Walker could play; the claim about the NAACP was likely a complete fiction.[66] On the trip to Kansas City, Walker was allowed to lodge in the team hotel, though he was not allowed to stay with his teammates, instead spending the night on a folding cot set up for him in a storage room. On the way home he was forced to sleep in the basement of a hotel in Effingham, Illinois, and was prohibited from eating in the dining room. In response, Wooden left the team that morning to eat breakfast with Walker in the basement. At one meal, according to Wooden, restaurant staff did not notice Walker until after the meal was served and then attempted to deny Walker his food, to which the team and Wooden protested by walking out. Walker thus remained a staunch defender of John Wooden. When Wooden announced that spring that he was leaving Indiana State to take the job at UCLA that would make him a legend, Walker's disappointment was palpable. Unsure of whether the next coach would treat him with as much consideration and fairness as Wooden or instead bring along Mr. J. C. with him, Walker simply wrote in his memoir that "a truly wonderful man is leaving."[67] After Wooden retired from UCLA in 1975, he was feted in Indiana at a testimonial dinner. As part of the festivities, the *Indianapolis News* solicited and bound up memories of Wooden from his Indiana days to be presented to him at the dinner, some of which they published in the paper. The first tribute they printed was from Clarence Walker: "I remember how you refused to schedule some teams away from home because of the very traumatic experiences of not allowing me to eat or sleep with the rest of the team, and the harassment by players and fans during the game. I remember you more for your stand for right in the face of adversity, rather than the great coach you turned out to be."[68] Walker closed his memoir of the 1948 season with a searing examination of the nature of man. Perhaps he was writing about Wooden or himself or both when he ended with "An important trait among men is their ability to assert themselves in relation to other men. It is not necessary to win all the little battles, but if and when human issues arise—we must take a stand—and this we must do by assertion."[69]

Although the ban on black players had been lifted, their treatment and accommodations in Kansas City remained an issue. Duer and Liston were justifiably relieved to be rid of the prohibition of black players but realized there was little they could do about how they were treated once in Kansas City. In a letter to a coach of an integrated team, Liston observed, "There is a social condition in Kansas City in which the NAIB has no influence and that is . . . colored players . . . must stay at the colored hotels." The best the NAIB could do for the time being, Liston acknowledged, was simply to let coaches know of the potential landmines that awaited integrated teams: "Coaches will be notified of the social condition and if they wish to enter the qualifying [tournament] knowing these conditions, they may, should they qualify for the National Intercollegiate Tournament."[70] By all accounts, Kansas City fans treated Walker warmly during the games. John Johnson, editor of *The Call*, asserted that Walker "was rewarded for his efforts by a fair amount of applause whenever he left the court" and that "the spectators for the most part appeared to favor the participation of the Negro player, for they applauded his play whenever he was recalled to the bench. No expressions of disapproval were heard."[71] Liston too observed the positive welcome that Walker got from the fans: "He was well received by the crowd and was treated like any other boy on the playing floor." Liston closed with a note of caution, though, foretelling of the NAIB's future struggles with the Kansas City hospitality industry: "He had to stay at the colored hotel, however."

Like so many similar struggles in dozens of other American cities following World War II, the struggle for integrated hospitality services in the Kansas City metro area occurred against the backdrop of significant demographic upheaval, rising social expectations, and a transformation of tactics by racial progressives on both sides of the color line. As they did in the wake of World War I, black Americans during and after World War II fled the South and its intertwined legacies of disenfranchisement, segregation, and lynching for the promise of economic opportunities created by the war in growing cities of the North and West. As a result, Kansas City's black population grew 49 percent in the 1940s, but they did not find much respite from Southern segregation either on the historically pro-Confederate Missouri side of the city or the antislavery Kansas side.[72] When an interracial alliance of parents tried to integrate the public schools in the Kansas suburb of South Park, the president of the school board baldly announced in an open meeting that "no nigger will get into South Park as long as I live." After black parents complained that the school board spent ninety thousand dollars building a new elementary school for whites, the board condescendingly provided the black school with a new mailbox and new lightbulbs.[73] And while the black population grew by almost half during the period, the city's white population in the same decade fell by 20 percent. Thus, many white Kansas Citians witnessed the postwar years as ones of discomfiting demographic change. Kansas City dealt with this demographic change the same way many cities did, by engaging in a de facto segregation largely enforced with the complicity of the local school board, real estate agents, bank lenders, and restrictive property covenants. The dividing line along Troost Avenue between white Kansas City and the black neighborhoods on the east side was so rigid that black residents referred to it as "the Troost Wall." Ground zero for this confrontation emerged at the downtown, city-owned Municipal Auditorium, home of the NAIB Tournament and located in Kansas City's central business district but also hard up against the Troost Wall. The city segregated the auditorium, which remained a particular offense to Kansas City's middle-class black population, and it soon emerged as a primary source of confrontation between segregationists and racial progressives.[74]

In February 1942 the black singer Paul Robeson played the auditorium after having been reassured by the booking agent that seating would be integrated. In reality the auditorium management frequently engaged in block seating to avoid criticisms by the city's black population whereby whole sections would be segregated but the sections would be scattered throughout the venue. Thus, while black faces might be seen all over the arena, they were only allowed to sit in sections next to other black faces. Robeson, who had vowed never to play a segregated venue, realized what had happened as he scanned the audience during his first set. At intermission he considered not coming back out but changed his mind and addressed the house to explain the nature of his displeasure. He acknowledged that he felt compelled to complete his set for those who paid for tickets, but instead scrapped his remaining set list and launched into a program of freedom songs, discomfiting some whites enough that they left.[75]

The Robeson concert spurred some activist Kansas City blacks to confront the issue of segregation at the auditorium and other public facilities with the city council. Both the mayor and the council replied that the leasing arrangements with promoters allowed the latter to set up whatever seating arrangements they desired, with city government having no authority in events not run by the city. These activists increasingly found common cause with white racial progressives, as in the 1943 case when the Kansas City Philharmonic Orchestra and black singer Carole Brice booked the auditorium. The trustees of the Philharmonic insisted on segregated seating, but both the conductor and the orchestra, all of whom were white, strenuously objected, leading to integrated seating for the event. As this kind of sentiment appeared more frequently, many white Kansas Citians looked with particular anxiety at racial discord occurring elsewhere—most notably the Detroit race riot of 1943—and joined with black activists to form an interracial committee aimed at defusing racial tension and achieving some progress on integrating public facilities. Even though the committee failed to achieve any lasting reforms, it marked a nascent white awareness of growing black frustrations in the city and revealed a progressive element to which NAIB officials might appeal as they introduced integrated college basketball to Kansas City.[76]

The Philharmonic had won integrated seating for their events, but other events remained rigidly segregated such that the Kansas City NAACP began picketing cultural events at the auditorium in November 1945.[77] It is unclear during this period if blacks were prohibited from attending the NAIB Tournament at all or were forced to do so under segregated conditions. When the tournament finally agreed to drop the ban on black players, one of the tangential issues that committee members raised was the matter of seating at the auditorium. Ray Hanson, who supported dropping the ban, then asked Liston, "Does this mean that if colored boys played[,] that colored people can also attend the games that are held in the Auditorium?"[78] *The Call* remained strangely silent on the matter, and it was not finally resolved until black voters demonstrated their might in the 1951 city council elections: the council passed an ordinance prohibiting discrimination at the auditorium, the airport, and the Starlight Theater at Swope Park, though pointedly not including the public swimming pool at Swope Park.[79] As integration slowly crept into American life and institutions such as college basketball, more and more black players found themselves in Kansas City in March of every year, and housing them remained the NAIB's number one logistical concern.

After watching Rosamond Wilson sit on the Morningside College bench with no hope of entering the game on that Thursday in March 1946, Al Duer committed himself to change the NAIB. But his inability to bring the association to his egalitarian views for a postwar America left the NAIB in a defensive, reactive position when Manhattan College made its principled stand. Once he replaced Liston as executive director, however, Duer positioned the organization into a much more proactive stance. In this regard his timing was perfect, as the tone of racial activism in Kansas City changed at almost the exact same moment. In addition to the challenges of segregation at the auditorium and other public facilities in the city, black parents in the southern suburbs on the Kansas side joined with white allies in 1948 to form the third NAACP chapter in the area, suing to challenge school segregation in the South Park development. And in the downtown area by the 1950s, women's social groups began challenging segregated lunch counters, bringing together local NAACP chapters, the Urban League, and local ministers.[80] At first the NAIB tried simply to manage the segregationist culture in Kansas City's hospitality industry by quietly working to negotiate accommodationist arrangements that did not directly challenge the discriminatory practices of the city's hotels and restaurants. By 1950, Duer's first full year in charge, the association quietly reached an agreement with a few "first class" Kansas City hotels that agreed to lodge teams with black players as long as teams agreed to avoid calling too much attention to their black teammates. The NAIB put together a single page of "Special Instructions" for coaches of integrated teams, and as an indication of how frequent this was becoming, the instructions were sent out as part of the tournament packet to all teams. First and foremost, the NAIB asked coaches of integrated squads to notify the executive secretary "that you have colored personnel before arrival in Kansas City," thereby allowing NAIB staff to make "special arrangements." Coaches were asked to abide by three restrictions, however. First, if teams wished to eat together, coaches should arrange with the hotel manager "for meals in a private dining area, otherwise, room service must be arranged for colored personnel." Second, when entering and leaving the hotel, blacks were expected to do so with their teams "and to avoid loitering in the lobby." Finally, black players were "requested not to have colored guests in the hotel but must arrange to meet friends outside the hotel." The NAIB stressed that "this is the first time group accommodations have been possible under any conditions, and we must avoid any incident which would be embarrassing to either the young men, the management of the cooperating hotels, or the NAIB."[81] Although these arrangements clearly continued to treat black players as second class, it marked an upgrade from the humiliating experiences of Rosamond Wilson and Clarence Walker. One coach from a historically black college acknowledged that such arrangements were an acceptable expedient and a step up from automatically putting black players in "negro hotels" or the Paseo YMCA.[82]

The housing issue, however, remained an almost constant line item in the NAIB Executive Committee's annual meeting minutes. Duer, unwilling to leave the issue to a committee, took charge of the matter personally and reviewed the existing agreement in November 1952; finding the accommodationist arrangement of two years earlier now distasteful, he declared his desires to see the second-class restrictions removed entirely. Duer discussed "the difficulties . . . of providing suitable rooms for colored team personnel over the past few years" and indicated that he had requested a meeting with the Kansas City Hotel Association to discuss the problem. Duer's willingness to leverage the position of the NAIB grew bolder as he began insinuating that hotels that accommodated NAIB needs would gain business in the future but that the pressure on these hotels would only get worse, informing them "that we will have more colored players to house each year."[83] By the fall of 1953 Duer and the organization grew increasingly impatient with the intractable stance of the city's hotels and his willingness to compromise was at an end. In late September, Duer wrote, "This situation is anything but satisfactory." He grew increasingly disgusted with the segregationist attitudes in the city, noting with frustration that the city had closed the public pool at Swope Park rather than comply with Kansas's integration law. The executive board embraced Duer's willingness to use the organization as a wedge to force the city's hotels to integrate and discussed possibly relocating the tournament to another city. Recognizing that no single hotel would take the step without some cover from the others, the board authorized Duer to meet with the Kansas City Hotel Association and "press them on the matter." When that meeting proved to be unsatisfactory, the executive board considered playing its trump card: leaving Kansas City entirely.[84] One delegate reminded the executive committee that the NCAA had recently instituted a policy whereby "they would not take their convention to a city where the hotels discriminated against Negroes."[85] Others too were increasingly unwilling to accommodate the city's segregationist sensibilities in contrast to the growing diversity of the schools that played in the tournament. Al Garton, the athletic director at Eastern New Mexico College, wrote to Duer decrying the stance of the city's hotels, and he too suggested moving the tournament out of Kansas City: "With the . . . membership as it now stands, it might be well for us to be thinking and inquiring of another city." Garton went so far as to begin vetting Indianapolis as a potential candidate.[86]

The hotel issue troubled Duer for reasons far beyond the practical issue of housing integrated basketball teams. Since its inception, tournament organizers had thought of the tournament as an egalitarian, inclusive event. Liston first envisioned it as a place where small colleges could compete fairly and equitably away from the predatory hypocrisy of the AAU Tournament. And then, after the NCAA began offering its tournament, closed to nonmembers and privileging the prominent big-time schools whose personnel dominated NCAA committees, Liston and Duer saw their event as an expression of the growing frustration of small schools that viewed the NCAA as an undemocratic, elitist institution. As a result, NAIB organizers described their event in terms of equality and democracy. When the *Kansas City Star* described the 1948 tournament as a meeting of teams "in democratic fashion" and "afford[ing] a chance to the small school," it did so without irony because it was referring to the organization's founding ethos. But Manhattan College's stance that year forced the group to reconsider the meaning of the event, particularly in the face of such personal struggles of Rosamond Wilson, Clarence Walker, John Wilson, and LeRoy Watts. Their unwillingness to do so without the threat of losing Liston's treasured Olympic berth was not to the organization's credit and spoke to the role that inertia and indifference often played in perpetuating racial exclusion. However, the willingness of the NAIA to embrace racial change after that, particularly its attempt to leverage its institutional prestige to integrate the Kansas City hospitality industry, marked a sophisticated social consciousness and organizational maturity. The actions of the NAIA appeared in even bolder relief when compared with the actions of the NCAA and its leaders, which seldom demonstrated either the organizational commitment or the social consciousness displayed by the NAIA.

The media controversy over Manhattan College's initial refusal, along with the public sympathy and threat to revoke the NAIB's Olympic bid, as well as the efforts by the professional leagues to sign Washington, Strode, Robinson, and Barksdale, demonstrated the changing racial consciousness in the United States after World War II. The public and media outcry over the exclusion of black players demonstrated that fewer and fewer Americans were willing to countenance such overt discriminatory practices in the wake of postwar social and political changes. It also marked an awareness of how such practices played against the backdrop of the Cold War with the Soviets over leadership of the "free" world. Thus, black activists within the college sports landscape took advantage of the profile and consciousness created by Manhattan's stand. Within three weeks, six black coaches, all members of the NABC and from three conferences representing forty-five different historically black colleges, petitioned the NABC "to study the possibilities of entering Colored College basketball teams into the NCAA Basketball Tournament."[87] Though the NCAA Tournament contained no explicit provision barring black players as had the NAIB event before 1948, its privileging of the big-time conferences—most notably the Atlantic Coast Conference, the Southern Conference, the Southeastern Conference, and the Southwest Conference, all of whose members practiced segregation—meant they refused to play HBCs and thus almost no HBC had any real chance of being invited to play in the NCAA Tournament.

HBCs in the early twentieth century ended up living in a largely insulated, parallel world of intercollegiate athletics. Like colleges with predominantly white enrollments, HBCs vigorously pursued competitive athletics in the late nineteenth and early twentieth centuries in largely the same forms and for largely the same reasons. As segregationist practices and racist sentiments hardened in the early twentieth century, however, black academics and intellectuals imposed upon college athletics at HBCs additional rationales that imbued athletics with the language of racial progress. As racial theories of the time argued that supposedly legitimate biological differences created black inferiority, black academics saw athletic excellence as a way to demonstrate what historian Patrick Miller has called "muscular assimilationism." Supporters of racial uplift sought to use muscular assimilationism to capture the positive attentions of white America and to demonstrate the beneficial character traits and physical exploits of black Americans, with the intent of demonstrating an unthreatening black assimilation to dominant cultural values. Muscular assimilationism, according to Miller, was not simply a counter to white racialist sentiments. It was also a source of race pride where blacks outside of academia not only took solace in the successes of other blacks but saw examples of excellence to inspire other black endeavors as well, thereby elevating all blacks and further weakening white supremacist arguments. Just as events of the 1930s changed America's higher education in general, they also heavily influenced education at HBCs. According to Miller, "Black educators and social commentators . . . saw in the Depression a historic moment . . . to confront the principles of equality and opportunity in practice, to denounce segregation and discrimination . . . and ultimately to expose the hollowness of high-sounding declarations concerning American freedom."[88]

As a result of efforts to pursue muscular assimilationism and in response to the realities imposed by segregation, HBCs created their own conferences and athletic peers. In 1946 the Colored Intercollegiate Athletic Association (CIAA) began hosting a conference basketball championship tournament. Quickly, the CIAA Tournament became a highly competitive event featuring outstanding basketball, but it also emerged as a central social and intellectual gathering among the aspirant black middle class in the host city of Washington, DC, as well as the college towns of the participating schools.[89] However, the CIAA Tournament did little to impress the leadership of the NCAA Basketball Tournament, whose champion was ignored when tournament invitations were handed out each year. NCAA officials claimed that CIAA teams and teams from other HBC conferences lacked the credentials to warrant inclusion. The fact that most white schools refused to play HBCs that would have elevated HBC credentials was one expression of the racial antipathy that marginalized HBC efforts. But many coaches and administrators at HBCs suspected that arguments claiming the subpar nature of HBC basketball were little more than a cover for thinly veiled racist sentiment that simply did not want to include HBCs in the NCAA Basketball Tournament. When Manhattan College's stand eventually forced the NAIB's hand, HBC coaches hoped to use that momentum by also forcing the NCAA's hand with the coaches' 1948 petition to the NABC for inclusion in the tournament.

In response to the request, Penn State's John Lawther, the NABC secretary, offered a sympathetic response but acknowledged that the NABC lacked the capacity to fully address the issue. Lawther assured the coaches that the NABC "has no color nor race lines but neither has it much administrative power. What we accomplish must be done through suggestion and Association prestige." He did, however, agree to forward the request to NABC president Howard Hobson and referred it to Tug Wilson at the NCAA.[90] When the group heard nothing back from the NCAA, the original six signatories of the NABC petition began circularizing other black coaches at the then four major HBC athletic conferences: the Southern Intercollegiate Colored Conference, the Mid-Eastern Athletic Conference, the Southwestern Athletic Conference, and the Colored Intercollegiate Athletic Association. Led by North Carolina College's John B. McLendon, the group stylized itself as the Committee on Integration into National Basketball Playoffs but would soon go through several appellations.

McLendon's committee emerged in the late 1940s as a typical expression of racial reform efforts both before and after World War II. These efforts were often led by civic-minded, usually well-educated black activists, ensconced within the professions and the property-owning black middle class, and referred to as "race men" and "race women." As much as circumstances allowed, these race men wrapped themselves within the institutional authorities of their employers and organizations, utilizing the language of freedom and equality in confronting the abundant local expressions of injustice and inequality apparent in countless areas of mid-century American life.[91] Few coaches better exemplified the quintessential race man like North Carolina College's John B. McLendon. Growing up in Kansas City, McLendon fell in love with the game of basketball and decided early in life that he wanted to be a coach. After realizing that James Naismith was then teaching at the University of Kansas, McLendon quickly found his way to the city of Lawrence and baldly asked the game's inventor to serve as his academic adviser. Naismith easily agreed and McLendon became his only black advisee. While at Kansas in the mid-1930s, McLendon integrated the university swimming pool by simply jumping in one afternoon. After McLendon got out, the pool director had the pool drained, to which McLendon replied, with Naismith's approval, that he would be back every day. Eventually, the university allowed for integrated swimming. Upon his hiring at Durham's North Carolina College (NCC) as head basketball coach, McLendon resented that the white papers never covered his team's games and the ensuing sense of inferiority that it created within his players, even though NCC was undefeated in 1944. In response he scheduled a game that year against the all-white and undefeated Duke University Medical School team. Because interracial play was illegal, the game occurred in a locked gym before empty bleachers, but NCC won the game.[92]

Thus, just as John Nichols and Schobie Barr represented the liberal arts world from whence they came, McLendon was embracing the tenets of both muscular assimilationism as well as the more aggressive civil rights style that had emerged from the Depression and that he had brought with him to the University of Kansas. McLendon soon learned that winning full inclusion into American life, and the NCAA Basketball Tournament, would take more than simply identifying and illustrating existing inequality. It would require confronting a toxic mixture of latent racism with colossal indifference as well as aligning himself and other race men with some unlikely allies. It also now interjected race into the multiple struggles within the NCAA. Delegates from the liberal arts colleges saw the willingness of big-time commercialized programs to exclude HBCs as yet another example of their ability to bend the institutional identity of the NCAA to their interests. And the smaller state institutions found in the HBCs' devotion to basketball excellence the promise of allies with whom to win access to the NCAA Tournament or the creation of championship events for the smaller schools. These three strands—the liberal arts reform impulse, the small school search for access, and the HBC demand for racial equality—now came together to force the NCAA to confront both its past and its future.

HOME RULE'S LAST REDOUBT

RACE, THE NCAA, AND COLLEGE BASKETBALL IN MID-CENTURY AMERICA (1950-1955)

At the end of the 1950 NCAA Annual Convention, which that year had been held in New York, the NCAA innocuously announced that the following year's event would be held in Dallas, Texas. It was only the second time in the association's history that the convention had been awarded to a Southern city, the first being New Orleans in 1937, and many in the media interpreted the decision not only as an example of the association's growth and increased national prestige but also as an attempt to show the flag in a region that had been only lukewarm about the association's designs on national guidelines for football and its efforts to assert itself as the standard-bearer on amateurism. What received no media attention at the time, however, was that the Hotel Adolphus in Dallas was segregated. The NCAA had held its conventions before in segregated facilities, but it seemed unaware of the changing social, cultural, and political outlooks and how the grounds of egalitarianism—or at least the appearance of it—were shifting beneath its feet. The 1951 NCAA Convention in Dallas would be held amid a changed landscape that included the advances of black pioneers in American professional sports as well as the growing commitment of the federal government, the American military, and the national Democratic Party to oppose segregation. It also rather inconveniently occurred just as its key leadership was then attempting to fend off concerns from its black membership of NCAA indifference to racial antipathy and to convince them that the inability of historically black colleges to gain access to the NCAA Basketball Tournament had nothing to do with race or a discriminatory selection process. In the rapidly evolving racial politics of postwar America, race men like North Carolina College's John McLendon and his allies on both sides of the color line successfully managed to embarrass an increasingly defensive NCAA while simultaneously supporting the NAIA in its forceful embrace of sporting equality.

The road to Dallas, however, began even earlier than the previous year's convention in New York. Its contours first appeared in the NCAA's bungled response to the petition from the HBCs seeking admission to the NCAA Basketball Tournament. McLendon and his committee examined the concerns of the NCAA Basketball Committee and attempted to identify compromises that might demonstrate their flexibility to the tournament committee. They naively assumed the NCAA would approach their request the same way. Acknowledging that the presence of Southern segregated schools in the NCAA Tournament meant that the current "plan of elimination of teams through district and regional play-offs . . . will not be integrated in our day," McLendon and his committee proposed that the four HBC conference champions play each other, with the top two advancing to the NCAA Tournament. Penn State's John Lawther, the executive secretary of the National Association of Basketball Coaches, who first fielded the petition, continued to offer his encouragement and advice, but by February 1949 the NCAA had yet to formally acknowledge the proposal.[1] As a result, McLendon addressed Tug Wilson directly, noting that their group had never received any response, and urged the NCAA to provide for "integration by the school year 1949–50." Wilson promised to bring it before the NCAA Tournament Committee but acknowledged that real authority to change the tournament format rested only with the NCAA Council. The tournament committee, however, found nothing in McLendon's proposal to like. According to Wilson, the committee insisted on maintaining an eight-team format with one representative from each of the NCAA's eight districts, which "would mean that if a colored team were selected from a district, there could be no other representation."[2]

The real issue was that members of the committee did not believe that any of the HBC teams were worthy of tournament consideration, then or anytime soon. Wilson noted that the committee members felt "the quality of competition at the present time is not equal to tournament caliber." Wilson then rather questionably suggested that the HBCs might better improve their tournament resumes if they played "other NCAA members" from their district, which was not only nearly impossible for HBCs in segregationist states but downright illegal in some of them. In closing he managed to insult both the HBCs and the NAIB Tournament by suggesting they "get into the small college tournament in Kansas City, where teams . . . are selected by the caliber of the basketball they play."[3] Wilson's reply suggests that he and the committee gave little serious consideration to both the tournament proposal and the very issues that kept black schools at a disadvantage in the first place. To suggest that HBCs play more schools in their district to get into the tournament implied that he had no real understanding of the practical consequences of segregation. The refusal of segregated white institutions to play them in the regular season is why the HBCs needed an alternate route to the tournament; to suggest otherwise appeared to mark either the indifference, ignorance, or hostility of Wilson and the tournament committee. And it was no small paradox that the NCAA, hostile to the NAIB from the beginning, now openly encouraged some of its own members to participate in the Kansas City event. Having tried to undermine and denigrate the NAIB event for the last decade, the NCAA and Tug Wilson were now only too happy to foist upon it the black schools they were in no hurry to admit into their own tournament.

In the wake of Wilson's response, many observers on both sides of the color line wondered about the willingness of NCAA leaders to fully embrace the process of integration. After it became apparent that the tournament committee had no real intention of addressing the exclusion of the HBCs, Penn State's John Lawther implied that the tournament committee never seriously considered the request from black schools, saying, "I am inclined to think they are trying to table the problem hoping that it will not be raised again."[4] Howard University's Edward Jackson wrote Wilson an impassioned letter in which he commented on the fallacy of keeping the black colleges out of the tournament on the assumption that black college basketball equaled inferior play while the committee did not make the same assumptions about white teams. As many postwar racial progressives increasingly did at the time, Jackson referred to the desegregation of other sports, particularly professional football and baseball, declaring such actions as "indicative of the times" and implying that the NCAA's passively segregationist tournament was retrograde in a changing postwar society.[5] McLendon too became more direct in labeling the NCAA as openly hostile to black basketball: "In all other NCAA area of sports, there is not such a door shut in our faces as in basketball." Wilson's further comments on the matter only emboldened the black coaches' assumptions that he was dissembling. Wilson again refused to acknowledge that the black schools faced a more difficult, if not insurmountable, process to qualify for the NCAA Tournament when he asserted that the committee believed "that any member of the NCAA should receive consideration from the Selection Committee" and that "if a team is not chosen to represent their district," it was because the committee felt confident that it was not as qualified as the team that was selected. Wilson offered no explanation as to how the committee might make the judgment when Southern white and black schools never faced each other and faced almost no common opponents, to which Edward Jackson declared, "We doubt very much if under the present arrangement that any of the Selection Committees for the Districts will have enough adequate information to make a comparative evaluation of our teams as against other district teams."[6]

Historically black colleges faced numerous difficulties in scheduling road games against traditionally white schools even north of formal Southern segregation. Besides finding coaches and athletic directors willing to schedule HBCs at all, black coaches had to deal with additional barriers. Almost never did white schools agree to play on the road against HBCs, placing the onus of travel expenses entirely upon chronically underfunded Jim Crow black colleges. Assuming they could find a white school willing to schedule them and afford to make the trip, HBCs also had to find suitable meal and lodging accommodations. In 1948 Oberlin College scheduled a track meet against Howard University, and in acknowledgment of the limited housing options in town, John Nichols arranged for the Howard team to stay on campus, maintaining, "It is only through some such arrangements that it is possible for them to make the trip." Nichols originally arranged for the team to stay in the Oberlin gym, but the school's prudential committee questioned such spartan facilities and the appearance of the school's unwillingness to "house colored boys the same as white boys," so the Howard team stayed in the Quadrangle residence house. Such sensitivity to the matter emerged as an expression of Oberlin's distinctive racial consciousness. Oberlin's origins as an abolitionist campus prior to the Civil War gave it a deserved reputation for racial liberalism well into the twentieth century. After World War II the school maintained a standing "interracial committee" charged with ensuring "that at Oberlin it is a normal and unchallenged practice that students of different races, religions, and nationalities attend class together, live in the same residence halls, eat in the same dining halls, receive scholarships and financial aid on an equal basis, and join together in extra-curricular activities."[7] Oberlin's consciousness on the matter, however, was not representative, even among its own peers. In an effort to follow Tug Wilson's advice about more fully inserting HBCs into the white athletic establishment, Mack Greene, Central State College's athletic director, applied to join the Ohio Athletic Conference (OAC). Oberlin warmly supported Greene's efforts, with Nichols personally sponsoring Central's application. Though the OAC was then struggling to maintain members and particularly to fill out a full football schedule, the conference rejected Central's application. Mount Union College's Nelson Jones argued that as a public school with lower tuition, Central State would enjoy an unfair competitive advantage in a conference of private schools. Greene responded with a lengthy breakdown of median family income of blacks in the United States, showing that in proportion to their income and relative to Central's tuition, its students actually paid more for tuition than those at Mount Union, and Greene and Nichols both urged the conference to reconsider. It did not.[8] Central State's experience demonstrated how little Tug Wilson and the NCAA leadership understood the difficulties faced by HBCs in pursuing a national collegiate sporting program and how hollow and dismissive was their suggestion to simply start playing white schools if they wanted access to the basketball tournament. Suspicions about Wilson and the NCAA only grew in 1951.

In the midst of the HBCs' efforts to gain access to the NCAA Basketball Tournament and their nagging suspicions that many within the NCAA hierarchy were at best indifferent to or ignorant of the practical constraints of segregation, the NCAA held their January 1951 annual convention in Dallas at the segregated Adolphus Hotel. A year earlier Mack Greene had written to NCAA president Hugh Willett to protest this indignity, declaring that the NCAA had an obligation to provide a convention site that welcomed all of its members and asking the NCAA to reconsider. Willett wrote back immediately that the matter would be discussed by both the NCAA Council and the executive committee and promised a reply. However, by May, Greene had received no response and, suspicious that nonresponses from the NCAA on matters of race were becoming a recurring tactic, feared that the council was simply ignoring the matter. He again contacted Willett, pressing him on the matter. After receiving Greene's second letter, Willett wrote the members of the council, tacitly revealing that Greene's fears were not unwarranted when he noted that Greene's refusal to let the matter drop necessitated a response and "makes unwise any further postponement of a statement regarding our position in the matter." Willett responded that the council gave "careful consideration" to the matter, though he hastened to note that its discussions occurred "without formal action." Willett flatly refused to consider moving the convention, declaring it "quite impossible at this time." In trying to defuse Greene's charges that the NCAA was sanctioning the exclusion of black delegates from the hotel's lodging and dining facilities, Willett rather lamely noted that "the Association has no further responsibility for housing . . . [and] . . . meals," and that each delegate "is responsible for making his individual reservations at whatever hotel may be able to accommodate him." All convention-goers "will eat when and where they can." Having described the situation as one in which all delegates would have to fend for themselves regardless of color, Willett thus absolved the NCAA of any moral obligation of placing delegates in the situation in the first place.[9]

As Greene and other black delegates stewed over this latest example of the NCAA leadership's seeming oblivion to the injustices of segregation, Greene found himself at a testimonial dinner in October to commemorate the selection of Jesse Owens as the "Greatest Track Athlete of the First Half of the Century," with the keynote address given by none other than Tug Wilson. In writing to Wilson after the event, Greene described his speech as "brilliant" and claimed that it provided him with "an answer to a previously unanswered question, namely, what should be the attitude of the NCAA in its programs towards" blacks? Greene pointed to how Wilson described Owens's famous rebuff of Adolf Hitler at the 1936 Berlin Olympics and how Owens rejected Hitler's claim that Owens was merely "an auxiliary citizen." But the complimentary nature of Wilson's remarks that night troubled Greene: "I find it most difficult to reconcile your Owens Testimonial pronouncement with the statement of President Willett" regarding the NCAA's lack of responsibility over the segregated facilities in Dallas. These kinds of actions illustrated the "auxiliary citizen status of the Negro members of the Association. . . . The NCAA moved its convention into an area of the United States where the social patterns are openly and pointedly against part of its membership." Greene asserted "the responsibility of the NCAA to provide equitable opportunities to all of its membership in every aspect of its program"; anything less was "discriminatory." He saw Wilson's testimonial address as exemplary of the same hypocrisy represented in selecting the Dallas convention site and the continued exclusion of the HBCs from the basketball tournament: "I find it impossible to reconcile the avowed principles of democracy and good sportsmanship upon which the Association is founded with the attitude that seems to oscillate between indifference and paternalism in the NCAA to the persistent appeal of Negro member institutions for full participation in all aspects of its program."[10]

Greene's use of Adolf Hitler's legacy as a standard-bearer for racist and un-American ideals was a common rhetorical tactic of race men during the period. In 1954 Rufus Clement, the president of Atlanta University, wrote in the pages of the *Journal of Negro Education* an essay on the fruits of muscular assimilationism since the end of World War II and the defeat of Hitler's vision of white supremacy. Clement declared that should the ghost of Hitler find itself at an American professional baseball game, "it would assuredly have a most uneasy afternoon," not only with the integration of Major League Baseball but with the growing prominence of blacks in almost all athletic endeavors. According to Clement, the sporting exploits of blacks demonstrated their athletic excellence as well as their elevated character and shared values with whites, the classic tenets of muscular assimilationism. Thus, not only "would the ghost of Hitler be completely disheartened," but, Clement implied, those who embraced racist sentiments stood outside the bounds of American ideals and in opposition to America's growing prominence as a global beacon of freedom and equality.[11] In his letter to Wilson, Greene also put the matter within the context of the United States' growing prominence as "defender of the free world" in the struggle against communism and the growing rhetoric of democracy in postwar America: "I want to be able to convince my students who have already received their induction papers into the Armed Forces of the United States that they are not going somewhere in the world to fight to perpetuate their auxiliary citizen status." The way to do that, Greene implied, was to make concrete challenges to segregation wherever it appeared, which was an effort that Greene found wanting in the NCAA. Greene described how one of his players, currently on an educational deferment from the army, asked him after the previous night's practice, "'If we win our conference championship this year, will we be permitted to play in the NCAA tournament?' I had no answer for him, Tug. The stock answers about 'patience' are not very effective with a youngster who just attended a memorial service for his buddy killed in action in Korea." Greene called on Wilson, Willett, and "the other strong men of the NCAA" to demonstrate to both black students and the supporters of segregation where they stood: "The NCAA must stop giving aid and comfort to the enemies of democracy" by the continued acceptance of segregationist and exclusionist policies like the Dallas selection and the exclusion of HBCs. "I won't be in Dallas this year to subject myself to the social indignities that Texas law declares I deserve," he wrote, "and I don't believe you would go there either, if the same discrimination was imposed upon you." Greene closed by giving Wilson, the ultimate defender of the Big Ten, something to think about one of Ohio State's favorite sons: "Think of the loss to America if, instead of going to high school in Cleveland, chance had planted Jesse Owens in Dallas!" Wilson never responded to Greene's letter.[12]

Wilson was apparently unmoved by Greene's impassioned missive, continuing to demonstrate the very hostility and indifference that Greene urged Wilson and the NCAA to abandon. As the spat over the Dallas convention site spilled onto the pages of the national media, Wilson, mindful of the role of the South in the origins of the Sanity Code, justified the selection of Dallas as an opportunity to strengthen NCAA relations with the South. "That particular section of the country, while never very active in NCAA affairs, has never had a convention or much else," he said. "When the invitation was proposed, everybody seemed delighted over the suggestion." In Wilson's mind the possibility of bringing Southern schools into the fold was more important than any potential message sent to delegates from HBCs. In the pages of the *Dallas Morning News*, Wilson grew resentful and catty over the implication that the NCAA failed to consider its black members, saying, "Ample provision has been made for Negro delegates. More, probably, than for the rest of us." And when black delegates charged that they would be barred from the hotel elevators, Wilson noted that convention business occurred on the second floor, requiring only a single flight of stairs. "Everybody will use the same footwork," he said. And any hopes that the NCAA might have been chastened by the firestorm over the location of the Dallas convention were dashed when the organization agreed to hold the 1951 swimming national championships at the segregated pool of the University of Texas.[13]

Although the criticisms about the Dallas convention and the implication of racial indifference and intolerance embarrassed the NCAA, the request of the HBCs for access to the basketball tournament overshadowed the simple fact that several interests within the NCAA were already unhappy with the existing structure of the tournament. Almost from the beginning, the event excluded worthy teams, and the inconsistent means by which some teams were selected by committee while others played off to gain entry exposed the NCAA to criticism. In response the NCAA Council approved in 1950 an expansion of the tournament to sixteen teams, beginning in 1951, leaving to the basketball tournament committee the process by which those sixteen teams were selected. John Bunn of Stanford simply proposed doubling the number of teams from each region, thereby keeping the East/West regional format intact and maintaining the existing discretion of the committee to select the additional teams. Both the Rocky Mountain Athletic Conference and the Association of New England Colleges, having chafed at the continued exclusion of their conference champions from the tournament, petitioned the tournament committee for automatic inclusion. On the eve of the Dallas convention, Arthur Lonborg, chairman of the basketball committee, solicited Walter Byers about the process by which such requests should be handled. Lonborg suggested that "it would be wise if we could get together in Dallas to discuss [Bunn's] proposal along with others that seem to keep coming in." One of those other proposals was yet another from John McLendon representing the HBCs, now going by the name of National Basketball Committee of Colored Colleges. Lonborg, like Byers and Wilson before him, responded to McLendon's proposal with more than a little disingenuousness. Though wanting "to go slow" on the question of expanding automatic bids, Lonborg had no intention of supporting a bid for HBCs, notifying McLendon that none were available for HBCs under the expanded format. Before the tournament's expansion, Wilson and the committee had justified rejecting the HBC proposal to include the one or two most outstanding black teams on the basis of the sanctity of the eight-team regional format. However, having abandoned that system the following year, Lonborg now justified the rejection of the HBC proposal on the number of other requests for automatic qualification, saying, "We have had many similar requests and if all were approved there would be no room for [at-large] teams."[14]

The new tournament format identified ten conferences, "which, through recent years, had previously provided the most outstanding basketball competition," whose champions received automatic entry into the tournament. Harold Olsen protested that sanctifying some conferences and excluding others from automatic bids "would accentuate" the differences between schools. Byers, however, disagreed, rather mystifyingly arguing that "it would give greater opportunity to the smaller schools to participate" even though the ten automatic bids all went to big-time conferences.[15] Byers's logic was that limiting the number of automatic bids increased the number of at-large bids. But his argument ignored the realization that only larger, big-time conferences received at-large bids. If Byers truly wanted to ensure access for "the smaller schools," he apparently never considered supporting calls for issuing automatic bids to all conference champions. For reasons that remain unclear, Byers reserved for himself the responsibility of notifying McLendon, telling Lonborg to notify the other two applicants of the committee's decision but that "I will handle from this office the petition from the colored colleges." Byers began by trying to assuage McLendon that the committee approved the current tournament plan "for one year only, and the operation of the tournament will be reviewed annually," implying that McLendon and the HBCs should be patient because they might be included in the coming years. Then Byers returned to Wilson's theme of two years earlier by claiming that the HBCs were not good enough yet to warrant entry: "When one of your schools has an outstanding basketball team, it will be considered for a member-at-large berth in the tournament field on the same basis as the other member schools in this Association." And in a comment to the media about the HBC proposal, Byers made the assurance that "no rule prohibited Negro teams and there is nothing to prevent the selection of an outstanding team." But then he immediately revealed "the difficulty in determining an outstanding Negro basketball team" due to the inability of HBCs to play white schools while also absolving the NCAA of any responsibility for the absence of black teams in the NCAA Tournament: "The NCAA can't force schools to play Negro teams."[16] As long as the big-time schools refused to play the HBCs, the NCAA could continue to claim that the HBCs lacked any credentials identifying themselves as "outstanding." And the NCAA's inability or unwillingness to press white schools on the matter provided a convenient rationale to continue to exclude HBCs. Nothing in the extant correspondence of either Byers or Wilson suggests they embraced openly racist sentiments, but their failure to acknowledge the injustice of the matter, and indeed their willingness to appear as defenders for it, only more deeply embittered men like McLendon and Greene.

In the wake of the decision made at Dallas, McLendon and the other black coaches redoubled their efforts to force the NCAA to accept more egalitarian policies. McLendon sent around the letters from Lonborg and Byers, asking other coaches their sentiments on the contents. Up to this point, McLendon and the black coaches had been content to patiently petition the system, quietly writing letters and gaining supporters like Lawther and Nichols where they might be found. They felt that the doubling of the tournament field in 1951 would bear fruit. Having been rejected with yet another round of derision and indifference, however, McLendon now decided to intensify the struggle. Abandoning the private correspondence and bureaucratic maneuvering of the past, he intended to use the letters publicly to illustrate some of the hypocrisy and dissembling of NCAA officials on the matter, indicating that the other coaches should let him know in their responses if they were unwilling to have their comments released for attribution. For McLendon, the decision to host the 1951 convention in segregated Dallas and the duplicity involved in yet again rejecting the HBCs' tournament request indicated the necessity of changing tactics: "It seems to me our fight begins now."[17] McLendon's public criticisms of the NCAA increased accordingly during this period. In a guest column in the black-oriented *Carolina Times*, McLendon blasted the NCAA's argument that the HBCs needed to play white schools. McLendon coached in the Colored Intercollegiate Athletic Association, which, like two other HBC conferences, fell squarely within the NCAA's District 3, encompassing a good portion of the former Confederacy. McLendon noted that "a few schools in the East will play CIAA opponents. However, there is not a single team in District Three which has the nerve, spine . . . or guts to play a CIAA opponent." The NCAA, according to McLendon, had little more spinal rigidity or intestinal fortitude to even urge interracial play. As far as he was concerned, the NCAA stood for "No Colored Athletes Allowed."[18]

McLendon was not the only black coach whose frustration and anger with the NCAA increased during this period. Howard University's Edward Jackson noted that while the letters from Byers and Lonborg contained less hostility than in previous exchanges, they continued to rely on the same message: "The time to change is always in the future, never in the present." The so-called patience doctrine had been the standard white fallback response to demands for racial change in virtually every aspect of the civil rights struggle, from voting rights to integration in the military to school desegregation. At every juncture, white apologists for segregation, anxious about what integration might entail, counseled the same thing: "Wait."[19] It was what finally prompted Martin Luther King to pen his book-length response, *Why We Can't Wait* (1964). Well before King's book, however, black leaders in and out of sports recognized the patience doctrine for what it was and disdained it as tired, disingenuous, and a thin veneer for outright racism. In counseling patience, whites suggested that blacks would achieve equality soon but inherently acknowledged the absence of it in the present and thus the auxiliary, purgatory-like existence of blacks in all aspects of American life. Hampton Institute's H. R. Jefferson decried this auxiliary status in the NCAA: "All Negro colleges that are members of the Association . . . are members of the Association and should not be denied equal opportunities to enjoy all the privileges and benefits of such membership. It is difficult for me to see how the NCAA or any of its officers can justly present any argument to the contrary." As far as Jefferson was concerned, the question was simply a matter of whether the HBCs were members or not. The unwillingness of many within the NCAA to answer that question in the affirmative soon led many to begin considering whether the NAIA might be a better fit for them.[20]

Another issue that troubled many black coaches was the NCAA's insistence on the HBCs to produce an "outstanding team" as measured against white opponents. It wasn't nearly good enough to win a conference championship, or even go undefeated, as West Virginia State College had done in 1948. The continued suggestion that black schools needed to play—and beat—white schools suggested that HBCs needed "to wait for the creation of a super team that would at long last be allowed to participate in the NCAA tournament." As Jackson pointed out, not only were white schools not held to the same standard, but "such a team may never come along." Just as whites used the patience doctrine to deflect demands for black equality, the expectations of the so-called Super Negro were also used to delay equal access. Because so many whites were ambivalent or downright hostile to integration, only black athletes with superstar talent were initially accepted into the white sporting establishment in the decades after World War II. Blacks of only average talent were almost always excluded, as coaches knew they could just as easily find middling white athletes to fill out their second string with less fear of social disruption. The black athletic pioneers of the time—from Jackie Robinson to Jim Brown at the professional level and players like Ernie Davis and Bill Garrett at the college level—were all not just good players but epically great ones. They were Hall of Famers who, by their limited numbers, helped create in the white mind the notion of the black athlete as Super Negro. Jackson and other black coaches understood that many within the NCAA basketball establishment believed that an "outstanding team" from the ranks of the HBCs might not have to be merely deserving and competitive but capable of winning the whole tournament before they would be allowed to participate.[21]

Even more troubling to HBC coaches and administrators was that the tools used by the NCAA Basketball Committee to help determine an "outstanding team" either relied on some of the same logic about lack of white opponents or, worse, used overtly racist practices. Like so many of the forces that shaped early college basketball, the processes by which potential tournament teams were ranked emerged out of a system first created for college football. With no formal NCAA championship system to identify an official NCAA football champion, various media outlets often attempted to identify a national champion based on subjective characteristics. But in the days before television and significant intersectional play, those rankings were little more than guesses and aggregations of various biases. In response, in 1929 Richard Dunkel created a mathematical formula intended to account for dozens of categories of data whereby football teams might be compared to one another in the language of numerical values, thus allowing the Dunkel Index to rate teams even if they never played each other or common opponents. In 1936 Dunkel also created the Dunkel Basketball Power Index, and with the expansion of the NCAA Tournament in the early 1950s, if not sooner, the NCAA Basketball Committee was consulting the index to inform some of its decisions regarding at-large teams. The problem was that the Dunkel Index did not rank every NCAA team and ranked almost no HBC teams. In 1954 Mack Greene brought up the matter with Dunkel, simply requesting an explanation and, assuming the black colleges had not been diligent in providing statistical data to the media, asked, "Would you please kindly advise where we have been delinquent?" Dunkel earnestly wrote back, saying he "would be delighted to include every one of the Negro colleges" in his rankings, but he lacked enough statistical data to include more than four of them. The culprit, according to Dunkel, was that the failure of the HBCs to play the mainstream white schools, which Dunkel labeled "the General colleges," left him without "a broad enough statistical base to expand the rankings to include all Negro colleges." Although Dunkel closed by genuinely assuring Greene "that it is our earnest desire to include all Negro colleges," he failed to realize that his reliance on "the General colleges" created a universal matrix only of predominantly white schools. Dunkel offered the same solution as had Wilson and Byers: play the white schools that would not actually schedule them.[22]

The Dunkel Index unintentionally relied on the same logic as the NCAA Tournament in holding HBCs accountable for the unwillingness of white schools to schedule them. Other publications in the world of higher education, however, were more intentional and explicit in holding the HBCs apart. The *Blue Book of College Athletics*, published in the postwar years by McNitt's Inc., billed itself as the "National Directory of College Athletics" and was a crucial tool for coaches and athletic directors in scheduling. In addition to contact names, the *Blue Book* also included institutional profiles and statistical information used by coaches and administrators in selecting possible opponents to fill out their schedules. Though the NCAA Tournament Committee never acknowledged using the *Blue Book* to select a team for the tournament, it was used throughout higher education as the go-to reference for unfamiliar teams and programs. Beginning in 1947 the *Blue Book* began signifying the HBCs with the letter "N" next to the school names. The designation brought stern criticism from black college personnel. Mack Greene described the practice as "un-American" and requested that McNitt's cease to so designate his school. Publisher H. A. McNitt wrote back only to inform Greene that the *Blue Book* was simply following "the same practice employed by the World Almanac and the United States Government in its listings of colleges and universities." Although other schools also complained to McNitt's, the *Blue Book* continued to designate HBCs with the pejorative "N." Central State College's president, Charles Wesley, compared its absurdity to signifying Notre Dame with a "C" for Catholic and Brandeis University with a "J" for Jewish. The problem, according to Wesley, was that making such designations marked schools and the groups of people who were enrolled there "as separate and distinct." In a familiar touchstone, Wesley compared such practices to methods by which the Nazis designated Jews for persecution.[23]

Describing supporters of segregation as un-American and undemocratic emerged as a common theme in the tactics of black activists. The campaign of the black coaches increasingly restricted the grounds upon which the NCAA could maneuver in excluding black teams from the tournament while simultaneously trying to marginalize as undemocratic the NCAA rationale for excluding black teams. Mack Greene explicitly noted that black educators enjoyed the opportunity "to do great service to the cause of democracy" and that challenging the NCAA on their exclusion from the basketball tournament was just such an opportunity. Such efforts, however, required the collective action of black educators willing to expose themselves and challenge discriminatory practices and attitude: "We cannot have progress and at the same time hold firmly to the status quo." The only way to win access to the basketball tournament and other aspects of college sports governance was to boldly call out the NCAA on its practices, as they had done with McNitt and Dunkel, and be willing to make concerted efforts to change the organization: "Our participation in the full scope of the NCAA affairs will be proportional to the efforts we put forth to achieve it." Henry Kean at Tennessee Agricultural and Industrial State College also called on black schools to commit themselves seriously to NCAA participation in order to undercut the organization's future efforts to continue excluding black schools. Not only did some conferences need to change the dates of their conference tournaments so as to avoid potential conflicts with possible NCAA play-in games, but black schools needed to implement the freshman rule before the NCAA accepted any plan to include black schools so that it could not be used against them in the future. Kean called upon his fellow coaches "to plug all the loopholes" to deprive the NCAA of any excuse to continue holding the HBCs at arm's length. For Kean, the black schools had to outmaneuver the NCAA and leave it with little ground upon which it could continue excluding the HBCs. Finally, Greene suggested that black schools take Byers and Wilson at their word that no formal prohibitions existed against black athletes and schools. He called upon HBCs to send eligible athletes to the various NCAA championship events to both demonstrate their desire to participate in the whole NCAA program and challenge whether these events were as inclusive as NCAA leadership claimed. Greene explicitly noted that black schools should attempt to qualify athletes for the swimming championships hosted by the University of Texas: "It is all right to lose in the event but LET'S NOT LOSE IN THE GREATER FIGHT FOR FULL CITIZENSHIP BY NOT ENTERING."[24]

By mid-1951 racial events in college athletics over the previous two years began coming into focus for race men like Mack Greene and John McLendon. The discussion over whether black players would be allowed in the NAIB Tournament and whether an HBC might be entered in the NCAA Basketball Tournament quickly revealed the tangential nefariousness of discrimination in a host of related issues, such as whether the Kansas City hotel industry would house black players, where the NCAA held its annual conventions, if and how black schools were listed in national publications, and whether championship events such as those at the University of Texas provided for all of the NCAA's membership. Realizing that the issue of discrimination in college sports was far larger than entrance into a basketball tournament, Mack Greene began a newsletter in April 1951, sent to every black college athletic administrator for whom he could find a mailing address. The first volume featured answers to a brief questionnaire he had sent out earlier and revealed not only a seething intensity against the NCAA but also an untapped desire to organize. H. R. Jefferson at Hampton Institute, using language and rhetoric similar to that of the small colleges in the NCAA, called for an annual meeting of "the major Negro conferences and associations." Asserting that existing institutional groups like the NCAA did not deal with and could not understand the distinct issues faced by HBCs, Jefferson envisioned a "meeting in which mutual problems could be discussed and procedures agreed upon." It was a sentiment echoed by A. W. Mumford of Southern University, who saw a unified black college effort as crucial "to secure full participation for all [Negro] members in the NCAA." However, like many small college delegates of white schools in the NCAA, many HBC representatives saw the NCAA in increasingly hostile and confrontational terms. Hampton's Jefferson declared the necessity for black schools "to present a united front to the NCAA." Like their small college compatriots, many saw the absence of black delegates from NCAA committees as indicative of a general indifference or hostility not just on the part of the leadership but from member schools as a whole. Mark Caldwell from West Virginia State College openly doubted whether "we can get more Negroes active on NCAA committees at this time." Howard's E. L. Jackson spoke for many of Greene's respondents by bluntly declaring, "I believe that the NCAA personnel at the top must change and I also believe that the present NCAA leadership is, if not positively anti-Negro, at least indifferent and would like to maintain the status quo as far as our group is concerned."[25]

As a result of the overwhelming response for organization, Greene called for a convention in Chicago of personnel from historically black colleges in August 1951. With faculty and administrators from campuses representing every HBC conference, as well as some conference personnel and other interested parties in attendance, the Chicago meeting created the National Athletic Steering Committee (NASC), devoted to "studying any and all problems of segregation and discrimination in intercollegiate athletics on a national level" and to working with schools, conferences, and national organizations to bring about equitable resolutions to those problems. In an effort to create a national clearinghouse for black college athletics, the NASC sent all HBCs an information sheet asking them to identify sports in which they competed, head coaches for each sport, athletic and faculty representatives, name and contact information for sports publicity personnel, and a request for an academic catalog from each school. Greene also lent the NASC the air of scholarly legitimacy by describing its efforts within the larger context of the social justice movement in the pages of the academic *Journal of Human Relations*. Although the NASC avoided specifically committing itself to the integration of the NCAA Basketball Tournament, it did pledge itself to host an eight-team tournament featuring the four HBC conference champions and four at-large teams, designed to deliver to the NCAA Tournament a consensus HBC representative. Though it remained as yet unclear if the winner of what became known as the Negro National Championship would be acceptable to the NCAA, the NASC hoped that having a mechanism already in place would be one less rationale for the NCAA to yet again exclude the black schools.[26]

Unable to get any traction from the NCAA leadership on the issues of either race or tournament access, Mack Greene turned to a sympathetic group within the organization on at least the latter issue: the NCAA College Committee. Having already become a confidante of Nichols in his efforts to get Central State College admitted to the OAC, Greene and Nichols now also became regular correspondents regarding small college issues. Having been primed by Nichols that identifying and scheduling like-minded opponents was one of the problems that small colleges faced, Greene considered asking the College Committee to consider the possibility of an NCAA policy regarding nondiscriminatory scheduling: "What can be done to increase freedom of scheduling among member colleges with equal education and athletic programs, disregarding race of contestants where there are no prohibitory laws?" Greene knew that the NCAA could never impose on Southern schools a policy prohibited by statute, but his question to Nichols was aimed more at Northern schools whose academic, financial, and enrollment profiles fit those of the HBCs but refused to schedule them anyway: "Is this subject still too 'hush-hush' for open consideration?" Whether he thought he could actually get the NCAA to embrace such a policy or simply wanted to put them on the defensive by making them reject such a request, in 1952 with the imprimatur of the NASC, Greene formally petitioned the NCAA Council asking it to issue a statement "encouraging inter-racial scheduling." The council managed to avoid Greene's maneuver by refusing to vote on the request at all, tabling it as essentially out of order, "as the NCAA is not a scheduling agency and does not recommend scheduling policies for any institution or conference." Though the council managed to extricate itself on the scheduling question, its legalistic dodge of the issue, without any sentiment of regret or sympathy for the difficulties of HBCs, further hardened the belief of Greene, McLendon, and the others that the NCAA leadership was "anti-Negro."[27]

The issue of scheduling and the NCAA Tournament revealed the transitional upheaval the NCAA found itself in during the period. Almost all delegates of big-time programs clung to the home rule principle as an article of faith, but the increasing complexity of college athletics forced some to abandon home rule when it served their interests. Since its inception, the NCAA Basketball Committee had relied on organizational resources to isolate opponents and manipulate events to their own benefit. The willingness of some schools to play in the NIT rather than the NCAA's event incited Phog Allen to call for the organization to compel member schools to play in the NCAA Basketball Tournament. Of course, the most obvious stage of transition was the passage and then rejection of the Sanity Code, which called for an abandonment of home rule entirely. Yet, Greene's proposal, which was rejected out of hand as an outlandish violation of home rule, was no different from Allen's call. The difference, of course, is that Greene's proposal did not serve the interests of the segregated all-white Southern schools that played big-time basketball, nor did it create any sense of social justice obligations within the nominally integrated but deeply ambivalent Northern schools that passively viewed segregation as no business of theirs.

It was at this time that the then NAIB began requiring membership to participate in their tournament, and though teams with black players now regularly participated in Kansas City, no HBCs belonged to the NAIB until Mack Greene sent in an application for Central State College in June 1951. Initially, Central State's application was approved for membership in July, followed shortly thereafter by an application from Tuskegee Institute. But after learning that both schools were "colored colleges," Al Duer put their applications on hold in order to confer with the NAIB's executive committee, noting that while he "would like nothing better than to permit every colored institution in the United States to take out memberships immediately," he thought "it would be unwise to rush headlong into this thing and have incidents happen that would deter our programs." Both Greene and Central's president, Charles Wesley, must have immediately sensed in Duer's letter the same kind of dissembling and obfuscation demonstrated by Wilson and Byers. Wesley responded with a confrontational letter blistering Duer for evading the issue and appearing to ask blacks yet again to wait patiently for the right moment for their inclusion, while criticizing Duer for lacking the nerve to either accept or reject Central's application. Greene's letter was less confrontational than Wesley's, but its tone nonetheless left Duer "quite disappointed," as it criticized Duer by reminding him that "an increasing number of administrators . . . in athletics . . . have shown courage and vision in the conduct of their programs with bi-racial team memberships." Greene implied that he was as yet unable to place Duer in that category.[28]

Duer's quick response, however, quickly dispelled any notions that he was of the same stripe as Tug Wilson and Walter Byers by acknowledging the difficulties faced by HBCs and pledging direct action. He expressed his approval of Greene's "very fine letter" and noted his agreement "with the viewpoint you have presented wholeheartedly." After assuring Greene that he would forward to the executive committee "a recommendation that we accept all colleges into membership on an equal basis," he pledged "to do all in my power to make the ideal you present a reality at the earliest possible time." In short order, Duer successfully shepherded Central State's application through to acceptance, winning the approval of the Southern white schools that so concerned Duer in the process. J. R. Ricks of Mississippi's Delta State Teachers College replied to Duer's query about the effects of Tuskegee's application and stated explicitly, "Speaking for this institution, we have no problem." Ricks acknowledged that Mississippi law prohibited his institution from playing Tuskegee, but he said he doubted that would be a problem, as "Tuskegee will not take the initiative and try to force competition." Ricks admitted that his correspondence with several schools showed a commitment to the NAIB that trumped white supremacy by acknowledging a broad belief "that a worthwhile and workable solution can be found . . . to admit Tuskegee to membership."[29] Central State too won what appeared to be easy admittance, along with their immediate eligibility for the Ohio District playoff, the winner of which earned a place on the bracket for the NAIB Tournament. Having found quick acceptance to the applications for Tuskegee and Central and what appeared to be nothing more than ambivalence from Southern schools, Duer charged ahead to lay the foundation for a wholesale admission of HBCs to the NAIB. Recognizing that most HBCs in the South would not enjoy the same ease of entry into their district playoff as Central, Duer proposed that the NAIB sanction the NASC Tournament, the so-called Negro National Championship, whose winner would gain automatic entry to the NAIB Tournament. Duer understood that such a separate-but-equal solution was only a temporary expediency and would end as soon as HBCs were able "to participate on an equal basis within their district" by entering their regular district playoff. With such a system in place, Duer assured the executive committee that "the NAIB will be taking a big step forward and will be able to hold its head up as a truly democratic organization." Cognizant of how the discussion to admit black players in 1948 seemed to drag on until the matter was forced upon the organization, Duer informed the executive committee that "it is imperative that a definite policy be worked out immediately." Recognizing he had found in Duer a kindred spirit, Greene happily informed the NASC membership of Duer's efforts by noting the undetermined outcome of their endeavor but said, "We are jogging along with real friends on the national athletic scene who seem headed for the same goal as ours." Furthermore, Greene both opened and closed the February 1952 NASC newsletter with the plea to his readership to **JOIN THE NAIB**, in bold, uppercase letters in thirty-six-point font.[30]

Although Duer was committed to the rapid integration of the NAIB, he had misjudged both his executive committee and the views of at least one of his district chairs. The NAIB Executive Committee unanimously approved the acceptance of HBCs into membership, but it "doubted the wisdom" of Duer's plan to sanction the 1952 NASC Tournament. Even Central State's eligibility for the Ohio District playoff appeared in jeopardy when Don Renninger of Findlay College, the Ohio District chairman, informed Duer that Central was ineligible because he had received no formal record of their membership before the deadline. When Duer tried to convince Renninger of Central's application date, Renninger tersely responded, "Consider my resignation if my decision is not sustained." Crestfallen, Duer informed Greene of Renninger's decision, complaining, "The old prejudice came to the front again." Undaunted, Greene now contacted Renninger directly, urging him to set aside "our personal prejudices" for "the principles of the institutions of which we are a part" in "an appeal to your better self to reconsider your position." Although Greene failed to persuade Renninger to relent in 1952, it likely caused a backlash that ultimately worked in favor of the HBCs. Meeting a month later on the eve of the 1952 now NAIA Tournament, the executive committee gave Duer everything he asked for and more. In addition to reasserting its previous endorsement of HBC membership, the committee now reversed its earlier hesitancies regarding the NASC Tournament by sanctioning it as an NAIA event and granting its champion automatic entry into the NAIB Tournament. Also, after empathically establishing Central State's membership in the Ohio District, the committee codified as policy what the NCAA had refused even to discuss—namely, a way to overcome the unwillingness of white schools to put historically black colleges on their schedules. The NAIA now created a district-at-large, to include any school in any geographic region of the country prohibited by local custom from participating in their district playoff. In a direct rebuke to Don Renninger, the committee ruled that it would "not accept the veto of any District Chair of an application made solely on the basis of race." In an acknowledgment of the NAIA's obligation to its newest and growing membership base, in 1954 NAIA president Al Wheeler created a Special Committee on Integration, which included himself, Duer, Mack Greene, and Morehouse College's Burwell Harvey.[31]

Duer's commitment of the NAIA to integration and the cause of democracy not only marked his own personal views but also created gains at the expense of the rival NCAA. Duer was aware of the racial indifference and hostility that the NCAA had shown the HBCs, but in growing the NAIA's black membership, he also managed to do so without demonizing or alienating his white Southern membership, something the NCAA appeared unable or unwilling to manage or even attempt. When Delta State's president, William Kethley, wrote to Duer to reiterate Ricks's earlier insistence of the impossibility "for us to schedule games against colored colleges," Duer offered a reassuring letter, sympathetic to Kethley's difficulties, if not to segregation itself, saying: "I fully realize that most of us on the Executive Committee are too far away from the problem to recommend a very wise solution." After explicitly asserting that "we are not asking any institution in your district to schedule games with colored colleges," Duer noted that "it was our aim to avoid this by placing them in their own District at Large. . . . Again, let me reassure you that we will take no action which is not approved by member institutions affecting your district." Throughout the exchange with Kethley and other correspondents involved in the NAIA's integration, Duer copied on all correspondence individuals on both sides of the color line, demonstrating his ability to address with transparency such complex issues without engaging in the duplicity so often perceived in the actions of NCAA leaders.[32] This style managed to win over Mack Greene and NASC personnel but also allowed Southern white coaches and administrators to see in Duer somebody who was genuinely sympathetic to their difficulties and sought to solve problems by consensus rather than fiat. Although Duer was outspoken in his personal opposition to segregation, his assurances to Southern coaches that the district-at-large insulated them from legal and political confrontation illustrated his understanding of the complexities of Southern racial politics. With such assurances, coaches in even such arch-segregationist environments as Mississippi and Louisiana were comfortable that admitting HBCs strengthened the NAIA without threatening segregation.[33] The NAIA's continued willingness to confront the exclusionist Kansas City hospitality industry, cajole its reticent white and Southern membership, and leverage its institutional authority to include the HBCs only hastened those schools' rapid embrace of the organization. By 1956 the district-at-large included forty-five schools, leading the executive committee to split it into two districts, thereby guaranteeing at least two HBC annual entrants in the NAIA Tournament. In 1958 the demand from the growing number of HBCs unable to hold playoff games in their regular districts required the committee to create a third at-large district.[34]

The actions of Duer and other NAIA personnel appeared in sharp contrast to those of the NCAA. At its outset the NASC reached out to the leadership of both the NCAA and the NAIA, appraising each of their organizational structure, agenda to affect integration, and willingness to work with both organizations. Duer responded wholeheartedly, and his actions regarding Central State's application and the confrontation with Renninger demonstrated his earnestness on the matter. Walter Byers too responded to the NASC's entreaties, encouraging the group in its efforts, saying, "The officers of the NCAA wish to convey their real interest in the project being undertaken by your group." However, Byers then informed Greene of "the consensus that the NCAA not officially designate or appoint representatives to the NASC" and that any involvement between the NASC and the NCAA should occur "on a personal and unofficial basis."[35] Likewise, when the NCAA Council again rejected the NASC proposal to place the winner of the Negro National Championship into the NCAA Tournament, the council nonetheless committed itself to "the harmonious integration of . . . NCAA activities" less than six months after tabling indefinitely a measure that would have addressed interracial scheduling. Byers enjoyed a standing invitation to the NASC's annual meeting, but he never attended. In contrast, Duer never missed.[36] Throughout the late 1940s and 1950s, Byers, Willett, and other members of the NCAA leadership regularly voiced platitudes of sympathy and support on matters of race, but their inaction on the subject only made the comments look that much hollower and more gratuitous. Their unwillingness to act on their pronouncements looked even more glaring in the face of the affirmative efforts of Duer and the NAIA.

By the early 1950s the NCAA could no longer blithely ignore the increasingly public criticisms of McLendon, Greene, and the NASC. In the wake of the ongoing fallout over the 1951 Dallas convention, many within the NCAA realized that it could not continue dismissing the presence of black players, coaches, and members at events. With Greene and the other black coaches continuing to embarrass the organization as undemocratic and indifferent at best and overtly hostile to blacks at worst, council members and committee chairs took stock of upcoming NCAA events, including the basketball tournament. With the expansion of the tournament first to sixteen and then to twenty-four teams, an increasing number of locales requested the privilege of hosting games in the event. Since at least 1950, the University of Kentucky's Adolph Rupp had been badgering the basketball committee to grant games to Lexington, with Rupp's efforts apparently winning for Lexington the 1953 Final Four. No Southern school had ever hosted the finals before, and only North Carolina had previously hosted any NCAA Tournament games in the Eastern regional. Less than eight months after the Dallas convention, however, committee chair Arthur Lonborg contacted Rupp about the consequences of black players in Lexington. Rupp evasively brushed off Lonborg's initial concerns by obliquely replying that should any integrated teams make the 1953 Final Four, any issues "could be handled." Lonborg wrote back to press Rupp on the matter, specifically inquiring about whether "suitable housing arrangements can be made for colored players." It is unclear what Rupp's answer was, but he likely was not sympathetic to the expectations of integrated facilities. Even though Kentucky was the first SEC school to integrate in football, it was one of the last to do so in basketball, and Rupp's past on the matter of race is less than admirable.[37] The details of the decision remain clouded, but the 1953 Final Four was eventually played in Kansas City, and Lexington did not host an NCAA Tournament until 1955, and even then only a first round Eastern regional likely to feature teams from Southern districts.[38] At roughly the same time, the NCAA also agreed to host its 1953 convention at Washington, DC's segregated Mayflower Hotel. But this time the NCAA quietly arranged with the hotel "that all members will receive the same cordial treatment in housing, eating, and meeting at the Mayflower." The Mayflower, however, did not make any public pronouncements and did not renounce its segregationist policies.[39]

The NCAA's monolithic ambivalence to athletic integration and the plight of HBCs began to crack as more black schools joined the NAIA, and those that belonged to the NCAA increasingly made common cause with the small colleges. The first defection from the NCAA's mask of indifference was so shocking that the NASC voted unanimously to respond to it with public gratitude. In 1952 Vanderbilt University's faculty athletic representative and dean of the School of Engineering, Fred J. Lewis, who served on the NCAA Council representing District 3, encompassing schools in most of the former Confederacy, sent an apparently unsolicited letter to every NCAA member school in his district. In it he addressed the growing clamor of HBCs, many of whom also resided in District 3, for full inclusion in the national athletic scene and their growing frustration with the patience doctrine. Lewis bluntly informed the letter's recipients that the blame lay entirely at their feet. Having been at Vanderbilt since 1925, Lewis was well-versed in Southern segregation and the institutional machinations by which Southern white schools pretended that the HBCs simply did not exist. Lewis pointed to the growing number of HBCs that were at that moment fleeing to the NAIA in droves and were doing so for one simple reason: the Southern white schools of the NCAA in District 3 would not play them. He also detailed the difficulties of HBCs to fill their schedules, the inconvenience and expense of having to travel long distances to find teams willing to play them, and the inanity of holding the HBCs out of the athletic mainstream by claiming they lacked the level of competition necessary to assert their legitimacy when the very same schools making that argument refused to schedule them in the first place.[40]

It is unclear what motivated Lewis's unsolicited letter; its origins remain hazy and its exact text is apparently lost to history. But while Lewis had been in the South for almost thirty years by the time he wrote the letter, he was not a native Southerner, nor was he apparently a man with whom to be trifled. A native of Massachusetts with an engineering PhD from Penn State who had previously taught at Lehigh University, Lewis had such an imposing reputation on campus that one profile written a year before his letter declared, "Practically nobody thinks of calling him Fred." Though Lewis maintained an air of formality with many on campus, he was not inured to man's capacity for inhumanity. Many former Eastern European Jewish refugees after World War II found their way to Vanderbilt and, while capable, lacked formal academic credentials due to the disruption of the war and the Nazi prohibition against Jews entering professional training. Those interested in Vanderbilt's engineering program in the late 1940s, such as Walter Ziffer, who had recently graduated from a far different institution in Auschwitz, found themselves in the dean's office asking Lewis "to take a chance. Lewis [invariably] did." Thus, Lewis insisted on taking people on their own merits and maintained a sharp cynicism for arbitrary expressions of inequality and unfair treatment. His letter was by far the most "honest and sympathetic explanation" of HBC struggles while affirming the responsibility that so many within white Southern higher education bore for those struggles. Mack Greene and the NASC were so enthused over Lewis's letter that they unanimously resolved to send him a letter of gratitude. While the tone and contents of Lewis's missive most assuredly linked with the NASC's agenda, it was met with such enthusiasm in large measure because it marked the kind of genuine empathy so lacking in communications from previous NCAA leaders.[41]

No sooner had Lewis boldly confronted the white Southern educational establishment about athletic segregation than Southern Methodist University's (SMU's) Edwin Mouzon Jr. suddenly revealed to the NCAA Council his apparent sympathies for the cause of equality when it came to the NCAA Basketball Tournament. In a case that is even less documented than Lewis's letter, Mouzon now sided with Mack Greene's proposal to enter an HBC team in the tournament. If Lewis could be written off as a closet integrationist and carpetbagger—or at least a lapsed Yankee—Mouzon was a blue-blooded Southerner to the hilt and a scion of one of Southern Methodism's first families. His father not only helped found SMU but also reunited the church by healing the rift within American Methodism created over slavery and the Civil War. Hardly an outspoken integrationist, Mouzon Sr. nevertheless understood the role race played in dividing the Church and was an ardent and public critic of the Ku Klux Klan, decrying the organization's activities at his postings in both North Carolina and Texas. A Texan by birth and an SMU alum, the younger Mouzon happily returned to Dallas when his alma mater came calling. He received his faculty appointment at SMU even before completing his doctorate in mathematics from the University of Illinois. He also absorbed his father's teaching on racial reconciliation and justice.[42]

Whatever back-channel discussions took place have been entirely obscured by the lapse of time, but in February 1953 Mouzon recommended that the council urge the NCAA Executive Committee to consider "selecting a negro college team, or qualifying the championship negro college team [the winner of the NASC Tournament], for the

NCAA basketball tournament." What is clear is that Mouzon's motion came at a pivotal time for the two institutions at the center of his life. In 1952 the American Methodist General Conference considered with vigorous debate a motion that advocated for the Church a significant social responsibility in ending segregation and charged it with racial reconciliation. The motion was narrowly defeated, but its sponsor did manage to pass a motion that "recommend[ed] all Methodist Schools of Theology admit qualified students without regards to race or color." Even though state law prohibited such integrationist activities at Duke in North Carolina and Emory in Georgia, SMU immediately complied, becoming the first Methodist institution of higher education to desegregate. Under the leadership of SMU president Umphrey Lee, the Dallas school successfully integrated and then quietly began using its moral capital to challenge other Methodist universities across the South. Mouzon did not teach in the theology school, but his personal lineage in the reformist wing of the Church made it impossible to believe that he was unaware of or unaffected by these events. And as Lewis and Mouzon were the only two Southerners on the council at the time, it seems implausible that they had not been in contact with each other on a matter as singularly touchy as race. The timing, however, suggests that Mouzon may have been equally encouraged by Lewis's letter to District 3 and the arrival of the first black students on SMU's campus just five months earlier. What is even more intriguing is that Mouzon's move occurred six full months before the Crowley Committee decided to refer the matter to the NCAA Basketball Committee, suggesting at least some connection.[43]

In addition to the growing prominence of race in so many aspects of American life and the unwillingness of a growing number to ignore it, the NCAA also had to deal with the increasing alliance between the HBCs and small colleges. As part of the lobbying efforts to win inclusion in the basketball tournament, Mack Greene and John McLendon urged HBC coaches, administrators, and faculty to participate in all manner of NCAA activities in order to demonstrate their willingness to contribute to the organization. As such, Greene, McLendon, and others rapidly found their way to the College Committee, and their easy collegial personalities, along with the dignity of their cause, rapidly won over friends and allies such as John Nichols at Oberlin, George Gauthier at Ohio Wesleyan, and Schober Barr from Franklin and Marshall. Getting little traction on the issue of scheduling from the NCAA Council on the top end of the organization, Greene now brought the matter up to the

College Committee and found a more receptive audience. By the end of 1952 the committee's annual report included a list of topics to address the following year; number one on the list was "the increase of freedom of scheduling, especially as it affects institutions with predominantly Negro enrollment."[44] Although the NASC did not formally testify at the Crowley Committee hearings, the committee was certainly aware of and sympathetic to their efforts, because two members of the three-man committee were none other than John Nichols and Fred Lewis. The committee apparently intended to hear from the NASC or asked for some guidance on the matter, because after its first hearing in April 1953, Walter Byers notified the committee that the NASC proposal for "an automatic at-large selection of the champion colored basketball . . . team for participation in the NCAA tournament" had already been presented to the NCAA Executive Committee, implying that the Crowley Committee need not pursue that matter further. Duly warned off, the Crowley Committee tabled its discussion. However, even though the committee never heard formal testimony from an NASC representative, it did ask for and receive the proposal from the executive committee. In its final report the executive committee recommended the legitimacy of the NASC proposal and bypassed the NCAA Council by forwarding it directly to the basketball committee.[45]

By the end of 1953, HBC delegates understood the NCAA in split terms. At the top were the big-time commercialized schools, many of which took their cues from or were in league with Walter Byers on the preservation of the NCAA as a trade association designed to protect the interests of the big-time schools. Some of these were segregated Southern white schools, while others simply rejected the notion of the NCAA as a vehicle for social change. At the bottom were the small colleges and their growing institutional presence resulting from the Crowley Committee recommendations. That dichotomy was never more visible than over a few months' period in 1953. Though Greene would have preferred that the NCAA simply expel any member school that refused to schedule any other member for reasons other than "educational, athletic or conference standards," he understood how little support that idea would receive in both the executive committee and the membership at large. The limited coercive power the NCAA had over its membership and the fractious vulnerability of the NCAA resulting from the Sanity Code aftermath made the NCAA leadership even less likely to pursue an aggressive policy with regard to racial progress. Greene then appeared before the executive committee to request that it simply issue

"an open statement to the membership that the practice of discriminatory scheduling . . . is undemocratic and un-American." He suggested
that until member scheduling practices came up to that standard, the
NCAA should implement some kind of "'stopgap measure' pending the
date when there will be fuller integration in American college athletics,
which will allow the colleges for Negroes holding active membership to
win a berth in NCAA team sport championships." The committee tabled
even that measure, however.[46] Conversely, Greene and his allies saw in
the small college officials nothing but kindred spirits. In a summary of
NASC–NCAA relations, Greene notified the NASC membership that
George Gauthier, sympathetic to the HBCs, represented the Small College Committee on the NCAA Committee on Committees and would
serve as a voice for HBC concerns. Because the small colleges now enjoyed a permanent vice presidency on the executive committee and the
NCAA Council, the HBCs now had allies on those powerful bodies to
counter the perceived indifference and opposition that already existed
there. In 1953–1954 that representative was Schober Barr, "another liberal thinker to whom we can appeal for our" interests. That same year,
the College Committee created official representation for each of the
eight districts, and John Nichols promptly nominated Mack Greene to
represent District 4, and Greene was duly elected.[47]

HBCs finally found some traction in the NCAA, or at least the College Committee, yet the organization never embraced them in the same
way as the NAIA. Duer pledged to white Southern coaches and administrators not to make things worse for them regarding integration,
but neither was he going to downplay the NAIA's policies or minimize
to the media and the public the meaning of the NAIA's action. In the
communications and public statements of the organization, the NAIA
unselfconsciously committed itself to integration as an expression of democracy and Americanism. In the December 1953 edition of the *NAIA
News*, association president Al Wheeler noted with equal parts pride
and exaggeration that the admission of "Negro colleges to membership
in the NAIA and participation in our tournament met with approval
from every angle," and in a jab at the Kansas City hospitality industry,
he commented on the particularly warm reception from Kansas City
fans. It was a theme that NAIA officials returned to again and again
throughout the 1950s, as in 1955 when Al Duer wrote in the program
for that year's tournament that the presence of "Negro schools" was an
example of the NAIA theme of "democracy in action."[48] The organization continued to bolster that rhetoric with action. Ten months after

Wheeler's reference to the warm Kansas City reception of black teams, when the Hotel Phillips refused yet again to house black players, the association made good on its promise and moved its headquarters to the Hotel Kansas Citian. In 1957 the NAIA not only pulled its football national championship game from Little Rock, Arkansas, in response to the crisis over the desegregation that year of the city's Central High School and the subsequent occupation of the town by the 101st Airborne Division, but it also refused to downplay the situation by explaining in both the game program and the media packet the role that civil rights played in the decision.[49]

The NAIA was more than willing to work with Southern schools to maintain their place in the organization, but if circumstances required a choice between segregation and democracy, the NAIA made clear its intentions. In 1953 executive committee member Glenn Martin once again stated his support of the admission of HBCs, calling it "a wise move." Moreover, Martin reassured Duer, "I would vote in favor of continuing" to support the HBCs even "at the expense of losing a few schools in the South who are unwilling to take part in our program under the present plans."[50] By 1959 the NAIA's executive committee began developing plans to phase HBCs out of the districts-at-large and into their natural geographic districts wherever state law allowed. Additionally, the NAIA took McLendon's proposal seriously and pledged "to aid Negro schools in scheduling games against white schools in the regular season." These and other proactive efforts by the NAIA to welcome HBCs only made the NCAA's halfhearted efforts look even worse. Race, according to Texas Southern University's Alexander Durley, made "the NAIA . . . the NCAA's Achilles' heel."[51]

Although Duer won the relatively easy admittance of HBCs to the NAIA and hoped to avoid confrontation with Southern white schools by segregating the HBCs in the districts-at-large, the NAIA soon faced a reckoning for those successes, testing their resolve. White schools in the Deep South were wary of the admission of HBCs but hoped to avoid home-state criticism and confrontation by simply refusing to play black schools, as evidenced by the correspondence of both Ricks and Kethley. The quickly shifting grounds of racial politics in the 1950s soon rendered that optimism obsolete. Imbued by the rhetoric of World War II, blacks, many of them veterans, intensified their demands for equality One manifestation of this was a slight uptick in black voter registration in Southern states, and another was President Truman's executive order desegregating the armed forces. Additionally, the national Democratic

CHAPTER 6

Party successfully included in its 1948 presidential platform a strongly worded plank calling for an end to segregation, notoriously spurring Deep South delegates to walk out of the convention and ultimately form a third-party segregationist challenge behind candidate Strom Thurmond. The dawning of the 1950s found the white South intensely uneasy about integration long before Martin Luther King's arrival on the national scene and the Supreme Court's 1954 decision to rule school segregation unconstitutional. Southern state legislatures and local communities began passing laws extending and more rigidly defining segregation. One aspect of that included a growing preoccupation with integrated sports. In response to efforts to integrate the minor leagues as part of the process begun with Jackie Robinson's desegregation of Major League Baseball, the Louisiana legislature considered in 1952 a bill that would have banned interracial sports, a matter also considered by the Georgia Assembly in 1955. The city council of Montgomery, Alabama, passed an ordinance in 1950 criminalizing interracial play within the city limits, and existing statewide school segregation statutes in Alabama prohibited integrated athletic contests as an expression of educational segregation. In 1953 Mississippi governor J. P. Coleman essentially issued an executive order of rather dubious legality banning interracial play within the state. The growing white Southern paranoia over the race question drove defenders of segregation to link integration with communism and other left-wing conspiracies, thus allowing them to see the matter in the gravest terms of national security. Thus, any and all examples of "creeping integration" were met with the sternest of responses.[52]

In this environment Southern white college coaches who had hoped they might remain an active NAIA member quarantined from integration by the districts-at-large felt the ground rapidly shifting beneath their feet. Even though the district-at-large proposal kept Southern white and black schools from having to compete against each other, the Alabama schools all voted against their admission solely because "state law prohibits white colleges from competing against colored colleges in the state."[53] Likewise, NAIA officials who had hoped that white Southern opposition to the HBCs would gradually dissipate soon realized that political opposition in the white South was making increasingly untenable the presence of segregated schools in an integrated NAIA. By the end of 1953 Duer and others began to consider the possibility of all Mississippi schools having to withdraw from the NAIA for political reasons, which was likely to initiate a stampede of schools from Alabama, Georgia, and Louisiana as well. As Southern segregationist attitudes became increasingly inflexible and irrational as the 1950s progressed, white Southerners grappled with the athletic isolation imposed by segregation. Segregated college football teams who refused to play integrated teams found themselves with no other postseason options than the Sugar Bowl, which *Washington Post* columnist Shirley Povich derided as "settling some kind of Dixie championship only," while the *Shreveport Times* foresaw a day when segregated teams "will find themselves . . . with no one to play on prestige fields and no one giving a hoot about them."[54] In describing the volatility and unpredictability of the South on the politics of race, Duer said, "They are awfully tense."[55] The environment in the South became even more tense after the 1954 *Brown v. Board of Education* decision and the onset of the Montgomery bus boycott in December 1955. Southern states, particularly in the Deep South, responded with the tactic of massive resistance, with none more emphatic than Louisiana. According to Neil McMillen, the Louisiana legislature eventually passed 131 segregationist acts and resolutions during the period, more than double any other Southern state. One of these acts explicitly outlawed all interracial athletic activity.[56]

The legislature created the Joint Committee on Segregation, headed by William Rainach, who also headed the statewide segregationist Citizens' Council. Rainach ruthlessly used both his public and private positions to ensure statewide racial orthodoxy, intimidating university officials on multiple campuses to do his bidding. Luther Marlar, the chair of District 10 in Louisiana, wrote to Duer in a panic in the summer of 1956, saying, "We have been ordered not to participate against any colored personnel at any place or time." Marlar believed "that no state institution (white) will be permitted to remain a member of the organization" due to its integrated membership. So hostile had the environment in Louisiana become that Marlar begged Duer "not to let it get into the paper that I have written you about this matter. It could very well cost me my job if this should leak out that I wrote to you."[57] Marlar's concerns were not idle paranoia considering that Rainach had orchestrated the removal of a member of the Louisiana State University (LSU) Board of Supervisors for having a black mistress and apparently had a mole within the office of LSU president Troy Middleton to keep informed of the activities of the state's flagship university.[58] With state laws or policies in Louisiana, Mississippi, and Alabama and one pending in Georgia now prohibiting participation in integrated events like the NAIA Tournament, many white Southern university presidents felt additional pressure to discontinue their membership in an integrated organization. As Marlar told

Duer that September, his university president would not countenance "paying dues to an organization that our state law forbids us to participate in." White Southern sentiments toward the NAIA were further inflamed when the organization named A. W. Mumford of Southern University to its executive committee, a move that was so resented in the South that John Ricks of Mississippi Southern College wrote to Duer to complain about the difficulties such actions created for Southern white schools in trying to remain in the NAIA. Duer wrote back to calm Ricks's frustration but attempted to chasten him by suggesting, "I think you will agree that with 45 all-Negro institutions that are all loyal and enthusiastic," such moves were neither unwarranted nor surprising. Nonetheless, by 1957 every public university in Louisiana and Mississippi had either withdrawn its membership or become inactive, a status Marlar secretly embraced for Southeastern Louisiana University and urged Duer to propose to others, a task that Marlar explained he could not undertake for himself: "I would write this letter but in view of the race problem it might be suicide." In a handwritten postscript, Marlar begged Duer's "pardon for the poor typing but I cannot use a secretary for a letter of this type."[59]

By the mid-1950s the NAIA abandoned its former relative indifference to the exclusion of black athletes and black teams and, under the leadership of Al Duer, instead fully embraced athletic integration and an organizational responsibility to use its institutional presence to hasten that process. It was a responsibility that the NCAA could not or would not take on, however. But the struggles of historically black colleges and the support they eventually received from the NAIA inadvertently became wrapped up in the larger turmoil within the NCAA over the role of championships, the sectarian infighting involving the small colleges, and the possible division into classifications. Quite simply, the NAIA's position as a safe haven for small colleges seeking a level playing field and for black colleges seeking access to the national sporting culture now made the NAIA an undeniable threat to the NCAA, a threat the NCAA had no intention of ignoring or tolerating.

CHAPTER 7

DEFENDING THE KINGDOM

THE NAIA WAR AND THE DIVISION OF THE NCAA (1955–1957)

In November 1955 Walter Byers stood before several dozen delegates from the NCAA's smaller institutions to open what the organization innocuously titled an "Invitational Workshop on College Athletics." The three-day NCAA-funded conference addressed all manner of small college athletic administration by focusing on matters such as staff professional development and institutional control but also acknowledged the liberal arts agenda by expressly commenting on the purpose of expanding participation in both intramural and intercollegiate athletics. Byers innocuously opened his remarks by noting his pleasure that so many found time in their schedule to attend the workshop but then proceeded to chastise his audience for their lack of loyalty, consideration, and deference. After questionably summarizing the postwar recruiting excesses and academic and point-shaving scandals of 1951 as having strengthened the NCAA, Byers then challenged those who had instead used those events to "complain that the NCAA is an organization of and for the big universities." Those critics, many of whom were now sitting in the room, had, according to Byers, denigrated the NCAA to outsiders, competitors, and the media by asserting that the NCAA "has done little or nothing for the smaller colleges." Worse than these "adverse criticisms and grievances by the score" was the unwillingness of the small college critics to recognize the "many services" provided to them by the NCAA but "are taken for granted." After having called them on the carpet for their apostasy, Byers then accused his audience of hypocrisy: "But when the criticism was sharpest, the increase in membership among the smaller institutions was highest—an increase which was unsolicited." In the span of a few short minutes, Byers indignantly criticized the small college delegates for their ingratitude while simultaneously implying that the NCAA had not asked for small college membership and were thus not obligated to their concerns.[1]

Byers's performance at the 1955 workshop was little more than a temper tantrum aimed at the portion of the membership whose concerns for the direction of the NCAA were implicit criticisms of the course that Byers had navigated, if not exactly charted. Byers was a stern taskmaster at the NCAA, seldom cultivating close relationships with either the professional staff or the academics from member schools; most either feared him or were intimidated by him. His control over the affairs of the professional staff extended to imposing a dress code, a ban on beverages at staffers' work stations, and a requirement for how the drapes should be drawn every afternoon at 5 P.M.[2] Byers no doubt resented the small college critics whom he saw as ungrateful, but their growing opposition to the big-time model that Byers stewarded could no longer go unnoticed. The level of small college dissatisfaction with the NCAA evident in the Crowley report and the growth of the NAIA demonstrated that the NCAA simply could not ignore the small colleges as they had for much of the organization's recent history. Nor could the NCAA leadership continue to ignore the NAIA threat by simply demeaning the organization as illegitimate. As a result, the mid-1950s witnessed the coalescence of several historical pressures in college athletics, including HBC demands for equality within the athletic establishment, liberal arts clamoring for reform, and small college insistence on access to championship events. In the face of such pressures, Walter Byers decided to marginalize the NAIA once and for all.

The Crowley Committee findings forced the NCAA to make substantive organizational concessions for the first time. The NCAA Council's acceptance of the Crowley recommendation to create a vice-president-at-large position for a delegate from the College Committee guaranteed for the first time a voice for the smaller schools in the highest level of the NCAA's organizational bureaucracy. The council also approved expanding the various rules committees to allow for small college representatives, though by simply adding a College Committee representative without having to remove an existing delegate from a big-time school.[3] While these concessions were reactive and intended to redress institutional isolation of the smaller schools, the council also understood that the College Committee delegates expected the NCAA to help identify and address "the numerous problems besetting the small athletic director" as an indefinite associational responsibility to smaller schools.

It was in this vein that the NCAA hosted the 1955 workshop, a fully funded three-day event held on the campus of the University of Chicago. Walter Byers's bombastic opening remarks, which were so critical of many small college members, came within his address on "The Purposes and Services of the NCAA." Byers briefly surveyed the association's recent history, where he noted that much of the NCAA's mile markers were points of crisis, claiming, "We have progressed by disaster." He subtly alluded to the NAIA by noting that throughout these "disasters," the membership agreed "that the hope for a better future in intercollegiate athletics in America lay within the NCAA," suggesting that as bad as things got, the situation was still better with the NCAA than without it. While Byers granted that the spike in NCAA membership since World War II "has been due primarily to smaller institutions," he acknowledged the institutional indifference to this member base when he correctly pointed out the difficulty the association faced in identifying what defined a small college or what they wanted out of the association. He basically admitted the NCAA leadership did not know how these members saw themselves or what they wanted, but he then rather disingenuously declared "there was quick unanimity that we should remain in one organization." Byers's less than subtle criticisms in his address did not go unnoticed in the completed evaluations solicited after the workshop. While the participants were highly favorable toward the workshop and its benefits as a whole, the number of negative responses to Byers's address was greater than for any other component of the workshop, suggesting that many participants resented his caustic tone and saw him as the handmaiden of the commercialized interests and his comments as little more than an unpleasant infomercial for that wing of the NCAA.[4]

In addition to the Chicago workshop and an effort to provide tangible institutional benefits to the smaller schools, the NCAA Council also attempted to address what the smaller schools saw as distinct competitive disadvantages faced by the smaller schools. Prior to the Chicago workshop, the council had urged the membership to recognize the financial and competitive difficulties that NCAA eligibility rules placed on smaller colleges, specifically the question of freshman eligibility. That question is older than the NCAA itself, but seldom did its defenders seek its imposition for the purposes of allowing freshmen time to orient themselves academically. Rather, its supporters generally came from the ranks of the biggest schools with enrollments large enough to field competitive teams from just three academic classes and enough financial wherewithal to field separate freshman teams while recognizing that such a rule put its smaller rivals at a competitive and financial disadvantage. In 1909 Harvard relied on its celebrity status as a football opponent by virtually extorting Dartmouth into accepting the freshman rule by otherwise refusing to schedule Dartmouth. A decade later, UC Berkeley likewise broke off football relations with its smaller rival across the Bay when Stanford insisted on allowing its freshmen to play on the varsity team. Though such heavy-handed tactics worked when the larger schools enjoyed the advantage, by the 1950s many became increasingly conscious of the electoral math: as the small schools had been telling themselves since before World War II, they enjoyed a voting majority in the association.[5]

Large school apprehension of the small school majority and the threat it entailed to the unity of the NCAA was not an abstraction in the 1950s. The small schools in the venerated Southern Conference, for example, banded together in 1952 to outvote their larger brethren to keep the freshman rule from being reimposed after its wartime suspension. The fact that the smaller schools managed to flex their electoral muscle was bad enough, but, worse, it led to division as the larger schools promptly bolted the conference over the matter to create the Atlantic Coast Conference.[6] The prospect of a similar fissure occurring within the NCAA prompted the membership to amend NCAA bylaws in 1954 granting an exemption to the freshman rule at "institutions with an undergraduate male enrollment of 750 or less." Although many schools just over that threshold grumbled about their exclusion, the exemption did head off some of the most disparate competitive inequalities.[7]

Having shored up the NCAA's rear flank, Walter Byers now decided to go on the offensive against the NAIA. Byers understood that the NAIA would continue to attract members as long as schools and those within the athletics establishment saw that organization as legitimate, and beginning in 1953 he sought to undermine that legitimacy, starting with the Crowley Committee. In good faith, Al Duer presented to the Crowley Committee on the role of the NAIA and suggested that the NCAA and the NAIA establish a joint committee charged with discussing mutual small college concerns. He also encouraged them to address "problems before they become friction areas" between the two organizations so as "to avoid serious conflict." In a letter to Crowley after his testimony, Duer noted that such a committee should enjoy an easy rapport, since "these two groups have much more in common than does the small college section of the NCAA and the large university section."[8] Unbeknownst to Duer, Byers had already conveyed to both the NCAA Council and Crowley his hostility toward the NAIA and his expectations of what the Crowley Committee should find with regard to the "Small College Question." Crowley responded to Duer's letter by parroting Byer's assertion that "no major friction . . . between the two organizations" would emerge as long as the NAIA accepted Byers's three demands: (1) to abandon its use of the word "national" to describe its championships, (2) to shutter its statistical service, and (3) to stop using NCAA rule books for football and basketball. Crowley also implied that the relationship between Duer and Byers was already strained by urging Duer to "endeavor to bring about a rapprochement by cooperating with Mr. Byers."[9] The personal rivalry between Duer and Byers became more open and hostile after that point. Byers directed a letter to Duer in March 1953 specifically laying out the NCAA's demands and alleging that the NAIA was engaging in confrontational tactics toward the NCAA. In September Byers sent another letter about the NAIA infringing on the NCAA's prerogative and refused to consider any compromise, to which Duer reported to his executive committee, "Personally, I find him very difficult to work with."[10] Duer was not the only NAIA official to clash with Byers. Al Wheeler, the NAIA president, sympathized with Duer: "You know, I just don't like the guy and I'm sure he doesn't feel very friendly towards the NAIA."

In his 1955 annual report to the NAIA's executive committee, Duer described the relationship between the two organizations as "in very bad repair, mainly because of [Byers's] attitude that we simply do not exist or have a right to mutual respect."[11] Byers consistently returned to the theme of the NAIA as an illegitimate usurper. As late as 1965, he emphatically claimed that the NAIA "had no right" to form a national organization that presumed to rival the NCAA, simply asserting by fiat that the NCAA "is the governing body for all of intercollegiate athletics."[12] The antipathy between the two became college athletics' worst-kept secret by the mid-1950s, such that Duer even joked about it on occasion. In 1956 Centenary College's athletic director, F. H. Delaney, sheepishly admitted to Duer that Byers had asked him to help provide information on regional teams for an NCAA event, to which Duer good-naturedly responded that Delaney had "joined the ranks of the 'rebel army.'" On a less jovial note at the same time, Duer remarked to one correspondent regarding the NCAA's appeals to smaller schools, "There is no doubt . . . their aim is to kill us if they can."[13] The severity of Byers's views toward the NAIA was not accepted by everyone in the NCAA leadership, however. Howard Hobson, former Oregon head coach and then Yale athletic director, described the NAIA as "a group worthy of participation" in the Olympic qualifying process. Such sentiments, however, did nothing to temper Byers's ruthlessness, and in 1974 Byers reneged on an agreement with Duer not to televise the NCAA Midwest regional in the Kansas City television market during the NAIA Tournament. Duer sent a harshly worded letter of protest, which Byers never answered.[14]

The hostility between the two executive directors was merely the opening salvo in Byers's attempt to delegitimize the NAIA, an effort that was readily apparent to the NAIA leadership. Near the end of 1953, Gus Miller, a member of the NAIA's executive committee from West Texas State College, asserted that Byers and the NCAA "just don't know the problems of the small college and apparently can't learn, but they would undermine the NAIA if they can. And they are trying." Duer shared the sentiment, informing his executive committee in January 1954 that "the NCAA is not only attempting to stimulate the 'Small College Section' of the NCAA but they are taking definite steps which will counteract our program."[15] To that end, the NCAA passed a rule for the 1954–1955 school year stating that any conference containing "over fifty members" could automatically affiliate with the NCAA without having to acquire allied membership. The Eastern Collegiate Athletic Conference (ECAC) was the only such conference in the nation, but many ECAC schools were already NAIA members. By eliminating the requirement of allied membership, the NCAA sought to lure ECAC schools and the possibility of an automatic conference berth in the NCAA Basketball Tournament.[16] The same year, Byers and the NCAA initiated a campaign to more directly involve the organization in the agendas of other bodies, such as the academic-minded Committee on Physical Education and Athletics (CPEA) and the professional American Association of Health, Physical Education, and Recreation (AAHPER), to bring those groups into the NCAA's orbit on its definition of amateurism and to accept the NCAA as the sole steward of college athletics. Although the CPEA agreed to "work more intimately with the NCAA," the AAPHER attempted to chart an independent course between the NCAA and the NAIA, the outcome of which was that "the AAPHER is not going to take a stand on any issue which will alienate the affections of any large and influential group," a position that Wheeler described as "somewhat disappointing." Though the AAPHER refused to get drawn into the NCAA's efforts to kill the NAIA, neither did it offer any criticisms of the very NCAA practices that led it to declare neutrality in the first place.[17]

The NCAA's most heavy-handed intervention with an outside organization came when the National Federation of State High School Athletic Association (NFSHAA) proposed a memorandum of understanding with the NAIA concerning football rules and officiating. The NAIA also sought to include the national governing body of junior college athletics. Once the NCAA learned of the proposed arrangement, however, Byers notified the NFSHAA executive director that any such alliance with the NAIA would terminate any future cooperation with the NCAA.[18] It was Byers's intention to isolate the NAIA and deprive it of allies both within and without the ranks of college athletics.

Delegitimating the NAIA with future members or potential allies certainly put the NAIA on the defensive, but Byers's most decisive move was to sanction a challenge to the one feature that made the NAIA distinctive and made the NCAA so vulnerable: its basketball tournament. The iconic representation of college athletics had always been college football, and the small schools had known for some time that trying to compete in the world of commercialized college football was a lost cause. The concessions to competitive and academic pragmatism necessary to succeed, as well as the expense, were more than many were willing or able to make. Nothing symbolized this stark reality better in the 1950s than the abandonment of big-time football by the Ivy League, the inventors of the game and all of its commercialized abuses. Basketball, however, was a game that many schools believed minimized financial and enrollment disparities, where different styles of play and skill sets could neutralize sheer size and strength, and where teamwork could overwhelm sheer talent. In short, basketball was a game the smaller colleges believed they could pursue competitively without prostituting their academic or character-development missions. Being kept out of the NCAA Basketball Tournament galled them in many ways far worse than the destruction of college football as they knew it. The NCAA's small liberal arts colleges desperately clung to the notion that their ability to pursue championship-caliber basketball helped justify their continued participation in the NCAA, through which they might still influence

CHAPTER 7

reform. Other smaller schools, particularly smaller state schools and regional campuses, less concerned with idealistic reform and more interested in a level playing field, looked longingly at the NAIA's annual tournament in Kansas City, with many holding dual membership to gain access or simply abandoning the NCAA outright. To continue the basketball status quo within the NCAA meant to continue hemorrhaging small public schools to the NAIA and alienating the private liberal arts colleges with the likelihood that they might eventually follow the path to Kansas City. The challenge was fraught with complications, however. If the NCAA attempted to challenge the NAIA with a rival tournament and failed, it would mark a wholesale abandonment of the NCAA by smaller schools interested in championship play, and it would bolster the arguments of the liberal arts colleges that claimed the NCAA served only the big-time commercialized schools.

The open warfare initiated by Byers against the NAIA, however, forced the liberal arts colleges to choose sides and, overwhelmingly, they chose the prestige and status of the NCAA and its well-known big-time members. Private, top-tier liberal arts colleges decided to swallow their distaste for the commercialized model that the NCAA enabled. Televised college football gave the NCAA a level of wealth, status, and name recognition that the NAIA could not match. The liberal arts delegates embraced the formal collegiality practiced by the barons of college athletics, where members who had known one another for years referred to each other in open meetings with a senatorial courtesy as "the gentlemen from Harvard" or "my esteemed colleague from Swarthmore," while rejecting the small state schools and open admissions policies of the parochial colleges that made up a substantial percentage of the NAIA membership. The comments included in the final Crowley Committee report revealed the deep divisions between the smaller state schools and the private liberal arts colleges over the primacy of reform, but that divide became more public when the College Committee, dominated by the liberal arts schools, voted unanimously in March 1954 "that whatever is done with regard to championships for smaller colleges should be completed in the existing framework of the NCAA." Although the College Committee "urge[d] the NCAA Council and the Executive Committee to continue their efforts to open the basketball . . . playoffs to more smaller-college qualifiers," it revealed its unwillingness to consider any joint arrangements with the NAIA.[19]

Having decided that the future of the liberal arts colleges lay solely within the NCAA, the College Committee still faced the discontent from many small schools over their inability to get into the NCAA Basketball Tournament. As George Lawson of Muhlenberg College said at the 1955 meeting of the College Committee, "I don't believe this committee gets any more questions on any one subject than on the National Collegiate Basketball Championship." At that year's meeting, the College Committee attendees peppered Dutch Lonborg, the basketball committee chair, about the difficulties of smaller schools gaining entrance, the inherent limitations of the HBCs, and the disparate advantages the larger, Eastern schools enjoyed. The questioning remained civil and the frustrations stayed beneath the surface, but for those who had followed the discussion for years, the earnestness of answers wrapped in duplicity and half-truths must have made listeners feel like they were trapped in a Kafka novel. Lonborg immediately acknowledged the skepticism of the room by taking great pains "to say from the very beginning that any team eligible to compete under the NCAA rules is looked over by our Selection Committees, and if strong enough to be selected, it will be selected. We want to make this point crystal clear to this group." Having repeated the canard about a level playing field, which almost no one in the room except Lonborg believed, Lonborg proceeded to catalog some of the very instances in the tournament's early years when arbitrary selections among teams determined who got bids and who stayed home. In an effort to avoid "excluding some very fine basketball teams from the tournament," Lonborg noted the expansion of the field to a larger bracket, with fifteen conference champions receiving automatic bids and anywhere from eight to ten additional schools receiving at-large bids.[20] The tournament's 1951 expansion to sixteen teams lasted only two years, before the NCAA immediately inflated it to twenty-two teams in 1953. The tournament field then fluctuated between twenty-four teams in 1954, 1955, and 1957; twenty-five teams in 1956; and twenty-three teams in 1957 and 1959.[21] The process by which the committee awarded the at-large bids particularly raised the hackles of Western schools when Lonborg announced that as a matter of policy, the committee reserved a majority of at-large bids for the Eastern schools. When the tournament operated with a sixteen-team field, the East and West brackets each received eight bids. With its expansion, however, the privileging of Eastern schools began with twelve Eastern schools and only ten Western schools in 1952. Eastern schools continued to receive two more bids than Western schools through the remainder of the decade, save for 1956. In that year the tournament field expanded to twenty-five teams, and Eastern schools received fourteen bids while the West received only eleven.

Though the NCAA was just then in the process of fielding the largest tournament field ever, with twenty-five teams, Lonborg attempted to deflect some of this concern by quickly acknowledging that it might "be necessary for us to enlarge our tournament to 32 teams so that we can get all the fine teams in the tournament." The NCAA Tournament would not expand to thirty-two teams until 1975, but many already felt the twenty-four-team field was obsolete and the imbalance of Eastern teams was becoming harder to justify.[22]

Knowing that the room wanted to talk about only one thing, Lonborg dispensed of his intentions to discuss the nuances of the committee's operations on matters such as seeding and the assignment of byes and opened up the discussion for questions on "the selection of teams," which "is pretty much the most important thing before this group" to-day. Kelly Thompson from Western Kentucky University immediately inquired about how his school's conference, which lacked an automatic bid, could secure one and protested how few small college conferences enjoyed the privilege of an automatic bid by asserting that several "other conferences represented here . . . feel that we have some pretty good arguments and logic" to justify their automatic inclusion. Lonborg hardly mollified his audience when he replied that all conferences were welcome to apply for automatic inclusion by submitting to the NCAA a list of the conference's schools, their size, and their schedules, acknowledging that school size was taken into account and that schools that could not get known teams to schedule them were at a disadvantage. It was an issue Mack Greene immediately picked up by challenging Lonborg on how the committee determined a team's "strength . . . where you don't know about the strength of the teams they have competed against." When Lonborg acknowledged that the committee often deferred to the subjective opinion of one of its two coach representatives, Greene incredulously responded, "Purely on the opinion of [one] fellow, without any specific factors?" Lonborg failed to assuage Greene and the other representatives of HBCs in the room when he further conceded that the committee also consulted "the various ratings" indexes like the Dunkel Index and the McNitt's *Blue Book*. John McLendon then suggested that as he understood the criteria, "the possibilities of the smaller colleges ever getting into the tournament are very small, on the basis of what you call 'strength.'" After asking McLendon to define "small college," Lonborg backtracked and said the committee did not consider enrollment size but simply looked at "strength of the team." With both Greene and McLendon unable to pin down Lonborg on how the committee determined strength, McLendon tried another tactic by asking if "competition between conferences help[ed]" and if more intersectional games might enhance a school's profile. Again Lonborg fell back on the dodge that such games only counted if intersectional games were between strong teams. At that point Lonborg abruptly excused himself from the meeting by announcing he had another meeting to attend and hastily left the room.[23]

It's unclear if Lonborg's awkward, if not dissembling, performance at the 1955 College Committee meeting infuriated the attendees with his circular logic, or simply convinced them that they were never going to be invited to the NCAA Tournament on their own merits, but the timing appears causative. At its March 1955 meeting the College Committee appointed a subcommittee of McLendon, Lawson, and Ralph Ginn of South Dakota State College to consider creating a separate small college basketball tournament. Unsurprisingly, the committee agreed unanimously to recommend the creation of a second NCAA Tournament for small schools, which was then discussed at length at the November 1955 Chicago workshop presided over by Byers. While the workshop generally agreed in the abstract that "national championships, as conducted by the NCAA, are consistent with educational objectives," the group in Chicago primarily concerned itself with one sport. "It was agreed that basketball is the logical sport to start a new classification of competition for smaller schools" and that "there is a greater demand for national championship play-offs in basketball than in any of the other sports."[24] Illustrating the demand for access to the basketball tournament, the soon-to-be-created College Division Tournament Committee sent out a questionnaire to prospective schools. Of the 208 respondents, 63 percent had never participated in the NCAA Basketball Tournament, but 94 percent expressed interest in a small college tournament. The NCAA Convention approved the new tournament at its 1956 convention to begin play the following year. The ease with which the council approved and forwarded the matter to the full convention suggests that the Chicago workshop was decisive in convincing Byers and others that a separate tournament was imperative to hold at bay the disenchantment of the smaller schools. While the Chicago workshop successfully recommended distinguishing the two tournaments as the College Division Tournament and the University Division Tournament, the College Committee also recommended to the council at the same convention that the NCAA "utilize the terminology 'university' and 'college' in differentiating between the larger and smaller institutions of the Association" even outside of the context of the tournaments, in essence creating a definitive two-tiered classification system within the NCAA. Unwilling to go that far, the council chose to take no action on the matter. Considering Byers had emphatically asserted in the wake of the Crowley report that the creation of the College Committee was "never designed or contemplated to be a separation of the two classes of institutions," the council's move in 1956 had Byers's fingerprints all over it.[25]

Byers now realized the necessity of a separate small college tournament to stave off the dismembering of the NCAA, yet he also saw in the circumstances the promise of possibility. He now attempted to strike at the one thing that he believed gave the NAIA any claim to equality with the NCAA as a voice in amateur sports: their participation in the Olympic basketball qualifying process. Now that the NCAA would be offering its own tournament, Byers presumed that by dint of the NCAA's institutional legitimacy, their tournament instantly relegated the NAIA event to the status of illegitimate sideshow. After agreeing to put the small college tournament on the January 1956 convention agenda, Byers contacted the US Olympic Committee and called for the exclusion of the NAIA champion from the upcoming Olympic qualifying process for the Summer Games in Melbourne. Byers attempted to use strong-arm tactics by threatening to refuse NCAA teams' participation in the process if it involved NAIA schools. The NCAA justified the exclusion of the NAIA by claiming that their participating made the qualifying process too drawn out and imposed upon the players "too great a loss of time away from campus" and their studies.[26]

It is unclear what role Byers's efforts played, but the location of the 1956 Summer Games significantly complicated the traditional Olympic qualifying process. Since its inception the US Olympic qualifying process had sought to identify an Olympic squad made up overwhelmingly of two teams that made the finals of the qualifying tournament rather than create a team of exceptional players from dozens of teams. Thus, the Olympic qualifying tournament involved champion teams from the AAU, the NCAA, and the NAIA. However, to account for the seasonal difference in the southern hemisphere, Melbourne Olympic organizers scheduled the games for November, meaning the Summer Olympics would be held during the American academic year, requiring significant missed class time. Worse, it meant that a potential Olympic team might be overwhelmingly made up from a collegiate championship team that had been crowned eight months earlier and included players who had graduated and were thus no longer eligible to play for their college teams even though their collegiate membership is what earned them the right to participate in the Olympic process. To avoid these problems, as well as a potential confrontation with the NCAA over the NAIA's continued participation, the USOC switched to a format involving college all-star teams made up of players from multiple teams. This would minimize the number of players from any one school forced to miss class time and would avoid the problem of a team qualifying with graduated seniors who were no longer eligible.[27] Though it also deprived both the NCAA and NAIA of the potential bragging rights of having one of its teams crowned as Olympic champion, Byers no doubt took satisfaction in further marginalizing the NAIA.

The never-resolved issue of what defined a "small college" now emerged in distinguishing between the college and university divisions. Rather than attempt a quantification of schools along lines of enroll-ment or budget, the committee simply deferred to the list of so-called major colleges established by the National Collegiate Association Bureau (NCAB), the NCAA's in-house statistical agency. Created before World War II but not officially subsidized by the NCAA until 1946 as part of the NCAA's aggressive efforts to establish itself as a trade association to support commercialized athletics, the NCAB's primary responsibility was to serve as a big-time intercollegiate statistical clearinghouse to the commercial media and to publish the NCAA's annual guidebooks for NCAA-sanctioned sports.[28] Surely, many small colleges noted the irony of the NCAB, whose creation they steadfastly opposed in 1946, ten years later arbitrarily determining the very nature of their identity and eligibility. Almost immediately the tournament committee linked College Division membership with their status as NCAA outliers. The committee required that only half of a conference's members need be NCAA members to qualify for an automatic berth and, recognizing "that, at the outset, several of the conferences would not be allied NCAA members," allowed a two-year exemption for those conferences to still earn automatic berths. However, the committee drew the line at prohib-iting non-NCAA member schools from participating, even if they won their conference championship. The University Division Tournament Committee determined that schools that qualified for the College Divi-sion but wished to participate in the University Division (in other words, those who aspired to play big-time commercialized sports) would be allowed to move up if the University Division Tournament Committee offered them an at-large bid. So troubling was the question of identity even within a conference that the Middle Atlantic States Athletic Conference decided in 1956 to create for basketball only separate university and college divisions for its member schools.[29]

While teams and conferences continued to wrestle with their proper place in the NCAA and its new upcoming basketball tournament, almost everyone agreed that the NAIA was the clear loser in the outcome. In its coverage of the NCAA Convention, the *New York Times* declared that the decision "virtually sealed the doom of the NAIA small college basketball tourney." When serious discussion of creating separate divisions within the NCAA appeared as far back as January 1955, Centenary College's F. H. Delaney immediately viewed a separate small college division as a swipe at the NAIA: "The NAIA has done a great service for the small college and seems to have their interests at heart. Would we be biting off our nose in that particular instance?"[30] Delaney operated under the presumption that the NAIA's early efforts for small colleges—in particular, their successful basketball tournament—fairly won for them a prerogative that the NCAA had no honorable right to challenge. After the NCAA created the College Division Tournament, others too saw the issue in similar terms. Many media outlets blasted the NCAA for its decision as unnecessary and driven solely by the search for revenue and a petty desire to destroy the NAIA. Ernest Mehl of the *Kansas City Star* promptly assigned the ethical high ground to the NAIA, describing that organization as "content to remain in its own circle, glorying in the ever increasing number of its member colleges, happy with the code of morals and sportsmanship by which it abides," in sharp contrast to the "headaches" created by the NCAA's commercialized model. Unaware and unconcerned with the NAIA Tournament's "steady rise," the NCAA, according to Mehl, "would be quite well pleased if the NAIA Tournament in Kansas City fell by the wayside."

Others, however, were not as circumspect in their criticisms of the NCAA. Charles Johnson of the *Minneapolis Star* described the NCAA's decision as nothing more than "power politics" and an example of that organization's "double talk." Bill Williams of the Baton Rouge *State Times Advocate* referred to the new tournament as a "low blow" by a ruthless and hypocritical NCAA out to "kill the NAIA." After cataloging the familiar litany of complaints made by small colleges over the years about an indifferent NCAA, Williams described the NCAA's newfound concern for small colleges as a trap that would "no doubt lure some of the unthinking smaller schools into an NCAA staged affair. To do so is to succumb to the wild song of Lorelei and, like the mariners, meet disaster on the rocks." Williams was not the only writer to turn to cultural or literary analogies in critically assessing the current state of the NCAA. Clyde McBride, writing in the *Kansas City Times*, saw the NCAA's move as a Mafioso, gangland-style violation of turf, describing the NCAA in familial and paternal terms and seeing its actions as "moving in on the NAIA." The editors of the *News Tribune* in Beaver Falls, West Virginia, described the NCAA as a "big octopus" intent on "set[ting] out its tentacles to do but one job and that is to swallow up the NAIA."[31]

Few, however, were as critical as Jack Fisher of the *Shreveport Times*: "Bluntly, it shapes up like this: the NCAA is out to put the NAIA out of business because it has been doing its job too well." Like Williams, Fisher commented on the NCAA's history of ignoring the interests of "the have-nots," leading to the creation of the NAIA and the notion "that 'small' and 'helpless' are not necessarily synonymous." Only naked greed and ruthlessness, according to Fisher, could "justify [the NCAA's] sudden solicitude for the little fellas after a long and dishonorable history of degrading them." What galled observers like Fisher was that the NCAA had either stood idly by or actively sanctioned the changes in college football that all but destroyed the game at the small college level and then claimed in 1956 to be looking out for the small colleges' interests. It was a theme the Associated Press' Whitney Martin also touched on. The NCAA, according to Martin, "has been concerned largely with larger schools" over the past several decades, leaving "those with small enrollments and small football teams pretty much shifting for themselves." Duer also made the connection to college football by asserting that regional television of big-time college football "has just about wrecked the small colleges." He prophesied that "within a few years the smaller schools will have to find a completely new method of financing their sports programs because of the inroads made by larger institutions" and the commercialized model at the expense of programs like the NAIA Basketball Tournament. "There is no excuse for it and no call for it," he said.[32]

While Al Duer and writers mostly located in NAIA media markets might be expected to defend the organization and criticize the NCAA, the setup and finances of the new College Division Tournament revealed much of the criticism's accuracy. The now labeled University Division Tournament Committee only begrudgingly expanded the size of the tournament field over the years and kept it at around twenty-four teams until 1975, whereas the College Division Tournament began play with a thirty-two-team field. After rejecting every proposal that would have included historically black colleges in the University Division Tournament, the College Division Tournament now enjoyed substantial room in its field to grant automatic bids to three HBC conferences, plus an at-large bid to ensure that the HBC entrants could play each other in the first round. Wary of the financial implications of such a large tournament, the NCAA contracted with a "community corporation" based in Evansville, Indiana, that provided the NCAA an $18,000 guarantee, in exchange for which Evansville won the right to host the quarter-finals, semifinals, and national championship game for the first four years. The original contract contained high hopes for the tournament's profitability, stating that the first $20,000 over the $18,000 guarantee would accrue to the corporation for future promotional purposes and that when revenues exceeded that $20,000 threshold, the corporation and the NCAA would split revenues with the corporation's profits to be directed to a reserve fund devoted to the future tournament expenses, up to $20,000. Once the corporation's reserve fund hit $20,000, all revenues accrued to the NCAA. Another provision, however, acknowledged the limited commercial appeal of the College Division Tournament in its early years. The contract stipulated that the championship game should be played on Saturday nights in years "when there is no conflict with games sponsored by the Indiana State High School Athletic Association." The financial returns from the NCAA's two tournaments in 1957 reveal the vastly different worlds in which they resided. The University Division Tournament, involving twenty-three teams and played in Kansas City's Municipal Auditorium, netted $176,500, the equivalent of more than $1.5 million in 2018. By comparison, the College Division Tournament, with thirty-two teams and played on the home court of the then named Evansville College, lost $10,425.[33]

In an effort to win over the HBCs, the NCAA Council named Mack Greene to the College Division Basketball Tournament Committee, granting the first committee appointment to an HBC delegate in NCAA history. Even with Greene's membership, however, the committee lacked the will or institutional gravitas to address the kinds of issues involving integrated play that the NAIA had marshaled almost a decade earlier. They essentially created a Jim Crow regional of the thirty-two-team bracket by ensuring for the first few years of the tournament that HBC conferences met one another in the first round. In the inaugural 1957 tournament, North Carolina Central University and Florida A&M University played each other the first round in the East Region while Mississippi's Jackson State University beat Philander Smith College in the Midwest Region. Sadly, for Jackson State, it was not opposition from an opponent but from their own state legislature that knocked them out that year. Political custom back home prohibited them from engaging in integrated play, thus requiring them to forfeit their second-round game against the University of South Dakota. Coincidentally, USD was one of the few teams to field an integrated starting lineup that year with black players Jim and Cliff Daniels starting for the Coyotes. In 1958 and 1959 the tournament continued to minimize the presence of black schools by placing all four HBCs in the same regional, thereby ensuring that only one could make it to the quarterfinals. No historically black colleges appeared in the University, or by then Division I, Tournament until Alcorn State University in 1980.[34]

At the 1956 NCAA Convention that approved the College Division Tournament, Al Duer gave an impassioned argument against its creation, citing the preexisting role of the NAIA, the predatory consequences of commercialism upon small college football, the historic exclusion of small colleges from the NCAA Tournament, and the obvious areas of conflict between the proposed tournament and the NAIA. In response, NCAA officials simply declared that the creation of the "College Division Tournament was in no sense aimed at the NAIA."[35] Yet, everything about the NCAA's decisions regarding the College Division Tournament suggest otherwise. Having spent almost twenty years arguing that a dearth of quality teams limited the University Tournament's expansion, the NCAA now created an additional tournament with a field a third larger than its existing tournament. Having spent much of its recent history attempting to overcome the home rule principle and elevate its institutional control in the form of television money and the Sanity Code, it now proposed a decentralized relationship with an outside contractor to run an event of its own creation. Having spent the early years of its basketball tournament decrying the NIT and the NAIB events, when it chose to acknowledge them at all, as marginal or illegitimate, it now located its new tournament in a locale where it played second fiddle to high school games. Having spent the better part of the last decade doing everything possible to exclude HBCs and avoid making segregated member institutions play them, it now included member schools in which it had no previous interest but now made up 13 percent of its competitors' membership base (and conveniently relegated them to a classification below the big-time commercialized segregated state schools who would now never have to play them). Having made no effort to address the inherent competitive limitations faced by HBCs and rebuffed with indifference the criticisms that NCAA actions appeared sympathetic to segregation, the NCAA now named one of its biggest critics to the tournament committee. Finally, having concerned itself with profits in every aspect of its tournament management since the days of Phog Allen, the NCAA now engaged in a venture that put them deeply in the red. The NCAA's protestations to the contrary, it appears that they created the event to appeal to as many schools as possible and overwhelmingly for the purpose of stanching the tide of membership loss to the NAIA.

Supporters of the NAIA knew that the NCAA College Division Tournament could not succeed if NAIA members refused to participate and stayed with the NAIA. Francis Hoover of Appalachian State College bluntly declared, "The issue will come down to a matter of loyalty of NAIA schools. If they remain loyal, the NCAA small college tournament will not be a success." One NAIA athletic director asserted that "it is an accepted fact that the small tournament is the one in Kansas City." Only an abandonment of it would allow the NCAA Tournament to gain any legitimacy, leaving Bill Zorn of Wisconsin State Teachers College to say, "I don't see why a small college would go with [the NCAA]—they have no voice, and never will have."[36] The problem was that some NAIA schools began to jump ship almost immediately. One of the earliest to bolt was Evansville College. Though Evansville had been a longtime NAIA member, it did so because the school's athletic board knew the NCAA Tournament Committee was never going to favor the Aces over Indiana or Purdue for a tournament invitation. The creation of the College Division now gave Evansville an opportunity to compete for championships against more comparable competition. And while Evansville's athletic board "discussed thoroughly" the option of maintaining memberships in both the NAIA and the NCAA, it decided to drop the former for financial reasons.[37]

For many schools, the NCAA label, regardless of the circumstances, carried more prestige and prominence. Longtime NAIA member Emporia State Teachers College left their loyalties in doubt by joining the NCAA for just that year because of a strong basketball team hoping to make their tournament. Emporia also maintained that basketball success might advertise the university, something that could benefit from the NCAA's sports media services. Emporia was not alone in this tactic; Beloit College, Lawrence Technical University, and Seattle University also used it. "Why? Big time publicity" and other "fringe" benefits, according to NAIA Executive Committee member Gus Fish.[38] Other long-standing NAIA members soon began choosing the NCAA permanently. Mississippi College's athletic director wrote in a letter to Duer, "We already hold membership in the NCAA and we feel we have nothing to gain in continuing holding membership in the two organizations." Duer received the same sentiment in letters from Loyola College (MD) and Wabash College, among others. In replying to a similar letter from Pennsylvania's Lebanon Valley College, Duer reiterated his usual conviction "that our organization is doubly more aware of the problems of the so-called 'small college' than any other organization," but schools accepted Byers's logic that the NCAA's wealth, status, and prominence more effectively served their athletic interests. So precipitous was the NAIA membership decline in response to the NCAA's actions that a separate file exists in the NAIA archives titled "Memberships Dropped, 1955–57."[39]

Race too almost surely played a role in the NAIA's membership woes in the latter 1950s. Just as its egalitarian and democratic policies attracted historically black colleges, they appear to have shaped the actions of many white institutions. As Southeastern Louisiana's Luther Marlar predicted, Southern political pressure ensured that "no state institution (white) will be permitted to remain a member" of the NAIA. Accordingly, longtime NAIA members such as Centenary College, Eastern Kentucky University, Lamar College, Louisiana Polytechnic Institute, Memphis State University, Middle Tennessee State College, Morehead State College, and Mississippi Southern College all quietly withdrew from the organization. All told, perhaps as many as two dozen Southern schools, mostly in the Deep South, dropped their membership as the NAIA refused to downplay its embrace of integration.[40] The role that race played in the decision of every school is impossible to measure, but it played a decisive role at enough schools to suggest that the departure of so many schools at the time was more than coincidental.

The fact that many schools chose the NCAA over the NAIA is not surprising given the significant divisions that had always lain just below the surface of the small college revolt against the NCAA. Since the 1930s schools like Oberlin, Johns Hopkins, and Franklin and Marshall identified themselves as "small colleges" because they opposed the big state universities' transformation of college football into a near-corporate enterprise. But size and athletic aspiration did not really mark the liberal arts agenda within the NCAA. Those schools wanted to use the NCAA to engage in what they thought was athletic and academic reform, not simply to create more championship opportunities with peers of their athletic profile. Although their definition of amateurism was really just less commercialized than the big-time purveyors (many of them also retained paid coaches, charged admission, and recruited athletes in some fashion), their only hope of ever creating uniform standards of eligibility, prohibiting subsidization of athletes, and, most important, weaning the athletic department from its reliance on the paying gate and outside sources of revenue derived from winning all lay within the prestige of the NCAA. These schools understood that the public acclaim and media attention afforded to winning athletic programs, particularly in college football, made it difficult for those beyond the pale to claim a place within the pantheon of academic leadership.

While the angst of the liberal arts colleges reached its apex after the scandal-ridden year of 1951 and Schober Barr's provocative call for the small colleges to seize control of the NCAA, a majority of them never seriously considered leaving that organization. The liberal arts colleges applauded the NAIA's efforts to provide a home for small colleges—and in particular, to try "saving college football"—but even the most ardent NCAA critics, like Oberlin's John Nichols, always held them at arm's length. Al Duer understood the division within the small college identity when he described "the leadership of the 'Small College' section of the NCAA" as "the typically super-academic and wealthy colleges—Johns Hopkins, Oberlin, Franklin and Marshall."[41] These were schools that had little in common, academically, financially, culturally, and socially, with the typical NAIA member that came from the ranks of small state schools and church-affiliated colleges of the South, Plains states, and the far West. Schools like Evansville, Wabash, Loyola, and Lebanon Valley that dropped out of the NAIA in 1955 when the NCAA created a place for them all fit the classic liberal arts profile: all private residential institutions, founded before the onset of industrialization, enjoying at least some endowed financial foundation, and benefiting from selective admissions policies. In the public's view, the NCAA's most notable members not only appeared prominently on the gridiron and the hardwood but also developed notable research agendas that won federal grants and national influence during the Cold War.[42] Though not every liberal arts school aspired to the same, they thought of themselves as interested players in the elite world of American academia.

While Duer recognized the difference and did not begrudge the NCAA's liberal arts colleges their identity, others within the NAIA were not as charitable. Joseph Hutton, Hamline University's director of athletics, decried the NCAA "small colleges" as "pious hypocrites

... who look down their noses at the NAIA."[43] In Hutton's opinion the NCAA's action was "nothing more than throwing another piece of bait ... to their small college" membership, who now snobbishly forsook the NAIA to ignore the NCAA's history of transgression against the smaller schools. Hypocrites or not, the liberal arts colleges were willing to forego championships in the hope that remaining within the NCAA allowed them the prestige and opportunity to continue to push for reform. Whether the liberal arts colleges liked it or not, the NCAA bestowed, in the words of Walter Byers, "prestige and so-called 'athletic accreditation' due to the NCAA standards and [its] enforcement." Put more simply, belonging to the NCAA wrapped a school in the public perception of big-time athletics, whether or not it actually pursued (or even liked) big-time athletics.[44] Fred Hess of Nebraska Wesleyan University described those who embraced Byers's notion of athletic accreditation thusly: "small schools coveting the distinction of being known with great athletic programs ... preferring to identify themselves with the NCAA even in a role of shirt-tail relative because of the pseudo prestige ... this association heaps upon them."[45]

The NCAA refused to acknowledge that the creation of the College Division in 1957 marked a formal classification system within the organization. Thus, the liberal arts colleges continued to call upon the organization for the kinds of reforms that Nichols, Bilheimer, and Houston had been advocating since the 1930s. The creation of the College Division Basketball Tournament and other similar events, however, undercut much of the internal momentum for reform, leaving fewer and fewer idealists to fantasize about flexing their electoral majority within the organization. Instead, many of the small colleges, now having their own championships for which to contend—not just in basketball but soon in baseball and other sports—began engaging in the same abuses and the same drift toward commercialism that their predecessors had decried. Having failed at convincing the big-time schools and having lost their small-enrollment confederates, the liberal arts colleges finally threw in the towel in 1973 and voted for a formal separation of the NCAA into three divisions. In a telling validation of what Barr, Houston, and Bilheimer had asserted for so many years about small college voting power, while 237 schools chose the commercialized topmost level (Division I), 427 schools chose the lower classifications, with more than half (233) choosing the lowest classification (Division III). What became Division II was basically a replica of the NAIA, a program run by those shut out of the big-time commercial strata by circumstance or choice, with rules and finances akin to their more moderate aspirations and budgetary realities. What became Division III, however, was the monument Nichols, Bilheimer, Houston, and Barr never lived to see. With the 1973 classification system, Division III schools were prohibited from granting athletic scholarships; coaches usually taught academic classes; championships were minimized (the first Division III basketball tournament was not held until two years after the division's creation); schools created far more competitive opportunities by fielding teams in more sports than schools in the other divisions; and schools funded their athletic programs out of their annual budgets with most events, even football games, operating without an admission charge.[46]

Beginning in the early 1960s the trajectories of the NCAA and the NAIA moved in divergent directions. Having survived the crisis years of the 1950s, NCAA membership began a steady period of growth. The single biggest fact in that growth, however, was the wealth and prominence accrued from the NCAA's college football television policy in the 1950s and 1960s, soon followed in the 1970s by money from the University Division Basketball Tournament. Though not all NCAA member schools enjoyed television exposure, they all indirectly benefited from the money the cartel model extracted from the television networks. Television exposure also created in the minds of an undiscerning viewing public the appearance of legitimacy and authenticity, and the college football they saw on television was NCAA college football. It was television, more than anything else, that created the popular notion that "real" college sports were governed by the NCAA.[47] Prospective member schools, like the liberal arts schools a decade before, overwhelmingly decided to throw in with the institutional and televised prestige of the NCAA.

When Congress passed Title IX of the 1972 Education Act, the NCAA could no longer ignore women's sports, just as they realized in the 1950s that they could no longer ignore the small colleges. And in the same way they saw the NAIA as a threat to their monopoly to be ruthlessly pursued, the NCAA determined that the Association of Intercollegiate Athletics for Women (AIAW) was an organization with which it could not coexist. The AIAW, like the liberal arts reformers and the small college partisans, represented an alternative narrative for college sports and, like many smaller schools, wanted to hold at bay the professionalizing impulses marked by the NCAA. Thus, they tried to limit scholarships, championships, and recruiting in an effort to strike some balance of "enough but not too much." Employing tactics learned in the fight against the NAIA, the NCAA went to war with the AIAW in 1979 by leveraging its finances and prestige, offering athletic scholarships, championship events, and paid travel for participating teams to lure women's programs from the AIAW. Even though the AIAW enjoyed a membership of almost a thousand schools on the eve of their battle with the NCAA, most of them abandoned the AIAW for the NCAA, and by 1983 the AIAW ceased operations.[48]

Walter Byers's comment to the small college workshop in 1955 that the NCAA "has progressed by disaster" was truer than he probably intended. Throughout its history, the NCAA has been marked by an inherently conservative approach, historically seeking to avoid any action and taking it only when forced. The very creation of the NCAA came only in reaction to the usurpations of the McCracken Conference and the brutality crisis of 1905; the efforts to expand offerings for the small colleges came only after they threatened to take over the association or leave it entirely in the early 1950s; and their efforts to address the racial disparities and inequities faced by some members resulted in tepid responses like ensuring accessible convention facilities. The embarrassing revelations of the Carnegie Report and the gambling and academic scandals of 1951 led to no action whatsoever other than empty platitudes. The big-time membership of the NCAA and the institutional drift of the professional staff, beginning with Tug Wilson and Walter Byers, sought as little change as possible to maintain the status quo. It is the reason that college athletics has witnessed so little structural change in more than one hundred years. In the face of liberal arts discontent over commercialization and committees, small college discontent over competitive equity, and HBC protests over racial inequalities, the NCAA imposed the chimerical without addressing the substantive. Creating the College Division Tournament, and later Division II itself, did nothing to address the ethical and moral concerns espoused by the liberal arts colleges, not did it impose any greater institutional will to ensure that all members enjoyed equal competitive standing regardless of race. But like the creation of the NCAA itself in 1905, the creation of the College Division Tournament helped buy off the reformist momentum in the early 1950s that potentially threatened the commercialized interests ensconced in the NCAA. Giving the small colleges their own tournament protected the tournament monopoly (and its revenues) of the big-time schools, and shunting the HBCs into the College Division alleviated (for a time) Southern concerns about interracial play. Thus, the creation of the College Division Tournament was actually motivated by the desire to protect the interests of the commercialized University Division schools.

The NAIA, on the other hand, while managing to avoid the AIAW's fate, foundered in the increasingly competitive and high-stakes cultural milieu of postwar American sports. While the NAIA's membership witnessed measurable growth again in the 1960s, it did not keep pace with that of the NCAA. Far more consequential than membership, however, was the NAIA's refusal or inability to match the NCAA in its pursuit of commercialized, profitable athletics. Duer first cautioned his membership in 1959 with his concerns of college sports as "a separate commercial or promotional adjunct" to the educational process. More than simply parrot the concerns that Nichols and others had been uttering since the 1930s against the commercialized power, Duer saw the real culprit as a cultural shift in American society. Restraining the spectacle of commercialized college athletics, according to Duer, "is contrary both to the present trend in the development of intercollegiate athletics nationally and also is in direct conflict with the major trends in our society."[49] Duer was not the only critic who noted this expanding embrace in American society of the collegiate athletic spectacle increasingly devoid of values. Harvard's James B. Conant penned an essay in *Look* magazine in 1961 criticizing the expectation that scholastic and intercollegiate athletics' primary role was to help build community, create publicity, and generate revenue through winning teams. Completely absent, according to Conant, was any concern for the development of the individual.[50]

This shift in the popular perception of the meaning of athletics was felt not merely in the amorphous public but also within the NAIA membership. In 1959 the NAIA passed legislation imposing penalties on members who skipped NAIA events for those sponsored by the NCAA, with Duer ominously observing, "We are coming to have more and more conflicts." By the NAIA's own count, 138 members also held membership in the NCAA and generally privileged those events over those of the NAIA. In 1962 the NAIA expanded the sanctions to conferences whose members strayed to NCAA's events.[51] At the NAIA's 1964 annual meeting, an exasperated Duer vented his growing frustration with the infidelity of member schools: "If you cannot see that dual memberships are going to weaken our organization and take away from you what you have sacrificed to gain, you are not reasoning and facing the facts. You are asking organizations to 'bid' for your participation and support. . . . If you are thinking this way without much loyalty to any organization or cause, I would not place much value on your membership or leadership."[52]

Nothing so starkly demonstrated the divergent directions of the NAIA and the NCAA like the growing financial disparity between the two organizations. To combat what many in the NAIA saw as the NCAA's efforts to slay the former organization, the NAIA linked itself with the AAU in its decades-long fight with the NCAA over the control of amateur sports. To preserve its cherished Olympic status and to demonstrate that it was a significant voice in college sports, the NAIA also attempted to play a greater role in US Olympic affairs. Joining these organizations, however, also increased their costs, as did their travel and lobbying efforts. In attempting to combat the NCAA's challenge by deepening its involvement in athletic organization, the NAIA took on financial obligations it increasingly struggled to meet. Three times in the 1960s, the NAIA finished in the red and even in profitable years imposed a spartan economy on its members and staff. One example of that was the NAIA policy that prohibited reimbursement of travel costs for committee meetings or other association business. Additionally, the organization's growth in numbers and number of sports offered increased their insurance premiums across the board in 1960, with football witnessing a 100 percent premium increase. Duer's legendary frugality kept the NAIA afloat, but consider that in 1960, a year the NAIA enjoyed a modest surplus, it witnessed total annual revenues of $65,000. By comparison, the NCAA's football contract with ABC television that same year brought in $6.3 million.[53]

Joseph Hutton's criticisms of liberal arts snobbery aside, the problem was not simply the NAIA's membership but its aspirations. In attempting to deflect Byers's criticisms throughout the early 1950s that the NAIA was a usurper and a threat to the NCAA, Al Duer consistently responded that the NAIA and the NCAA could coexist because the NAIA only desired to advocate for the small colleges and provide them with resources and opportunities that the NCAA did not. Even as the NCAA began the process by which it attempted to make the NAIA obsolete, Duer declared, "We have no desire to enter into open conflict with any organization."

The NAIA, according to Duer, merely emerged as a "protest of the failure of any other organization to aid in solving [the small college's] problems or to give its membership an opportunity to participate in either activities or policy making."[54] By its own definition, the NAIA did not want to be "the voice of college sports" or the defining purveyor of amateurism. It assumed that setting its expectations lower would allow it to occupy a low-key and underserved but necessary niche in the otherwise high-profile world of cut-throat college athletics. But it ceded to the NCAA the prestige necessary both to affect the moral and educational reform desired by the liberal arts colleges and to create an equally prominent standing necessary to attract new members. Thus, in one of the many paradoxes of college athletics, even though the NCAA was the purveyor of much of what the liberal arts colleges opposed, they needed the organization's prominence to combat that which it created. The NAIA's unwillingness to go to war against the NCAA left it unprepared to respond to the kinds of tactics that Byers employed against them. While the NAIA merely sought to exist on the margins of college athletics to serve the small college interests, the NCAA played for keeps in all of its dealings. As a result, the NAIA made the proverbial mistake of bringing a knife to a gunfight.

CONCLUSION

The early years of college basketball were years of intense conflict within college sports in general and the game itself. Though local, inchoate, and sometimes petty in their origins, those struggles ultimately helped create the modern NCAA that is well-financed, highly regulatory, and completely in thrall to the interests of the big-time commercialized schools. And while these conflicts maintained immense significance for the future of college athletics, they were also evocative of both systemic transformations and structural continuities affecting American culture and society during the period. The economic failure represented by the Depression, the grand crusade for freedom in the form of World War II, and the disorienting years of the early Cold War wrought tremendous changes that challenged traditional modes of elitist and paternalist dominance, elevated racial equality to a national standard, and transformed higher education. But the end of the period saw elites still largely in control of American society, little different from before.

From the 1930s through the 1950s the NCAA faced an almost unrelenting series of challenges in the form of a fractured membership along lines of reform, changing ideals on the issue of race, and external challenges in the form of economic upheaval, manpower shortages on account of the war, and scandal at almost every turn. Walter Byers was not exaggerating when he asserted that the NCAA had "progressed by disaster." And yet, by the early 1960s the NCAA had easily cleared the shoals of disaster without much reform or even accountability to the public, only to stumble into yet another point-shaving scandal in basketball in 1961 but to emerge from that one too, not much different from before. And while Byers deserves a substantial amount of credit for keeping the whole venture from foundering, the outcome has its origins in the wars of college basketball.

Since its inception the NCAA succeeded in attracting the schools that pursued big-time commercialized athletics only by avoiding actions that threatened big-time commercialized athletics. To ensure that the NCAA abided by the home rule principle, representatives from the big-time schools dominated the committee and bureaucratic structure of the NCAA to ensure that little came before the membership that threatened the big-time agenda. Actively excluded from, or ambivalent to, the power structure of the NCAA, the majority of members were increasingly appalled by the actions of the big-time programs in the mid-twentieth century. The naked ambivalence to the Carnegie Report in 1929, the presumption that commercialized sports like football and basketball should be privileged to the detriment of others during the economic crisis of the Depression, the unwillingness to fully support the war effort by diverting varsity resources to inductee physical training in the early 1940s, and the postwar academic, recruiting, and gambling scandals all demonstrated that those schools pursued college athletics for different reasons and different values. In an effort to standardize many practices in football, many within the big-time camp proposed the Sanity Code, dressed it up as "reform," and presumed that the liberal arts reformers would join them. The code's ultimate failure marked not only the deep divide within the membership over the question of reform but also a possible breaking point for many smaller schools who considered leaving the NCAA.

This was not the first time that the big-time schools attempted to serve their own interests by assuming the mantle of reform and hoping the real reformers would not notice. Supporters of the NCAA sanctioning its own basketball championship also wrapped their argument within the established reformist rhetoric of the period. Creating a tournament run by and for collegiate interests would allow the NCAA to arrest the drift of postseason basketball toward the pattern of college football bowl games. However, though its supporters called for the NCAA Basketball Tournament in the language of reform and as a privilege to its membership, its implementation only served the interests of the big-time commercialized programs. Consequently, it revealed the habit of the big-time commercialized institutions to direct the energies of the NCAA to their own needs and prerogatives but to do so in the language of amateurism. Many smaller NCAA member schools were ambivalent about the tournament, knowing they had no intention or hope of participating in it, but its creation and subsequent operation became part of their argument about the ability of the commercialized programs to bend the NCAA to their interests. Thus, in their battle with outside interests over control of basketball, the big-time schools managed to further alienate the majority of the organization's own delegates.

In what can only be described as the "miracle of television" did the NCAA manage to avoid almost certain destruction. At the same time the Sanity Code rose and fell, some big-time commercialized programs began selling off the television broadcast rights to their football games, triggering the rest of the college football world to react with alarm. In the ruthlessly naked world of supply-and-demand capitalism, many big-time schools realized that a handful of schools were going to get fabulously wealthy broadcasting their games while the rest would fall hopelessly behind in the never-ending financial arms race of big-time college football. Those below the big-time level also faced the very real prospect of significantly reduced live gate receipts as fans stayed home to watch high-profile games for free on television. Thus, a fearful membership readily turned to the NCAA not only to more effectively package and negotiate television contracts but also to forge a cartel to limit team appearances and create an artificially restricted market, thereby sharing the wealth while limiting the consequences to the membership. Some of that wealth went into enforcement, assuring the public that the NCAA now enjoyed the tools to defend amateurism against overzealous purveyors of corruption and self-interest. In selling college football to the television networks, the NCAA succeeded in convincing most Americans that the organization was, indeed, the voice of college sports.

Such an image, however, was possible only because the threat of secession and abandonment had been diverted by the Crowley reforms, the most notable of which was the creation of a separate basketball tournament for the smaller schools. The substantial concessions to the liberal arts and smaller state schools allowed Walter Byers and the big-time programs within the NCAA not only to hold together its fractious constituency but also to portray to the public a single product to be consumed by the television networks and a single vigilant organization to defend the interests of amateurism as the public desired to think of it. The creation of an empowered, financed, and regulatory NCAA came only with the assent of its noncommercialized membership, the vast majority of which had long ago given up on playing football in the public eye. That assent came only with concessions and cooptation represented by the NCAA's stratification into university and college divisions, the creation of two separate basketball tournaments, and the opening of committee access to smaller schools. And yet, amazingly, this new modern NCAA was not substantially different from its predecessor in that it continued to privilege the interests of highly competitive, commercialized athletics. Thus, division among the schools that cared more about basketball than football actually strengthened the position of the NCAA's big-time interests. As a result, in the face of overwhelming crises and criticisms, the commercialized athletics programs within the NCAA managed to have their cake and eat it too.

The NCAA's successful navigation of the changing educational and social landscape in a democratic society after World War II was not as easily matched by the liberal arts colleges, which struggled to confront those same changes. The liberal arts educational curriculum for more than a century focused on critical and classical analysis in smaller classes amid a broad aesthetic and athletic extra curriculum, largely rejecting the notion of academic preparation for a specific trade and instead teaching broad intellectual skills that would be transferable to multiple jobs. But by the early twentieth century, such expensive, handcrafted academic preparation faced increasing pressure from large state schools with not only their massive lecture halls and publicly subsidized tuition but also their curricula aimed at specific economic endeavors and an undergraduate culture that elevated a packaged extra curriculum to be consumed rather than in which to participate. As the market demanded more affordable and accessible higher education in the postwar years, an undergraduate culture wrapped around watching big-time athletics became a near universal deliverable. The backhanded validation of the liberal arts model came in the mid-twentieth century when larger schools began implementing honors programs, creating liberal arts curricula within the environment of commercialized mass education, thus allowing interested students to have both their (Friedrich) Nietzsche and their (Ray) Nitschke. The liberal arts athletic reform measures were as much an effort to stanch the encroachment of the large state schools on their enrollment as it was an ideological opposition to the consequences of commercialized athletics.

While the episode illustrates the tremendous resilience of big-time athletics in the face of crisis and organized calls for reform, it is also illustrative of larger shifts in American society during the period. The 1920s witnessed perhaps the last time when most Americans readily deferred to and accepted elitist notions of economic, social, and political control. Although democracy allowed for the participation in public life of most Americans, that participation simply validated a public agenda set by organizations, institutions, and individuals who came significantly from the ranks of the white, native-born, and Protestant majority. The oft-repeated slogan during the pro-business administrations of the period—that what was good for the Republican Party was good for America—represented that many claimed to know what was best for America, while many more simply accepted their logic. Organizations like the AAU and later the NCAA elevated a fictional notion of amateur athletics as a superior form that few Americans challenged or questioned and then used it as a vehicle to dominate nonprofessional sports in America, excluding those who did not fit their model or defer to their authority. The transparent disdain for Jews, Catholics, and immigrants seen in the comments of many college basketball leaders represented the ubiquity of such sentiments. The dominance of American society by such naked elitism soon ran up against imposing historical forces in the form of the Depression and World War II.

The collapse of the economy beginning in 1929 and the financial ruination of millions of hardworking Americans did much to challenge the notion that the few "knew best" for the many. Although the period decisively did not witness the overthrow of corporate capitalism or the two-party political system, it did witness a surge of economic, social, and political populism that challenged the authority of established elites. These populists wrapped themselves in antielitist tropes of democracy, fairness, and access to criticize a system rigged against the everyman. Political and social critics like Louisiana senator Huey P. Long, the Detroit radio priest Father Charles Coughlin, and civic activist and administrator Francis Townsend all created national followings during the 1930s by criticizing how elites had manipulated the system to their advantage, ignored the exploitations of the masses, excluded them from avenues of dialogue and change, and generally disdained the honest, if not common, strivings of many Americans. In this regard, Emil Liston too wrapped himself in the populist rhetoric of the period, arguing first that the AAU Tournament and then later the NCAA Tournament were undemocratic and exclusive by unfairly shutting out most colleges from the egalitarian and meritocratic world of competitive athletics.

Though Liston came by his Depression-era populism honestly, he was uniquely situated for his message to enjoy great resonance with his target demographic. Located on the Plains and on the periphery of the Dust Bowl, Liston spoke to a population made famous by John Steinbeck's *Grapes of Wrath*, who were wracked by agricultural disaster and felt they had been abandoned by America. The small colleges of the Plains states and the arid West who took in the sons of the Dust Bowl felt a strong need to prove their worth and recover their self-respect. Yet when institutions like the NCAA not only refused such schools entry into their tournament but then also derided them as irrelevant, it further elevated Liston as the voice of the region's athletic downtrodden and dismissed. If Liston was not college basketball's version of Tom Joad, he was close.

White populists like Liston represented one challenge to the presumed cultural authority of America's sporting elites; the criticisms and strivings of black Americans represented yet another. Imbued by wartime rhetoric that elevated the United States as the defenders of freedom against fascist tyranny and racism, black Americans began challenging long-standing discriminatory laws and customs that stood outside the American creed and the international image crafted by the United States. Opposition to segregation in the military, voter registration campaigns, and threats of direct action in the 1940s demonstrated an end to black Americans' willingness to quietly endure a second-class existence. As in society at large, the sporting elites in the NCAA at first dismissed, disdained, and derided these populist and racial challenges to their cultural monopoly. The extent to which critics like Phog Allen and Harold Olsen attempted to undermine and isolate Liston through their media and public influences, and the way Tug Wilson responded to requests for racial equality by dissembling and simply putting off the entreaties of race men like Mack Greene and John McLendon, demonstrated that elites were not yet comfortable with or perhaps even aware of the larger changes taking place in American society.

These populist and racial critics eventually forced upon the NAIA and the NCAA a responsiveness borne from those organizations' own aspirations and rhetoric. Both athletic sanctioning bodies presumed a level of authority and legitimacy with the public and other organizations, and their fumbling acquiescence to change marked an emerging acknowledgment that no longer could such institutions simply dismiss external challenges. When the NAIA's policy of racial exclusion came to light, it was the threat of losing their automatic bid into the Olympic qualifying process that decisively forced change upon the organization. It could have easily continued to exclude black players and still fill a tournament field, particularly with its Southern members, but the NAIA's desires to achieve a level of public legitimacy by gaining entry to the Olympic tournament forced them to choose between old prejudices and future aspirations. And while the housing issue showed that the NAIB and Kansas City still had much to address before exhibiting the fullest forms of equality, Al Duer embraced the possibility of positioning the NAIA along lines of racial and social equality as he quickly grasped that the NAIA had stolen a march on the NCAA.

The NCAA too found itself caught during the period between its own rhetoric and practice. In its confrontations with the AAU and the NAIA, the NCAA insisted that it alone was the legitimate expression of amateur status—"*the* voice of college sports," according to one NCAA partisan. Walter Byers's almost childish rants about the NAIA's use of the word "national" as an infringement of NCAA prerogative was one expression of that. But as institutions like the NCAA claimed to be "national," the meaning and responsibility of the term was transformed in the postwar years. As American ideals shifted, organizations that claimed to speak with one voice for a broad constituency increasingly needed to ensure that its values were in line with those changing American ideals or be out of step with popular opinion and forfeit their nationalist legitimacy. Thus, the NCAA began moderate efforts to distance itself from claims of racial discrimination by more carefully vetting its convention sites and eliciting guarantees of equal accommodations at its championship locales.

Here was the promise of mid-century American democratic rhetoric. The innate fairness and justice of black demands for equality nested themselves in the self-interests of institutions, giving tangible meaning to the argument that everyone benefited from freedom's expansion. As the orbits in which these organizations operated became more prominent by their own desires and actions, the more they opened themselves to criticism and condemnation when their conduct conflicted with popular expectations. Quite simply, racist policies and practices were becoming bad for business and public perception.

The NCAA's "national" aspirations also forced the organization to belatedly acknowledge the majority of its membership in the form of the small colleges. If the NCAA intended to serve as "the voice of college sports," particularly to protect the interests of commercialized athletics, it needed most colleges as members. The threat of secession by the liberal arts colleges and the medium-time schools threatened to undermine the authority of the NCAA and its dominant faction, the schools that pursued big-time commercialized athletics. But the creation of prominent "national" events demonstrated the difficulty of serving only the interests of the big-time minority. In its origins the NCAA Basketball Tournament was inherently exclusive: it not only rejected nonmembers, but its selection committee also kept out those whom it deemed unworthy. The NCAA then did everything possible to make its tournament attractive and desirable—to achieve, in other words, the legitimacy it sought as the sole presence of college athletics. But having elevated its legitimacy, the organization had the temerity to be put off when the rest of its membership wanted to participate.

The response of the NCAA's powerbrokers to smaller school demands for greater organizational and competitive equity and HBC refusals to accept explicitly discriminatory practices was at first dismissive and clumsy. Yet when faced with the possible dissolution or delegitimization of the NCAA, the commercialized programs shrewdly made concessions that quelled the insurgency yet left the interests of the big-time commercialized programs still at the center of the NCAA's agenda. Having successfully managed to co-opt, redirect, and simply deflect the reformist pressures of the late 1950s while providing the illusion of reform and inclusion, NCAA elites managed the trick again in the early 1970s when faced with the so-called Robin Hood reforms that demanded greater revenue sharing in college football and in the early 1980s with the arrival of women's athletics. Most recently in 2015, the so-called autonomy plan once again demonstrated the NCAA's privileged member demographic by essentially allowing the five most commercialized conferences to set their own rules within the organization. In each instance the association faced tremendous external and internal pressures and the possibility of revolutionary change yet managed to emerge little different from before with the interests of commercialized athletics as the organization's primary concern. It is in this fashion that the NCAA operates as a trade association designed to protect its product in the marketplace.

The postwar years in American history are traditionally seen as ones of immense transformation and democratic expansion. The civil rights movement, widespread opposition to the war in Vietnam, growing concerns over the Cold War, second-wave feminism, and the Twenty-Sixth

Amendment all suggested revolutionary challenges to the status quo of American politics, society, and economy. However, institutions, organizations, and individuals quickly recovered and managed to create systems that addressed demands for greater access but effectively left elites in control of society as before. As a result, by the beginning of the twenty-first century, the corporate and political power structure of the United States remains largely unchanged, still in the hands of a predominantly white, male, upper-class elite. The story of NCAA elites holding off the insurgencies of the postwar years is the story of America during the period—not one of revolutionary and democratic change but one of continuity and elite persistence. The question, then, is not really how did the NCAA manage to survive but, rather, how did its critics ever hope to succeed?

NOTES

NCAA	National Collegiate Athletics Association
NHC	City College of New York, Nat Holman Collection
NWDS	Northwestern University, Walter Dill Scott Papers
OPE/I12	Oberlin College, Physical Education Records I12
OPE/I3	Oberlin College, Physical Education Records I3
OPE/I4	Oberlin College, Physical Education Records I4
OPE/V2	Oberlin College, Physical Education Records V2
OPE/V3	Oberlin College, Physical Education Records V3
OWFM	Ohio Wesleyan University, Faculty Meeting Minutes
OWS	Oberlin College, William Stevenson Papers
POP	University of Pennsylvania, Records of the Office of the President
RDA	Ohio State University, Records of the Director of Athletics
SMUFS	Southern Methodist University, Faculty Staff Vertical Files
TMP	Emory University, Thomas McDonough Papers
TPE/A	Tufts University, Department of Physical Education/ Athletics Records
TVF	Tufts University, Vertical Files

INTRODUCTION

1. See, for example, Brian Ingrassia, *The Rise of Gridiron University: Higher Education's Uneasy Alliance with Big-Time Football* (Lawrence: University of Kansas Press, 2012), showing this impulse beginning with the dawn of the twentieth century and the Progressive movement.

2. See, for example, John Rozier, *Out of the Grandstand and Onto the Playing Field: A History of the Division of Health, Physical Education, Recreation, and Athletics at Emory University, 1880–1983* (Atlanta: Emory University Press, 1983), as an expression of competitive participatory athletics.

3. The scholarly literature on reform and the early NCAA is extensive, but the definitive treatments are Ronald A. Smith, *Sports and Freedom, The Rise of Big-Time College Athletics* (New York: Oxford University Press, 1988); Ronald A. Smith, *Pay for Play: A History of Big-Time College Athletic Reform* (Champaign: University of Illinois Press, 2011); John Sayle Watterson, *College Football: History, Spectacle, Controversy* (Baltimore: Johns Hopkins University Press, 2000); and John R. Thelin, *Games Colleges Play: Scandal and Reform in Intercollegiate Athletics* (Baltimore: Johns Hopkins University Press, 1996).

4. The authoritative works on reform and college football's place in the academy are R. Smith, *Sports and Freedom* and *Pay for Play*; Watterson, *College Football*; Thelin, *Games Colleges Play*; and Ingrassia, *Rise of Gridiron University*, which authoritatively demonstrates that many big-time schools willingly embraced big-time sports as opposed to merely being unable to restrain them. For a more cynical examination, see Murray Sperber, *Onward to Victory: The Crises That Shaped College Sports* (New York: Henry Holt, 1998).

5. Neil D. Isaacs, *All the Moves: A History of College Basketball* (Philadelphia: J. B. Lippincott, 1975); Terry Frei, *March 1939: Before the Madness—The Story of the First NCAA Basketball Champions* (Lanham, MD: Taylor Trade Publishing, 2014); J. Samuel Walker and Randy Roberts, *The Road to Madness: How the 1973-1974 Season Transformed College* Basketball (Chapel Hill: University of North Carolina Press, 2016); Seth Davis, *When March Went Mad: The Game That Transformed Basketball* (New York: St. Martin's Griffin, 2010); and Peter C. Bjarkman, *Hoopla: A History of College Basketball* (Indianapolis: Masters Press, 1996).

6. Chad Carlson, *Making March Madness: The Early Years of the NCAA, NIT, and College Basketball Championships* (Fayetteville: University of Arkansas Press, 2017); Milton Katz, *Breaking Through: John B. McLendon, Basketball and Civil Rights Pioneer* (Fayetteville: University of Arkansas Press, 2010); Aram Goudzousian, *Bill Russell and the Basketball Revolution* (Berkeley: University of California Press, 2010); Jeffrey Lane, *Under the Boards: The Cultural Revolution in Basketball* (Lincoln: University of Nebraska Press, 2007).

CHAPTER 1. BASKETBALL'S CIVIL WAR

1. Scott Morrow Johnson, *Phog: The Most Influential Man in Basketball* (Lincoln: University of Nebraska Press, 2016), 105–106; "Basketball Rule Reduces Dribble," *New York Times*, April 10, 1927, 52; "See Cleaner Court Game Next Season," *Middletown Daily Herald*, April 15, 1927, 16.

2. Johnson, *Phog*, 105–106; "Basketball Rule Reduces Dribble," *New York Times*, April 10, 1927, 52; "Valley Coaches to Protest New Basketball Rules, *Chicago Tribune*, April 25, 1927, 27; PCC Nixes New Dribble Rule," *Stanford Daily*, April 29, 1927, 2; "Executive Board May Rescind Dribble Rule as Protests Grow," *New York Times*, May 1, 1927, 55; "Basketball Rules Committee Rescinds One-Bound Dribble," *New York Times*, May 19, 1927, 23.

3. On early college football and its excesses, see Ronald A. Smith, *Sports and Freedom: The Rise of Big-Time College Athletics* (New York: Oxford University Press, 1988); John Sayle Watterson, *College Football: History, Spectacle, Controversy* (Baltimore: Johns Hopkins University Press, 2000); and Mark F. Bernstein, *Football: The Ivy League Origins of an American Obsession* (Philadelphia: University of Pennsylvania Press, 2001).

4. The first McCracken Conference included Army, Columbia, Fordham, Haverford, New York University, Rochester, Rutgers, Swarthmore, Syracuse, Union College, and Wesleyan University (CT). While the majority of schools were not represented by men of great standing within the game, Army was represented by the decidedly influential, and future president of the NCAA, Palmer Pierce. Watterson, *College Football*, 74.

5. On the crisis of 1905 and the creation of the NCAA, see R. Smith, *Sports and Freedom*, 191–208; Watterson, *College Football*, 64–119; Ronald A. Smith, *Pay for*

Play: A History of Big-Time College Athletic Reform (Champaign: University of Illinois Press, 2011), 42–59.

6. W. Burlette Carter, "The Age of Innocence: The First 25 Years of the National Collegiate Athletic Association, 1906 to 1931," *Vanderbilt Journal of Entertainment and Technology Law*, (Spring 2006): 211–91.

7. R. Smith, *Pay for Play*, 52–54.

8. Carter, "Age of Innocence"; and Winifred R. Tilden, "Shall We Have Universal Physical Education?" *Iowa Homemaker* 1 (1921): 7–8.

9. R. Smith, *Pay for Play*, 61–62.

10. Jack Falla's appendixes demonstrate the preponderance of certain schools and certain individuals on these committees, which is backed up by the NCAA's annual yearbooks and meeting minutes in the 1940s and 1950s when the personnel from the small colleges began to complain about the committee dominance of these individuals. Jack Falla, *NCAA: The Voice of College Sports—A Diamond Anniversary History, 1906–1981* (Mission, KS: National Collegiate Athletic Association, 1981).

11. On football's growth in the 1920s, see Raymond Schmidt, *Shaping College Football: The Transformation of an American Sport, 1919–1930* (Syracuse, NY: Syracuse University Press, 2007); and Watterson, *College Football*, 143–76. On the Carnegie Report, see John R. Thelin, *Games College Play: Scandal and Reform in Intercollegiate Athletics* (Baltimore: Johns Hopkins University Press, 1994), 13–37; and R. Smith, *Pay for Play*, 59–70.

12. Murray Sperber, *Onward to Victory: The Crises That Shaped College Sports* (New York: Henry Holt, 1998), 172, discusses early opposition to bowl games. See Robert M. Ours, *Bowl Games: College Football's Greatest Tradition* (New York: Westholme Publishing, 2004) for the financial arrangements and shenanigans of the early games.

13. Tony Ladd and James Mathisen, *Muscular Christianity: Evangelical Protestants and the Development of American Sport* (Ada, MI: Baker Publishing, 1999); and Clifford Putney, *Muscular Christianity: Manhood and Sports in Protestant America, 1880–1920* (Cambridge, MA: Harvard University Press, 2003).

14. Chad Carlson, *Making March Madness: The Early Years of the NCAA, NIT, and College Basketball Championships* (Fayetteville: University of Arkansas Press, 2017), 3.

15. On the AAU's early history and their half-century dispute with the NCAA, see Arnold W. Flath, *A History of Relations between the National Collegiate Athletic Association and the Amateur Athletic Union of the United States, 1905–1963* (Champaign, IL: Stipes Publishing, 1964). For more context and a more recent examination of the NCAA's struggle with the AAU, see Joseph M. Turrini, *The End of Amateurism in American Track and Field* (Chicago: University of Illinois Press, 2010), particularly chapter 1. On the struggle of early basketball, see Albert G. Applin II, "From Muscular Christianity to the Market Place: The History of Men's and Boys' Basketball in the United States, 1891–1957," PhD diss., Univer-

sity of Massachusetts, 1982; and Marc Thomas Horger, "Play by the Rules: The Creation of Basketball and the Progressive Era, 1891–1917," PhD diss., Ohio State University, 2001.

16. On the inability to replicate British amateurism in the United States, see Donald J. Mrozek, *Sport and American Mentality, 1880–1910* (Knoxville: University of Tennessee Press, 1983).

17. Flath, *History of Relations*, 121–23; see particularly the dispute over USC's Charles Paddock in 1923. On Didrikson, see Susan E. Cayleff, *Babe: The Life and Legend of Babe Didrikson Zaharias* (Champaign: University of Illinois Press, 1996), 50–52.

18. Applin, "Muscular Christianity," 161–91; Blair Kerchoff, *Phog Allen: The Father of Basketball Coaching* (Indianapolis: Masters Press, 1996), 96–97; James E. Krause, *Guardians of the Game: A Legacy of Leadership* (Overland Park, KS: Ascend Books, 2008), 10–13, 29–35. Though Allen was joined initially by Nat Holman, head coach of the City College of New York, in his call for an independent college rules committee, as soon became apparent, Holman eventually emerged as a Judas figure in the eyes of the college coaches.

19. Kerchoff, *Phog Allen*, 96–97; and Krause, *Guardians of the Game*, 10–13, 29–35.

20. "A Change of Emphasis Is Needed," NABC Bulletin no. 1, 1936–1937, "National Basketball Coaches, 1934–1937," box 12, RDA. The NABC began publishing the bulletin in 1933 as a way to maintain contact with its membership between its annual meetings and as a way to standardize coaching practices and ensure uniform implementation of the rules. See Thomas Robert Somerville, "A History of the National Association of Basketball Coaches of the United States," PhD diss., Ohio State University, 1980, 72–73.

21. "Intersectional Contests Point to Basketball Improvement," NABC Bulletin no. 3, 1936–1937, "National Basketball Coaches, 1934–1937," box 12, RDA.

22. Bob Kuska, *Hot Potato: How Washington and New York Gave Birth to Black Basketball and Changed America's Game Forever* (Charlottesville: University of Virginia Press, 2006), 81, 86–88.

23. Letter from "June" [Hamilton] to [Lynn] "Saint" [John], March 30, 1933, "Correspondence, Salmon, H. H.," box 4, RDA.

24. Letter from Harold Swaffield to Floyd Rowe, May 8, 1935, "Basketball Rules Committee Correspondence, 1935–40 (2 of 3)," box 3, RDA.

25. Letter from C. W. Whitten to L. W. St. John, May 15, 1935, "Basketball Rules Committee Correspondence, 1935–40 (2 of 3)," box 3, RDA.

26. Letter from Avery Brundage to L. W. St. John, December 27, 1934, "Basketball Rules Committee Reorganization, 1933–40," box 4, RDA.

27. Letter from L. W. St. John to J. H. Crocker, November 25, 1935, "Basketball Rules Committee Correspondence, 1935–40 (1 of 3)," box 3, and "Is Basketball Going Backwards?," NABC Bulletin no. 1, 1936–1937, "National Basketball Coaches, 1934–1937," box 12, both found in RDA.

28. Letter from John Griffith to L. W. St. John, April 17, 1935, "Basketball Rules Committee Correspondence, 1935–40 (2 of 3)," box 3, RDA.

29. Letter from L. W. St. John to H. H. Salmon, December 20, 1935, "Basketball Rules Committee Correspondence, 1935–40 (1 of 3)," box 3, RDA.

30. Letter from John Brown to L. W. St. John, April 8, 1936, and letter from L. W. St. John to H. V. Porter, April 13, 1936; both found in "Basketball Rules Committee Correspondence, 1935–40 (1 of 3)," box 3, RDA. On Smith's salary, see letter from L. W. St. John to Floyd Rowe, April 28, 1936, "Basketball Rules Committee: Reorganization, 1929–1940," box 4, RDA.

31. Neil D. Isaacs, *All the Moves: A History of College Basketball* (Philadelphia, J. B. Lippincott, 1975), 22; and Carlson, *Making March Madness*, 11–12.

32. Report on Study of Special Interpretation of the Rules, "Basketball Rules Committee Correspondence, 1935–40 (1 of 3)," box 3, RDA.

33. Ibid.

34. Isaacs, *All the Moves*, 28.

35. "Is Basketball Going Backwards?," NABC Bulletin no. 1, 1936–1937, "National Basketball Coaches, 1934–1937," box 12, RDA. Phog Allen too saw duplicity in Holman's actions and motivations regarding the rules. See Forrest C. Allen to L. W. St. John, February 4, 1937, "Basketball Rules Committee Correspondence, 1937–40," box 4, RDA.

36. Letter from L. W. St. John to Walter Meanwell, January 20, 1937, "Basketball Rules Committee Correspondence, 1931–1940," box 4, RDA.

37. Letter from L. W. St. John to Hugo Goldsmith, November 20, 1936, "Basketball Rules Committee Reorganization, 1933–40 (3 of 3)," box 4, RDA.

38. Rather amazingly, Holman lacks a full-length biography. The thumbnail sketch here is drawn from "Nat Holman, Famous Athletic Star and Coach, Will Be Physical Director in New Building," *YMHA Bulletin*, May 23, 1930, NHC; "Nat Holman Is Dead at 98; Led CCNY Champions," *New York Times*, February 13, 1995, B7. See also Stanley Cohen, *The Game They Played* (New York: Da Capo Press, 1986).

39. Brad Austin, *Democratic Sports: Men's and Women's College Athletics during the Great Depression* (Fayetteville: University of Arkansas Press, 2015), 50–51.

40. Tom Graham and Rachel Cody Graham, *Getting Open: The Unknown Story of Bill Garrett and the Integration of College Basketball* (New York: Atria Books, 2006), 105.

41. "Is Basketball Going Backwards?," NABC Bulletin no. 1, 1936–1937; "National Basketball Coaches, 1934–1937," box 12, RDA.

42. Forrest C. Allen to L. W. St. John, February 4, 1937, "Basketball Rules Committee Correspondence, 1937–40," box 4, RDA.

43. The Eastern Intercollegiate Basketball League (EIBL) began play in 1901 and was the forerunner to the modern-day Ivy League, which considers its basketball competition a direct continuation of the EIBL.

44. "Trans-Continental Trip Emphasizes Need for Uniform Interpretations" and "The Other Side of the Screen"; both found in NABC Bulletin no. 3, 1936–1937; "National Basketball Coaches, 1934–1937," box 12, RDA.

45. "Basketball," *Sport Pictorial*, January 1936, 4.

46. "Trans-Continental Trip Emphasizes Need for Uniform Interpretations," and "The Other Side of the Screen," both found in NABC Bulletin no. 3, 1936–1937, National Basketball Coaches, 1934–1937, box 12, RDA.

47. The reference to "shorter races" is found in Forrest C. Allen to L. W. St. John, February 4, 1937, "Basketball Rules Committee Correspondence, 1937–40," box 4, RDA. On Allen's advocacy of the twelve-foot goal and other innovations that he claimed protected the degradation of the game, see Johnson, *Phog*, 13–22.

48. Letter from L. W. St. John to Hugo Goldsmith, November 20, 1936, "Basketball Rules Committee Reorganization, 1933–40," box 4, RDA.

49. Letter from Forrest C. Allen to L. W. St. John, December 17, 1936, and letter from L. W. St. John to Forrest Allen, December 22, 1936; both found in "Basketball Rules Committee Reorganization, 1933–40," box 4, RDA.

50. Letter from Forrest Allen to E. S. Hickey, December 17, 1936, "Basketball Rules Committee Reorganization, 1933–40," and letter from Walter Meanwell to L. W. St. John, January 15, 1937, "Basketball Rules Committee Correspondence, 1937–40"; both found in box 4, RDA.

51. Is Basketball Going Backwards?," NABC Bulletin no. 1, 1936–1937; "National Basketball Coaches, 1934–1937," box 12, RDA.

52. Elliot Gorn, *Dillinger's Wild Ride: The Year That Made America's Public Enemy Number One* (New York: Oxford University Press, 2011); see particularly chapters 1 and 2. Alan Brinkley, *Voices of Protest: Huey Long, Father Coughlin, and the Great Depression* (New York: Vintage Press, 1983), discusses the growing prominence of demagoguery during the period. Rural anxiety of, and antipathy toward, cities did not originate with the Depression, reaching a fever pitch at least a decade earlier; see Lynn Dumenil, *The Modern Temper: American Culture and Society in the 1920s* (New York: Hill and Wang, 1995).

53. Carson Cunningham, *American Hoops: U.S. Men's Olympic Basketball from Berlin to Beijing* (Lincoln: University of Nebraska Press, 2009), 8–9 and 420n25; Kerchoff, *Phog Allen*, 109–110; Adolph H. Grundman, "A.A.U.–N.C.A.A. Politics: Forrest C. 'Phog' Allen and America's First Olympic Basketball Team," *OLYMPIKA: International Journal of Olympic Studies* 5 (1996): 111–26.

54. "The Sporting Eye," *The Cowl*, January 17, 1936, 5.

55. "The Sporting Eye," *The Cowl*, February 7, 1936, 4.

56. Adolph Grundman, *The Golden Age of Amateur Basketball: The AAU Tournament, 1921–1968* (Lincoln: University of Nebraska Press, 2004), 7, 18–19, 31–32; Kerchoff, *Phog Allen*, 97–101; Johnson, *Phog*, 120–23.

57. Grundman, *Golden Age*, 7, 18–19, 31–32.

58. Letter from Forrest Allen to W. E. Meanwell, May 5, 1936, "AAU," box 1,

FCA-BC. The entire episode is discussed in Kerchoff, *Phog Allen*, 105–113; Cunningham, *American Hoops*, 19; and Grundman, *Golden Age*, 48–53.

59. Kerchoff, *Phog Allen*, 113; Grundman, *Golden Age*, 52.

CHAPTER 2. SEARCHING FOR CHAMPIONS AND FINDING ENEMIES

1. Letter from H. G. Olsen to Forrest C. Allen, November 26, 1938, and letter from Forrest C. Allen to H. G. Olsen, November 28, 1938; both found in "NCAA Basketball Tournament 1937–39 III," box 16, FCA-BC; letter from Marshall Diebold to Forrest C. Allen, November 23, 1939, and letter from Marshall Diebold to Butch Grover, November 23, 1939; both found in "National Intercollegiate Basketball, 1939–1940," box 16, FCA-BC.

2. Roger Kahn, "Success and Ned Irish," *Sports Illustrated*, March 27, 1961, 39–46. "Ticket Sale Grows for Benefit Games," December 5, 1930, 36; "Benefit Games Set for Six Quintets," January 4, 1931, S4; "Six Quintets Play in Garden Tonight," January 19, 1931, 22; "Six Metropolitan College Fives Will Play in Garden for Benefit of the Unemployed," November 12, 1931, 33; "College Quintets Ready for Carnival," December 24, 1931, 24; "Fives Help Charity in a Triple-Header," December 18, 1932, S3; all found in *New York Times*.

3. Peter C. Bjarkman, *Hoopla: A History of College Basketball* (Indianapolis: Masters Press, 1996), 35–36; Kahn, "Success and Ned Irish." An excellent thumbnail sketch of Irish, including a critic's view of his perceived caustic personality, is Stanley Frank, "Basketball's Big Wheel," *Saturday Evening Post*, January 15, 1949, 131–34. The Olympic anecdote is found in Carson Cunningham, *American Hoops: U.S. Men's Olympic Basketball from Berlin to Beijing* (Lincoln: University of Nebraska, Press, 2009), 27.

4. "Basketball: N.Y.U. Quints Make It More Popular Than Football," *Newsweek*, January 18, 1936, 29–30.

5. "The Pride of Peoria: Its Little Known Bradley Tech Makes Basketball History," *Newsweek*, January 9, 1939, 31–32.

6. Charles Davies Employment Contracts, "Charles Davies," DVPF.

7. Bjarkman, *Hoopla*, xvi, 39.

8. Letter from E. S. Liston to J. Lyman Bingham, January 15, 1936, "Liston Correspondence," box: Early NAIA History, NAIA. See also Francis Lentz Hoover, "A History of the National Association of Intercollegiate Athletics," DPE diss., Indiana University, 1958, 29–31.

9. 1937 Basketball Tournament Report, "Men's Basketball, 1921–1957," Vertical Files, NAIA; "Star Cage Games Here," *Kansas City Star*, February 28, 1937, 4B; Hoover, "History of the NAIA," 31–34; Danny Stooksbury, *National Title: The Unlikely Tale of the NAIB Tournament* (Bradenton Beach, FL: Higher Level Publishing, 2010), 7–15.

10. "Field of 8 Teams," March 7, 1937, B2; "Sporting Comment," March 8, 1937, 10; "Sporting Comment," March 14, 1937, B1; all found in *Kansas City Star*.

11. Hoover, "History of the NAIA," 38–43; Stooksbury, *National Title*, 20–25.

12. "Sporting Comment," *Kansas City Star*, November 14, 1937, B1.

13. "Best U.S. College Quintets to Be Matched in Writers' Garden Tournament in March," *New York Times*, February 2, 1938, 25; "Field Completed in Court Tourney," *New York Times*, March 7, 1938, 22.

14. "Bushnell and Salmon to Aid in Tourney," *New York Times*, February 16, 1938, 25.

15. "Making a Bid Too Late," and "City College Slighted?"; both found in *New York Times*, March 12, 1938, 22.

16. Bjarkman, *Hoopla*, 48; "Letters to the Sports Editor," *New York Times*, February 26, 1938, 12; "On Basketball Courts," *New York Times*, February 9, 1938, 26, and February 15, 1938, 18. See also "L.I.U. Five Earned Top Ranking in U.S.," December 24, 1939, 50, and "DePaul's Quintet Will Oppose L.I.U.," March 11, 1940, 23; both found in *New York Times*. The New Jersey event is described in Chad Carlson, *Making March Madness: The Early Years of the NCAA, NIT, and College Basketball Championships* (Fayetteville: University of Arkansas Press, 2017), 31.

17. "Writer Cage Tourney Tops," *Brooklyn Daily Eagle*, March 10, 1939, 21; Terry Frei, *March 1939: Before the Madness—The Story of the First NCAA Basketball Champions* (Lanham, MD: Taylor Trade Publishing, 2014), 140.

18. "On Basketball Courts, *New York Times*, December 21, 1938, 32.

19. Letter from H. V. Porter to F. C. Allen, December 8, 1939, "National Intercollegiate Basketball, 1939–1940," box 16, FCA-BC.

20. On the early NIT-NCAA relationship, see Chad Carlson, "A Tale of Two Tournaments: The Red Cross Games and the Early NCAA-NIT Relationship," *Journal of Intercollegiate Sport* 5 (2012): 260–80.

21. Frei, *March 1939*, 36.

22. "Court Title Tourney Planned by N.C.A.A.", *New York Times*, December 15, 1938, 38. The contents of Olsen's letter are found in the minutes of the NABC's 1938 Chicago meeting, *Proceedings, Annual Convention of the NABC, April 4–5, 1938*, NCAA Men's Basketball Committee, vol. 1, NCAA. Krause suggests that the coaches' original intentions stemmed from the success of the Garden doubleheaders. James E. Krause, *Guardians of the Game: A Legacy of Leadership* (Overland Park, KS: Ascend Books, 2008), 14–15.

23. *Proceedings, Annual Convention of the NABC, April 4–5, 1938*, NCAA Men's Basketball Committee, vol. 1, NCAA.

24. The NABC hosted at its 1935 convention a series of exhibitions designed to demonstrate differing styles of play and to seek conformity on rules interpretations. The success of the 1935 exhibitions inspired the organization to try planning some kind of tournament the following year, but the plans never came to fruition; see Carlson, *Making March Madness*, 29–31. To this day the NABC holds its annual meeting in conjunction with the Final Four and ensures almost 100 percent attendance, because coaches who do not attend the annual meeting are denied their free tickets to the Final Four. Andy Katz, "Coaching Summit

All about Change," *ESPN.com.*, October 2, 2002, https://www.espn.com/mens
-college-basketball/columns/story?columnist=katz_andy&id=1637752.

25. *Proceedings, Annual Convention of the NABC, April 4–5, 1938*, and *Proceedings, The National Association of Basketball Coaches, March 26–27, 1939*; both found in NCAA Men's Basketball Committee, vol. 1, NCAA; "Court Title Tourney Planned by N.C.A.A.," *New York Times*, December 15, 1938, 38.

26. Frei, *March 1939*, 44–45.

27. "College Basketball," 8, *1939 Annual Basketball Guide*, NCAA; "Report of Tournament and Olympic Committee," *Proceedings, National Association of Basketball Coaches, March 26–27, 1939*, 9, NCAA Men's Basketball Committee, vol. 1, NCAA.

28. "Report of Tournament and Olympic Committee," *Proceedings, The National Association of Basketball Coaches, March 26–27, 1939*, 9, NCAA Men's Basketball Committee, vol. 1, NCAA. Terry Frei argues that the ability of several teams to play their way into the eight-team bracket reveals a tournament in excess of eight teams. Frei, *March 1939*, 95–100.

29. "Report of Tournament and Olympic Committee," *Proceedings, National Association of Basketball Coaches, March 26–27, 1939*, 9, NCAA Men's Basketball Committee, vol. 1, NCAA.

30. Letter from H. G. Olsen to Forrest C. Allen, February 1, 1939, "NCAA Basketball Tournament 1937/38–1938/39 III," box 16, FCA-BC.

31. Letter from H. V. Porter to F. C. Allen, December 8, 1939, "National Intercollegiate Basketball, 1939–1940," box 16, FCA-BC.

32. Letter from H. G. Olsen to Forrest C. Allen, February 1, 1939, "NCAA Basketball Tournament 1937/38–1938/39 III," box 16, FCA-BC.

33. Letter from H. G. Olsen to Saint [Lynn St. John], undated, and letter from Forrest C. Allen to H. G. Olsen, March 6, 1940; both found in "NCAA Basketball Tournament 1938–41," box 13, RDA.

34. "Court Title Tourney Planned by N.C.A.A.," *New York Times*, December 15, 1938, 38.

35. Letter from H. G. Olsen to Forrest C. Allen, February 1, 1939, "NCAA Basketball Tournament 1937/38–1938/39 III," box 16, FCA-BC.

36. Even after the NCAA expanded the tournament in 1950 to sixteen teams, it continued to privilege the largest and most prominent conferences by granting automatic entrance to the champions of the ten most notable conferences, which even one of the tournament's supporters felt "would accentuate the major and minor classifications." See letter from Walter Byers to Harold Olsen, July 10, 1950, "NCAA Committees 1950–51," box 4, FCA-AL.

37. Smith Barrier, *Tobacco Road: Basketball in North Carolina* (New York: Leisure Press, 1983), 70, 47, 39; Bjarkman, *Hoopla*, 67.

38. Letter from Phillip O. Badger to Harold Olsen, February 8, "NCAA Basketball Tournament 1938–41," box 13, RDA.

39. Letter from Harold Olsen to Phillip O. Badger, February 26, 1940, "NCAA Basketball Tournament 1938–41," box 13, RDA.

40. Letter from H. G. Olsen to Forrest C. Allen, February 1, 1939, and Bulletin 3 [undated] from H. G. Olsen; both found in "NCAA Basketball Tournament 1937/38–1938/39 III," box 16, FCA-BC.

41. Letter from Forrest Allen to H. G. Olsen, March 6, 1940, "NCAA Basketball Tournament 1938–1941," box 13, RDA.

42. "Three National Cage Champs to be Named in Tourneys Soon," *Kansas City Star*, February 1, 1939, B1.

43. "College Basketball," 8, *1939 Annual Basketball Guide*, NCAA.

44. "Report of Tournament and Olympic Committee," *Proceedings, The National Association of Basketball Coaches, March 26–27, 1939*, 9, NCAA Men's Basketball Committee, vol. 1, NCAA.

45. Letter from L. W. St. John to J. W. St. Clair, January 21, 1938, folder 31, box 3, RDA.

46. "1939 Report of the NCAA Basketball Tournament Committee," *1939 NCAA Annual Proceedings*, NCAA.

47. Letter from Phillip O. Badger to H. G. Olsen, December 21, 1938, "NCAA Basketball Tournament 1938–1941," box 13, RDA.

48. "College Tourney a Go, Say Writers," January 21, 1939, *New York Times*, 32; "Met. Basketball Writers Vote Dates for 2d College Tourney," *New York Herald Tribune*, January 25, 1939, B1.

49. "Met. Basketball Writers Vote Dates for 2d College Tourney," *New York Herald Tribune*, January 25, 1939, B1; "On Basketball Courts," *New York Times*, December 21, 1938, 32; "College Invitation Tournament to Be Held in March by Basketball Writers, *New York Times*, January 25, 1939, 29.

50. "Met. Basketball Writers Vote Dates for 2d College Tourney," *New York Herald Tribune*, January 25, 1939, B1.

51. Ibid.

52. "College Invitation Tournament to Be Held in March by Basketball Writers," *New York Times*, January 25, 1939, 29.

53. Letter from Phillip Badger to W. B. Owens, January 27, 1939, and letter from Phillip Badger to Everett Morris, January 27, 1939; both found in "NCAA Basketball Tournament 1938–41," box 13, RDA.

54. Letter from L. W. St. John to Phillip O. Badger, April 24, 1940, folder 31, box 3, RDA.

55. Letter from Phillip Badger to Ned Irish, March 13, 1939, "NCAA Basketball Tournament 1938–41," box 13, RDA.

56. Ibid.

57. "On Basketball Courts," *New York Times*, February 9, 1940, 26; "Close Contests Loom at Garden in National Basketball Tourney," *New York Times*, March 10, 1940, 81; "Met. Basketball Writers Vote Dates for 2d College Tourney," *New*

York Herald Tribune, January 25, 1939, B1. On Irish's continuing loyalty to and prominence with the NIT, see Carlson, "Tale of Two Tournaments."

58. Letter from Philip O. Badger to H. G. Olsen, February 23, 1940, "NCAA Basketball Tournament 1938–41," box 13, RDA. Equally confusing was Everett Morris's public offer in 1939, from the dais of the writers' annual awards banquet, to turn over the management and profits of the NIT to the New York–area schools if they agreed to form a proposed Metropolitan Intercollegiate Conference. It is unclear what became of the proposal, but the conference never came to fruition. Frei, *March 1939,* 165.

59. Carlson, "Tale of Two Tournaments," 151–201. In contrast, Peter Bjarkman sees the arrangement between the two tournaments in far less hostile terms, describing the two as mutual beneficiaries of college basketball's growth during the period, "cooperatively sharing an ever-expanding wealth," Bjarkman, *Hoopla,* 58.

60. "Tense Fray Looms on Garden Court," March 22, 1947, 18; "Holy Cross Downs City College Five," March 23, 1947, S1; and "Crusaders Annex 23rd in a Row," March 26, 1947, 33; all found in *New York Times.* "Basketball: Study Hour?" *Newsweek,* April 7, 1947, 77–78.

61. Letter from H. G. Olsen to Forrest C. Allen, November 18, 1938, "NCAA Basketball Tournament 1937/38–1938/39 III," box 16, FCA-BC.

62. "Basketball Rebounds," *New York Tribune,* December 13, 1938, B1.

63. Letter from H. G. Olsen to Forrest C. Allen, November 26, 1938, "NCAA Basketball Tournament 1937/38–1938/39 III," box 16, FCA-BC.

64. Ibid.

65. Letter from Forrest C. Allen to H. G. Olsen, November 28, 1938, "NCAA Basketball Tournament 1937/38–1938/39 III," box 16, FCA-BC.

66. Letter from John L. Griffith to W. B. Owens, March 29, 1939, "NCAA Basketball Tournament, 1933–41," box 13, RDA. Griffith struggled throughout his career to reconcile his ideological desire to see mass participation with his personal views on varsity competition. Inevitably, the latter won out over the former, and he was a consistent supporter of bending the institutional will of both the Big Ten and the NCAA toward big-time commercialized athletics. See Matthew Lindaman, *Fit for America: Major John L. Griffith and the Quest for Athletics and Fitness* (New York: Syracuse University Press, 2018).

67. On Allen's early career at Baker, see Kerchoff, *Phog Allen,* 26; on Liston's assumptions about their relationship, see Stooksbury, *National Title,* 62; on the dedication of the new Baker gym, see NABC Bulletin 2, 1936–1937, "National Basketball Coaches, 1934–1937," box 12, RDA.

68. Letter from Forrest C. Allen to H. G. Olsen, November 16, 1938, "NCAA Basketball Tournament 1937/38–1938/39 III," box 16, FCA-BC.

69. Letter from Forrest C. Allen to E. J. Hickox, February 12, 1940, "National Intercollegiate Basketball, 1939–1940," box 16, FCA-BC. Allen's enmity toward Liston only increased in 1945 when Liston took issue with Allen's concerns for the threat of gambling in college basketball. Liston also took issue with Allen's

"deplorable lack of faith in the American youth and meager confidence in the integrity of coaches." The early 1950s revealed that Liston's confidence in either was woefully misplaced. Kerchoff, *Phog Allen*, 144.

70. "Basketball Rebounds," *New York Herald-Tribune*, December 14, 1938, B2.

71. "NCAA Basketball Tournament 1940, Bulletin 2," February 23, 1940, "NCAA Basketball Tournament, 1933–41," box 13, RDA.

72. Letter from Marshall Diebold to Forrest C. Allen, November 23, 1939, and letter from Marshall Diebold to Butch Grover, November 23, 1939; both found in "National Intercollegiate Basketball, 1939–1940," box 16, FCA-BC.

73. Letter from Marshall Diebold to Forest C. Allen, November 23, 1939, "National Intercollegiate Basketball, 1939–1940," box 16, FCA-BC.

74. Letter from John W. Bunn to William C. Owens, December 12, 1939, "National Intercollegiate Basketball, 1939–1940," box 16, FCA-BC.

75. Letter from H. G. Olsen to Forrest C. Allen, November 26, 1938, "NCAA Basketball Tournament, 1937/38–1938/39, III," box 16, FCA-BC.

76. Letter from H. G. Olsen to Forrest C. Allen, December 6, 1939, "NCAA Basketball Tournament, 1937/38–1938/39, III," box 16, FCA-BC.

77. Letter from Edward J. Hickox to Coach, December 12, 1939, "History of the NAIA," unnamed/unnumbered box, NAIA.

78. Letter from Forrest C. Allen to George Bowles, January 21, 2939, "NCAA Basketball Tournament, 1937/38–1938/39, III," box 16, FCA-BC.

79. Letter from Edward J. Hickox to Coach, December 12, 1939, "History of the NAIA," unnamed/unnumbered box, NAIA.

80. Letter from E. S. Liston to Edward J. Hickox, December 13, 1939, "History of the NAIA," unnamed/unnumbered box, NAIA.

81. Krause, *Guardians of the Game*, 16–21; Kerchoff, *Phog Allen*, 122–29.

82. Letter from Forrest C. Allen to John Bunn, April 25, 1940, "George Edwards–NCAA, 1941–1942," box 9, FCA-BC.

83. Kerchoff, *Phog Allen*, 127.

84. Carlson, *Making March Madness*, 217.

85. Letters from A. C. Lonborg to Walter Byers, August 29, 1950, and September 7, 1950; both found in "NCAA Tournament, 1950–51," box 4, FCA-AL.

CHAPTER 3. THE CITADEL OF HOME RULE

1. 1950 Small College Group Meeting minutes, *1949 NCAA Yearbook*, 128, NCAA. Nichols appeared to miss the irony of an Oberlin faculty member as a critic of big-time football when Oberlin had once been, in the words of one writer, "king of the gridiron." See Nat Brandt, *When Oberlin Was King of the Gridiron: The Heisman Years* (Oberlin, OH: College Press, 2001).

2. See John Thelin, *A History of American Higher Education* (Baltimore: Johns Hopkins University Press, 2004), 205–259; Helen Lefkowitz Horowitz, *Campus Life: Undergraduate Cultures from the End of the Eighteenth Century to the Present* (Chicago: University of Chicago Press, 1987), 118–92; David O. Levine, *The*

American College and the Culture of Aspiration, 1915–1940 (New York: Cornell University Press, 1988), 113–35; and Marc Edward Goulden, "From Country Club to Rat Race: A Social History of College Students, 1920–1960," PhD diss., University of Wisconsin, 1995, 562–693. The notion of the liberal arts in decline, what Bruce Kimball calls "the declension narrative," predates this period and continues well into the twentieth century, and not always accurately according to Kimball. Total numbers of students going into the liberal arts colleges (depending on one's definition of such) actually *increased* during the twentieth century. What declined was the percentage of students going into liberal arts colleges relative to the growing state universities. The key here for the purposes of my argument is the sense of liberal arts advocates that the defining undergraduate experience was shifting away from the small residential liberal arts colleges and toward the larger state universities. Thus, they were perceiving, correctly, a cultural shift rather than a statistical one. See Bruce Kimball, "The Declension Narrative, the Liberal Arts College, and the University," in *The Evolution of Liberal Arts in the Global Age*, ed. Peter Marber and Daniel Araya, 15–32 (New York: Routledge, 2017).

3. "Trend toward Professionalism Is Strongly Condemned at Session of NCAA," *New York Times*, December 29, 1936, 24. Nichols's criticisms and calls for reform within the NCAA occurred while others made similar efforts outside the organization. On the activities of Frank Porter Graham at the University of North Carolina, see Richard Stone, "The Graham Plan of 1935: An Aborted Crusade to De-Emphasize College Athletics," *North Carolina Historical Review* (July 1987): 274–93. On the activities of Robert Hutchinson at the University of Chicago, see Robin Lester, *Stagg's University: The Rise, Decline, and Fall of Big-Time Football at the University of Chicago* (Urbana: University of Illinois Press, 1995), 164–86.

4. Betty Spears and Richard Swanson, *History of Sports and Physical Education in the United States* (Dubuque, IA: William C. Brown, 1988), 130–34. On neurasthenia and Victorian concerns with industrialization, see Harvey Green, *Fit for America: Health, Fitness, Sport, and American Society* (Baltimore: Johns Hopkins University Press, 1986), 136–66.

5. Spears and Swanson, *History of Sports*, 130–34, 184–85, 228–30.

6. On the concerns over the perceived political and economic weaknesses of Western governments, see Ira Katznelson, *Fear Itself: The New Deal and the Origins of Our Time* (New York: Liveright Press, 2014), 29–57. On the shift in higher education in response to these phenomena, see Christopher P. Loss, *Between Citizens and the State: The Politics of American Higher Education in the 20th Century* (Princeton, NJ: Princeton University Press, 2011), 7–71; Levine, *American College and the Culture of Aspiration*, 89–112 (quote on p. 87); and Thelin, *History of American Higher Education*, 268–69.

7. On the role of athletics as a tool of capitalism and democracy during the Depression, see Brad Austin, *Democratic Sports: Men's and Women's College Athletics during the Great Depression* (Fayetteville: University of Arkansas Press, 2015), 1–30. The Williams quote is found in Spears and Swanson, *History of Sports*, 130.

8. Curtis Whitefield Tong, "John Herbert Nichols, MD: A Life of Leadership in Physical Education and Athletics," PhD diss., Ohio State University, 1969, 118.

9. Ibid., 46–48, 64–66. Biographical material is also found in the finding aid to the John Herbert Nichols Papers, Oberlin College Archives. While at Rush, Nichols met legendary University of Chicago football coach Amos Alonzo Stagg, who had Nichols officiate Maroons scrimmages. Nichols eventually emerged as one of the top officials in the Midwest and, as such, was the head official at the University of Illinois's 1924 game against Michigan to dedicate Memorial Stadium in which Red Grange had his legendary six-touchdown performance.

10. Tong, "John Herbert Nichols," 80.

11. John Rozier, *Out of the Grandstand and Onto the Playing Field: A History of the Division of Health, Physical Education, Recreation, and Athletics at Emory University, 1880–1983* (Atlanta: Emory University Press, 1983), 13, 24, 30–36.

12. Letter from J. H. Nichols to Dr. G. W. Grant, March 13, 1940, "Athletic Director's Correspondence, 1937–1954," box 4, OPE/I3.

13. John Sayle Watterson, *College Football: History, Spectacle, Controversy* (Baltimore: Johns Hopkins University Press, 2002), 153–76, 185–86; and Melvin Henry Gruensfelder, "A History of the Origins and Development of the Southeastern Conference," MS thesis, University of Illinois, 1964, 65–67.

14. Ronald A. Smith, *Pay for Play A History of Big-Time College Athletic Reform* (Champaign: University of Illinois Press, 2011), 90–91.

15. Letter from Clarence Houston to Leonard Carmichael, December 5, 1940, folder 6, box 41, TPE/A.

16. "Obituaries," *Baltimore Sun*, September 22, 1992, 56.

17. Letter from J. H. Nichols to Edwin H. Wood, January 25, 1937, "Athletic Director's Correspondence, 1937–1954," box 5, OPE/I3.

18. "C. E. Bilheimer Retires in June," *Gettysburg College Bulletin*, April 1953, 25, and "Gettysburg's Athletic Program and Its Administration," *Gettysburg Alumni News*, December 1932, 8; both found in "Clarence Bilheimer," GVF.

19. Letter from J. H. Nichols to H. C. Willett, December 20, 1946, and letter from C. E. Bilheimer to J. H. Nichols, December 15, 1949; both found in "NCAA Small College, 1944–50," box 4, OPE/V2. *1937 NCAA Convention Proceedings*, 32nd Annual Convention, December 28–30, 1937, New Orleans, LA, NCAA; and *1938 NCAA Convention Proceedings*, 33rd Annual Convention, December 27, 1938, New York, NY, NCAA.

20. "Obituaries," *Baltimore Sun*, September 22, 1992, 56.

21. Meeting minutes of the Small College Group, 1939 *NCAA Convention Proceedings*, 34th Annual Convention, December 28–30, 1939, Los Angeles, CA 111–15, NCAA.

22. Brad Austin, "Protecting Athletics and the American War Defenses at Ohio State and across the Big Ten during the Great Depression," *Journal of Sport History* (Summer 2000): 247–70.

23. Letter from J. H. Nichols to Arch Ward, January 13, 1940, "Athletic Director's Correspondence, 1937–54," box 5, OPE/I3.

24. Letter from J. H. Nichols to G. W. Grant, March 13, 1940, "Athletic Director's Correspondence, 1937–1954," box 5, OPE/I3.

25. "The College Football Handicap," January 15, 1940, 22; "Running Back Some Long Kicks," January 28, 1940, 32; "Post Entry in the Football Free-for-all," February 5, 1940, 24; all found in *New York Times*. See also letter from J. H. Nichols to Arch Ward, January 30, 1940, and letter from J. H. Nichols to John Kieran, February 12, 1940, "Athletic Director's Correspondence, 1937–1954," box 5, OPE/I3.

26. "Post Entry in the Football Free-for-all," *New York Times*, February 5, 1940, 24.

27. Meeting minutes of the Small College Group, 1940 *NCAA Convention Proceedings*, 35th Annual Convention, December 30–31, 1940, New York, NY, NCAA.

28. Meeting minutes of the Small College Group, *1941 NCAA Convention Proceedings*, 36th Annual Convention, December 30–31, 1941, Detroit, MI, NCAA.

29. Letter from J. H. Nichols to William H. Hughes, November 8, 1940, "Athletic Director's Correspondence, 1937–1954," box 4, OPE/I3. On the physical education curriculum at Johns Hopkins, see "Obituaries," *Baltimore Sun*, September 22, 1992, 56, and "Obituary: Marshall Turner," *JHU Gazette*, April 17, 2006, 24. At Emory, see Rozier, *Out of the Grandstand*, 34. On required PE at Franklin and Marshall, see oral interview with J. Schober Barr, April 4, 1985, FMOHP.

30. Paula Welch, *History of American Physical Education and Sport* (Springfield, IL: Charles C Thomas, 1996), 176–77.

31. Meeting minutes of the Small College Group, *1945 NCAA Convention Proceedings*, 40th Annual Convention, January 12, 1945, St. Louis, MO, NCAA.

32. Ibid.

33. Letter from J. H. Nichols to William H. Hughes, November 8, 1940, "Athletic Director's Correspondence, 1937–1954," box 4, OPE/I3.

34. Meeting minutes of the Small College Group, *1945 NCAA Convention Proceedings*, 40th Annual Convention, January 12, 1945, St. Louis, MO, NCAA.

35. "NCAA Studies Ways to Aid Nation in War," *Chicago Tribune*, September 5, 1942, 19; Meeting minutes of the Small College Group, *1942 NCAA Convention Proceedings*, 37th Annual Convention, December 30, 1942, New York, NY, NCAA.

36. Letter from Phillip O. Badger to J. H. Nichols September 21, 1942, "Correspondence, 1941–1948," box 2, OPE/I3. On the navy's V-12 athletic programs, see James G. Schneider, *The Navy V-12 Program: Leadership for a Lifetime* (Boston: Houghton Mifflin, 1987), 262–70.

37. Letter from J. H. Nichols to Carl Wittke, March 10, 1942, "Dean Carl Wittke, 1938–1945," box 8, OPE/I3.

38. Blair Kerchoff, *Phog Allen: The Father of Basketball Coaches* (Dallas: Masters Press, 1996), 134.

39. Notes of discussion, June 22, 1943, with cover letter from L .K. Butler to J. H. Nichols, June 23, 1943; letter from L. K. Butler to J. H. Nichols, July 29, 1943; and letter from L. K. Butler to J. H. Nichols August 5, 1943; all found in "J. H. Nichols Correspondence, 1928–1953," box 4, OPE/I3.

40. Schneider, *Navy V-12 Program*, 262–70; Donald W. Rominger Jr., "From Playing Field to Battleground: The United States Navy V-5 Preflight Program in World War II," *Journal of Sport History* (Winter 1985): 252–64. On the ASTP, see Louis E. Keefer, *Scholars in Foxholes: The Story of the Army Specialized Training Program* (Jefferson, NC: McFarland, 1988), 131–39; Theodore W. Forbes, "The NCAA since 1942," DEd diss., Columbia University, 1955, 66–68. On the effects of the war on college football, see Kurt Edward Kemper, *College Football in American Culture in the Cold War Era* (Urbana: University of Illinois Press, 2009), 7–16.

41. Contribution of College P. E. to National Preparedness, "Contribution of College P.E. to National Preparedness, 1940–1942," box 1, OPE/I12; "NCAA Studies Ways to Aid Nation in War," *Chicago Tribune*, September 5, 1942, 19.

42. Meeting minutes of the Small College Group, *1944 NCAA Convention Proceedings*, 39th Annual Convention, January 2, 1945, New York, NY, NCAA. Beginning in 1945 the NCAA moved its annual convention from December to January, thus there was no convention held in the calendar year 1944. However, for the next several years, the NCAA identified its convention hearings by the calendar year that preceded them, because that document included all of the annual reports and other activities that occurred during the year. Thus, the official publication of the January 1945 convocation was titled the *1944 NCAA Convention Proceedings*.

43. Ibid.

44. Meeting minutes of the Small College Group, *1947 NCAA Convention Proceedings*, 41st Annual Convention, January 9, 1947, New York, NY, NCAA.

45. "College Physical Education for Peace and Defense," file 15, box 68, TMP.

46. Meeting minutes of the Small College Group, *1946 NCAA Convention Proceedings*, 40th Annual Convention, January 9, 1946, St. Louis, MO, NCAA.

47. Meeting minutes of the Small College Group, *1944 NCAA Convention Proceedings*, 39th Annual Convention, January 12, 1945, New York, NY, NCAA.

48. Letter from J. H. Nichols to C. E. Bilheimer, January 25, 1940, "Morrison, W. R., 1937–1952," box 7, OPE/I3.

49. Letter from C. Ward Macy to Clarence P. Houston, October 7, 1948, "NCAA Correspondence, 1941–1948," box 2, OPE/V3.

50. Letter from John C. Truesdale to J. H. Nichols, December 8, 1947, and letter from William R. Reed to J. H. Nichols, December 7, 1946; both found in "NCAA Correspondence, 1941–1948," box 2, OPE/V3.

51. Letter from K. L. Wilson to T. J. Davies, December 27, 1945, no file designation, box 757, CGA. For a sympathetic discussion of the motivations of the Big 10

Conference, see John Talbott Powell, "The Development and Influence of Faculty Representation in the Control of Intercollegiate Sport within the Intercollegiate Conference of Faculty Representatives from Its Inception in January 1895 to July 1963," PhD diss. University of Illinois, 1965.

52. Biographical materials found in "Houston, Clarence P.," TVF. The correspondence with Nichols is found in letter from Clarence P. Houston to J. H. Nichols, January 17, 1945, "NCAA Small Colleges, 1944–50," OPE/V3.

53. See, for example, letter from "Danny" [George Daniel] to "Nich" [J. H. Nichols], December 23, 1950, "Correspondence, 1949–50," box 3, OPE/V3. Daniel, commissioner of the Ohio Athletic Conference, urged Nichols to vote against the proposed fees, calling them "a mighty big increase."

54. Meeting minutes of the Small College Group, *1946 NCAA Convention Proceedings*, 40th Annual Convention, January 9, 1946, St. Louis, MO, NCAA.

55. Letter from J. H. Nichols to Clarence P. Houston, February 27, 1945, and Memorandum for Small College Committee from Clarence P. Houston (n.d.); both found in "Correspondence, 1941–1948," box 2, OPE/V3. Meeting minutes from the Small College Group, *1946 NCAA Convention Proceedings*, 40th Annual Convention, January 9, 1946, St. Louis, MO, NCAA.

56. Letter from J. H. Nichols to Arch Ward, January 13, 1940, "Athletic Director's Correspondence, 1937–1954," box 5, OPE/I3; letter from J. H. Nichols to E. H. Wilkins, [n.d.], "Development, 1931–1950," box 1, OPE/I4.

57. R. Smith, *Pay for Play*, 94. On the Sanity Code, see R. Smith, *Pay for Play*; 88–98, and Watterson, *College Football*, 209–214.

58. Letter from K. L. Wilson to Leonard Carmichael, June 25, 1945; letter from Clarence P. Houston to Leonard Carmichael, July 19, 1945; and letter from Leonard Carmichael to Kenneth L. Wilson; all found in "Intercollegiate Athletic Association, 1908–1946," box 41, TPE/A.

59. "Resolutions Presented to NCAA Resolutions Committee by NCAA Small College Group," [n.d.], "NCAA Small Colleges, 1944–1950," box 4, OPE/V3. On the historical limitations of presidential reform, see R. Smith, *Pay for Play*, particularly chapters 3, 8, 9, and 17.

60. Letter from G. Wilson Schaeffer to J. H. Nichols, December 11, 1947 (emphasis in original), and letter from John C. Truesdale to J. H. Nichols, December 8, 1947; both found in "NCAA Correspondence, 1941–1948," box 2, OPE/V3.

61. R. Smith, *Pay for Play*, 96.

62. Meeting minutes of the Small College Group, *1950 NCAA Convention Proceedings*, January 14, 1950, New York, NY, 128–62, NCAA.

63. Letter from Clarence P. Houston to W. H. Gill, March 1, 1948, no file designation, box 757, CGA.

64. Letter from J. H. Nichols to Walter Byers [n.d. 1948], "NCAA Correspondence, 1941–1948, box 2, OPE/V3.

65. Letter from Walter Byers to J. H. Nichols, January 23, 1948, and letter from

Walter Byers to J. H. Nichols, October 10, 1948; both found in "NCAA Correspondence, 1941–1948;" box 4, OPE/V3.

66. Letter from J. H. Nichols to Clarence P. Houston, October 2, 1948, "NCAA Correspondence, 1941–1948," box 4, OPE/V3; letter from Clarence P. Houston to J. H. Nichols, November 2, 1948, "Correspondence, 1942–1948," box 2, OPE/V3.

67. On the limits of presidential reform in intercollegiate athletics, see R. Smith, *Pay for Play*, 34–41, 164–86.

68. Nichols originally set the bar at one thousand male enrollments in the late 1930s but had revised it upward to two thousand by 1950. Meeting minutes of the Small College Group, *1950 NCAA Convention Proceedings*, January 14, 1950, New York, NY, 128–62, NCAA.

69. Meeting minutes of the Small College Group, *1947 NCAA Convention Proceedings*, January 9, 1947, New York, NY, NCAA.

70. "Address of President R. C. Hutchinson-Lafayette College," and letter from J. H. Nichols to Arthur Winters, February 3, 1950; both found in "Athletics Director Correspondence, 1937–1954," box 4, OPE/I3.

71. Letter from Malcolm E. Morrell to J. H. Nichols, December 10, 1949, "NCAA Small Colleges, 1944–1950," box 4, OPE/V3.

72. Meeting minutes of the Small College Group, 1950 NCAA Convention Proceedings, January 14th, 1950, New York, NY, NCAA.

73. Meeting minutes of the Small College Group, *1947 NCAA Convention Proceedings*, January 9, 1947, New York, NY, NCAA.

74. Letter from Clarence P. Houston to J. H. Nichols, November 1, 1950, "NCAA Nominating Committee 1950," box 3, OPE/V3.

75. Letter from Walter Byers to J. H. Nichols, February 2, 1950, "Correspondence, 1949–1950," box 2, OPE/V3.

76. Memo to president, faculty representatives, and athletic directors from K. L. Wilson, November 30, 1949, "Athletics, 1947–1959," box 4, OWS.

77. Letter from Walter Byers to J. H. Nichols, February 2, 1950, "Correspondence, 1949–1950," box 2, OPE/V3.

78. Ronald A. Smith and Jay W. Helman, "A History of Eligibility Rules among Big-Time Athletic Institutions" (unpublished paper written for the NCAA; in the author's possession). I am grateful to Ron Smith for providing me with this paper. See also R. Smith, *Pay for Play*, 196–206.

79. Meeting minutes of the Ohio Athletic Conference, March 13, 1950, and letter from George Gauthier to president of Oberlin College, September 22, 1950; both found in "Athletics, 1947–1959," box 4, OWS.

80. Letter from Al Duer to W. A. Herrington, February 6, 1950, "Executive Committee, 1949–1951," box: Early NAIA History, NAIA; letter from F. G. Welch to J. H. Nichols, October 23, 1950, "NCAA Small Colleges, 1944–50," box 4, OPE/V3.

81. Letter from F. G. Welch to J. H. Nichols, October 23, 1950, "NCAA Small Colleges, 1944–50," box 4, OPE/V3.

82. Letter from J. H. Nichols to Robert Kane, May 1, 1950, "Correspondence, 1937–54," box 4, OPE/I3.

83. Letter from E. Wilson Lyon to John H. Nichols, February 24, 1950, "Letters received by the Director of Athletics, 1937–54," box 4, OPE/I3.

84. Letter from Eli [Marsh] to J. H. Nichols, April 18, 1952, "NCAA Council 1952," box 1, OPE/V3; letter from J. H. Nichols to Alison W. Marsh, April 24, 1952, "NCAA Correspondence, 1951–52," box 2, OPE/V3.

85. Falla, *NCAA*, appendix D, 260–64, and appendix E, 265–67.

86. "The Platoon System," *Bowdoin Alumnus*, February 1953, and "Malcolm Morrell," BVF.

87. Letter from E. LeRoy Mercer to Hugh C. Willett, August 1, 1950, "PE Dept., 1950–55," box 60, POP.

88. Letter from Robert J. Kane to J. H. Nichols, April 12, 1950, "Letters received by the Director of Athletics, 1937–54," box 4, OPE/I3.

89. Letter from J. H. Nichols to Robert Kane, May 1, 1950, "Correspondence, 1937–54," box 4, OP/I3.

90. Letter from J. H. Nichols to S. W. Cram, November 13, 1950, "Correspondence, 1949–59," box 2, OPE/V3.

91. College Roundtable Meeting minutes, January 11, 1951, *1950 NCAA Yearbook*, NCAA.

92. Letter from J. H. Nichols to E. W. Lyon, February 7, 1950, "Correspondence, 1937–54," box 4, OPE/I3.

93. Letter from J. L. Morrill to J. H. Nichols, December 24, 1952, "NCAA Council 1953," box 1 OPE/V3.

94. On the point-shaving scandal in college basketball, see Charles S. Rosen, *The Scandals of '51: How the Gamblers Almost Killed College Basketball* (New York: Seven Stories Press, 1999); Stanley Cohen, *The Game They Played* (New York: Farrar, Strauss, and Giroux, 2001); and Murray Sperber, *Onward to Victory: The Crises That Shaped College Sports* (New York: Henry Holt, 1998), 285–343. On the William and Mary scandal, see Joan Gosnell, "Kickoffs and Kickbacks: The 1951 Football Scandal at William and Mary," MA thesis, College of William and Mary, 1990. On the scandal at West Point, see James Blackwell, *On Brave Old Army Team: The Scandal That Rocked a Nation, West Point 1951* (Novato, CA: Presidio Press, 1996); and Frank Deford, "Code Breakers," *Sports Illustrated* (November 13, 2000), 82–98.

95. As an example, Colorado College sent their policies around in the spring of 1951, Earlham College circulated theirs that summer, and Oberlin sent theirs in the spring of 1952. The optimism that motivated this process is discussed in letter from J. H. Nichols to Howard M. Olson, May 18, 1951, "Letters, 1951–52," box 1 OPE/I4. As an example of the internal discussions regarding gambling and the policies created to address it, see letter from Clarence P. Houston to Leonard

Carmichael, February 16, 1945, and letter from Leonard Carmichael to Clarence P. Houston, February 19, 1945; both in folder 3, box 41, TPE/A. On the internal discussions regarding aid to athletes, see "Minutes of Committee on Student Aid," October 31, 1952, unnamed folder, box 112, CAF.

96. Ronald A. Smith, *Sports and Freedom: The Rise of Big-Time College Sports* (New York: Oxford University Press, 1988), 134–46. See also R. Smith, *Pay for Play*, 25–33.

97. Small College Group Meeting minutes [undated], *1949 NCAA Yearbook*, NCAA; letter from Malcolm E. Morrell to C. E. Bilheimer, June 28, 1951, "NCAA College Committee, 1951–53," box 1, OPE/V3.

98. College Roundtable Meeting minutes, January 11, 1951, *1950 NCAA Yearbook*, NCAA.

99. Letter from J. H. Nichols to Roelif Loveland, November 27, 1951, "Athletic Director's Correspondence, 1937–1954," box 5, OPE/I3.

100. "Official Notice of the 46th Annual Convention of the NCAA," with notations from Nichols, in "Correspondence, 1951–52," box 2 OPE/V3.

101. "Annual Report of the Director of Athletics," April 10, 1952, folder 63, box 1, BAR.

102. "A Report to the Ohio Wesleyan University faculty on Intercollegiate Athletics," included in Faculty Minutes, October 13, 1952, OWFM.

103. College Meeting Minutes, January 8, 1953, *1952–53 NCAA Yearbook*, NCAA.

104. "Statement of the NCAA Council" [undated], "NCAA Committees, 1950–51," box 4, FCA-AL. Not everyone in the NCAA leadership was as dismissive as the council's official statement. NCAA president Hugh Willett from USC said in the wake of the scandals, "We are examining and re-evaluating our whole athletic program and I assure you we are doing quite a bit of soul searching to determine to what extent we ourselves may be responsible for the present situation." "NCAA Re-Examining Program, Says Willett," *Los Angeles Times*, August 5, 1951, pt. 2, p. 2.

CHAPTER 4. BARBARIANS AT THE GATE

1. On the betting scandal and aftermath at Kentucky, see Murray Sperber, *Onward to Victory: The Crises That Shaped College Sports* (New York: Henry Holt, 1998), 327–43.

2. On Barr's background, see "Barr None," *Franklin and Marshall Magazine*, Summer 2003, 9–14, and "Excerpts from Address by Prof. Sponaugle, 5/10/63," "Barr, J. Schober—Bio," FMA. Barr's comments are found in College Roundtable Meeting minutes, January 11, 1952, *1951 NCAA Yearbook*, NCAA.

3. Letter from S. W. Cram to George Daniel, November 3, 1950, "NCAA Small College 1944–50," box 3, OPE/V3; College Roundtable Meeting minutes, January 11, 1951, *1950 NCAA Yearbook*, NCAA. As to the confusion that emerged about what direction to take after the 1950 convention, see letter from R. E. Peters to

Max Farrington and J. H. Nichols, April 15, 1950, and letter from J. H. Nichols to R. E. Peters, April 25, 1950; both found in "Report of the NCAA Survey Committee," box 3, OPE/V3.

4. College Roundtable Meeting minutes, January 11, 1951, *1950 NCAA Yearbook*, NCAA.

5. Mass letter from George Springer to Dear Sir, September 19, 1951, "Letters received by the Director of Athletics, 1937–54," box 4, OPE/I3.

6. Letter from George Springer to George Daniel, October 2, 1951, "Letters received by the Director of Athletics, 1937–54," box 4, OPE/I3.

7. Hugh Hawkins, "The Making of the Liberal Arts College Identity," *Daedalus* 128, no. 1 (1999): 1–25.

8. On the NAIB's early years, see Danny Stooksbury, *National Title: The Unlikely Tale of the NAIB Tournament* (Bradenton Beach, FL: Higher Level Publishing, 2010), 1–62; Francis Lentz Hoover, "A History of the National Association of Intercollegiate Athletics," PE.D. diss., Indiana University, 1958, 46–49.

9. Letter from Angus Nicoson to E. S. Liston, October 7, 1947, and letter from E. S. Liston to Angus Nicoson, October 10, 1947; both found in "Membership Lists Prior to 1951," box: National Membership, 1941, 1957–, 1964, NAIA.

10. Stooksbury, *National Title*, 124–26; Hoover, "History of the NAIA," 62–64. The growing small college interest in the NAIB event caused the Ohio Athletic Conference, all of whom were NCAA members, to allow all of its member schools to participate in the NAIB event beginning in 1951. Meeting Minutes of the Ohio Athletic Conference, December 4, 1950, "Athletics, 1947–1959," box 4, OWS. NCAA members holding dual membership in the NAIA was not at all uncommon, as schools tended to enjoy the prestige of the former but the competitive equity of the latter. See Kurt Edward Kemper, "'Movin' on Up': College Sports and Athletic Realignment in the 1950s," paper delivered to the South Dakota Historical Society Annual History Conference, 2012, Pierre, SD (in author's possession).

11. Stooksbury, *National Title*, 136–40; Hoover, "History of the NAIA," 62–64.

12. "Emil Smith Liston," *(Baker University) News-Bulletin*, November 1949, 2.

13. Letter from W. A. Miller to A. O. Duer, November 5, 1949, "NAIB History," unnamed/unnumbered box, NAIA; see also Hoover, "History of the NAIA," 77–79.

14. "Welcome to the National Intercollegiate Basketball Championship Tournament," 1947 NAIB Program, 3, Basketball Vertical Files, NAIA.

15. Letter from Emil Liston to Al Duer, July 16, 1947, "Liston Correspondence," box: Early NAIA History 1940s, 1950s, 1960s, NAIA.

16. "Toughest of Them All," 1950 NAIB Program, 23, Basketball Vertical Files, NAIA.

17. Letter from Al Duer to W. A. Herrington, February 6, 1950, "Executive Committee, 1948–1951," box: Early NAIA History, NAIA.

18. Hoover, "History of the NAIA," 71–83; letter from S. W. Cram to J. H. Nichols, March 7, 1951, NCAA Correspondence 1951–52, box 2, OPE/V3.

19. Hoover, "History of the NAIA," 80–86. On member pressures to expand NAIB offerings, see letter from Al Duer to W. A. Herrington, February 6, 1950, "Executive Committee, 1948–1951," box: Early NAIA History, NAIA.

20. Letter from Al Duer to George Daniel, December 21, 1951, "Letters received by the Director of Athletics, 1937–54," box 4, OPE/V3.

21. "How We Got Here," 1956 NAIA Program, 7, Basketball Vertical Files, NAIA.

22. Letter from W. A. Miller to Al Duer, November 3, 1954, "Executive Committee, 1950–53," box: Early NAIA History, NAIA.

23. "How to Save College Football," in "Executive Committee, 1950–53," box: Early NAIA History, NAIA.

24. Letter from J. H. Nichols to E. W. Lyon, February 7, 1950, 1937–1954, box 4, OPE/I3.

25. "Siwash" was a common mid-century euphemism for small residential liberal arts colleges, popularized by George Fitch's successful 1910 novel *Good Old Siwash*, based on Fitch's liberal arts alma mater, Knox College.

26. "How to Save College Football," and letter from Al Duer to Gus Miller, November 22, 1954; both found in "Executive Committee, 1950–53," box: Early NAIA History, NAIA.

27. Letter from J. H. Nichols to C. E. Bilheimer, April 17, 1951, "NCAA College Committee, 1951–52," box 3, OPE/V3.

28. Letter from J. H. Nichols to Walter Byers, December 15, 1951, "Correspondence 1951–52," box 2, OPE/V3.

29. Round Table Meetings, Small College Committee Minutes, January 11, 1951, *1950 NCAA Yearbook*, NCAA.

30. Letter from John Truesdale to C. E. Bilheimer, June 29, 1951, "NCAA College Committee, 1951–53," box 1, OPE/V3.

31. Letter from J. H. Nichols to Walter Byers, October 2, 1951, "NCAA College Committee, 1951–53," box 1, OPE/V3.

32. Letter from C. E. Bilheimer to J. H. Nichols, May 22, 1951, "NCAA College Committee, 1951–52," box 3, OPE/V3.

33. Letter from Howard Olson to C. E. Bilheimer, June 30, 1951, "NCAA College Committee 1951–53," box 1, OPE/V3.

34. Letter from C. E. Bilheimer to J. H. Nichols, May 22, 1951, "NCAA College Committee 1951–52," box 3, OPE/V3.

35. Letter from Howard Olson to C. E. Bilheimer, June 30, 1951, "NCAA College Committee 1951–53," box 1, OPE/V3.

36. Letter from J. H. Nichols to Walter Byers, October 2, 1951, "NCAA College Committee 1951–53," box 1, OPE/V3.

37. Letter from J. H. Nichols to Father Wilfred Crowley, December 8, 1953, "Athletic Director's Correspondence 1937–54," box 5, OPE/I3.

38. Letter from Hugh Willett to C. E. Bilheimer, June 4, 1951, "NCAA Executive Committee Meeting 1951," box 1 OPE/V3.

39. Letter from J. H. Nichols to Hugh Willett, May 5, 1952, and letter from H. C. Willett to J. H. Nichols, May 19, 1952; both found in "NCAA Correspondence 1951–52," box 2, OPE/V3. Some schools began discussing withdrawal at the 1951 College Committee Meeting. Round Table Meetings, Small College Committee Minutes, January 11, 1951, *1950 NCAA Yearbook*, NCAA.

40. Letter from E. LeRoy Mercer to C. E. Bilheimer, June 6, 1951, and letter from Howard Olson to C. E. Bilheimer, June 30, 1951; both found in "NCAA College Committee 1951–53," box 1, OPE/V3. See also Round Table Meeting Minutes, College Meeting, January 10, 1952, *1951 NCAA Yearbook*, NCAA.

41. Letter from Malcolm Morrell to C. E. Bilheimer, June 28, 1951, "NCAA College Committee 1951–53," box 1, OPE/V3. Biographical material on Morrell can be found in "The fairness of Holmes, the devotion of Yawkey, and a skill something like Mayor Curley's," *Bowdoin Alumnus*, March 1967, 2–5, and "In Memory," *Bowdoin Alumnus* (Winter 1968/69): 38–39.

42. Round Table Meetings, College Meeting, January 8, 1953, *1952–53 NCAA Yearbook*, NCAA.

43. Round Table Meetings, College Meeting, January 10, 1952, *1951–52 NCAA Yearbook*, NCAA.

44. Biographical material on Barr can be found in "Barr, J. Schober," FMA; and Christopher Rabb, "Barr None," *Franklin and Marshall Magazine*, Summer 2003, 11–14.

45. Round Table Meetings, College Meeting, January 10, 1952, *1951–52 NCAA Yearbook*, NCAA.

46. Peter Zahorsky, "A History of Intercollegiate Athletics at South Dakota State College," MA thesis, South Dakota State College, 1959, 66–69, 71; Vernon Schoolmeester, "A History of Intercollegiate Basketball at South Dakota State University," MA thesis, South Dakota State University, 1969, 41–42; Round Table Meetings, College Meeting, January 10, 1952, *1951–52 NCAA Yearbook*, NCAA; Kemper, "'Movin' on Up.'" The concept of "medium-time" athletics is developed in Mark Bernstein, *Football: The Ivy League Origins of an American Obsession* (Philadelphia: University of Pennsylvania Press, 2001).

47. Round Table Meetings, College Meeting, January 10, 1952, *1951–52 NCAA Yearbook*, NCAA.

48. Round Table Meetings, College Meeting, January 8, 1953, *1952–53 NCAA Yearbook*, NCAA.

49. Appendix B, Minutes of the NCAA Council, January 6–7, 1953, "NCAA Council 1953," box 1, OPE/V3.

50. "Marshall S. Turner, 90, Head of Athletics at Johns Hopkins," *Baltimore Sun*, April 15, 2006, 39.

51. Letter from J. H. Nichols to Marshall Turner, February 17, 1953, "NCAA 1952–53," box 2, OPE/V3.

52. Minutes of the NCAA Executive Committee, March 22–23, 1953, *1952–53 NCAA Yearbook*, NCAA.

53. Letter from Wilfred Crowley to J. H. Nichols, March 6, 1953, with handwritten notes from Nichols attached, and letter from Marshall Turner to Nick, August 1, 1952; all found in "NCAA College Committee 1951–1953," box 1, OPE/V3. See also letter from J. H. Nichols to W. H. Crowley, March 27, 1953, "1937–54," box 4, OPE/I3.

54. Letter from J. H. Nichols to Victor O. Schmidt, February 25, 1953, and letter from J. H. Nichols to Wilfred H. Crowley, May 14, 1953; both found in "Athletic Director's Correspondence, 1937–1954," box 5, OPE/I3.

55. Special Committee on Small College–NCAA Relations, April 16–17, 1953, "NCAA College Committee, 1951–53," box 1, OPE/V3.

56. "Analysis of Survey and Report, by the NCAA Special Committee on Small College Relations," "NCAA Small College Committee Report 1953," box 1, OPE/V3.

57. "Appendix of Comments," in "Analysis of Survey and Report, by the NCAA Special Committee on Small College Relations," "NCAA Small College Committee Report 1953," box 1, OPE/V3.

58. "Report and Recommendations of Special Committee on Small College and NCAA Relations," "NCAA Small College Committee Report 1953," box 1, OPE/V3.

59. Letter from A. B. Moore to Walter Byers, December 7, 1953, "NCAA—Byers, Walter—1953," box 4, AFAR.

60. "Report and Recommendations of Special Committee on Small College and NCAA Relations," "NCAA Small College Committee Report 1953," box 1, OPE/V3.

61. "Analysis of the 'Small College' Situation," NCAA Council Minutes, February 17, 1953, *1952–53 NCAA Yearbook*, NCAA; letter from Wilfred H. Crowley to J. H. Nichols, May 19, 1953, "Small College Committee April 16–17," box 1, OPE/V3. In 1955 Byers disingenuously claimed that only ninety-five NCAA schools ever joined the NAIA. Theodore W. Forbes, "The NCAA since 1942," EdD diss., Columbia University, 1955, 190.

62. "Analysis of the 'Small College' Situation," NCAA Council Minutes, February 17, 1953, *1952–53 NCAA Yearbook*, NCAA.

63. Ibid.

64. Memorandum from Walter Byers to Faculty Representatives and Athletic Directors, November 5, 1953, "NCAA Small College Committee Report 1953," box 1, OPE/V3.

65. NCAA Council Meeting Minutes, undated, "NCAA College Committee, 1951–52, box 1, OPE/V3.

CHAPTER 5. REBELS WITH A CONSCIENCE

1. "Unusual Tournament Makes Kansas City Nation's BB Capital This Week," *Kansas City Star*, March 8, 1948, 20.

2. In the De La Salle tradition, men who take orders to join the De La Salle

Order give up their birth names and are known simply by a single name following the egalitarian "Brother."

3. "Special Meeting" agenda, March 2, 1948, and letter from Brother Thomas
to Brother Eusebius, March 2, 1948; both in "f.4 Correspondence 1944–53," box
5, MAA.

4. "Special Meeting" agenda, March 2, 1948; letter from Brother Thomas to
Brother Eusebius, March 2, 1948; letter from Brother B. Thomas to E. S. Liston,
March 2, 1948; telegram from Brother Eusebius to NAIB Kansas City, March 2,
1948; all in "f.4 Correspondence 1944–53," box 5, MAA. See also, "Manhattan's
Five Is Out of Tourney," *New York Times*, March 2, 1948, 37. It is also possible that
Manhattan officials were already aware of the NAIB policies from their former
coach John "Honey" Russell, who was then at Seton Hall University. Russell had
served on the NAIB's executive committee in 1946 when Morningside brought
a black player who then sat on the bench during Morningside's games. "Men's
Basketball, 1921–1957," Vertical files, NAIA.

5. Telegram from E. S. Liston to Brother Eusebius, March 2, 1948, and telegram
from Brother Eusebius to E. L. [*sic*] Liston, March 3, 1948; both in "f.4 Correspondence 1944–53," box 5, MAA.

6. "Higher Sportsmanship," *New York Herald-Tribune*, March 8, 1948, and
"Manhattan Five's Racial Stand Alters Negro Bias," March 31, 1948; both in "BB
1943, 1945–49," box 15, MAC. "A Partial List of Letters Congratulating . . .," and
"Administration's Decision on Non-Participation in NAIB"; both in "f.4 Cor-
respondence 1944–53," box 5, MAA. "Balk at NAIB Ruling," *Kansas City Times*,
March 5, 1948, 20. LIU was joined in their protest by New York University and
City College of New York, also with large Jewish undergraduate populations.
Adolph H. Grundman, *The Golden Age of Amateur Basketball: The AAU Tourna-
ment, 1921–1968*, (Lincoln: University of Nebraska Press, 2004), 45–46.

7. Though Barksdale was invited to integrate the NBA in 1948, his more lu-
crative outside business interests allowed him to demure. Two years later, Nat
Clifton, Chuck Cooper, and Earl Lloyd integrated the NBA. Barksdale eventually
joined them the following year, becoming the first black player to play in the
NBA All-Star game. Chad Carlson, "Basketball's Forgotten Experiment: Don
Barksdale and the Legacy of the United States Olympic Basketball Team," *Inter-
national Journal of the History of Sport* (May 2010): 1330–59; *BOUNCE: The Don
Barksdale Story*, documentary film (Oakland, CA: Doug Harris Films, 2008).

8. Charles Martin, *Benching Jim Crow: The Rise and Fall of the Color Line in
Southern College Sports, 1890–1980* (Urbana: University of Illinois Press, 2004);
the seven players are identified on pp. 68–69. For a discussion of the difficul-
ties faced by black college football players during the time, see Lane Demas,
Integrating the Gridiron: Black Civil Rights and American College Football (New
Brunswick, NJ: University of Rutgers Press, 2010).

9. Brad Austin, "Protecting Athletics and the American War Defenses at Ohio

State and across the Big Ten during the Great Depression," *Journal of Sport History* (Summer 2000): 247–70.

10. Tom Graham and Rachel Graham Cody, *Getting Open: The Unknown Story of Bill Garrett and the Integration of College Basketball* (New York: Atria Books, 2006), 116–17.

11. Mark Soderstrom, "Weeds in Linnaeus' Garden: Sciences, Segregation, Eugenics, and the Rhetoric of Racism at the University of Minnesota and the Big Ten, 1900–1945," PhD diss., University of Minnesota, 2004, 275–81. The University of Minnesota's football program also had a particularly controversial record on race coming out of the 1930s, having been Iowa State University's opponent in the 1923 game that resulted in the death of Cyclones player Jack Trice and the University of Iowa's opponent in a 1934 game that resulted in such a severe injury to the Hawkeyes' Ozzie Simmons that the schools threatened to break off relations. Jaime Schultz, *Moments of Impact: Injury, Racialized Memory, and Reconciliation in College Football* (Lincoln: University of Nebraska Press, 2015).

12. "Probes Ban on Cagers in Big 10," *Pittsburgh Courier*, February 27, 1943, 19.

13. Graham and Graham, *Getting Open*, 91–93.

14. "An Open Letter to K. L. (Tug) Wilson, Commissioner, Big Ten Conference," *Hammond (IN) Times*, March 24, 1947, 25.

15. Graham and Graham, *Getting Open*, 101–126.

16. Letter from K. L. Wilson to Walter D. Scott, January 5, 1936, folder 3, box 31, NWDS.

17. Martin, *Benching Jim Crow*, 69–70, 77.

18. "College Players Protest Paper's Ban against Negro Coach," *Pittsburgh Courier*, February 22, 1941, 17.

19. Letter from Harry Henshel to Louis Wilke, March 4, 1948, and letter from Louis Wilke to E. S. Liston, March 4, 1948; both in "History of the NAIA," unnamed/unnumbered box, NAIA. "Olympic Committeeman Suggests U.S. Trials Drop NAIB Winner," *New York Times*, March 4, 1948, 25.

20. "Olympic Committeeman Suggests U.S. Trials Drop NAIB Winner," *New York Times*, March 4, 1948, p. 25.

21. Letter from E. S. Liston to Brother B. Eusebius, March 19, 1948, "Colored Players," unnamed/unnumbered box, NAIA.

22. "The Wise Owl," *St. Joseph (MO) News Press*, March 5, 1948, 17.

23. Letter from E. S. Liston to Brother B. Eusebius, March 19, 1948, "Colored Players," unnamed/unnumbered box, NAIA; "Olympic Committeeman Suggests U.S. Trials Drop NAIB Winner," *New York Times*, March 4, 1948, 25; letter from E. S. Liston to Al Duer, February 10, 1947, "Liston Correspondence," box: Early NAIA History, NAIA; "Manhattan Accepts NAIB Bid with Tourney Dropping Negro Ban," *New York Times*, March 6, 1948, 17.

24. "Proceedings—First Annual Meeting NAIB," NAIA Records, unnamed/unnumbered box, NAIA.

25. Letter from E. S. Liston to Kenneth Mercer, March 30, 1948, "Colored Players," unnamed/unnumbered box, NAIA; "The NAIA Changed Basketball, and Kansas City," *Kansas City Star*, March 12, 2011, https://meacswacsports.blogspot.com/2011/03/naia-changed-basketball-and-kansas-city.html.

26. Letter from E. S. Liston to Al Duer, February 10, 1947, "Liston Correspondence," box: Early NAIA History, NAIA.

27. The identities and affiliations of those present were taken from "Proceedings—First Annual Meeting NAIB," NAIA Records, unnamed/unnumbered box, NAIA.

28. Email from Martha Imperato to the author, March 14, 2011, in the author's possession.

29. Email from Elise Blas to the author, March 1, 2011, in the author's possession.

30. "Legacy of Davies Can't Be Forgotten," author unknown, paper dated January 21, 1983, and newspaper clippings; all in "Davies, Charles," DVPF.

31. Email from Laurie Langland to the author, March 15, 2011, in the author's possession.

32. Emails from Bill Shaman to the author, March 16, 2011, and March 18, 2011; both in the author's possession.

33. "Santa Barbara Star Barred from Meet," *Pittsburgh Courier*, March 15, 1941, 17. Santa Barbara's student newspaper, *The Gaucho,* wrote a scathing editorial of the school's decision, but that was the only local public comment on the matter. See Martin, *Benching Jim Crow,* 70–71.

34. Tom Gallagher, "Color Ban Prevented Morningside Player from Competing," *Sioux City Journal,* March 10, 2006, https://siouxcityjournal.com/news/color-ban-prevented-morningside-player-from-competing/article_69fdab66-d149-5741-b1cc-f39ded34e300.html; Jody Ewing, "A Game, Life Well Played," *Sioux City Weekender,* September 4, 2003, https://jodyewing.com/features/al-buckingham. Buckingham's recollections in the *Sioux City Journal* piece fifty-seven years after the fact are slightly flawed. He implied that Morningside was invited to the tournament three straight years and that the prohibitions on Wilson were lessened with each passing year. Morningside was not invited the following year, and Wilson played for Morningside in 1947 only.

35. "Color Ban Prevented Morningside Player from Competing," *Sioux City Journal,* March 10, 2006, online edition; "The NAIA Changed Basketball, and Kansas City," *Kansas City Star,* March 12, 2011, online edition.

36. See, for example, letter from A. O. Duer to E. S. Liston, February 4, 1947, and letter from A. O. Duer to E. S. Liston, February 24, 1947; both in "Liston Correspondence," box: Early NAIA History, NAIA. Letter from Ray Hanson to E. S. Liston, March 4, 1948, "Colored Players," unnamed/unnumbered box, NAIA.

37. 1946 NAIB Championship Program, Men's Basketball 1921–57, Vertical Files, NAIA.

38. Letter from A. O. Duer to E. S. Liston February 4, 1947, "Liston Corre-spondence," box: Early NAIA History, NAIA.

39. Letter from A. O. Duer to E. S. Liston February 24, 1947, "Liston Corre-spondence," box: Early NAIA History, NAIA.

40. Letter from A. O. Duer to E. S. Liston February 4, 1947, "Liston Corre-spondence," box: Early NAIA History, NAIA.

41. Letter from E. S. Liston to A.O. Duer, February 10, 1947; see also letter from E. S. Liston to A. O. Duer, February 18, 1947; both in "Liston Correspondence," box: Early NAIA History, NAIA.

42. Letter from E. S. Liston to A. O. Duer, February 10, 1947, "Liston Cor-respondence," box: Early NAIA History, NAIA.

43. "Racial Ban Lifted Too Late for U. of D.," *The Cue*, Dubuque University, March 11, 1948, 4; letter from Ken Mercer to E. S. Liston, March 27, 1948, "Colored Players," unnamed/unnumbered box, NAIA.

44. Letter from Edward Ronsheim to Chairman Basketball Division USOC, February 21, 1948, "History of the NAIA," unnamed/unnumbered box, NAIA. On Wilson and Anderson College, see Graham and Graham, *Getting Open*, 91–94, 193.

45. Letter from E. S. Liston to John R. Wooden, December 31, 1946, "NAIA History," unnamed/unnumbered box, NAIA; letter from E. S. Liston to A. O. Duer, February 15, 1947, "Liston Correspondence," box: Early NAIA History, NAIA. On the status of Indiana State's mid-season struggles, see "Sycamore Sports," *Indiana Statesman*, April 3, 1947, 6.

46. Email from John Matthew Smith to the author, September 10, 2014, in the author's possession

47. The commentary, both scholarly and anecdotal, on Wooden's views on race is broad, but most of it is from late in Wooden's life. The most thorough is Seth Davis's excellent biography, *Wooden: A Coach's Life* (New York: Henry Holt, 2014). For Wooden's relationships with black players later in his career, see John Matthew Smith, *The Sons of Westwood: John Wooden, UCLA, and the Dynasty That Changed College Basketball* (Urbana: University of Illinois Press, 2013); "Standing Tall—Indiana State Remembers John Wooden," Indiana State Univer-sity, June 7, 2010, https://www2.indstate.edu/news/news.php?newsid=2289; Jeff Eisenberg, "A Forgotten Aspect of John Wooden: His Impact on Race Relations," *Yahoo! Sports*, June 3, 2010, http://topcollegebb.blogspot.com/2011/06/forgotten -aspect-of-john-wooden-his.html; "A Milestone Deserving of Permanent Com-memoration," *Terre Haute Tribune-Star*, June 23, 2010, https://www.tribstar.com/opinion/mark-bennett-a-milestone-deserving-of-permanent-commemoration/article_052315cd-7b26-535a-93ba-021134284e21.html; Ted Green, "A Lasting Moral Victory," *IndyStar.com*, June 6, 2010, http:// archive.indystar.com/article/20100606/NEWS/100729009/A-lasting-moral-victory. The quote from Smith is in an email from John Matthew Smith to the author, September 10, 2014, in the

author's possession. The anecdote about Wooden's daughter is in Davis, *Wooden*, 88; and the anecdote about the Louisville convention is in Pat Williams, *How to Be Like Coach Wooden: Life Lessons of Basketball's Greatest Leader* (Deerfield Beach, FL: HCI, 2006), 19.

48. Letter from E. S. Liston to A. O. Duer, February 15, 1947, "Liston Correspondence," box: Early NAIA History, NAIA.

49. John Wooden, with Steve Jamison, *My Personal Best: Life Lessons from an All-American Journey* (New York: McGraw Hill, 2004), 76–80.

50. "Sycamore Sports," *Indiana Statesman*, March 13, 1947, 6.

51. Letter from E. S. Liston to Brother B. Thomas, March 19, 1948, and letter from Ray Hanson to E. S. Liston, March 3, 1948; both in "Colored Players," unnamed/unnumbered box, NAIA.

52. All telegrams are in the folder "Colored Players," unnamed/unnumbered box, NAIA. See also "Manhattan Accepts NAIB Bid with Tourney Dropping Negro Ban," *New York Times*, March 6, 1948, 17.

53. Telegram from Peggy Brown to Emil Liston, March 5, 1948, and letter from Carlos Harrison to Emil Liston, March 6, 1948; both in "Colored Players," unnamed/unnumbered box, NAIA.

54. "NAIB Drops Rule Barring Negro Players," and "NAIB Sees the Light," *Kansas City Call*, March 12, 1948, 8.

55. Clarence Walker memoir, in the author's possession. I am deeply grateful for Johnny Smith's willingness to provide this document to me. While Clarence Walker's presence may not have been welcomed in Sankey's Café, as late as 1944 the café explicitly welcomed a Jewish clientele by advertising in a local Jewish paper to announce, "Greetings to our Jewish Friends," *Jewish Post*, April 7, 1944, 4.

56. Calling ahead to ascertain lodging restrictions relative to blacks was a practice that Wooden learned from his days coaching at South Bend Central. Davis, *Wooden*, 83.

57. Walker memoir.

58. Ibid.

59. Davis, *Wooden*, 92. Prior to the 1948 tourney, the media again noted that the previous year's team did not play in the NAIB "due to a conflict with final examination week." "Sycamores Bid for National Hardwood Crown," *Indiana Statesman*, March 17, 1948, 1.

60. Walker memoir.

61. Wooden, *My Personal Best*, 76–80.

62. "Standing Tall—Indiana State Remembers John Wooden," June 7, 2010, https://www2.indstate.edu/news/news.php?newsid=2289.

63. Walker memoir; Davis, *Wooden*, 94; "Sycamores Bid for National Hardwood Crown," *Indiana Statesman*, March 17, 1948, 1.

64. "Coach Praises Player," *Kansas City Call*, March 19, 1948, 7.

65. 1948 NAIB Championship Tournament Program, Men's Basketball 1921–1957, Vertical Files, NAIA.

66. The episode is apparently not mentioned at all in the Tirey Papers at Indiana State University's Archives in Cunningham Memorial Library, even though Wooden later claimed that Tirey personally intervened to implore the coach to play. And Davis's thoroughly researched biography discusses the Walker episode in detail and turned up no mention of the NAACP's involvement. Davis, *Wooden*, 90–94.

67. James E. Krause, *Guardians of the Game: A Legacy of Leadership* (Overland Park, KS: Ascend Books, 2008), 178; Walker memoir.

68. "Wooden Hero to Many," *Indianapolis News*, December 11, 1975, 44.

69. Walker memoir.

70. Letter from E. S. Liston to Kenneth Mercer, March 30, 1948, "Colored Players," unnamed/unnumbered box, NAIA.

71. "Coach Praises Player," and "Sport Light," *Kansas City Call*, March 19, 1948, 7–8; letter from E. S. Liston to Kenneth Mercer, March 30, 1948, "Colored Players," unnamed/unnumbered box, NAIA.

72. Kevin Fox Gotham, *Race, Real Estate, and Uneven Development: The Kansas City Experience, 1900–2000* (Albany: SUNY Press, 2002), 94; Dorothy Hodge Davis, "Changing Discriminatory Practices in Department Store Eating Facilities, in Kansas City, Missouri," MSW thesis, University of Kansas, 1960. To be sure, Kansas state law gave the appearance of a more tolerant attitude than Missouri state law, which was openly segregationist. However, as Gretchen Cassel Eick has shown, Kansas's antidiscriminatory statutes were widely ignored in large measure because they lacked much enforcement mechanisms. See Gretchen Cassel Eick, *Dissent in Wichita: The Civil Rights Movement in the Midwest, 1954–1972* (Urbana: University of Illinois Press, 2001), 17–25. Kansas also maintained a bizarre provision that allowed school segregation in "first-class towns" of more than one hundred thousand residents but prohibited it in the vast majority of the state's smaller communities; see Milton S. Katz, "A Pioneer in Civil Rights: Esther Brown and the South Park Desegregation Case of 1948," *Kansas History* (Winter 1995): 235–47.

73. Katz, "Pioneer in Civil Rights," 235–47.

74. Gotham, *Race, Real Estate, and Uneven Development*, 91–99.

75. Sherry L. Schirmer, *A City Divided: The Racial Landscape of Kansas City, 1900–1960* (Columbia: University of Missouri Press, 2002), 189–92.

76. Ibid.; Gotham, *Race, Real Estate, and Uneven Development*, 91–99.

77. Schirmer, *City Divided*, 196.

78. Letter from Ray Hanson to E. S. Liston, March 4, 1948, "Colored Players," unnamed/unnumbered box, NAIA.

79. Schirmer, *City Divided*, 197–98.

80. Katz, "Pioneer in Civil Rights"; and Davis, "Changing Discriminatory Practices."

81. Special Instructions to Coaches with Colored Players on Squad, "Colored Players," unnamed/unnumbered box, NAIA.

82. Meeting minutes of the Executive Committee, November 14, 1952, "Executive Committee, 1950–53," box: Early NAIA History, NAIA.

83. Meeting minutes of the Executive Committee, March 6–13, 1952, and November 13, 1952; both in Executive Committee, 1950–53, box: Early NAIA History, NAIA.

84. Meeting minutes of the Executive Committee, September 24, 1953, and letter from A. G. Wheeler to A. O. Duer, September 30, 1953; both in "Executive Committee, 1950–53," box: Early NAIA History, NAIA.

85. Meeting minutes of the Executive Committee, November 14, 1952, "Executive Committee, 1950–53," box: Early NAIA History, NAIA.

86. Letter from Al Garton to A. O. Duer, October 5, 1953, "Executive Committee, 195–53," box: Early NAIA History, NAIA.

87. Letter to the National Intercollegiate Basketball Association from T. L. Hill and J. B. McLendon, March 23, 1948, MKP.

88. Patrick B. Miller, "Muscular Assimilationism: Sport and the Paradoxes of Racial Reform," in *Race and Sport: The Struggle for Equality On and Off the Field*, ed. Charles K. Ross, 146–82 (Jackson: University Press of Mississippi, 2005). The quote is from Patrick B. Miller, "Sports as 'Interracial Education': Popular Culture and Civil Rights Strategies during the 1930s and Beyond," in *The Civil Rights Movement Revisited: Critical Perspectives on the Struggle for Racial Equality in the United States*, ed. Patrick B. Miller, Therese Frey Steffen, and Elisabeth Schaffer-Wunsche, 21–37 (Piscataway, NJ: Transaction Publishers, 2001). See also Patrick B. Miller, "Holding Center Stage: Race Pride and the Extracurriculum at Historically Black Colleges and Universities," in *Affect and Power: Essays on Sex, Slavery, Race, and Religion*, ed. David Libby, Paul Spickard, and Susan Ditto, 141–58 (Jackson: University Press of Mississippi, 2004).

89. John B. McLendon, "The First CIAA Championship Basketball Tournament," CNC.

90. Letter to the National Intercollegiate Basketball Association from T. L. Hill and J. B. McLendon, March 23, 1948, and letter from John Lawther to J. B. McLendon, March 26, 1948; both found in MKP. The institutional isolation that HBCs faced is exemplified in the communication between McLendon and Lawther. The initial petition is addressed to the "National Intercollegiate Basketball Association," which was the umbrella group of the Joint Rules Committee, suggesting that McLendon and his group lacked a thorough awareness of the governing bodies of collegiate basketball that had held HBCs at more than arm's length.

91. The concept of "race men" is best explained in Douglas Flamming, *Bound for Freedom: Black Los Angeles in Jim Crow America* (Berkeley: University of California Press, 2005), 7, 104–109, 126–29.

92. Scott Ellsworth, *The Secret Game: A Wartime Story of Courage, Change, and Basketball's Lost Triumph* (New York: Back Bay Books, 2016); Milton S. Katz, *Breaking Through: John B. McLendon, Basketball Legend and Civil Rights Pioneer* (Fayetteville: University of Arkansas Press, 2007), 6–46. See also Jacqueline Imani

Bryant, "Basketball Coach John B. McLendon, the Noble Revolutionary of U.S. Sport, April 5, 1915–October 8, 1999," *Journal of Black Studies* (May 2000): 720–34.

CHAPTER 6. HOME RULE'S LAST REDOUBT

1. Letter to Coach from J. B. McLendon, January 29, 1949, and letter from John Lawther to J. B. McLendon, February 24, 1949; both found in MKP.

2. Letter from J. B. McLendon to Kenneth Wilson, February 26, 1949, and letter from K. L. Wilson to J. B. McLendon, March 12, 1949; both found in MKP.

3. Letter K. L. Wilson to J. B. McLendon March 29, 1949, MKP.

4. Letter from H. R. Jefferson to J. B. McLendon, April 6, 1949, MKP; Lawther's comments are contained therein.

5. Letter Edward Jackson to K. L. Wilson, April 11, 1949, MKP.

6. Letter from J. B. McLendon to K. L. Wilson May 17, 1949; letter from K. L. Wilson to Edward Jackson, May 26, 1949; and letter from Edward Jackson to K. L. Wilson, June 6, 1949; all found in MKP.

7. Letter from J. H. Nichols to W. R. Morrison, January 15, 1948, and letter from W. R. Morrison to J. H. Nichols, March 4, 1948; both found in "Morrison, W. R. 1937–1952," box 7, OPE/I3; and Proposed Policy—Interracial Committee, January 29, 1947, "Interracial Committee," box 3, OWS. The presence of such a social justice committee at Oberlin is not surprising given its history, specifically within the context of race. Oberlin's reputation as a radical campus was firmly established when it allowed for black enrollment before the Civil War, becoming the first integrated institution of higher learning in the United States well before abolitionism enjoyed any widespread respectability. Its reputation for radicalism increased even further when it also allowed women to enroll in 1837, not only making it the first coeducational institution of higher learning but also, and far more controversially, placing white women and black men together in the same institution. See Nat Brandt, *The Town That Started the Civil War: The True Story of the Community That Stood Up to Slavery—and Changed a Nation Forever* (New York: Random House, 1991), and J. Brent Morris, *Oberlin, Hotbed of Abolitionism: College, Community, and the Fight for Freedom and Equality in Antebellum America* (Chapel Hill: University of North Carolina Press, 2014).

8. Letter from Mack Greene to Nelson Jones, November 24, 1952; letter from Mack Greene to William Morgan, November 24, 1952; and letter from J. H. Nichols to Mack Greene, December 8, 1952; all found in "Letters Received by the Director of Athletics, 1937–54," box 4, OPE/I3.

9. Letter from Mack Greene to Hugh Willett, February 12, 1950; letter from Hugh Willett to Mack Greene, February 14, 1950; letter from Hugh Willett to NCAA Council, May 15, 1950; and letter from Hugh Willett to Mack Greene, May 15, 1950; all found in "NCAA Correspondence, 1949–50," box 2, OPE/V3.

10. Letter from Mack Greene to Kenneth Wilson," December 5, 1950, "NCAA Committees, 1950–51," box 4, FCA-AL.

11. Rufus E. Clement, "Racial Integration in the Field of Sports," *Journal of Negro Education* (Summer 1954): 222–30.

12. Letter from Mack Greene to Kenneth Wilson," December 5, 1950, "NCAA Committees, 1950–51," box 4, FCA-AL.

13. "NCAA Accused of Discrimination," *New York Times*, January 8, 1951, 31; "Southern Schools Join Fight against Sanity Code in NCAA," *New York Times*, January 9, 1951, 43; "Jim Crowism Charges Draw Denial by NCAA," *Dallas Morning News*, January 8, 1950, part 3, 1.

14. Letter from J. B. McLendon to Hugh Willett, December 22, 1950; letter from A. C. Lonborg to Walter Byers, December 28, 1950; letter from A. C. Lonborg to Asa Bushnell, December 28, 1950; letter from J. B. McLendon to Gus Lonborg, January 5, 1951; and letter from A. C. Lonborg to J. B. McLendon, January 19, 1951; all found in "NCAA Committees, 1950–51," box 4, FCA-AL.

15. Letter from Walter Byers to Harold Olsen, July 10, 1950, "NCAA Committees, 1950–51," box 4, FCA-AL.

16. Letter from Walter Byers to A. C. Lonborg, January 19, 1951, "NCAA Committees, 1950–51," box 4, FCA-AL; letter from Walter Byers to J. B. McLendon, January 23, 1951, MKP; "Jim Crowism Charges Draw Denial by NCAA," *Dallas Morning News*, January 8, 1950, part 3, 1.

17. Letter from J. B. McLendon to National Basketball Committee Members, January 24, 1951, MKP.

18. Pamela Grundy, *Learning to Win: Sports, Education, and Social Change in Twentieth-Century North Carolina* (Chapel Hill: University of North Carolina Press, 2001), 188.

19. Letter from Edward Jackson to J. B. McLendon, January 30, 1951, MKP.

20. Martin Luther King, *Why We Can't Wait* (New York: Harper and Row, 1964); letter from H. R. Jefferson to J. B. McLendon, January 31, 1951, MKP.

21. Letter from Edward Jackson to J. B. McLendon, January 30, 1951, MKP. On the image of the black athlete in the white mind and the emergence of a Super Negro character, see Amy Bass, *Not the Triumph but the Struggle: The 1968 Olympics and the Making of the Black Athlete* (Minneapolis: University of Minnesota Press, 2004), 37–80. See also John Hoberman, *Darwin's Athletes: How Sport Has Damaged Black America and Preserved the Myth of Race* (New York: Mariner Books, 1997), 187–207.

22. Letter from Mack Greene to Dunkel's Sports Research Service, January 12, 1954, and letter from Dick Dunkel, January 16, 1954; both found in National Athletic Newsletter, March 1, 1954, MKP.

23. Letter from Mack Greene to McNitts Inc., March 28, 1949; letter from H. A. McNitt to Mack M. Greene, March 31, 1949; letter from Mack Green to H. A. McNitt, April 5, 1949; letter from H. A. McNitt to Mack Greene, May 9, 1949; all found in National Athletic Newsletter, July 14, 1952. Letter from Mack Greene to Charles Wesley, November 18, 1952, and letter from Charles Wesley to Mack Greene, November 25, 1952; both found in MKP.

24. Letter from Mack Greene to Athletic Directors and Administrators, February 6, 1951, and letter from Henry Kean to J. B. McLendon, February 12, 1951; both found in MKP.

25. National Athletic Newsletter, April 26, 1951, MKP.

26. National Athletic Newsletter, September 4, 1951, MKP; Mack C. Greene, "Intercollegiate Athletics at the Social Frontier," *Journal of Human Relations* (Summer 1953): 5–18; National Athletic Steering Committee Information Sheet, folder 31, box 2, ABH.

27. Letter from Mack Greene to J. H. Nichols, July 3, 1952, "Small College Committee," and Meeting minutes of the NCAA Council, August 15–17, 1953, "Council Hearing 1953"; both found in box 1, OPE/V3.

28. Letter from A. O. Duer to Charles Wesley, October 31, 1951; letter from A. O. Duer to Mack Greene, October 31, 1951; and letter from Mack Greene to A. O. Duer, November 6, 1951; all found in MKP.

29. Letter from J. R. Ricks to A. O. Duer, November 27, 1951, folder 8, box 1, DDA.

30. Letter from A. O. Duer to NAIB Executive Committee, November 1951, "Executive Committee, 1950–53," box: Early NAIA History, NAIA; National Athletic Newsletter, February 6, 1952, MKP.

31. Milton S. Katz and John B. McLendon, *Breaking Through: The NAIA and the Integration of Intercollegiate Athletics in Post–World War II America* (Downers Grove, IL: Maxaid, 1988), 14–16; Milton S. Katz, *Breaking Through: John B. McLendon, Basketball Legend and Civil Rights Pioneer* (Fayetteville: University of Arkansas Press, 2007), 70–73; National Athletic Newsletter, March 1, 1954, MKP.

32. Letter from W. M. Kethley to A. O. Duer, December 11, 1952, and letter from A. O. Duer to W. M. Kethley, December 31, 1952; both found in folder 8, box 1, DDA.

33. Letter from A. O. Duer to H. Lee Prather, September 24, 1953, and letter from H. Lee Prather to A. O. Duer, September 28, 1953; both found in "Executive Committee, 1953–1954," box: Early NAIA History, NAIA.

34. M. Katz and McLendon, *Breaking Through*, 16; M. Katz, *Breaking Through*, 70–73; National Athletic Newsletter, March 1, 1954, MKP.

35. Letter from Walter Byers to Mack Greene, undated [Sept.–Nov. 1951], in National Athletic Newsletter, November 20, 1951, and March 1, 1954; both found in MKP.

36. National Athletic Newsletter, March 1, 1954, MKP.

37. Few figures from the period are as polarizing and complicating on the issue of race as Rupp. Don Barksdale claimed that he enjoyed a very positive relationship with Rupp during the latter's tenure as assistant coach for Team USA at the 1948 Olympics. Chad Carlson, "Basketball's Forgotten Experiment: Don Barksdale and the Legacy of the United States Olympic Basketball Team," *International Journal of the History of Sport* (May 2010): 1330–59. Yet Rupp's own

actions and pronouncements complicate that image. He steadfastly refused to recruit black players even after other teams in the University of Kentucky athletic department integrated. And several eyewitnesses claim he referred to black players during the famous 1966 NCAA championship game against the all-black Texas Western College (TWC) lineup as "coons" while also scoffing at the TWC logo by asking sarcastically, "What's that stand for? Two White Coaches?" Frank Fitzpatrick, *And the Walls Came Tumbling Down: Kentucky, Texas Western, and the Game That Changed American Sports* (New York: Simon and Schuster, 1999), 129–47; the TWC reference is on 39–40. Curry Kirkpatrick, "The Night They Drove Old Dixie Down," *Sports Illustrated*, April 1, 1991, 70–83.

38. Letter from A. C. Lonborg to Adolph Rupp, September 3, 1951, "NCAA Committees, 1950–51," box 4, FCA-AL. From 1939 to 1950 the NCAA championship location hosted a single game between the regional champions from the East and West. Beginning in 1951 the championship location featured the national semifinals, the final game, and, until 1981, the third-place consolation game, thus beginning the notion of the Final Four.

39. National Athletic Newsletter, February 6, 1952, MKP. The Mayflower's segregationist practices notwithstanding, the hotel was ironically given the nickname "the second-best address in Washington" [after the White House] by Harry Truman, who ordered the desegregation of the armed forces and definitively committed the Democratic Party to a civil rights agenda.

40. The text of Lewis's letter is not known to exist, but it is discussed at length in National Athletic Newsletter, February 6, 1952, MKP.

41. The material on Lewis is found in "Vanderbilt Portraits No. 15," *Vanderbilt Alumnus*, March 1951, 4, and "In the Face of Destruction," *Vanderbilt Magazine*, March 11, 2008, https://news.vanderbilt.edu/vanderbiltmagazine/in_the_face _of_destruction; National Athletic Newsletter, February 6, 1952, MKP.

42. Meeting minutes of the NCAA Council, February 6, 1953, NCAA. On Mouzon's family and background, see "Award to Dr. Edwin D. Mouzon, Jr." and "SMU Athletic Era Ends," *Dallas Morning News* clipping; both found in SMUFS.

43. Meeting minutes of the NCAA Council, February 6, 1953. On integration of both the Methodist Church and SMU specifically, see Scott A. Cashion, "'And So We Moved Quietly': Southern Methodist University and Desegregation, 1950–1970," PhD diss., University of Arkansas, 2013; quote on p. 15.

44. Letter from Marshall Turner to J. H. Nichols, August 1, 1952, "NCAA College Committee, 1951–53," box 1, OPE/V3.

45. Special Committee on Small College–NCAA Relations, April 1953; and Report and Recommendations of Special Committee on Small College–NCAA Relations, both found in "NCAA College Committee, 1951–53," box 1, OPE/V3.

46. Meeting minutes of the NCAA Executive Committee, March 22–23, 1953, NCAA.

47. National Athletic Newsletter, March 1, 1954, MKP.

48. NAIA News, October 1953, "NCAA Programs, Proposed Amendments

153–54," box 3, OPE/V3; 1955 NAIA Championship Tournament Program, Men's Basketball 1951–57, Vertical Files, NAIA.

49. Letter from A. O. Duer to Executive Committee, January 20, 1954, "Executive Committee, 1950–53," box: Early NAIA History, NAIA; and 1957 NAIA Holiday Bowl Press Book, Football 1954–57, Vertical Files, NAIA.

50. Letter from Glenn Martin to Al Duer, November 5, 1953, "Executive Committee 1950–53," box: Early NAIA History, NAIA.

51. Carol Braxton Land, "A History of the National Association of Intercollegiate Athletics," PhD diss., University of Southern California, 1977, 6–7, 50.

52. For a lengthy discussion of the intersection of race, sports, and politics in the South during this time, see Kurt Edward Kemper, *College Football in American Culture in the Cold War Era* (Champaign: University of Illinois Press, 2008), 83–89.

53. Minutes of the Executive Committee, November 14, 1952, under cover of letter from A. G. Wheeler to A. O. Duer, November 17, 1952, "Executive Committee 1950–53, box: Early NAIA History, NAIA.

54. Kemper, *College Football*, 80–81, 90.

55. Letter from Roswell D. Merrick to A. O. Duer, November 2, 1953, and letter from A. O. Duer to Roswell Merrick, November 18, 1953; both found in "Executive Committee 1950–53, box: Early NAIA History, NAIA.

56. Kemper, *College Football*, 83–89; Neil R. McMillen, *The Citizens' Council: Organized Resistance to the Second Reconstruction, 1954–1964* (Champaign: University of Illinois Press, 1971), 59–72.

57. Letter from Luther Marlar to A. O. Duer, July 11, 1956, and letter from Al Duer to Luther Marlar, July 13, 1956, "District 18, 1956–57," unnumbered/unnamed box, NAIA.

58. Kemper, *College Football*, 94–102.

59. Letter from Luther Marlar to A. O. Duer, September 5, 1956; letter from Luther Marlar to A. O. Duer, January 24, 1957; letter from Joe Aillet to A. O. Duer, October 12, 1957; letter from Al Duer to Joe Aillet, October 16, 1957; and letter from Luther Marlar to A. O. Duer, January 8, 1959; all found in "District 18, 1956–57," unnumbered/unnamed box, NAIA. Letter from A. O. Duer to John Ricks, November 8, 1956, "District 19 Alabama/MS 1956–57," unnumbered/unnamed box, NAIA.

CHAPTER 7. DEFENDING THE KINGDOM

1. "NCAA Invitational Workshop on College Athletics, November 20, 1955," file 15, box 68, TMP.

2. Steve Rushin, "Inside the Moat," *Sports Illustrated*, March 3, 1997, 68–78; William Rhoden, "The Vision of Walter Byers, a Flawed Leader, Still Shapes the NCAA," *New York Times*, May 30, 2015, SP4; Jack McCallum, "In the Kingdom of the Solitary Man," *Sports Illustrated*, October 6, 1986, 64–78.

3. "Report and Recommendations of Special Committee on Small College and

NCAA Relations," "NCAA Small College Committee Report 1953," box 1, OPE/V3.

4. "NCAA Invitational Workshop on College Athletics, November 20, 1955," file 15, box 68, TMP.

5. For an authoritative discussion of the freshman rule, see Ronald A. Smith and Jay W. Helman, "A History of Eligibility Rules among Big-Time Athletic Institutions." The document was prepared in the 1990s at the behest of the NCAA and remains, to my knowledge, unpublished. Ron Smith graciously provided me a copy and it remains in my possession.

6. Ibid.

7. "Eligibility Rules for 1954 National Collegiate Championship Events," NCAA Meeting, September 1954, box 3, OPE/V3.

8. Letter from A. O. Duer to W. H. Crowley, April 20, 1953, "NCAA College Committee 1951–53," box 1, OPE/V3.

9. Letter from Wilfred H. Crowley to A. O. Duer, April 21, 1953, "NCAA College Committee 1951–53," box 1, OPE/V3.

10. Meeting minutes of district chairs and presidents, March 9, 1953, "1953 Minutes of Meetings," box: National Membership, 1941, 1957–1964, NAIA; Executive Committee minutes, September 24, 1953, "Executive Committee 1950–53," box: Early NAIA History, NAIA.

11. Letter from A. G. Wheeler to A. O. Duer, September 30, 1953, "Executive Committee 1950–53," box: Early NAIA History, NAIA; Executive Secretary's Annual Report to Executive Committee 1955, "Secretary's Report, 1955–56," box: Early NAIA 1940s, 1950s, 1960s, NAIA.

12. NAIA Policy Statement, August 5, 1965, "NAIA History," unnamed/unnumbered box, NAIA.

13. Letter from F. H. Delaney to A. O. Duer, October 9, 1956, and letter from A. O. Duer and F. H. Delaney, October 15, 1956; both found in "Division 18—Louisiana—1956-7," unnamed/unnumbered box, NAIA; letter from Al Duer to Fred Hess, January 13, 1956, "A. O. Duer Correspondence—Personal 1956," box: Early NAIA History, NAIA.

14. Letter from Howard Hobson to Arthur C. Lonborg, June 29, 1951, "NCAA Committees 1950–53," box 4, FCA-AL; and letter from A. O. Duer to Walter Byers, April 24, 1974, "Basketball Tournament—Historical," unnamed/unnumbered box, NAIA.

15. Letter from W. A. Miller to Al Duer, September 28, 1953, "Executive Committee 1950–53," box: Early NAIA History, NAIA; letter from A. O. Duer to Executive Committee, January 20, 1954, "Executive Committee 1950–53," box: Early NAIA History, NAIA.

16. Letter from A. O. Duer to Executive Committee, January 20, 1954, "Executive Committee 1950–53," box: Early NAIA History, NAIA.

17. Letter from Thomas E. McDonough to John Nichols, April 7, 1954, "NCAA Meeting September 1954," box 3, OPE/V3; and letter from Al Wheeler to Execu-

tive Committee, December 10, 1954, "Executive Committee 1950–53," box: Early NAIA History, NAIA.

18. Minutes of the Executive Committee Annual Meeting March 10–15, 1958, "Minutes 1957–58," box: Early NAIA History 1940s, 1950s, 1960s, NAIA.

19. Letter from Theodore Harder to Presidents et al., April 22, 1954, "Executive Committee 1950–53," box: Early NAIA History, NAIA.

20. College Round Table Meeting minutes, January 6, 1955, *1954 NCAA Yearbook*, 214–15, NCAA.

21. Morgan G. Brenner, *College Basketball's National Championships: The Complete Records of Every Tournament Ever Played* (Lanham, MD: Scarecrow Press, 1999), 192–97.

22. College Round Table Meeting minutes, January 6, 1955, *1954 NCAA Yearbook*, 215, NCAA.

23. Ibid., 215–18.

24. College Round Table Meeting minutes, January 10, 1956, *1955 NCAA Yearbook*, 218, NCAA; "NCAA Invitational Workshop on College Athletics, November 20, 1955," file 15, box 68, TMP.

25. Results of College Division Basketball Tournament Questionnaire, f. 34, box 2, ABH; "NCAA Basketball Tournament for Small Colleges Approved," *New York Times*, January 12, 1956, 21; NCAA Council Minutes, January 8–10, 6, *1955 NCAA Yearbook*, NCAA.

26. Executive Secretary's Annual Report to Executive Committee 1955, "Secretary's Report, 1955–56," box: Early NAIA 1940s, 1950s, 1960s, NAIA.

27. Carson Cunningham, *American Hoops: U.S. Men's Olympic Basketball from Berlin to Beijing* (Lincoln: University of Nebraska Press, 2009), 140–41.

28. Minutes of the NCAA College Basketball Tournament Committee, June 4–5, 1956, 3, *1956 NCAA Yearbook*, NCAA; David Nelson, *The Anatomy of a Game: Football, the Rules, and the Men Who Made the Game* (Cranbury, NJ: Associated University Press, 1994), 209. Nelson asserts that by the end of the 1950s, "the NCAB became a completely owned and operated subunit of the NCAA."

29. Minutes of the NCAA College Basketball Tournament Committee, June 4–5, 1956, 1; Minutes of the NCAA University Division Basketball Tournament Committee, June 25–26, 1956, 4; Minutes of the NCAA Executive Committee, August 19, 1956, 5; all found in *1956 NCAA Yearbook*, NCAA.

30. "NCAA Basketball Tournament for Small Colleges Approved," *New York Times*, January 12, 1956, 21; College Committee Mid-Year Meeting minutes, March 24–25, 1954, 223, *1954 NCAA Yearbook*, NCAA.

31. "Sporting Comment," *Kansas City Star*, January 17, 1956, 21. All other media clippings are found in "Press Booklets—NCAA," unnamed/unnumbered box, NAIA.

32. "Press Booklets—NCAA," unnamed/unnumbered box, NAIA; and "Writer Says NCAA 'Poaching,'" "History," box: Early NAIA 1940s, 1950s, 1960s, NAIA.

33. Letter from A. J. Bergstrom to William Traylor, August 22, 1957 [labeled

as Appendix D], and Executive Committee Minutes, May 30, 1957; both found in *1957 NCAA Yearbook*, NCAA; and NCAA Council Minutes, April 30–May 2, 1956, 10, *1956 NCAA Yearbook*, NCAA. The NCAA continued to renew the contract such that the tournament remained in Evansville until 1977.

34. On the bracketing of the 1957 tournament, see "Appendix A—1957 College Division Basketball Bracket Report," *1957 NCAA Annual Yearbook*, A-26, NCAA. On Jackson State's forfeit, see Charles Martin, *Benching Jim Crow: The Rise and Fall of the Color Line in Southern College Sports, 1890–1980* (Chicago: University of Illinois Press, 2010), 246–47. The proscription against integrated games involving Mississippi schools in NCAA basketball tournaments was not limited to black schools. As evidence of the state's reactionary extremism on the subject of integration, in 1959, 1961, and 1962, Mississippi State University won the Southeastern Conference and its automatic berth in the NCAA Tournament but refused the invitation in deference to a state legislature that threatened to withhold funding to any state school that participated in integrated athletic events. Mississippi State finally accepted the invitation in 1963 but only after sneaking out of Starkville in the middle of the night so as to avoid any possible court injunctions prohibiting them from playing. Russell J. Henderson, "The 1963 Mississippi State University Basketball Controversy and the Repeal of the Unwritten Law: 'Something more than a game will be lost,'" *Journal of Southern History* (November 1997): 827–54; Michael Lenehan, *Ramblers: Loyola Chicago 1963—The Team That Changed the Color of College Basketball* (Chicago: Agate Midway, 2013); Jason A. Peterson, *Full Court Press: Mississippi State University, the Press, and the Battle to Integrate College Basketball* (Oxford: University Press of Mississippi, 2016); Kyle Veazey, *Champions for Change: How the Mississippi State Bulldogs and Their Coach Defied Segregation* (New York: History Press, 2012).

35. NCAA Council Minutes, January 8–10, 1956, 8, *1955 NCAA Yearbook*, NCAA.

36. "Press Booklets—NCAA," unnamed/unnumbered box, NAIA.

37. Letter from Bob Hudson to A. O. Duer, October 3, 1956, "Membership Dropped, 1955–57," box: National Membership 1941, 1957–, 1964, NAIA.

38. Letter from Gus Fish to Al Duer, November 4, 1954, "Executive Committee, 1950–53," box: Early NAIA History, NAIA.

39. Letter from S. L. Robinson to A. O. Duer, January 16, 1957; letter from Garland Frazier to A. O. Duer, August 9, 1955; letter from A. O. Duer to Ellis R. McCracken, April 4, 1957; and letter from Emil G. Rietz to A. O. Duer, May 28, 1956; all found in "Membership Dropped, 1955–57," box: National Membership 1941, 1957–, 1964, NAIA.

40. Membership data is taken from Jack Falla's appendix on NCAA membership against known Southern NAIA schools at the time. Jack Falla, *NCAA: The Voice of College Sports* (Mission, KS: National Collegiate Athletic Association, 1981), 252–58.

41. Letter from A. O. Duer to Executive Committee, January 20, 1954, "Executive Committee 1950–53," box: Early NAIA History, NAIA.

42. On the perceptions of institutional prestige and the growing prominence of large research institutions, see Rebecca S. Lowen, *Creating the Cold War University: The Transformation of Stanford* (Berkeley: University of California Press, 1997). For how such academic concerns for prestige affected athletics, see Kurt Edward Kemper, *College Football and American Culture in the Cold War Era* (Urbana: University of Illinois Press, 2008), 47–79.

43. "Press Booklets—NCAA," unnamed/unnumbered box, NAIA.

44. "NCAA Invitational Workshop on College Athletics, November 20, 1955," file 15, box 68, TMP. The notion of "athletic accreditation" continues to convince many administrators of the academic legitimacy conveyed by big-time athletics. In 2003 South Dakota State University (SDSU) moved from Division II to Division I, and its president, Peggy Miller, described the move as an opportunity to also move up into "Division I academics." "SDSU to Officially Declare Intent to Go Division I Today," *Argus Leader*, August 15, 2003, C1.

45. "NCAA Invitational Workshop on College Athletics, November 20, 1955," file 15, box 68, TMP.

46. Joseph N. Crowley, *Into the Arena: The NCAA's First Century* (Indianapolis: NCAA, 2006), 41–43; Falla, *NCAA*, 229–34.

47. Ronald A. Smith's *Play-by-Play: Radio, Television, and Big-Time College Sport* (Baltimore: Johns Hopkins University Press, 2001) discusses the extended nuances of the NCAA's television policies as well as the way in which media exposure shaped public understanding of college sports.

48. Welch Suggs, *A Place on the Team: The Triumph and Tragedy of Title IX* (Princeton, NJ: Princeton University Press, 2006), 45–65.

49. "From the Executive Secretary," *NAIA News*, vol. 7, March 1958, 4, NAIA.

50. James B. Conant, "Athletics: The Poison Ivy in Our Schools," *Look*, January 17, 1961, 49–53.

51. Carol Braxton Land, "A History of the National Association of Intercollegiate Athletics," PhD diss., University of Southern California, 1977, 43–45, 124–25.

52. Address to the Annual Meeting, March 13, 1964, NAIA.

53. Land, "History of the NAIA," 144, 221; Phillip Hochberg and Ira Horowitz, "Broadcasting and CATV: The Beauty and Bane of Major College Football," *Law and Contemporary Problems* (Winter 1973): 112–28.

54. "NCAA Invitational Workshop on College Athletics, November 20, 1955," file 15, box 68, TMP.

BIBLIOGRAPHY

ARCHIVAL AND MANUSCRIPT MATERIAL

Atlanta University Consortium, Atlanta, GA. Archives Research Center—Robert Woodruff Library: Burwell Harvey Collection (ABH).

Bowdoin College, Bowdoin, ME. Special Collections and Archives: Athletic Records 4.2.1 (BAR); Vertical Files (BVF).

City College of New York, New York, NY. Archives and Special Collections—Morris Raphael Cohen Library: Nat Holman Collection (NHC).

Colorado College, Colorado Springs, CO. Special Collections and Archives: General Athletics Records (CGA); Athletics Records—Rocky Mountain Faculty (CAF).

Delta State University, Greenville, MS. University Archives—Charles Capps Archives and Museum: Records of the Director of Athletics (DDA).

Duquesne University, Pittsburgh, PA. University Archives: Vertical Personnel Files (DVPF).

Emory University, Atlanta, GA. University Archives: Thomas McDonough Papers (TMP).

Franklin and Marshall College. Lancaster, PA. Archives and Special Collections: Franklin and Marshall Oral History Project (FMOHP); Department of Athletics (FMA).

Gettysburg College, Gettysburg, PA. Special Collections and College Archives: Vertical Files (GVF).

Manhattan College, Riverdale, NY. Archives and Special Collections: Athletics Administration Records (MAA); Athletics Clippings (MAC).

Milton Katz Papers (MKP). Katz copied letters pertaining to the National Athletic Steering Committee from the Offices of the Big Ten, but the conference disposed of them sometime in the early 2000s. Katz graciously provided the author with a copy of his files.

National Association of Intercollegiate Athletics, Kansas City, KS. Records of the NAIA (NAIA). NAIA records are unorganized and not maintained for public usage. They do not conform to standard conventions of archival nomenclature or identification, and some boxes have no identification whatsoever. As a result, all files have the same identifier.

National Collegiate Athletics Association, Indianapolis, IN. Records of the NCAA (NCAA). While the NCAA maintains a library for research the association has conducted, NCAA records of the association's business and history are quite limited and not organized as manuscript collections. Most exist as bound volumes of the association's various meetings and committee reports aggregated by year. As a result, all files have the same identifier.

Northwestern University, Chicago, IL. University Archives—Deering Library: Walter Dill Scott Papers (NWDS).

Oberlin College, Oberlin, OH. Department of Special Collections: Physical Education Records I3 (OPE/I3); Physical Education Records I4 (OPE/I4); Physical Education Records V2 (OPE/V2); Physical Education Records V3 (OPE/V3); Physical Education Records I12 (OPE/I12); William Stevenson Papers (OWS).

Ohio Wesleyan University, Delaware, OH. OWU Historical Collection: Faculty Meeting Minutes (OWFM).

Ohio State University, Columbus, OH. University Archives: Records of the Director of Athletics 9.E-1 (RDA).

Southern Methodist University. SMU Archives—DeGolyer Library: Faculty Staff Vertical Files (SMUFS).

Tufts University, Medford, MA. University Archives—Tisch Library: Department of Physical Education/Athletics Records (TPE/A); Vertical Files (TVF).

University of Alabama, Tuscaloosa, AL. University Archives—Hoole Special Collections Library: Records of the Faculty Representative for Athletics (AFAR).

University of Kansas, Lawrence, KS. University Archives—Kenneth Spencer Research Library. Papers of Forrest C. Allan: Basketball Coaches Correspondence (FCA-BC); Athletic Directors Correspondence—Arthur Lonborg (FCA-AL).

University of North Carolina, Chapel Hill, NC. Special Collections—Wilson Library: The Collection of North Caroliniana (CNC).

University of Pennsylvania, Philadelphia, PA. University Archives and Records Center: Records of the Office of the President (POP).

BIBLIOGRAPHY

SECONDARY MATERIALS

Applin II, Albert G. "From Muscular Christianity to the Market Place: The History of Men's and Boys' Basketball in the United States, 1891–1957." PhD diss., University of Massachusetts, 1982.

Austin, Brad. *Democratic Sports: Men's and Women's College Athletics during the Great Depression*. Fayetteville: University of Arkansas Press, 2015.

———. "Protecting Athletics and the American War Defenses at Ohio State and across the Big Ten during the Great Depression." *Journal of Sport History* (Summer 2000): 247–70.

Barrier, Smith. *Tobacco Road: Basketball in North Carolina*. New York: Leisure Press, 1983.

"Basketball: N.Y.U. Quints Make It More Popular than Football." *Newsweek*, January 18, 1936, 29–30.

Bass, Amy. *Not the Triumph but the Struggle: The 1968 Olympics and the Making of the Black Athlete*. Minneapolis: University of Minnesota Press, 2004.

Bernstein, Mark F. *Football: The Ivy League Origins of an American Obsession*. Philadelphia: University of Pennsylvania Press, 2001.

Bjarkman, Peter C. *Hoopla: A History of College Basketball*. Indianapolis: Masters Press, 1996.

Blackwell, James. *On Brave Old Army Team: The Scandal That Rocked a Nation, West Point 1951*. Novato, CA: Presidio Press, 1996.

Brandt, Nat. *The Town That Started the Civil War: The True Story of the Community That Stood Up to Slavery—and Changed a Nation Forever*. New York: Random House, 1991.

———. *When Oberlin Was King of the Gridiron: The Heisman Years*. Oberlin, OH: College Press, 2001.

Brenner, Morgan G. *College Basketball's National Championships: The Complete Records of Every Tournament Ever Played*. Lanham, MD: Scarecrow Press, 1999.

Brinkley, Alan. *Voices of Protest: Huey Long, Father Coughlin, and the Great Depression*. New York: Vintage Press, 1983.

Bryant, Jacqueline Imani. "Basketball Coach John B. McLendon, the Noble Revolutionary of U.S. Sport, April 5, 1915–October 8, 1999." *Journal of Black Studies* (May 2000): 720–34.

Carlson, Chad. "Basketball's Forgotten Experiment: Don Barksdale and the Legacy of the United States Olympic Basketball Team." *International Journal of the History of Sport* (May 2010): 1330–59.

———. *Making March Madness: The Early Years of the NCAA, NIT, and College Basketball Championships*. Fayetteville: University of Arkansas Press, 2017.

———. "A Tale of Two Tournaments: The Red Cross Games and the Early NCAA-NIT Relationship." *Journal of Intercollegiate Sport* 5 (2012): 260–80.

Carter, W. Burlette. "The Age of Innocence: The First 25 Years of the National

Collegiate Athletic Association, 1906 to 1931." *Vanderbilt Journal of Entertainment and Technology Law* (Spring 2006): 211–91.

Cashion, Scott A. "'And So We Moved Quietly': Southern Methodist University and Desegregation, 1950–1970." PhD diss., University of Arkansas, 2013.

Cayleff, Susan E. *Babe: The Life and Legend of Babe Didrikson Zaharias.* Champaign: University of Illinois Press, 1996.

Clement, Rufus E. "Racial Integration in the Field of Sports." *Journal of Negro Education* (Summer 1954): 222–30.

Cohen, Stanley, *The Game They Played.* New York: Farrar, Strauss, and Giroux, 2001.

Conant, James B. "Athletics: The Poison Ivy in Our Schools." *Look,* January 17, 1961, 49–53.

Crowley, Joseph N. *Into the Arena: The NCAA's First Century.* Indianapolis: NCAA, 2006.

Cunningham, Carson. *American Hoops: U.S. Men's Olympic Basketball from Berlin to Beijing.* Lincoln: University of Nebraska Press, 2009.

Davis, Dorothy Hodge. "Changing Discriminatory Practices in Department Store Eating Facilities, in Kansas City, Missouri." MSW thesis, University of Kansas, 1960.

Davis, Seth. *When March Went Mad: The Game That Transformed Basketball.* New York: St. Martin's Griffin, 2010.

———. *Wooden: A Coach's Life.* New York: Henry Holt, 2014.

Deford, Frank. "Code Breakers." *Sports Illustrated* (November 13, 2000): 82–98.

Demas, Lane. *Integrating the Gridiron: Black Civil Rights and American College Football.* New Brunswick, NJ: Rutgers University Press, 2010.

Dumenil, Lynn *The Modern Temper: American Culture and Society in the 1920s.* New York: Hill and Wang, 1995.

Eick, Gretchen Cassel. *Dissent in Wichita: The Civil Rights Movement in the Midwest, 1954–1972.* Urbana: University of Illinois Press, 2001.

Ellsworth, Scott. *The Secret Game: A Wartime Story of Courage, Change, and Basketball's Lost Triumph.* New York: Back Bay Books, 2016.

Ewing, Jody. "A Game, Life Well Played." *Sioux City Weekender,* September 4, 2003, https://jodyewing.com/features/al-buckingham.

Falla, Jack. *NCAA: The Voice of College Sports—A Diamond Anniversary History, 1906–1981.* Mission, KS: National Collegiate Athletic Association, 1981.

Fitzpatrick, Frank. *And the Walls Came Tumbling Down: Kentucky, Texas Western, and the Game That Changed American Sports.* New York: Simon and Schuster, 1999.

Flamming, Douglas. *Bound for Freedom: Black Los Angeles in Jim Crow America.* Berkeley: University of California Press, 2005.

Flath, Arnold W. *A History of Relations between the National Collegiate Athletic Association and the Amateur Athletic Union of the United States, 1905–1963.* Champaign, IL: Stipes Publishing, 1964.

Forbes, Theodore W. "The NCAA since 1942." DEd diss., Columbia University, 1955.

Frank, Stanley. "Basketball's Big Wheel." *Saturday Evening Post*, January 15, 1949, 131–34.

Frei, Terry. *March 1939: Before the Madness—The Story of the First NCAA Basketball Champions*. Lanham, MD: Taylor Trade Publishing, 2014.

Gallagher, Tom. "Color Ban Prevented Morningside Player from Competing." *Sioux City Journal*, March 10, 2006, https://siouxcityjournal.com/news/color -ban-prevented-morningside-player-from-competing/article_69fdab66-d149 -5741-b1cc-f39ded34e300.html.

Gorn, Elliot. *Dillinger's Wild Ride: The Year That Made America's Public Enemy Number One*. New York: Oxford University Press, 2011.

Gosnell, Joan. "Kickoffs and Kickbacks: The 1951 Football Scandal at William and Mary." MA thesis, College of William and Mary, 1990.

Gotham, Kevin Fox. *Race, Real Estate, and Uneven Development: The Kansas City Experience, 1900–2000*. Albany: SUNY Press, 2002.

Goudzousian, Aram. *Bill Russell and the Basketball Revolution*. Berkeley: University of California Press, 2010.

Goulden, Marc Edward. "From Country Club to Rat Race: A Social History of College Students, 1920–1960." PhD diss., University of Wisconsin, 1995.

Graham, Tom, and Rachel Cody Graham. *Getting Open: The Unknown Story of Bill Garrett and the Integration of College Basketball*. New York: Atria Books, 2006.

Green, Harvey. *Fit for America: Health, Fitness, Sport, and American Society*. Baltimore: Johns Hopkins University Press, 1986.

Greene, Mack C. "Intercollegiate Athletics at the Social Frontier." *Journal of Human Relations* (Summer 1953): 5–18.

Gruensfelder, Melvin Henry. "A History of the Origins and Development of the Southeastern Conference." MS thesis, University of Illinois, 1964.

Grundman, Adolph H. "A.A.U.–N.C.A.A. Politics: Forrest C. 'Phog' Allen and America's First Olympic Basketball Team." *OLYMPIKA: The International Journal of Olympic Studies* 5 (1996): 111–26.

———. *The Golden Age of Amateur Basketball: The AAU Tournament, 1921–1968*. Lincoln: University of Nebraska Press, 2004.

Grundy, Pamela. *Learning to Win: Sports, Education, and Social Change in Twentieth-Century North Carolina*. Chapel Hill: University of North Carolina Press, 2001.

Harris, Doug. *BOUNCE: The Don Barksdale Story*. Oakland, CA: Doug Harris Films, 2008.

Hawkins, Hugh. "The Making of the Liberal Arts College Identity." *Daedalus* 128, no. 1 (1999): 1–25.

Henderson, Russell J. "The 1963 Mississippi State University Basketball Controversy and the Repeal of the Unwritten Law: 'Something more than a game will be lost.'" *Journal of Southern History* (November 1997): 827–54.

Hoberman, John. *Darwin's Athletes: How Sport Has Damaged Black America and Preserved the Myth of Race*. New York: Mariner Books, 1997.

Hochberg, Phillip, and Ira Horowitz. "Broadcasting and CATV: The Beauty and Bane of Major College Football," *Law and Contemporary Problems* (Winter 1973): 112–28.

Hoover, Francis Lentz. "A History of the National Association of Intercollegiate Athletics." DPE diss., Indiana University, 1958.

Horger, Marc Thomas. "Play by the Rules: The Creation of Basketball and the Progressive Era, 1891–1917." PhD diss., Ohio State University, 2001.

Horowitz, Helen Lefkowitz. *Campus Life: Undergraduate Cultures from the End of the Eighteenth Century to the Present*. Chicago: University of Chicago Press, 1987.

Ingrassia, Brian. *The Rise of Gridiron University: Higher Education's Uneasy Alliance with Big-Time Football*. Lawrence: University of Kansas Press, 2012.

Isaacs, Neil D. *All the Moves: A History of College Basketball*. Philadelphia: J. B. Lippincott, 1975.

Johnson, Scott Morrow. *Phog: The Most Influential Man in Basketball*. Lincoln: University of Nebraska Press, 2016.

Kahn, Roger. "Success and Ned Irish." *Sports Illustrated,* March 27, 1961, 39–46.

Katz, Andy. "Coaching Summit All about Change." *ESPN.com,* October 2, 2002, https://www.espn.com/mens-college-basketball/columns/story?columnist=katz_andy&id=1637752.

Katz, Milton S. *Breaking Through: John B. McLendon, Basketball and Civil Rights Pioneer*. Fayetteville: University of Arkansas Press, 2010.

———. "A Pioneer in Civil Rights: Esther Brown and the South Park Desegregation Case of 1948." *Kansas History* (Winter 1995): 235–47.

Katz, Milton S., and John B. McLendon, *Breaking Through: The NAIA and the Integration of Intercollegiate Athletics in Post–World War II America*. Downers Grove, IL: Maxaid, 1988.

Katznelson, Ira. *Fear Itself: The New Deal and the Origins of Our Time*. New York: Liveright Press, 2014.

Keefer, Louis E. *Scholars in Foxholes: The Story of the Army Specialized Training Program*. Jefferson, NC: McFarland, 1988.

Kemper, Kurt Edward. *College Football in American Culture in the Cold War Era*. Urbana: University of Illinois Press, 2009.

———. "'Movin' on Up': College Sports and Athletic Realignment in the 1950s." Paper delivered to the South Dakota Historical Society Annual History Conference, October 19, 2012, Pierre, South Dakota.

Kerchoff, Blair. *Phog Allen: The Father of Basketball Coaching*. Indianapolis: Masters Press, 1996.

Kimball, Bruce. "The Declension Narrative, the Liberal Arts College, and the

University." In *The Evolution of Liberal Arts in the Global Age,* edited by Peter Marber and Daniel Araya, 15–32. New York: Routledge, 2017.

King, Martin Luther. *Why We Can't Wait.* New York: Harper & Row, 1964.

Kirkpatrick, Curry. "The Night They Drove Old Dixie Down." *Sports Illustrated,* April 1, 1991, 70–83.

Krause, James E. *Guardians of the Game: A Legacy of Leadership.* Overland Park, KS: Ascend Books, 2008.

Kuska, Bob. *Hot Potato: How Washington and New York Gave Birth to Black Basketball and Changed America's Game Forever.* Charlottesville: University of Virginia Press, 2006.

Ladd, Tony, and James A. Mathisen. *Muscular Christianity: Evangelical Protestants and the Development of American Sport.* Ada, MI: Baker Publishing, 1999.

Land, Carol Braxton. "A History of the National Association of Intercollegiate Athletics." PhD diss., University of Southern California, 1977.

Lane, Jeffrey, *Under the Boards: The Cultural Revolution in Basketball.* Lincoln: University of Nebraska Press, 2007.

Lenehan, Michael. *Ramblers: Loyola Chicago 1963—The Team That Changed the Color of College Basketball.* Chicago: Agate Midway, 2013.

Lester, Robin. *Stagg's University: The Rise, Decline, and Fall of Big-Time Football at the University of Chicago.* Urbana: University of Illinois Press, 1995.

Levine, David O. *The American College and the Culture of Aspiration, 1915–1940.* New York: Cornell University Press, 1988.

Lindaman, Matthew. *Fit for America: Major John L. Griffith and the Quest for Athletics and Fitness.* New York: Syracuse University Press, 2018.

Loss, Christopher P. *Between Citizens and the State: The Politics of American Higher Education in the 20th Century.* Princeton, NJ: Princeton University Press, 2011.

Lowen, Rebecca S. *Creating the Cold War University: The Transformation of Stanford.* Berkeley: University of California Press, 1997.

Martin, Charles. *Benching Jim Crow: The Rise and Fall of the Color Line in Southern College Sports, 1890–1980.* Urbana: University of Illinois Press, 2004.

McCallum, Jack. "In the Kingdom of the Solitary Man." *Sports Illustrated,* October 6, 1986, 64–78.

McMillen, Neil R. *The Citizens' Council: Organized Resistance to the Second Reconstruction, 1954–1964.* Champaign: University of Illinois Press, 1971.

Miller, Patrick B. "Holding Center Stage: Race Pride and the Extracurriculum at Historically Black Colleges and Universities." In *Affect and Power: Essays on Sex, Slavery, Race, and Religion,* edited by David Libby, Paul Spickard, and Susan Ditto, 141–58. Jackson: University Press of Mississippi, 2004.

———. "Muscular Assimilationism: Sport and the Paradoxes of Racial Reform." In *Race and Sport: The Struggle for Equality On and Off the Field,* edited by Charles K. Ross, 146–82. Jackson: University Press of Mississippi, 2005.

———. "Sports as 'Interracial Education': Popular Culture and Civil Rights Strategies during the 1930s and Beyond." In *The Civil Rights Movement Revisited: Critical Perspectives on the Struggle for Racial Equality in the United States,* edited by Patrick B. Miller, Therese Frey Steffen, and Elisabeth Schaffer-Wunsche, 21–37. Piscataway, NJ: Transaction Publishers, 2001.

Morris, J. Brent, *Oberlin, Hotbed of Abolitionism: College, Community, and the Fight for Freedom and Equality in Antebellum America.* Chapel Hill: University of North Carolina Press, 2014.

Mrozek, Donald J. *Sport and American Mentality, 1880–1910.* Knoxville: University of Tennessee Press, 1983.

Nelson, David. *The Anatomy of a Game: Football, the Rules, and the Men Who Made the Game.* Cranbury, NJ: Associated University Press, 1994.

Ours, Robert M. *Bowl Games: College Football's Greatest Tradition.* New York: Westholme Publishing, 2004.

Peterson, Jason A. *Full Court Press: Mississippi State University, the Press, and the Battle to Integrate College Basketball.* Oxford: University Press of Mississippi, 2016.

Powell, John Talbott. "The Development and Influence of Faculty Representation in the Control of Intercollegiate Sport within the Intercollegiate Conference of Faculty Representatives from Its Inception in January 1895 to July 1963." PhD diss., University of Illinois, 1965.

"The Pride of Peoria: It's Little Known Bradley Tech Makes Basketball History." *Newsweek,* January 9, 1939, 31–32.

Putney, Clifford. *Muscular Christianity: Manhood and Sports in Protestant America, 1880–1920.* Cambridge, MA: Harvard University Press, 2003.

Rabb, Christopher. "Barr None." *Franklin and Marshall Magazine* (Summer 2003): 11–14.

Rominger, Jr., Donald W. "From Playing Field to Battleground: The United States Navy V-5 Preflight Program in World War II." *Journal of Sport History* (Winter 1985): 252–64.

Rosen, Charles S. *The Scandals of '51: How the Gamblers Almost Killed College Basketball.* New York: Seven Stories Press, 1999.

Rozier, John. *Out of the Grandstand and Onto the Playing Field: A History of the Division of Health, Physical Education, Recreation, and Athletics at Emory University, 1880–1983.* Atlanta: Emory University Press, 1983.

Rushin, Steve. "Inside the Moat." *Sports Illustrated,* March 3, 1997, 68–78.

Schirmer, Sherry L. *A City Divided: The Racial Landscape of Kansas City, 1900–1960.* Columbia: University of Missouri Press, 2002.

Schmidt, Raymond. *Shaping College Football: The Transformation of an American Sport, 1919–1930.* Syracuse, NY: Syracuse University Press, 2007.

Schneider, James G. *The Navy V-12 Program: Leadership for a Lifetime.* Boston: Houghton Mifflin, 1987.

Schoolmeester, Vernon. "A History of Intercollegiate Basketball at South Dakota State University." MA thesis, South Dakota State University, 1969.

Schultz, Jaime. *Moments of Impact: Injury, Racialized Memory, and Reconciliation in College Football.* Lincoln: University of Nebraska Press, 2015.

Smith, John Matthew. *The Sons of Westwood: John Wooden, UCLA, and the Dynasty That Changed College Basketball.* Urbana: University of Illinois Press, 2013.

Smith, Ronald A. *Pay for Play: A History of Big-Time College Athletic Reform.* Champaign: University of Illinois Press, 2011.

———. *Play by Play: Radio, Television, and Big-Time College Sport.* Baltimore: Johns Hopkins University Press, 2001.

———. *Sports and Freedom: The Rise of Big-Time College Athletics.* New York: Oxford University Press, 1988.

Smith, Ronald A., and Jay W. Helman. "A History of Eligibility Rules among Big-Time Athletic Institutions." Unpublished; in the author's possession.

Somerville, Thomas Robert. "A History of the National Association of Basketball Coaches of the United States." PhD diss., Ohio State University, 1980.

Spears, Betty, and Richard Swanson. *History of Sports and Physical Education in the United States.* Dubuque, IA: William C. Brown, 1988.

Sperber, Murray. *Onward to Victory: The Crises That Shaped College Sports.* New York: Henry Holt, 1998.

Stone, Richard. "The Graham Plan of 1935: An Aborted Crusade to De-Emphasize College Athletics. *North Carolina Historical Review* (July 1987): 274–93.

Stooksbury, Danny. *National Title: The Unlikely Tale of the NAIB Tournament.* Bradenton Beach, FL: Higher Level Publishing, 2010.

Suggs, Welch. *A Place on the Team: The Triumph and Tragedy of Title IX.* Princeton, NJ: Princeton University Press, 2006.

Thelin, John R. *Games Colleges Play: Scandal and Reform in Intercollegiate Athletics.* Baltimore: Johns Hopkins University Press, 1996.

———. *A History of American Higher Education.* Baltimore: Johns Hopkins University Press, 2004.

Tilden, Winifred R. "Shall We Have Universal Physical Education?" *Iowa Homemaker* 1 (1921): 7–8.

Tong, Curtis Whitefield. "John Herbert Nichols, MD: A Life of Leadership in Physical Education and Athletics." PhD diss., Ohio State University, 1969.

Turrini, Joseph M. *The End of Amateurism in American Track and Field.* Chicago: University of Illinois Press, 2010.

Veazey, Kyle. *Champions for Change: How the Mississippi State Bulldogs and Their Coach Defied Segregation.* New York: History Press, 2012.

Walker, J. Samuel, and Randy Roberts. *The Road to Madness: How the 1973–1974 Season Transformed College Basketball.* Chapel Hill: University of North Carolina Press, 2016.

Watterson, John Sayle. *College Football: History, Spectacle, Controversy.* Baltimore: Johns Hopkins University Press, 2000.

Welch, Paula. *History of American Physical Education and Sport.* Springfield, IL: Charles C Thomas, 1996.

Williams, Pat. *How to Be Like Coach Wooden: Life Lessons of Basketball's Greatest Leader.* Deerfield Beach, FL: HCI, 2006.

Wooden, John, with Steve Jamison. *My Personal Best: Life Lessons from an All-American Journey.* New York: McGraw Hill, 2004.

Zahorsky, Peter. "A History of Intercollegiate Athletics at South Dakota State College." MA thesis, South Dakota State College, 1959.

INDEX

opposition to segregation by, 144–46,
149–50, 156; racial progressivism of, 159–
61, 183–87, 193–94; relations with Byers,
202–3; relations with Crowley Commit-
tee, 201–2
Duke University, 164, 191
Dunkel Index, 178, 180, 207
Duquesne University, 39, 50
Durley, Alexander, 194
Dyche, Schubert, 95

Eastern Collegiate Athletics Conference,
203
Eastern Intercollegiate Basketball League
(EIBL), 12, 29, 48–49
Eastern Kentucky University, 152, 216
Edwards, George, 41
Effrat, Louis, 44, 54
Emergency Unemployment Relief Commit-
tee, 36
Emery, Dan, 125
Emory University, 74–75, 80, 191
Emporia State University, 116, 215, 217
Erickson, Charles Dee, 142
Eusebius, Brother, 135–36, 145, 150
Evansville College, 2, 215
Exum, William, 129

Fisher, Jack, 211
Florida A&M University, 217
football, college, 6, 21, 36, 226; abuses of,
7, 12–13, 16–17; bowl games, 36; college
basketball fears of, 45–47; effects of segregation on, 196; reform literature of, 7–8;
small-college decline of, 116–17, 204
Franklin and Marshall College, 80, 123, 124,
216, 217
Frei, Terry, 46
Frost, Reuben, 143

Garrett, Bill, 139, 147, 177
Garton, Al, 161
Gauthier, George, 105, 191
Gettysburg College, 77
Ginn, Ralph, 208
Gorn, Elliot, 31
Graham, Tom, 28
Grapes of Wrath (Steinbeck), 230
Great Depression, 226, 229; effects on ath-
letics of, 78–79; effects on higher educa-
tion of, 73
Greene, Mack, 213, 230; criticism of NCAA
convention, 170–73; critique of ratings
indices, 178–79; efforts to desegregate

NAIA, 183–86; efforts to desegregate
NCAA, 179–83, 187–88, 190–93; and
NCAA basketball tournament, 207–8
Gregory, Kenneth, 48
Griffith, John, 24, 62, 138, 246n66
Grover, Butch, 63, 64
Gulick, Luther, 18

Hanson, Ray, 143, 150, 158
Harlem Globetrotters, 143
Harrison, Carlos, 151
Harvard University, 201
Harvey, Burwell, 186
Hawkins, Hugh, 111
Henry, Ralph, 131
Henshel, Harry, 140, 141, 150
Herrington, William, 150
Hess, Fred, 218
Hickey, E.S., 30
Hickox, Edward, 64–65
Historically Black Colleges (HBCs), 5, 7,
133–34; access to NCAA tournament
of, 162–65, 167–69, 172, 174–75; athletic
segregation of, 2, 162–64; NCAA tourna-
ment segregation of, 213–14; role of ath-
letics at, 6, 162–63
Hitler, Adolf, 171, 172
Hobson, Howard, 46, 56, 164, 203
Hogan, Frank, 103
Holman, Nat, 26–30, 36, 47, 52, 56, 64,
239n18
"home rule" principle, 14–25, 35, 82, 99, 183
Hoover, Francis, 215
Houston, Clarence, 85, 104, 218; small col-
lege leadership of, 87–88, 91–92, 94–95,
98
Hull, Jimmy, 138
Hutchinson, R.C., 96
Hutton, Joseph, 140–41, 146, 217–18

Iba, Henry, 41
Indiana Central College, 112
Indiana State University, 147–48
Indiana University, 138, 139, 147, 154, 215
integration, 194–95, 230; southern opposi-
tion to, 195–97
Intercollegiate Athletic Association of the
United States, NCAA
Intercollegiate Tournament. *See* National
Association of Intercollegiate Athletics
Tournament
Irish, Edward "Ned," 38, 42; involvement
with NIT, 56–59
Isaacs, Neil, 25

Ivy League, 111, 204. *See also* Eastern Intercollegiate Basketball League

Jackson, Edward, 168, 176, 177, 181
Jackson State University, 214
Jacobs, Randall, 82, 83
Jaworski, Chet, 49
Jefferson, H. R., 177, 181
Jewish Welfare Board, 28
Johns Hopkins University, 79–80, 111,
125–26, 216, 217
Johnson, Charles, 211
Johnson, Glenn, 147
Johnson, John, 151, 159
Joint Rules Committee, 20, 21, 23, 35; 1927
meeting of, 11, 20, 43; proposed restruc-
turing of, 22–23
Julian, Alvin, 59

Kane, Robert, 102
Kansas City (MO), 164; segregation in 142,
156–61, 265n72
Kansas City Athletic Club, 33, 61, 62
Kansas City Hotel Association, 160
Kansas City Philharmonic, 158
Kaufman, Nate, 28
Kean, Henry, 180
Kenyon College, 99–100
Keoghan, George, 140
Kethley, William, 186, 194
Kieran, John, 79
King, Martin Luther, 176, 195
Klueh, Duane, 153

Lafayette College, 96
Lamar University, 216
Lawrence Technical University, 215
Lawson, George, 206, 208
Lawther, John, 164
Lebanon Valley College, 216, 217
Lee, Umphrey, 191
Lehigh University, 189
Leib, Karl, 83
Leinbach, Elizabeth, 139
Levine, David, 73
Lewis, Fred, 126, 189–90, 191
"liberal arts agenda," 72–74, 106–7
liberal arts colleges: academic challenges to,
228–29, 247–48n2; alliance with HBCs,
165; changes to, 71; concerns over Cold
War fitness, 84–85; critique of big-time
athletics, 71, 74, 76–77; critique of NCAA,
99–103, 107–9, 122–24; excluded from
NCAA governance, 86–87, 101–2, 119–20;

Nichols as supporter of, 69–70; prefer-
ences for NCAA, 205, 216–18; role of ath-
letics in, 4, 6; support of WWII efforts,
80–84; views on 1951 scandals, 103–4
Liston, Emil, 40, 41–42, 42, 53, 54, 159, 161;
betrayed by critics, 62–65, 230, 246n69;
management of discrimination clause by,
136–37, 141, 145–46, 149–50, 156; as popu-
list icon, 229–30
Lonborg, Arthur, 41, 64, 67, 174–75, 188,
206–8
Long, Huey, 229
Long Island University, 49, 137
Losee, Ferron, 125
Louisiana Polytechnic Institute, 216
Louisiana State University, 196
Loyola College (MD), 216, 217
Loyola University (Chicago), 49
Luna Park, 82
Lyon, E. Wilson, 100, 118

Macy, C. Ward, 86
Madison Square Garden, 38, 43, 57, 59, 67
Major League Baseball, 137, 172
Manhattan College, 135–37, 140, 146, 147,
161, 162, 163
Marlar, Luther, 196–97, 216
Marsh, A. W., 84, 101
Marshall University, 152
Martin, Charles, 137
Martin, Glenn, 194
Martin, Whitney, 53, 212
Mason-Dixon Conference, 111
McBride, C. E., 48, 60–62, 146, 212
McCracken, Branch, 28, 139
McCracken Conference, 220, 237n4
McDonald, Don, 152
McDonough, Thomas, 75
McLendon, John, 167, 173, 175, 191, 207–8,
230; critique of NCAA, 175–76; formative
years, 164–65, 168–69
McMillen, Neil, 196
McNitt, H. A., 179, 180
Meanwell, Walter, 11, 30
Mehl, Ernest, 211
Memphis State University, 216
Mercer, Ken, 147
Mercer, T. Leroy, 101–2, 122
Messersmith, Lloyd, 84
Metcalf, T. Nelson, 80
Methodist Episcopal Church, 142
Metropolitan Basketball Writers Associa-
tion, 42, 43, 44, 54, 58, 60; decisions to
continue NIT by, 55–56

compared with University Division, 212–13; creation of, 7, 208–9; historically black colleges in, 1; 1947 Tournament, 114; 1958 Tournament, 1–2; rationale for, 220–21

National Collegiate Athletics Association (NCAA) University Division Tournament, 36, 39, 51–52, 58, 121, 161; classification of teams, 210–11; compared with College Division, 212–13; competition with NAIA Tournament, 63–65; competition with NIT, 52–53, 59–60; creation of, 45–48; early finances of, 65–67; expansion of, 125, 173–75, 244n36; HBC access to, 162; 1939 Tournament, 48–49; popular elevation of, 232; selection of teams for, 47–48, 49–53; small college criticism of, 206; sponsorship with NABC, 45–48, 65–66

National Federation of State High School Athletic Associations, 23, 192–93, 204

National Football League, 137

National Invitation Tournament (NIT), 3, 45, 50, 53, 54, 57; comparisons to Rose Bowl, 43–44; criticisms of, 43–45; efforts to undermine, 54–60; origins of, 42–43

National Rules Committee, 24

National Small College Athletics Association (NSCAA), 110–11, 115, 116

Navy V-5 program, 83

Navy V-12 program, 82, 83

NCAA. *See* National Collegiate Athletics Association

New York City: criticism of, 12, 26, 28–29

New York Giants, 37

New York University, 37, 38–39, 51–52

Nichols, John H., 96, 106, 114, 165, 191, 217, 218; background of, 73–74, 249n9; Cold War concerns of, 84; concerns of NAIA by, 118, 120; criticism of big-time athletics by, 76–81, 89, 117; Crowley Committee participation of, 126–27; doubts about NCAA of, 88–89, 100–101, 102; frustration with Byers, 98–99; 1936 NCAA address of, 69–70, 71–72, 75; 1950 NCAA address of, 69, 70–71; opposition to championships by, 119; response to 1951 scandals, 104–5, 121; support for HBCs, 169–70, 182, 193; support for presidential advisory committee of, 94–95; support of WWII by, 80;

North Carolina College, 164, 213

North Carolina State University, 50

Northeastern University, 88

Northwestern University, 48, 138

Notre Dame, 140, 152

Oberlin College, 79, 82, 83, 216, 217; social justice efforts at, 169–70, 267n7

O'Hara, John, 140

Ohio Athletic Conference, 99–100, 170, 182

Ohio State University, 28, 74, 79, 81, 90, 139

Oklahoma A&M University, 49, 52

Olsen, Harold G., 54, 55, 56, 58, 59, 66, 174; enticement to Badger by, 51–52; hostility towards NAIA by, 36, 60–62, 64; support for NCAA tournament, 45–50

Olson, Howard, 119, 120, 122

Owens, Jesse, 131, 171–73

Owens, William Brownlee, 46, 47, 54, 60–62

Pacific Coast Conference, 12, 75, 76; support of NCAA expansion, 90, 91

Parsons, Edward, 89, 98

Paseo YMCA, 144, 160

Pepperdine University, 114, 144

Philander Smith College, 214

physical education, 72–73

Pierce, Palmer 237n4

Porter, Henry Van Arsdale "H.V.," 44, 48, 54

post-pivot play, 25, 29–30; AAU-YMCA support of, 25–26; opposition to, 25–26

Povich, Shirley, 196

Prather, Lee, 150

Providence College, 32

Purdue University, 138, 215

Queensbridge College, 140

Rainach, William, 196

Reilly, Joseph, 34, 40, 41, 61

Renninger, Don, 185–86, 187

Rice Institute, 49, 52

Ricks, J. R., 184, 194, 197

Robeson, Paul, 157–58

Robinson, Jackie, 137, 162, 177, 195

Rocky Mountain Athletic Conference, 174

Ronsheim, Edward, 147

Rowe, Floyd, 25

Rupp, Adolph, 26, 41, 45, 50, 59, 121; Final Four lobbying efforts of, 188; reputation on race of, 269n37

Salmon, Hamilton, 23, 24, 32, 43, 47

Sanity Code, 69, 70, 95, 103, 173, 183, 226; consequences of, 109, 115, 121; demise of

Kurt Edward Kemper is a professor of history and the director of the General Beadle Honors Program at Dakota State University. He is the author of *College Football and American Culture in the Cold War Era*.

Bloomer Girls: Women Baseball Pioneers   *Debra A. Shattuck*
I Fight for a Living: Boxing and the Battle for Black Manhood, 1880–1915
   Louis Moore
The Revolt of the Black Athlete: 50th Anniversary Edition   *Harry Edwards*
Pigskin Nation: How the NFL Remade American Politics   *Jesse Berrett*
Hockey: A Global History   *Stephen Hardy and Andrew C. Holman*
Baseball: A History of America's Game   *Benjamin G. Rader*
Kansas City vs. Oakland: The Bitter Sports Rivalry That Defined an Era
   Matthew C. Ehrlich
The Gold in the Rings: The People and Events That Transformed the
   Olympic Games   *Stephen R. Wenn and Robert K. Barney*
Before March Madness: The Wars for the Soul of College Basketball
   Kurt Edward Kemper

REPRINT EDITIONS

The Nazi Olympics   *Richard D. Mandell*
Sports in the Western World (2d ed.)   *William J. Baker*
Jesse Owens: An American Life   *William J. Baker*

The University of Illinois Press
is a founding member of the
Association of University Presses.

———————————————

Composed in 11.25/13.5 Adobe Minion Pro
with Abraham and AT Crillee display
by Jim Proefrock
at the University of Illinois Press
Manufactured by Sheridan Books, Inc.

University of Illinois Press
1325 South Oak Street
Champaign, IL 61820-6903
www.press.uillinois.edu